Practice Problems
for the
FE-CIVIL CBT Exam

Indranil Goswami, Ph.D., P.E.

Second Printing

February, 2015

Table of Contents

PREFACE	i
MATHEMATICS (54 problems)	
Questions	1-18
Solutions	19-40
PROBABILITY & STATISTICS (35 problems)	
Questions	41-53
Solutions	54-66
COMPUTATIONAL TOOLS (15 problems)	
Questions	67-74
Solutions	75-80
ETHICS & PROFESSIONAL PRACTICE (14 problems)	
Questions	81-87
Solutions	88-90
ENGINEERING ECONOMICS (22 problems)	
Questions	91-98
Solutions	99-108
STATICS (29 problems)	
Questions	109-124
Solutions	125-140
DYNAMICS (21 problems)	
Questions	141-151
Solutions	152-162
MECHANICS OF MATERIALS (30 problems)	
Questions	163-176
Solutions	177-190
MATERIALS (15 problems)	
Questions	191-196
Solutions	197-202
FLUID MECHANICS (29 problems)	
Questions	203-215
Solutions	216-228
HYDRAULICS & HYDROLOGIC SYSTEMS (36 problems)	
Questions	229-244
Solutions	245-258
STRUCTURAL ANALYSIS (28 problems)	
Questions	259-273
Solutions	274-288

STRUCTURAL DESIGN (29 problems)

    Questions   289-301

    Solutions   302-314

GEOTECHNICAL ENGINEERING (38 problems)

    Questions   315-332

    Solutions   333-346

TRANSPORTATION (36 problems)

    Questions   347-361

    Solutions   362-374

ENVIRONMENTAL (30 problems)

    Questions   375-387

    Solutions   388-398

CONSTRUCTION (18 problems)

    Questions   399-407

    Solutions   408-414

SURVEYING (18 problems)

    Questions   415-423

    Solutions   424-431

Preface

This book was written to assist the student preparing for the new Civil FE Examination. It consists of approximately 500 practice problems of difficulty level appropriate for the new FE (Fundamentals of Engineering) examination. As of January 2014, the FE Civil exam will consist of approximately 110 questions in the following subject areas:

MATHEMATICS	7-11 problems
PROBABILITY & STATISTICS	4-6 problems
COMPUTATIONAL TOOLS	4-6 problems
ETHICS & PROFESSIONAL PRACTICE	4-6 problems
ENGINEERING ECONOMICS	4-6 problems
STATICS	7-11 problems
DYNAMICS	4-6 problems
MECHANICS OF MATERIALS	7-11 problems
MATERIALS	4-6 problems
FLUID MECHANICS	4-6 problems
HYDRAULICS & HYDROLOGIC SYSTEMS	8-12 problems
STRUCTURAL ANALYSIS	6-9 problems
STRUCTURAL DESIGN	6-9 problems
GEOTECHNICAL ENGINEERING	9-14 problems
TRANSPORTATION	8-12 problems
ENVIRONMENTAL	6-9 problems
CONSTRUCTION	4-6 problems
SURVEYING	4-6 problems

In this book, there are approximately 500 multiple-choice practice problems and solutions. They are organized in the same order as in the official (NCEES) syllabus. Whenever appropriate, solutions include specific suggestions and relevant strategic advice.

When attempting the problems, the student is advised to use a digital (PDF) copy of the FE Reference Handbook (9th edition), so that they can get accustomed to navigating it in electronic form, rather than as a paper document. Make sure that you use the most current version (9th edition) because there have been significant changes in content and organization from the 8th to the 9th edition.

On the actual exam, the examinee will have 5 hours and 20 minutes to answer 110 questions. That is an average pace of about 3 minutes per problem. The first 55 questions will represent the first half of the exam. A break will be offered after the first half is completed, no matter how long it takes. After the break, the examinees may use the remainder of his/her time to complete the second half of the exam. Thus, an examinee may take only an hour to complete the first 55 questions and after the break, will have more than 4 hours available to do the remaining 55 questions. Another examinee may do exactly the opposite.

In these practice problems, I have tried to keep the difficulty level of the questions at a reasonable level. Some are easier than others. However, some of the questions, in spite of being more difficult than the '3-minute' variety, have been retained because they reinforce a critical area of learning. On the actual test, there will invariably be a mix of questions of various difficulty levels and a well-prepared examinee will be able to recognize quickly whether a particular problem is easy enough to attempt right away, or one that should be put aside and come back to later. This is a very important strategy for an exam as fast-paced and as diverse as the FE exam.

A point to be emphasized is that this book does not contain review material. Solutions to problems are detailed enough to *inform* the reader about specific concepts and strategies relevant to the problem, but quite possibly not enough to instruct fully. For that, the reader is advised to use other books and manuals written specifically for that purpose. For the GENERAL topics still included in the FE-CIVIL exam (Mathematics, Probability and Statistics, Computational Tools, Ethics, Engineering Economics, Statics, Dynamics, Mechanics of Materials, Materials and Fluid Mechanics), a manual written for the General topics review will suffice. Similarly, there are several books written with the Civil discipline review in mind.

Addendum for the second printing: All reported typos and other errors have been corrected. In some instances, additional steps have been added to further clarify the solutions.

Mathematics

Mathematics Topics on FE Civil Examination 7–11 problems
Approximately 7% of exam

A. Analytic geometry
B. Calculus
C. Roots of equations
D. Vector analysis

Mathematics Topics on FE Civil Examination

Problem 1
Which of the following is a line which is perpendicular to the line 3x + 7y + 2 = 0?
- A. 7x + 3y + 8 = 0
- B. 3x − 7y + 1 = 0
- C. 7x − 3y + 5 = 0
- D. 3x + 7y + 1 = 0

Problem 2
What is the equation of the line shown in the figure?

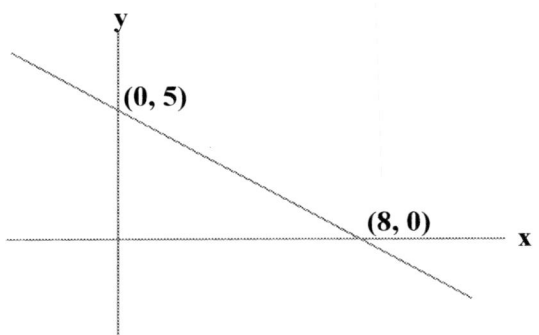

- A. 8x + 5y - 25 = 0
- B. 8x − 5y = 0
- C. 5x + 8y + 25 = 0
- D. 5x + 8y − 40 = 0

Problem 3
What is the equation of the directrix of the parabola whose equation is: $4x^2 + 3x + 7y - 2 = 0$?
- A. y − 45/28 = 0
- B. y − 45/56 = 0
- C. y + 45/28 = 0
- D. y + 45/56 = 0

Mathematics Topics on FE Civil Examination

Problem 4
What is the eccentricity of the ellipse whose equation is: $4x^2 + y^2 - 3x + 7y - 2 = 0$
 A. 0.87
 B. 0.75
 C. 0.50
 D. 0.25

Problem 5
What is the area of the ellipse whose equation is: $4x^2 + y^2 - 3x + 7y - 2 = 0$
 A. 541
 B. 172
 C. 93
 D. 23

Problem 6
What is the angle between the asymptotes of the hyperbola whose equation is
$$9(x - 2)^2 - 16(y - 5)^2 = 144$$
 A. 37
 B. 74
 C. 126
 D. 143

Problem 7
What is the following conic section?
$$5x^2 + 8xy + 3y^2 + 7x - 8y + 1 = 0$$
 A. Circle
 B. Ellipse
 C. Parabola
 D. Hyperbola

Problem 8
What is the cofactor matrix of the matrix A shown below?

$$A = \begin{bmatrix} 2 & 3 & 1 \\ 7 & -2 & 4 \\ 5 & -4 & 8 \end{bmatrix}$$

A. $\begin{bmatrix} 0 & 36 & -18 \\ 28 & 11 & -23 \\ 14 & 1 & -25 \end{bmatrix}$

B. $\begin{bmatrix} 0 & 28 & 14 \\ 36 & 11 & 1 \\ -18 & -23 & -25 \end{bmatrix}$

C. $\begin{bmatrix} 0 & -28 & 14 \\ -36 & 11 & -1 \\ -18 & 23 & -25 \end{bmatrix}$

D. $\begin{bmatrix} 0 & -36 & -18 \\ -28 & 11 & 23 \\ 14 & -1 & -25 \end{bmatrix}$

Problem 9
What is the classical adjoint of the matrix A shown below?

$$A = \begin{bmatrix} 2 & 3 & 1 \\ 7 & -2 & 4 \\ 5 & -4 & 8 \end{bmatrix}$$

A. $\begin{bmatrix} 0 & 36 & -18 \\ 28 & 11 & -23 \\ 14 & 1 & -25 \end{bmatrix}$

B. $\begin{bmatrix} 0 & 28 & 14 \\ 36 & 11 & 1 \\ -18 & -23 & -25 \end{bmatrix}$

C. $\begin{bmatrix} 0 & -28 & 14 \\ -36 & 11 & -1 \\ -18 & 23 & -25 \end{bmatrix}$

D. $\begin{bmatrix} 0 & -36 & -18 \\ -28 & 11 & 23 \\ 14 & -1 & -25 \end{bmatrix}$

Problem 10
Which of the following choices is a root of the following equation?

$$z^5 + 22.63 - 22.63j = 0$$

A. $z = -1.98 + 0.31j$
B. $z = 1.3 + 2.3j$
C. $z = 3 + 4j$
D. $z = 1.41 + 1.41j$

Problem 11

What is the angle between the lines AB and CD shown in the figure?

A. 26°
B. 74°
C. 106°
D. 116°

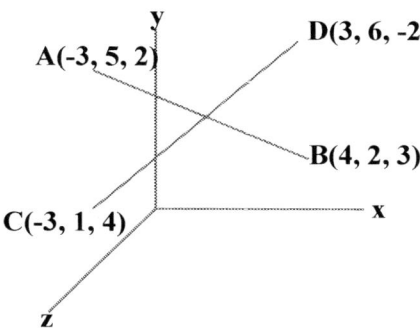

Problem 12

What is the area of the triangle ABC shown below?

A. 9.58
B. 12.35
C. 16.25
D. 32.50

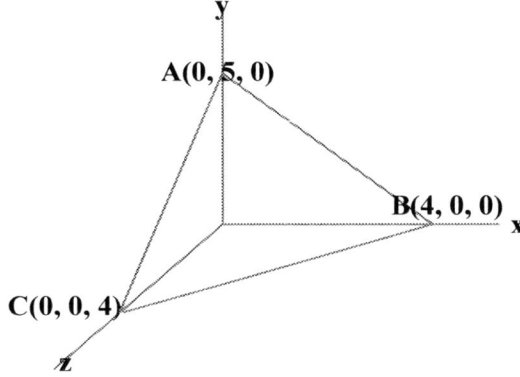

Problem 13
A tangent is drawn from the point (10,1) to the circle with center at (4,6) and radius 3. What is the angle α between the tangent and the radial line?

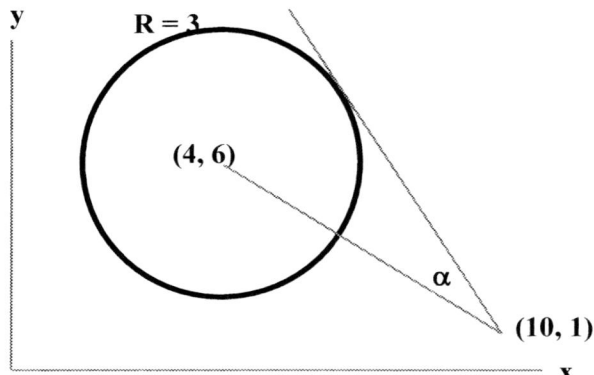

A. 22.6 degrees
B. 24.6 degrees
C. 36.8 degrees
D. 65.4 degrees

Problem 14
Given the following equation, which of the following relationships is true?
$$xy^2 - x = 10$$
A. $x = 1 - \log(1+y) - \log(y-1)$
B. $x = antilog\{1 - \log(1+y) - \log(y-1)\}$
C. $x = antilog\{1 - \log(1+y) - \log(1-y)\}$
D. $x = antilog\{10 - \log(1+y) - \log(y-1)\}$

Problem 15
A surface is characterized by the following equation:
$$3x^2y + y^3z + 4xy^2z^2 = 8$$
What is the equation of the vector normal to this surface at the point (1, 1, 1)?

A. 2i - 4j + 3k
B. 2i + 4j - 3k
C. 3i - 4j + 3k
D. i - 2j + 2k

Mathematics Topics on FE Civil Examination

Problem 16

What is the sum of the series shown below?

-5, 2, 9, ... , 128

    A. 1169
    B. 2337
    C. 1230
    D. 2460

Problem 17

What is the maximum value of the function y(x) in the interval 0 < x < 3?

$$y = 2x^3 - 8x^2 + 8x - 12$$

    A. -9.63
    B. +9.63
    C. -6.0
    D. 12.4

Problem 18

What is the maximum value of the function y(x) in the interval 1 < x < 3?

$$y = 2x^3 - 8x^2 + 8x - 12$$

    A. -10
    B. -6
    C. 6
    D. 10

Problem 19

Given that the matrix A shown below has a determinant = 72, what is the determinant of the matrix B?

$$A = \begin{bmatrix} 1 & 2 & 3 & 4 \\ 5 & 6 & 7 & 8 \\ 1 & 3 & 2 & 1 \\ 3 & 4 & 2 & 6 \end{bmatrix}; B = \begin{bmatrix} 1 & 3 & 2 & 1 \\ 5 & 6 & 7 & 8 \\ 2 & 4 & 6 & 8 \\ 3 & 4 & 2 & 6 \end{bmatrix}$$

    A. 72
    B. -72
    C. 144
    D. -144

Mathematics Topics on FE Civil Examination

Problem 20
Which is a solution to the differential equation below?
$$4\frac{d^2y}{dx^2} - 7\frac{dy}{dx} + 3y = 0$$

A. $y = 7e^{3x} - 3e^{-4x}$
B. $y = 7e^{0.75x} - 3e^{x}$
C. $y = 7e^{3x} - 3e^{4x}$
D. $y = 7e^{-0.75x} - 3e^{-4x}$

Problem 21
What is a valid solution to the differential equation below?
$$\frac{d^2y}{dx^2} + 6\frac{dy}{dx} + 25y = 4\sin x$$

A. $y = e^{-3x}(A \cos 4x + B \sin 4x) + Cx \sin x$
B. $y = e^{-3x}(A \cos 4x + B \sin 4x) + C \sin x$
C. $y = e^{3x}(A \cos 4x + B \sin 4x) + C \sin x$
D. $y = e^{3x}(A \cos 4x + B \sin 4x) + Cx \sin x$

Problem 22
What is a valid solution to the differential equation below?
$$\frac{d^2y}{dx^2} + 16y = 4\sin 4x$$

A. $y = (A + Bx + Cx^2) \cos 4x$
B. $y = (A + Bx + Cx^2) \sin 4x$
C. $y = (A + Bx) \cos 4x + (C + Dx) \sin 4x$
D. $y = (A + Bx) \cos x + (C + Dx) \sin x$

Problem 23
What is the Laplace Transform of the function below?
$$f(t) = e^{5t} \sin(3t + 5)$$

A. $F(s) = \frac{3 \sin 5 + (s-5) \cos 5}{s^2 - 10s + 34}$
B. $F(s) = \frac{3 \cos 5 + (s-5) \sin 5}{s^2 - 6s + 34}$
C. $F(s) = \frac{3 \cos 5 + (s-5) \sin 5}{s^2 - 10s + 34}$
D. $F(s) = \frac{3 \sin 5 + (s-5) \cos 5}{s^2 - 6s + 34}$

Mathematics Topics on FE Civil Examination

Problem 24
Newton's method is to be used to extract roots for the equation shown below:
$$2x^3 - 8x^2 + 8x - 12 = 0$$
Assuming an initial estimate x = 0, what is the new value of x after two iterations?
  A. -1
  B. -2
  C. -3
  D. -5

Problem 25
What is the estimate of the integral shown below if the Trapezoidal rule is used, dividing the domain into 6 equal intervals?
$$\int_0^6 f(x)dx = \int_0^6 (2x^3 - 8x^2 + 8x - 12)\, dx$$
  A. 154
  B. 144
  C. 120
  D. 58

Problem 26
What is the estimate of the integral shown below if the Forward Rectangular rule is used, dividing the domain into 6 equal intervals?
$$\int_0^6 f(x)dx = \int_0^6 (2x^3 - 8x^2 + 8x - 12)\, dx$$
  A. 154
  B. 144
  C. 120
  D. 58

Mathematics Topics on FE Civil Examination

Problem 27

What is the estimate of the integral shown below if the Simpson's rule is used, dividing the domain into 6 equal intervals?

$$\int_0^6 f(x)dx = \int_0^6 (2x^3 - 8x^2 + 8x - 12)\,dx$$

A. 154
B. 144
C. 120
D. 58

Problem 28

What is the Taylor Series for the function f(x) = sin²(x)?

A. $f(x) = x + x^2 - \frac{x^3}{6} + \cdots$

B. $f(x) = x - x^2 - \frac{x^3}{3} + \cdots$

C. $f(x) = x^2 - \frac{x^4}{6} + \frac{2x^6}{15} \cdots$

D. $f(x) = x^2 - \frac{x^4}{3} + \frac{2x^6}{45} \cdots$

Problem 29

What is the following integral?

$$\int x^2 e^{5x}\,dx$$

A. $e^{5x}\left(\frac{x^2}{5} + \frac{2x}{25} + \frac{2}{125}\right)$

B. $e^{5x}\left(\frac{x^2}{5} + \frac{2x}{25} - \frac{2}{125}\right)$

C. $e^{5x}\left(\frac{x^2}{5} - \frac{2x}{25} + \frac{2}{125}\right)$

D. $e^{5x}\left(\frac{x^2}{5} - \frac{2x}{25} - \frac{2}{125}\right)$

Mathematics Topics on FE Civil Examination

Problem 30
What is the value of the following definite integral?

$$\int_0^4 \frac{dx}{3x^2 - 5x + 3}$$

A. 2.38
B. 1.44
C. 82.33
D. 49.40

Problem 31
Given the differential equation:

$$\frac{dy}{dt} = y \sin t + 2y \cos t$$

and the initial condition y(0) = 1, what is the value of y at t = 0.5, if Euler's method is used to simulate the solution?

A. 1.25
B. 1.50
C. 1.75
D. 2.00

Problem 32
The number of tickets sold to a theme park in the year 2000 was 1,456,120. If the ticket sales are expected to increase by 2% every year, what is the total number of tickets sold during the 10-year period 2001-2010?

A. 15.5 million
B. 15.9 million
C. 16.1 million
D. 16.3 million

Problem 33

A parallelopiped is formed by drawing edges OA, OB and OC radiating out from the origin O and constructing opposite edges parallel to these rays. Coordinates are in cm. What is the volume of the parallelopiped?

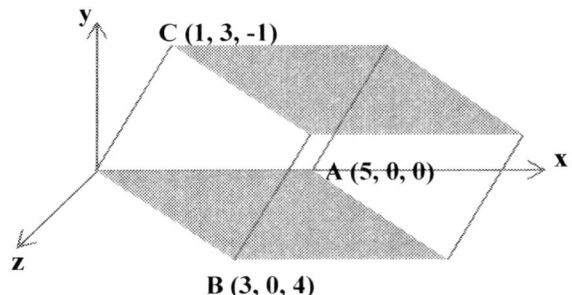

A. 60 cm³
B. 80 cm³
C. 96 cm³
D. 120 cm³

Problem 34

For the triangle shown below, what is the angle A?

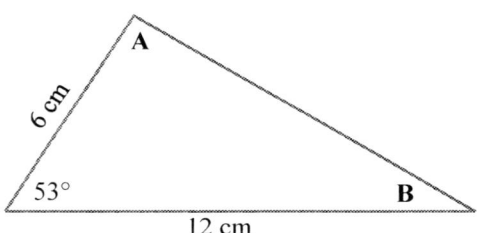

A. 81.3°
B. 82.1°
C. 82.8°
D. 83.5°

Problem 35

Calculate the following: $(-0.9 + 1.2j)^7$

A. 16.7 + 3.5 j
B. − 16.7 + 3.5 j
C. 16.7 − 3.5j
D. − 16.7 − 3.5j

Problem 36

What are the coordinates of the inflection point of the curve defined by the equation below?

$y = 3x^3 - 4x^2 - 9x + 5$

    A. x = 0.44, y = 0.48
    B. x = 0.65, y = 8.34
    C. x = 0.44, y = -7.39
    D. x = 0.65, y = -5.00

Problem 37

What is the radius of curvature of the curve defined by the function y(x) at the origin?

$y = 3x^3 - 4x^2 - 9x + 5$

    A. r = 93
    B. r = 85
    C. r = 78
    D. r = 71

Problem 38

What is the limit shown below?

$$\lim_{x \to 1} \frac{4x^4 - 2x^3 + x^2 - 3}{5x^3 - 4x^2 - 1}$$

    A. 11/9
    B. 12/7
    C. 10/3
    D. 14/5

Problem 39

What is the limit shown below?

$$\lim_{x \to \infty} \frac{4e^{3x}}{5x^3}$$

    A. 0
    B. 1
    C. 10/3
    D. ∞

Mathematics Topics on FE Civil Examination

Problem 40
Evaluate the following limit:
$$\lim_{x \to 0^+} x \ln x$$

A. 0
B. 1
C. ½
D. ∞

Problem 41
Given the function: $y(x) = (2x)^x$

What is the derivative $\frac{dy}{dx}$?

A. $\frac{dy}{dx} = x^{2x}[1 + \ln(2x)]$
B. $\frac{dy}{dx} = (2x)^x[1 + \ln(2x)]$
C. $\frac{dy}{dx} = x^x[1 + 2\ln(x)]$
D. $\frac{dy}{dx} = (2x)^x[1 + 2\ln(2x)]$

Problem 42
Convert the following polar equation into rectangular form:
$3r^2 \sin 2\theta + 2r^2 - 2 = 0$

A. $x^2 + y^2 + 3xy = 0$
B. $x^2 + 2y^2 + 3xy = 1$
C. $x^2 - y^2 + 3xy = 0$
D. $x^2 + y^2 + 3xy = 1$

Problem 43
Find the area defined by the following expressions:
(i) $3x^2 - 2 < y < 5$
(ii) $x > 0$

A. 7.1
B. 5.6
C. 4.8
D. 3.6

Mathematics Topics on FE Civil Examination

Problem 44

What is the Laplace transform of $4\frac{d^2y}{dx^2} - 3\frac{dy}{dx} + \sin 3x$

Boundary conditions are:

(i) At x = 0, y = 1

(ii) At x = 0, y' = ½

A. $s(4s - 3)F(s) + 4s - 1 + \frac{3}{s^2+9}$

B. $s(4s - 3)F(s) + 1 - 4s + \frac{3}{s^2-9}$

C. $s(4s - 3)F(s) + 4s + \frac{3}{s^2-9}$

D. $s(4s - 3)F(s) + 1 - 4s + \frac{3}{s^2+9}$

Problem 45

What is the determinant of the matrix shown below?

$$\begin{bmatrix} 2 & 1 & 3 \\ 7 & 4 & 2 \\ -2 & 2 & 5 \end{bmatrix}$$

A. 45
B. 59
C. 67
D. 97

Problem 46

The polar form of a vector is (10, 130°). The rectangular form is:

A. 7.66 + 6.43j
B. 6.43 - 7.66j
C. - 6.43 + 7.66j
D. - 7.66 - 6.43j

Problem 47

What are the direction cosines of the vector 5i + 6j – 3k?

A. $u_x = 0.60$; $u_y = 0.72$; $u_z = -0.36$
B. $u_x = 0.72$; $u_y = 0.36$; $u_z = -0.56$
C. $u_x = 0.60$; $u_y = 0.72$; $u_z = 0.36$
D. $u_x = 0.72$; $u_y = 0.36$; $u_z = 0.56$

Mathematics Topics on FE Civil Examination

Problem 48
What is the proper decomposition of the following function into partial fractions?
$$f(x) = \frac{3x - 7}{(x-4)^2(2x^3 + 1)}$$

A. $f(x) = \frac{A}{x-4} + \frac{Bx+C}{(x-4)^2} + \frac{Dx^2+Ex+F}{(2x^3+1)}$

B. $f(x) = \frac{A}{x-4} + \frac{B}{(x-4)^2} + \frac{Cx^2+Dx+E}{(2x^3+1)}$

C. $f(x) = \frac{Ax+B}{(x-4)^2} + \frac{Cx^2+Dx+E}{(2x^3+1)}$

D. $f(x) = \frac{A}{x-4} + \frac{B}{(x-4)^2} + \frac{C}{(2x^3+1)}$

Problem 49
A vector function **F**(x,y,z) is shown below. What is the curl of the function?
$$F(x, y, z) = 4xy^2z\boldsymbol{i} + 5x^2y^3z\boldsymbol{j} + 2x^2y^2z^2\boldsymbol{k}$$

A. $[4x^2yz^2 - 5x^2y^3]\boldsymbol{i} + [4xy^2 - 4xy^2z^2]\boldsymbol{j} + [10xy^3z - 8xyz]\boldsymbol{k}$

B. $[4xyz^2 - 5x^2y^3]\boldsymbol{i} + [4xy^2 - 4xy^2z^2]\boldsymbol{j} + [10xy^3z - 8xyz]\boldsymbol{k}$

C. $[4xyz^2 + 5x^2y^3]\boldsymbol{i} + [4xy^2 - 4xy^2z^2]\boldsymbol{j} + [10xy^3z - 8xyz]\boldsymbol{k}$

D. $[4x^2yz^2 - 5x^2y^3]\boldsymbol{i} + [4xy^2 + 4xyz^2]\boldsymbol{j} + [10xy^3z - 8xyz]\boldsymbol{k}$

Problem 50
A vector function **F**(x,y,z) is shown below. What is the divergence of the function?
$$F(x, y, z) = 4xy^2z\boldsymbol{i} + 5x^2y^3z\boldsymbol{j} + 2x^2y^2z^2\boldsymbol{k}$$

A. $4y^2z^2 + 15x^2y^2z$

B. $4xy^2z + 19x^2yz$

C. $4y^2z + 15x^2y^2z$

D. $4y^2z + 19x^2y^2z$

Problem 51

What is the Fourier series for the function shown below?

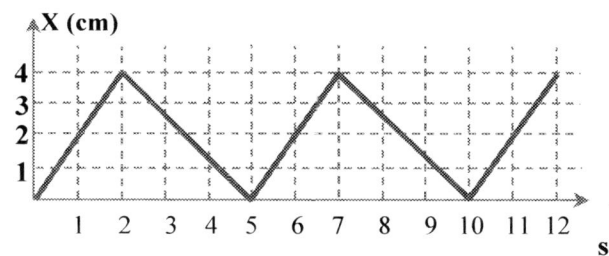

A. $X(t) = 4 - 1.53 \cos\frac{\pi t}{5} - 0.15 \cos\frac{2\pi t}{5} + \cdots + 0.50 \sin\frac{\pi t}{5} - 0.20 \sin\frac{2\pi t}{5} + \cdots$

B. $X(t) = 2 + 1.3 \cos\frac{2\pi t}{5} - 0.15 \cos\frac{4\pi t}{5} + \cdots$

C. $X(t) = 2 - 1.53 \cos\frac{2\pi t}{5} - 0.15 \cos\frac{4\pi t}{5} + \cdots + 0.50 \sin\frac{2\pi t}{5} - 0.20 \sin\frac{4\pi t}{5} + \cdots$

D. $X(t) = 4 + 0.50 \sin\frac{2\pi t}{5} - 0.20 \sin\frac{4\pi t}{5} + \cdots$

Problem 52

What is the magnitude of the angle θ that satisfies the following equation?
$$\cos 2\theta + 5 \cos \theta - 6 = 0$$

A. θ = 60°
B. θ = 45°
C. θ = 0°
D. θ = 30°

Problem 53

Solve the following equation for the angle θ
$$5 \sin \theta + 12 \cos \theta = 10$$

A. θ = 62°20′
B. θ = 17°06′
C. θ = 43°12′
D. θ = 51°29′

Problem 54

A track is laid out in the shape shown below. The straights are connected by semicircular segments. If a runner's path is offset 1 m outside the track edge shown, how many laps must be run to complete a 10 km race?

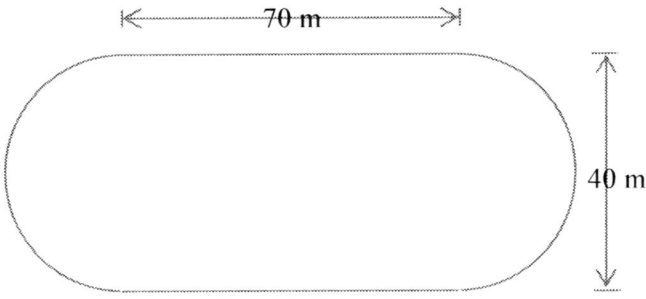

A. 37
B. 38
C. 39
D. 40

Mathematics Solutions

Mathematics Topics on FE Civil Examination

Solution 1
The coefficients A and B in the general form of the equation yield the slope m = - A/B
For two lines which are perpendicular, the slopes are negative reciprocal of each other ($m_1 = -1/m_2$).
This means that the A:B relationship will be reversed and undergo a change in sign.
The original equation has A = 3 and B = 7
The perpendicular line will have A = +7 and B = − 3 (or A = −7 and B = + 3)

Answer is C

Solution 2
The double intercept form of a straight line can be used here:
$$\frac{x}{8} + \frac{y}{5} = 1 \Rightarrow 5x + 8y = 40$$
The slope-intercept form of the straight line can also be used. The y-intercept is 5 and the slope can be computed using m = Δy/Δx = -5/8
Therefore, the equation is: $y = mx + b = -\frac{5}{8}x + 5 \Rightarrow 8y = -5x + 40 \Rightarrow 5x + 8y = 40$

Answer is D

Solution 3
The handbook shows a parabola with a vertical directrix. For such a parabola, the y term is quadratic and the x term is linear. In the question, the x term is quadratic and the y term is linear. Thus, the standard form would be: $(x - h)^2 = 2p(y - k)$
First step: Divide the equation by 4
$$x^2 + \frac{3}{4}x + \frac{7}{4}y - \frac{1}{2} = 0$$
Second step: Complete the square in the x-quadratic:
$$\left(x + \frac{3}{8}\right)^2 + \frac{7}{4}y - \frac{1}{2} = \left(\frac{3}{8}\right)^2$$
Third step: Move the y terms to the right side:
$$\left(x + \frac{3}{8}\right)^2 = -\frac{7}{4}y + \frac{1}{2} + \left(\frac{3}{8}\right)^2 = -\frac{7}{4}y + \frac{41}{64}$$
Fourth step: Write the y term in standard form
$$\left(x + \frac{3}{8}\right)^2 = 2\left(-\frac{7}{8}\right)\left(y - \frac{41}{7 \times 16}\right) = 2\left(-\frac{7}{8}\right)\left(y - \frac{41}{112}\right)$$
Therefore, the directrix is at: $y = k - \frac{p}{2} = \frac{41}{112} - \frac{1}{2} \times -\frac{7}{8} = \frac{41}{112} + \frac{7}{16} = \frac{90}{112} = \frac{45}{56}$

Answer is B

Mathematics Topics on FE Civil Examination

> Note that the handbook gives the directrix equation for the special case "when h = k = 0, directrix is x = - p/2" The more general case when h and k are not zero would be: the equation of the directrix is x = h – p/2
> Similarly, when the parabola opens up/down instead of right/left, the equation of the directrix is y = k – p/2

Solution 4

The handbook shows an ellipse with axes that are horizontal and vertical. Such an ellipse would have no mixed (xy) terms. In order to extract the a and b coefficients (all that's needed for the calculation of eccentricity), one needs to simply see that the standard form will be like

$$\frac{(x-h)^2}{1^2} + \frac{(y-k)^2}{2^2} = 1 \rightarrow a = 1; b = 2$$

Calculation of the rest is not necessary for this question. Therefore, the ratio of minor axis to major axis = a/b = 1/2 = 0.5

Therefore, eccentricity, $e = \sqrt{1 - 0.5^2} = 0.866$

Answer is A

> Note that the handbook gives the eccentricity equation for the special case "when h = k = 0" This expression for the eccentricity is dependent only on the length of the minor and the major axes and therefore is true for the more general case when h and k are not zero as well

Solution 5

In this case, it is not enough to simply calculate the ratio b/a, but the actual lengths 'a' and 'b', because the area is asked for.

The given equation can be adapted into the standard form by the completion of squares:

Step 1: Complete the squares

$$4\left[x^2 - 2\left(\frac{3}{8}\right)x + \left(\frac{3}{8}\right)^2\right] + \left[y^2 + 2\left(\frac{7}{2}\right)y + \left(\frac{7}{2}\right)^2\right] - 2 = 4\left(\frac{3}{8}\right)^2 + \left(\frac{7}{2}\right)^2 = \frac{205}{16}$$

$$4\left[x - \frac{3}{8}\right]^2 + \left[y + \frac{7}{2}\right]^2 = \frac{237}{16}$$

$$\frac{\left(x - \frac{3}{8}\right)^2}{\frac{237}{64}} + \frac{\left(y + \frac{7}{2}\right)^2}{\frac{237}{16}} = 1$$

Therefore, semi-major axis length = √(237/16) and semi-minor axis length = √(237/64)
Therefore, area, A = πab = 23.27

Answer is D

Solution 6

The slope of the asymptotes of any hyperbola is given by ± b/a

The given equation can be adapted into the standard form by reducing the right side to 1:

$$\frac{(x-2)^2}{16} - \frac{(y-5)^2}{9} = 1$$

Therefore, a = 4 and b = 3

$$\tan \theta = \pm \frac{3}{4} \Rightarrow \theta = \pm 36.9°$$

Therefore, the acute angle between the asymptotes = 2θ = 73.8° and the obtuse angle = 106.2°

Answer is B

Solution 7

The necessary conditions for a CIRCLE are: A = C ≠ 0 and B = 0. These conditions are not met. Therefore, it is either an ellipse, parabola or hyperbola. The discriminant is calculated as

$$B^2 - 4AC = 8^2 - 4 \times 5 \times 3 = 4 > 0$$

Since the discriminant is greater than zero, the equation describes a hyperbola.

Answer is D

Solution 8

Choose one of the positions on the original matrix for which the entries in the answer choices are unique. This will allow you to choose the correct answer with the minimum amount of work.

For example, for the number 3 in the (1, 2) position (row 1, column 2) in the matrix A, the 4 choices for cofactor are 36, 28, -28, and -36, which are all different.

The cofactor of 3 is (with a change in sign because (1, 2) is an odd position), is the determinant

$$-\begin{vmatrix} 7 & 4 \\ 5 & 8 \end{vmatrix} = -36$$

Answer is D

> In any problem where the answer choices contain multiple entities (as in each matrix contains 9 elements), look for an entity that has unique choices amongst the 4 answer choices. This will allow you to choose the correct answer without solving the entire problem.

Mathematics Topics on FE Civil Examination

Solution 9

Choose one of the positions on the four given answer choices for which the entries are unique. This will allow you to choose the correct answer with the minimum amount of work.

For example, for the (3, 2) position (row 3, column 2), the 4 choices for the adjoint are 1, -23, 23 and -1, which are all different.

Now, remember that the adjoint is obtained by transposing the cofactor matrix. Therefore, entries in the (3, 2) position of the adjoint will originate from the (2, 3) position of the original matrix. The cofactor of $A_{23} = 4$ is (with a change in sign because (2, 3) is an odd position), is the determinant

$$-\begin{vmatrix} 2 & 3 \\ 5 & -4 \end{vmatrix} = 23$$

This number will occupy the (2, 3) position in the cofactor matrix, but move to the (3, 2) position in the adjoint matrix.

Answer is C

Solution 10

$$z^5 = -22.63 + 22.63j$$

The magnitude of the complex number on the right = 32 and the angle = $\tan^{-1}$ (22.63/-22.63) = 135 = $3\pi/4$
Therefore,

$$z^5 = 32e^{j\frac{3\pi}{4}}$$

The first root is

$$z_1 = 32^{1/5}e^{j3\pi/20} = 2e^{j3\pi/20}$$

The fact that the root has a magnitude of 2 eliminates options B and C.

This can be represented by a vector at angle of 27°
The other roots will be spaced equally (72° apart) around the 2π radians of the circle (spaced $2\pi/5$). Therefore, the other roots are:

$$z_2 = 2e^{j(3\pi/20+2\pi/5)} = 2e^{j11\pi/20}$$
$$z_3 = 2e^{j(3\pi/20+4\pi/5)} = 2e^{j19\pi/20}$$
$$z_4 = 2e^{j(3\pi/20+6\pi/5)} = 2e^{j27\pi/20}$$
$$z_5 = 2e^{j(3\pi/20+8\pi/5)} = 2e^{j35\pi/20}$$

These are represented by vectors at angles 99, 171, 243 and 315 degrees respectively. Option A has magnitude = 2 and angle = 171 degrees.

Answer is A

As soon as it is obvious that the magnitude of the complex number is 32 and the fifth root will have magnitude = fifth root of 32 = 2, you should scan the answer choices. In this case, this examination will eliminate choices B and C.

Note that your calculator will yield $\tan^{-1}(22.63/-22.63) = -45$. It is important to recognize that the angle should actually be taken as $-45 + 180 = 135$, which is a second quadrant angle, as appropriate for the complex number $-22.63 + 22.63j$

Also note that for the exponential form of complex numbers, it is essential to express the angle in radians.

Solution 11
The dot product is a convenient way to calculate the angle between two vectors, since the result of the operation is a scalar.

Vector **AB** = 7i − 3j + k
Vector **CD** = 6i + 5j − 6k
AB·CD = (7)(6) + (-3)(5) + (1)(-6) = 21
$|AB| = \sqrt{7^2 + 3^2 + 1^2} = \sqrt{59}$
$|CD| = \sqrt{6^2 + 5^2 + 6^2} = \sqrt{97}$

$$\cos\theta = \frac{21}{\sqrt{59}\sqrt{97}} = 73.9°$$

Answer is B

Solution 12
Vector **AB** = 4i − 5j
Vector **AC** = − 5j + 4k
AB X AC = − 20k − 16j − 20i
$|AB \times AC| = \sqrt{20^2 + 16^2 + 20^2} = \sqrt{1056} = 32.5$
Therefore, area of the triangle = ½ (32.5) = 16.25

Answer is C

The cross product is a convenient way to calculate the area of a trapezoid whose sides can be expressed as vectors. The magnitude of the cross product is the area of the trapezoid and the unit vector of the cross product is the vector normal to the plane of the trapezoid.

Solution 13
The general form of the circle shown is:
$$(x-4)^2 + (y-6)^2 = 3^2$$
The length of the tangent (to the point of tangency) is calculated as:

Mathematics Topics on FE Civil Examination

$$\sqrt{(x'-h)^2 + (y'-k)^2 - r^2} = \sqrt{(10-4)^2 + (1-6)^2 - 3^2} = 7.21$$

$\tan \alpha = 3/7.21 = 0.416$

$\alpha = 22.6°$

Answer is A

Solution 14

$$xy^2 - x = x(y^2 - 1) = x(y-1)(y+1) = 10$$
$$\log x + \log(y-1) + \log(y+1) = \log 10 = 1$$
$$\log x = 1 - \log(y-1) - \log(y+1)$$
$$x = antilog\{1 - \log(y-1) - \log(y+1)\}$$

Answer is B

Solution 15

The scalar function
$$f(x, y, z) = 3x^2y + y^3z + 4xy^2z^2 - 8$$
has the gradient given by:

$$\nabla f = \boldsymbol{i}\frac{\partial f}{\partial x} + \boldsymbol{j}\frac{\partial f}{\partial y} + \boldsymbol{k}\frac{\partial f}{\partial z} = (6xy + 4y^2z^2)\boldsymbol{i} + (3x^2 + 3y^2z + 8xyz^2)\boldsymbol{j} + (y^3 + 8xy^2z)\boldsymbol{k}$$

At the point (1, 1, 1), this is the vector 10**i** + 14**j** + 9**k**

A vector normal to this gradient vector will have a zero dot product with 10**i** + 14**j** + 9**k**
2**i** - 4**j** + 3**k**   Dot product = 20-56+27 = 9
2**i** + 4**j** - 3**k**   Dot product = 20+56-27 = 49
3**i** - 4**j** + 3**k**   Dot product = 30-56+27 = 1
i - 2**j** + 2**k**   Dot product = 10-28+18 = 0

Answer is D

Solution 16

The series is an arithmetic series with first term = -5 and constant difference d = 7
The number of terms can be calculated from
$$128 = -5 + (n-1) \times 7 \Rightarrow n = 20$$
Sum of the 20-term series:
$$S = \left(\frac{a+l}{2}\right)n = \frac{-5+128}{2} \times 20 = 1230$$

Answer is C

Mathematics Topics on FE Civil Examination

Solution 17
The first derivative dy/dx is
$$\frac{dy}{dx} = 6x^2 - 16x + 8$$
Equating dy/dx to zero, we get:
$$3x^2 - 8x + 4 = 0 \Rightarrow x = 0.667, 2.0$$

Both of these extrema are within the given domain 0 < x < 3

The second derivative d^2y/dx^2 is
$$\frac{d^2y}{dx^2} = 12x - 16$$

At x = 0.667, d^2y/dx^2 < 0. This is a MAXIMUM
At x = 2.0, d^2y/dx^2 > 0. This is a MINIMUM

To find the maximum value of the function, evaluate y(0.667) = -9.63
However, since a closed domain is given, one must also evaluate the function at the domain boundaries (x = 0 and x = 3).

At x = 0, y = -12
At x = 3, y = -6 (Thus, if we are looking for the absolute maximum of the function within this domain, the value at x = 3 is the desired answer, even though t is not a *true* extremum.

Answer is C

Solution 18
Note the difference between this problem and the previous one. The domain for the function has been changed.
The first derivative dy/dx is
$$\frac{dy}{dx} = 6x^2 - 16x + 8$$
Equating dy/dx to zero, we get:
$3x^2 - 8x + 4 = 0 \Rightarrow x = 0.667, 2.0$
Of these, the only one within the domain 1 < x < 3 is x = 2
The second derivative d^2y/dx^2 is
$$\frac{d^2y}{dx^2} = 12x - 16$$
At x = 2.0, d^2y/dx^2 > 0. This is a MINIMUM
So, a true maximum does not exist within the domain 1 < x < 3
To find the maximum value of the function, evaluate the function at the two boundaries:
y(1) = -10

Mathematics Topics on FE Civil Examination

y(3) = -6

Answer is B

Solution 19

The two matrices are closely related in the following way: If row 1 and row 3 from matrix A are interchanged, and then row 3 is doubled (every cell in the row is doubled), then we get matrix B.

A row interchange causes the determinant to change sign. Multiplying a row (or column) by a factor causes the determinant to get multiplied by that factor. The set {1,2,3,4} that occurs in row 3 after the row interchange is doubled to the set {2,4,6,8}.

Therefore, determinant of matrix B is 72 x -1 x 2 = -144

Answer is D

Solution 20

This is a homogeneous, ordinary differential equation with constant coefficients. Trying the exponential solution y = e^{mx}, the characteristic equation is:
$4m^2 - 7m + 3 = 0$

Roots are: $m = \frac{7 \pm \sqrt{7^2 - 4 \times 4 \times 3}}{2 \times 4} \Rightarrow m = \frac{3}{4}, 1$

y = $Ae^{0.75x}$ + Be^x

With the given information (i.e. without any boundary conditions, there is no way to determine coefficients – only choice B has the correct pattern.

Answer is B

Solution 21

This is a nonhomogeneous ordinary differential equation with constant coefficients. For the homogeneous solution, trying the exponential solution y = e^{mx}, the characteristic equation is:
$m^2 + 6m + 25 = 0$

Roots are: $m = \frac{-6 \pm \sqrt{6^2 - 4 \times 1 \times 25}}{2 \times 1} \Rightarrow m = -3 \pm 4i$

This can be expressed in 4 different ways:
$y_H = Ae^{(-3+4i)x} + Be^{(-3-4i)x}$
$y_H = e^{-3x}(Ae^{4ix} + Be^{-4ix})$
$y_H = e^{-3x}(A_1 \cos 4x + B_1 \sin 4x)$
$y_H = Ce^{-3x} \cos(4x + \varphi)$

The particular solution will have the same form as the right hand side of the differential equation
$y_P = C \sin x$

The complete solution will be of the form:
$$y = y_H + y_P = e^{-3x}(A \cos 4x + B \sin 4x) + C \sin x + D \cos x$$

With the given information (i.e. without any boundary conditions, there is no way to determine coefficients – only choice B has the correct pattern.

Answer is B

Solution 22
This is a nonhomogeneous ordinary differential equation with constant coefficients. For the homogeneous solution, trying the exponential solution $y = e^{mx}$, the characteristic equation is:
$m^2 + 16 = 0$
Roots are: $m = \pm 4i$
This can be expressed in 3 different ways:
$y_H = Ae^{4ix} + Be^{-4ix}$
$y_H = A_1 \cos 4x + B_1 \sin 4x$
$y_H = C \cos(4x + \varphi)$

$$y_H = A \cos 4x + B \sin 4x$$

The particular solution will have the same form as the right hand side of the differential equation
$y_P = C \sin 4x + D \cos 4x$. However, this function already exists in the homogeneous solution. To make it unique, we multiply it with the simplest polynomial in the series x, x^2, x^3, etc.

The complete solution will be of the form:
$$y = y_H + y_P = A \sin 4x + B \cos 4x + Cx \sin 4x + Dx \cos 4x$$

With the given information (i.e. without any boundary conditions, there is no way to determine coefficients – only choice C has the correct pattern.

Answer is C

Solution 23
$f(t) = e^{5t} \sin(3t + 5) = e^{5t}(\cos 5 \sin 3t + \sin 5 \cos 3t)$
$$F(s) = \cos 5 \frac{3}{(s-5)^2 + 9} + \sin 5 \frac{s-5}{(s-5)^2 + 9}$$

Mathematics Topics on FE Civil Examination

$$F(s) = \frac{3\cos 5 + (s-5)\sin 5}{s^2 - 10s + 34}$$

Answer is C

Solution 24

$f(x) = 2x^3 - 8x^2 + 8x - 12$
$f'(x) = 6x^2 - 16x + 8$
$x_0 = 0; f(x_o) = -12; f'(x_o) = 8;$
$x_1 = 0 - \dfrac{-12}{8} = 1.5$
$x_1 = 1.5; f(x_1) = -11.25; f'(x_1) = -2.5;$
$x_2 = 1.5 - \dfrac{-11.25}{-2.5} = -3$

Answer is C

Solution 25

The domain 0 < x < 6 is to be divided into 6 equal intervals. Therefore, the function must be evaluated at x = 0, 1, 2, 3, 4, 5, 6

f(a) = f(0) = -12
f(b) = f(6) = 180
f(1) = -10
f(2) = -12
f(3) = -6
f(4) = 20
f(5) = 78

$$\int_0^6 f(x)dx = \frac{1}{2}[-12 + 2(-10 - 12 - 6 + 20 + 78) + 180] = 154$$

Answer is A

Solution 26

The domain 0 < x < 6 is to be divided into 6 equal intervals. Therefore, the function must be evaluated at x = 0, 1, 2, 3, 4, 5, 6

f(a) = f(0) = -12
f(1) = -10
f(2) = -12
f(3) = -6
f(4) = 20
f(5) = 78

$$\int_0^6 f(x)dx = 1 \times [-12 - 10 - 12 - 6 + 20 + 78] = 58$$

Answer is D

Solution 27
The domain 0 < x < 6 is to be divided into 6 equal intervals. Therefore, the function must be evaluated at x = 0, 1, 2, 3, 4, 5, 6

f(a) = f(0) = -12
f(b) = f(6) = 180
f(1) = -10
f(2) = -12
f(3) = -6
f(4) = 20
f(5) = 78

$$\int_0^6 f(x)dx = \frac{1}{3}[-12 + 4(-10 - 6 + 78) + 2(-12 + 20) + 180] = 144$$

Answer is B

Of the three methods (problems 25-27), the Simpson's rule is the only one that yields the exact answer (in this case).

Solution 28
f(x) = sin²(x)
f'(x) = 2sin(x)cos(x) = sin(2x)
f''(x) = 2cos(2x)
f'''(x) = -4sin(2x)
f''''(x) = -8cos(2x)
and so on ...

At x = 0, f(0) = 0; f'(0) = 0; f''(0) = 2; f'''(0) = 0; f^{IV}(0) = - 8 and so on ...

Taylor's Series (about a = 0) is:
$$f(x) = 0 + \frac{0}{1!}(x - 0) + \frac{2}{2!}(x - 0)^2 + \frac{0}{3!}(x - 0)^3 + \frac{-8}{4!}(x - 0)^4 + \cdots$$
$$f(x) = x^2 - \frac{x^4}{3}\cdots$$

Answer is D

Solution 29
Using u = x^2 and dv = e^{5x}dx → v = 1/5 e^{5x}
udv = d(uv) − vdu

Mathematics Topics on FE Civil Examination

$\int u\,dv = uv - \int v\,du$

$$\int x^2 e^{5x}\,dx = x^2 \frac{1}{5}e^{5x} - \int \frac{1}{5}e^{5x} 2x\,dx = \frac{x^2}{5}e^{5x} - \frac{2}{5}\int xe^{5x}\,dx$$

Now we must perform the integral

$$\int xe^{5x}\,dx$$

Once again, using u = x and dv = $e^{5x}dx \rightarrow v = 1/5\ e^{5x}$

$$\int xe^{5x}\,dx = x\frac{1}{5}e^{5x} - \int \frac{1}{5}e^{5x}\,dx = \frac{x}{5}e^{5x} - \frac{1}{5}\int e^{5x}\,dx = \frac{x}{5}e^{5x} - \frac{1}{25}e^{5x}$$

Therefore, the original integral is:

$$\int x^2 e^{5x}\,dx = \frac{x^2}{5}e^{5x} - \frac{2}{5}\int xe^{5x}\,dx = \frac{x^2}{5}e^{5x} - \frac{2}{5}\left(\frac{x}{5}e^{5x} - \frac{1}{25}e^{5x}\right)$$

$$= e^{5x}\left(\frac{x^2}{5} - \frac{2x}{25} + \frac{2}{125}\right) = e^{5x}\left(\frac{25x^2 - 10x + 2}{125}\right)$$

Answer is C

A shortcut for the case where the 'u' function is a polynomial is illustrated in the table below.
Step 1: List the polynomial as the u function and the other function as v.
Step 2: Successively differentiate u and integrate v until the derivative of the polynomial (u) becomes zero.
Step 3: Starting at the top of the table, assign alternating signs (+ and -) to the expressions.
Step 4: Starting with the upper left corner ($+x^2$ in this case), form products diagonally by multiplying it with the function in the cell 'below and to the right'. Continue accumulating these products until the zero is reached in the 'u' column.

	u (differentiate)	v (integrate)
+	x^2	e^{5x}
-	$2x$	$\frac{1}{5}e^{5x}$
+	2	$\frac{1}{25}e^{5x}$
-	0	$\frac{1}{125}e^{5x}$

$$+(x^2)\left(\frac{1}{5}e^{5x}\right) - (2x)\left(\frac{1}{25}e^{5x}\right) + (2)\left(\frac{1}{125}e^{5x}\right)$$

Solution 30
This is one of the standard forms in the handbook.
a = 3; b = -5; c = 3 → $4ac - b^2 = 11 > 0$. This is case 27a

$$I = \frac{2}{\sqrt{4ac-b^2}}\tan^{-1}\frac{2ax+b}{\sqrt{4ac-b^2}} = \frac{2}{\sqrt{11}}\tan^{-1}\left(\frac{6x-5}{\sqrt{11}}\right)$$

Mathematics Topics on FE Civil Examination

Evaluated between the limits x = 0 and x = 4, we get:

$$I = \frac{2}{\sqrt{11}}\left[\tan^{-1}\left(\frac{19}{\sqrt{11}}\right) - \tan^{-1}\left(\frac{-5}{\sqrt{11}}\right)\right] = 1.437$$

Answer is B

Note: Your calculator must be in RADIAN mode when evaluating this integral.

Solution 31

At t = 0:

$$\frac{dy}{dt} = y(0)\sin 0 + 2y(0)\cos 0 = 0 + 2 \times 1 = 2$$

$$y(0.5) = y(0) + \Delta t \left(\frac{dy}{dt}\right)_{t=0} = 1 + 0.5 \times 2 = 2.0$$

Answer is D

Solution 32

Sales in 2000 = 1,456,120
Sales in 2001 = 1,456,120 x 1.02 = 1,485,242
We have a geometric series with first term a = 1,485,242; rate of growth, r = 1.02; number of terms, n = 10.
The sum of the series is calculated as:

$$S_n = a\left(\frac{r^n - 1}{r - 1}\right) = 1,485,242 \times \frac{1.02^{10} - 1}{1.02 - 1} = 16,262,990$$

Answer is D

Solution 33

OA = 5i
OB = 3i + 4k
OC = i + 3j - k

The volume of the parallelepiped is calculated as the scalar triple product (absolute value).
The scalar triple product is calculated as:

$$\vec{OA} \cdot (\vec{OB} \times \vec{OC}) = \begin{vmatrix} 5 & 0 & 0 \\ 3 & 0 & 4 \\ 1 & 3 & -1 \end{vmatrix} = -60 \ cm^3$$

Volume of the parallelepiped is 60 cm^3

Answer is A

Solution 34

Designating the side opposite the angle of 53° as 'x', we can use the law of cosines to find side length 'x'

$$x^2 = 6^2 + 12^2 - 2 \times 6 \times 12 \times \cos 53 = 93.34$$

Mathematics Topics on FE Civil Examination

x = 9.66 cm

Now, using law of sines,
$$\frac{x}{\sin 53} = \frac{12}{\sin A} \Rightarrow A = \sin^{-1}\left(\frac{12 \sin 53}{9.66}\right) = 82.8°$$

Answer is C

Solution 35

Anything to do with powers and roots is best done using polar coordinates. The first step is to convert (-0.9+1.2j) to polar coordinates:
$$\sqrt{0.9^2 + 1.2^2} = 1.5$$
$$\theta = \tan^{-1}\left(\frac{1.2}{-0.9}\right) = -53.13° \text{ or } 126.87°$$

The second quadrant angle (126.87°) is appropriate, since the vector is a second quadrant vector. However, the angle MUST be expressed in radians.
$$\theta = 126.87° = 2.2143 \ rad$$
$$-0.9 + 1.2j = 1.5e^{2.2143j} \Rightarrow (-0.9 + 1.2j)^7 = (1.5e^{2.2143j})^7 = 17.086e^{15.5j}$$
$$e^{15.5j} = -0.9785 + 0.2065j$$
$$17.086e^{15.5j} = 17.086(-0.9785 + 0.2065j) = -16.72 + 3.53j$$

Answer is B

> Note that all 4 answer choices have the same magnitude. So, just calcualting the angle of the resulting vector is enough.
> The angle of -0.9 + 1.2j is 126.87°
> 126.87 x 7 = 888.1°
> Remove 2 complete revolutions (720°), we have the angle 168.1°, which is a second quadrant angle. Only choice (B) is in the second quadrant.

Solution 36

At the point of inflection, the curvature = 0. Therefore, the second derivative is zero.
$$y = 3x^3 - 4x^2 - 9x + 5$$
$$\frac{dy}{dx} = 9x^2 - 8x - 9$$
$$\frac{d^2y}{dx^2} = 18x - 8$$

Setting the second derivative to zero, x = 0.444.
Therefore, y = 0.478

Answer is A

Solution 37

$$y = 3x^3 - 4x^2 - 9x + 5$$

$$\frac{dy}{dx} = 9x^2 - 8x - 9; \quad \left.\frac{dy}{dx}\right|_{x=0} = -9$$

$$\frac{d^2y}{dx^2} = 18x - 8; \quad \left.\frac{d^2y}{dx^2}\right|_{x=0} = -8$$

Curvature is calculated as:

$$\kappa = \frac{\frac{d^2y}{dx^2}}{\left[1 + \left(\frac{dy}{dx}\right)^2\right]^{3/2}} = \frac{-8}{[1 + (-9)^2]^{3/2}} = -0.0108$$

Radius of curvature: $\rho = \left|\frac{1}{\kappa}\right| = 92.8$

Answer is A

Solution 38

At x = 1, this limit has the indeterminate form 0/0

Therefore, one must replace the numerator and denominator functions with their derivatives.

$$\lim_{x \to 1} \frac{4x^4 - 2x^3 + x^2 - 3}{5x^3 - 4x^2 - 1} = \lim_{x \to 1} \frac{16x^3 - 6x^2 + 2x}{15x^2 - 8x} = \frac{12}{7}$$

Answer is B

Solution 39

At $x \to \infty$, this limit has the indeterminate form ∞/∞

Therefore, one must replace the numerator and denominator functions with their derivatives.

$$\lim_{x \to \infty} \frac{4e^{3x}}{5x^3} = \lim_{x \to \infty} \frac{12e^{3x}}{15x^2}$$

This is still of the form ∞/∞. So we continue taking derivatives:

$$\lim_{x \to \infty} \frac{12e^{3x}}{15x^2} = \lim_{x \to \infty} \frac{36e^{3x}}{30x} = \lim_{x \to \infty} \frac{108e^{3x}}{30} = \frac{\infty}{30}$$

Answer is D

Solution 40

L'Hôpital's rule only applies to the quotient form, not the product form. However, we can convert the product to a quotient form as below:

$$\lim_{x \to 0^+} x \ln x = \lim_{x \to 0^+} \frac{\ln x}{1/x}$$

This form has the ∞/∞ form. Again, taking derivatives:

Mathematics Topics on FE Civil Examination

$$\lim_{x \to 0^+} \frac{\ln x}{1/x} = \lim_{x \to 0^+} \frac{1/x}{-1/x^2} = \lim_{x \to 0^+} (-x) = 0$$

Answer is A

Solution 41

$$y = (2x)^x \Rightarrow \ln y = x \ln(2x)$$

Taking derivatives of both sides:

$$\frac{1}{y}\frac{dy}{dx} = \ln(2x) + x \frac{1}{2x} 2 = 1 + \ln(2x)$$

$$\frac{dy}{dx} = y[1 + \ln(2x)] = (2x)^x [1 + \ln(2x)]$$

Answer is B

Solution 42

Using x = r cos θ and y = r sin θ

$$3r^2 (2 \sin\theta \cos\theta) + 2(x^2 + y^2) - 2 = 0$$
$$6(r \cos\theta)(r \sin\theta) + 2(x^2 + y^2) - 2 = 0$$
$$6xy + 2(x^2 + y^2) - 2 = 0$$
$$x^2 + y^2 + 3xy = 1$$

Answer is D

Solution 43

The region is shown below:

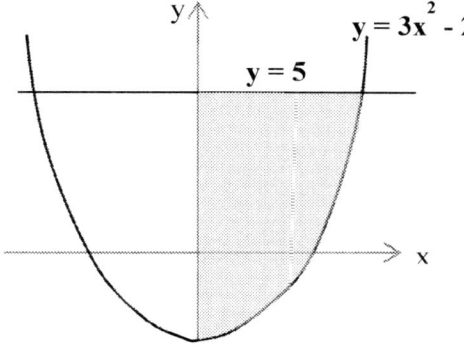

The vertex of the parabola is at (0, -2)

Point of intersection of the parabola and the line y = 5 is at (1.528, 5)

Mathematics Topics on FE Civil Examination

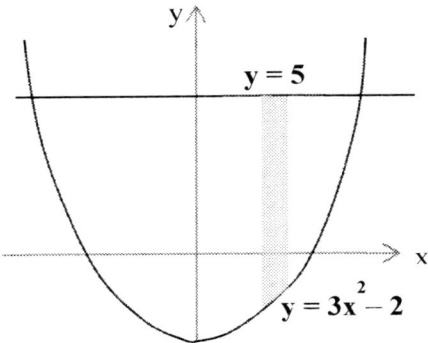

Height of vertical strips y = 5 − (3x² − 2) = 7 − 3x²

$$A = \int dA = \int_0^{1.528} y\,dx = \int_0^{1.528}(7 - 3x^2)\,dx = (7x - x^3)_0^{1.528} = 7.128$$

Answer is A

Solution 44

Laplace transform of d²y/dx² is:

$$s^2 F(s) - sy(0) - y'(0) = s^2 F(s) - s - \frac{1}{2}$$

Laplace transform of dy/dx is:

$$sF(s) - y(0) = sF(s) - 1$$

Laplace transform of sin 3x is:

$$\frac{3}{s^2 + 9}$$

$$4\left(s^2 F(s) - s - \frac{1}{2}\right) - 3(sF(s) - 1) + \frac{3}{s^2 + 9}$$

$$(4s^2 - 3s)F(s) + 1 - 4s + \frac{3}{s^2 + 9}$$

$$s(4s - 3)F(s) + 1 - 4s + \frac{3}{s^2 + 9}$$

Answer is D

Solution 45

Instead of following the traditional approach of reducing a 3x3 matrix to a series of 2x2 matrices, the following approach is much more convenient for calculating the determinant. However, this method WILL NOT work for larger matrices.

Construct an augmented matrix by copying the first 2 columns of the matrix on the right of the original matrix as shown.

$$\begin{bmatrix} 2 & 1 & 3 & | & 2 & 1 \\ 7 & 4 & 2 & | & 7 & 4 \\ -2 & 2 & 5 & | & -2 & 2 \end{bmatrix}$$

Diagonals are then drawn – one set starting at the top left corner and going down and to the right; another set starting at the top right corner and going down and to the left. The determinant is the difference between the products of the first set of diagonals and the products of the second set of diagonals.

Mathematics Topics on FE Civil Examination

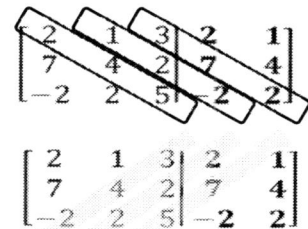

Determinant: $\Delta = (2 \times 4 \times 5 + 1 \times 2 \times -2 + 3 \times 7 \times 2) - (3 \times 4 \times -2 + 2 \times 2 \times 2 + 1 \times 7 \times 5) = 78 - 19 = 59$

Answer is B

Solution 46

This can be worked out by using:
$x = r \cos \theta = 10 \cos 130 = -6.43$
$y = r \sin \theta = 10 \sin 130 = 7.66$
Therefore, the vector is -6.43 + 7.66j

> However, if one notices that the angle of 130 degrees puts this vector in the second quadrant and the only answer choice in the second quadrant is (C), then no computations are necessary.

Answer is C

Solution 47

Magnitude of the vector: $\sqrt{5^2 + 6^2 + 3^2} = 8.367$

Unit vector: $\underline{u} = \dfrac{5i + 6j - 3k}{8.367} = 0.598\boldsymbol{i} + 0.717\boldsymbol{j} - 0.359\boldsymbol{k}$

Answer is A

Solution 48

The denominator can be decomposed into two factors: (x-4) repeated twice and (2x³+1) repeated once.

Partial fractions originating from the two repeat instances of (x-4) will be: $\dfrac{A}{x-4}$ and $\dfrac{B}{(x-4)^2}$

Partial fractions originating from the one instance of (2x³+1) will be: $\dfrac{Cx^2 + Dx + E}{(2x^3 + 1)}$ with numerator one order lower than the denominator.

Answer is B

Solution 49

The curl of a vector function is given by:

Mathematics Topics on FE Civil Examination

$$\begin{vmatrix} i & j & k \\ \frac{\partial}{\partial x} & \frac{\partial}{\partial y} & \frac{\partial}{\partial z} \\ (4xy^2z) & (5x^2y^3z) & (2x^2y^2z^2) \end{vmatrix}$$

$$= i\left[\frac{\partial}{\partial y}(2x^2y^2z^2) - \frac{\partial}{\partial z}(5x^2y^3z)\right] + j\left[\frac{\partial}{\partial z}(4xy^2z) - \frac{\partial}{\partial x}(2x^2y^2z^2)\right]$$

$$+ k\left[\frac{\partial}{\partial x}(5x^2y^3z) - \frac{\partial}{\partial y}(4xy^2z)\right]$$

$$= [4x^2yz^2 - 5x^2y^3]i + [4xy^2 - 4xy^2z^2]j + [10xy^3z - 8xyz]k$$

Answer is A

Solution 50

The divergence of a vector function is given by:

$$\left(i\frac{\partial}{\partial x} + j\frac{\partial}{\partial y} + k\frac{\partial}{\partial z}\right) \cdot [(4xy^2z)i + (5x^2y^3z)j + (2x^2y^2z^2)k]$$

$$= \frac{\partial}{\partial x}(4xy^2z) + \frac{\partial}{\partial y}(5x^2y^3z) + \frac{\partial}{\partial z}(2x^2y^2z^2)$$

$$= 4y^2z + 15x^2y^2z + 4x^2y^2z = 4y^2z + 19x^2y^2z$$

Answer is D

Solution 51

The function is periodic with period T = 5 sec. Therefore, the fundamental frequency w_0 = $2\pi/T = 2\pi/5$. The waveform is neither purely odd [X(-t) = - X(t)], nor purely even [X(-t) = X(t)]

Average value: $\bar{X} = \frac{\int_0^5 Xdt}{\int_0^5 dt} = \frac{10\ cm-sec}{5\ sec} = 2\ cm$

Therefore, the general structure of the Fourier series should be:

$$X(t) = 2 + \sum_{n=1}^{\infty}\left(a_n \cos\frac{2n\pi t}{5} + b_n \sin\frac{2n\pi t}{5}\right)$$

Answer is C

Solution 52

Using the identity:

$$\cos 2\theta = 2\cos^2\theta - 1$$

The equation becomes

$$2\cos^2\theta - 1 + 5\cos\theta - 6 = 0$$

$$2\cos^2\theta + 5\cos\theta - 7 = 0$$

Solving the quadratic:

$$\cos\theta = \frac{-5 \pm \sqrt{5^2 - 4\times 2 \times -7}}{4} = \frac{-5 \pm 9}{4} = 1, -3.5$$

The only viable solution is $\cos\theta = 1 \rightarrow \theta = 0$

Mathematics Topics on FE Civil Examination

Answer is C

> Given the multiple-choice nature of the test, trying out each of the four answer choices may well be less time consuming than solving the equation.

Solution 53

Since $\sqrt{(5^2 + 12^2)} = 13$, we divide both sides by 13:

$$\frac{5}{13}\sin\theta + \frac{12}{13}\cos\theta = \frac{10}{13}$$

Since the fractions 5/13 and 12/13 are complementary, we can write them as:

$$\cos\alpha = \frac{5}{13} \text{ and } \sin\alpha = \frac{12}{13}; \ \alpha = 67.38°$$

$$\cos\alpha \sin\theta + \sin\alpha \cos\theta = \sin(\theta + \alpha) = \frac{10}{13} = \sin 50.29 = \sin 129.71$$

$$\theta + \alpha = \sin^{-1}\left(\frac{10}{13}\right) = 50.3, 129.71$$

Therefore, θ + 67.38 = 129.71
θ = 62.33° = 62°20′

Answer is A

Solution 54

If the runner follows a path parallel to and offset 1 m to the outside of the track shown, the two semicircular portions add up to a full circle of diameter 42 m. The perimeter of such a circle is πD = 131.95 m. Therefore, the total length of the track is 131.95 + 140 = 271.95 m
No of laps = 10,000÷271.95 = 36.77

Answer is A

Probability & Statistics

Probability and Statistics Topics on FE Civil Exam   **4–6 problems**
Approximately 4% of exam

A. Measures of central tendencies and dispersions (e.g., mean, mode, standard deviation)
B. Estimation for a single mean (e.g., point, confidence intervals)
C. Regression and curve fitting
D. Expected value (weighted average) in decision making

Probability & Statistics Topics on FE Civil Examination

Problem 1

A bolt manufacturing process is being set up for production of 25 mm diameter bolts. A sample of 7 bolts is taken and the diameters are measured (mm) as: 24.6, 24.8, 24.9, 25.1, 25.2, 25.0, 25.0. What is the sample variance?

- A. 0.0395 mm^2
- B. 0.0583 mm^2
- C. 0.0750 mm^2
- D. 0.0917 mm^2

Problem 2

What is the probability that two people in a group of ten share the same birthday?

- A. 0.002
- B. 0.01
- C. 0.12
- D. 0.18

Problem 3

Pat can choose two modes of transportation to go to work - by car or by public transit. Her probability of being late for work is 40% by car and 15% by public transit. Pat drives to work 65% of the time and public transit 35% of the time. If she is late for work one day, what is the probability that she drove to work that day by car?

- A. 0.77
- B. 0.79
- C. 0.81
- D. 0.83

Problem 4

A large group (N = 235) of elementary school kids has their height measured. The mean height is 102 cm and the standard deviation is 1.56 cm. What is the probability that a child's height is less than 1.0 m?

- A. 6%
- B. 8%
- C. 10%
- D. 12%

Probability & Statistics Topics on FE Civil Examination

Problem 5
A group of 10 students from elementary school have their height measured. The sample mean is 102 cm and the sample standard deviation is 1.56 cm. What is the 90% confidence interval about the mean?
    A. 100 cm to 104 cm
    B. 100.5 cm to 103.5 cm
    C. 101.1 cm to 102.9 cm
    D. 101.6 cm to 102.4 cm

Problem 6
Respondents in 5 different categories were asked the question: "Will hosting the Superbowl be of economic benefit to the local community?" Their responses (20 respondents in each category) are summarized below. The numbers of negative responses in each category are recorded.

Category	Negative answer
Business owner	4/20
Student	6/20
Adult male	14/20
Adult female	10/20
Senior	16/20

Is there significant difference (at the 90% confidence level) between the different groups?
    A. Difference is significant because Chi square value is greater than critical value
    B. Difference is not significant because Chi square value is greater than critical value
    C. Difference is significant because Chi square value is less than critical value
    D. Difference is not significant because Chi square value is less than critical value

Problem 7
A 20-point quiz is administered to fourth and fifth graders. Two samples are taken from each group. 7 students are sampled from the fourth grade population, with a sample mean = 12 and sample variance = 2.23. 13 students are sampled from the fifth grade population, with a sample mean = 17 and sample variance = 3.24.
At the 95% confidence level, is the variance different between fourth and fifth graders?
    A. Difference is significant because the variance ratio is greater than critical value
    B. Difference is not significant because the variance ratio is greater than critical value
    C. Difference is significant because the variance ratio is less than critical value
    D. Difference is not significant because the variance ratio is less than critical value

Probability & Statistics Topics on FE Civil Examination

Problem 8

The table below shows summary of speed data for 100 cars observed on the highway. What is the mean speed?

Speed Range (km/hr)	Frequency
40 – 46	12
46 – 52	19
52 – 58	41
58 – 64	21
64 – 70	7

    A. 53.7 kmph
    B. 54.5 kmph
    C. 57.1 kmph
    D. 58.7 kmph

Problem 9

The table below shows summary of speed data for 100 cars observed on the highway. What is the standard deviation of the speed data?

Speed Range (km/hr)	Frequency
40 – 46	12
46 – 52	19
52 – 58	41
58 – 64	21
64 – 70	7

    A. 3.7 kmph
    B. 4.5 kmph
    C. 5.9 kmph
    D. 6.4 kmph

Problem 10

The table below shows summary of speed data for 100 cars observed on the highway. What is the median speed?

Speed Range (km/hr)	Frequency
40 – 46	12
46 – 52	19
52 – 58	41
58 – 64	21
64 – 70	7

    A. 53 kmph
    B. 55 kmph
    C. 59 kmph
    D. 61 kmph

Probability & Statistics Topics on FE Civil Examination

Problem 11
A random variable x has the probability density function shown below.

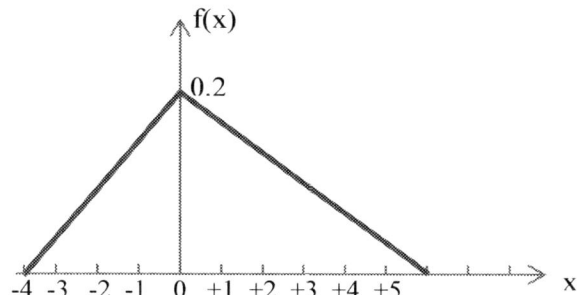

What is the expected value of the quadratic function $y(x) = 2x^2$?
- A. 9.33
- B. 7.20
- C. 5.08
- D. 2.13

Problem 12
A slightly biased coin has a 53% probability of showing 'heads'. If the coin is tossed 90 times, what is the probability that heads will turn up exactly 40 times?
- A. 7.5%
- B. 4.6%
- C. 2.3%
- D. 1.9%

Problem 13
A machine part has an expected probability of failure = 1%? If a sample of 20 parts is tested, what is the probability that the entire sample is deflect-free?
- A. 81.8%
- B. 80.0%
- C. 76.5%
- D. 72.1%

Probability & Statistics Topics on FE Civil Examination

Problem 14

Given the following x, y data, what is the equation of the least squares line of best fit?

x	y
0	12
1	23
2	32
3	40

A. y = 8.6x + 12.0
B. y = 9.3x + 11.8
C. y = 0.11x − 1.36
D. y = 9.3x + 12.8

Problem 15

A bag contains 10 green, 6 yellow and 4 red balls. How many unique sequences of 20 balls can be made by drawing from the bag?

A. 21.9 million
B. 27.9 million
C. 38.8 million
D. 42.1 million

Problem 16

Two groups of children were weighed as part of the state mandated health evaluation process. The data for the two groups are presented below:

Group 1	Group 2
Fourth graders	Fifth graders
N = 45	N = 55
Mean = 32.5 kg	Mean = 35.2 kg
Std. Deviation = 2.1 kg	Std. Deviation = 1.9 kg

What is the variance of the combined group of 100 students?

A. 3.97
B. 5.77
C. 7.17
D. 8.02

Problem 17

The overall cost of a project is defined by the function C below, where P is number of personnel units and M is number of material units.

$$C = 45P + 12M$$

P and M are normally distributed random variables with the following characteristics:

P: Mean = 120; Standard deviation = 3.1

M: Mean = 230; Standard deviation = 6.5

What is the probability that the cost of the project will exceed the budgeted amount of 8400?

    A. 4.2%
    B. 5.1%
    C. 5.4%
    D. 6.7%

Problem 18

A loaded dice has 6 possible outcomes, with the following probability mass function:

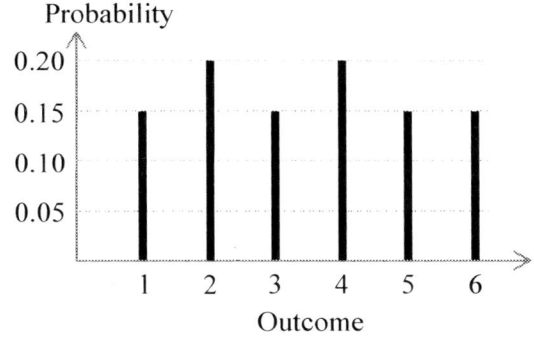

What is the expected value on a single throw of the dice?

    A. 3.15
    B. 3.45
    C. 3.65
    D. 3.75

Problem 19

The probability density function f(x) for a random variable is shown below. The random variable x is bounded by the values -2 and +6. What is the probability that x will be in the range $-1 \leq x \leq 3$?

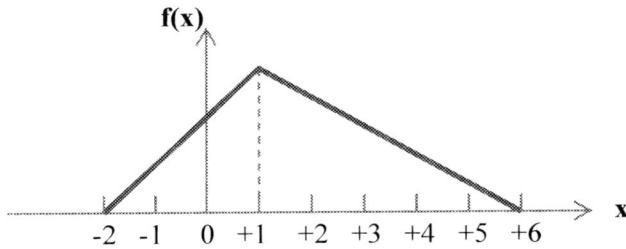

A. 0.73
B. 0.68
C. 0.64
D. 0.61

Problem 20

Approximately how many different ways is it possible to arrange the letters in the word COMBINATIONS?

A. 32 million
B. 60 million
C. 80 million
D. 479 million

Problem 21

At a high school, 63% of all students own a scientific calculator and 37% own a scientific calculator as well as an optical microscope. What is the probability that a student owns a microscope if it is known that he/she owns a calculator?

A. 23%
B. 26%
C. 59%
D. 100%

Probability & Statistics Topics on FE Civil Examination

Problem 22

A random variable X is normally distributed with known standard deviation = 6.8. A sample of 21 observations of X results in a sample mean = 28.5. What is the 90% confidence interval for the population mean?

    A. $25.59 \leq \mu \leq 31.41$
    B. $26.60 \leq \mu \leq 30.40$
    C. $25.94 \leq \mu \leq 31.06$
    D. $26.06 \leq \mu \leq 30.94$

Problem 23

A random variable X is normally distributed. A sample of 21 observations of X results in a sample mean = 28.5 and sample standard deviation = 6.8. What is the 90% confidence interval for the population mean?

    A. $25.59 \leq \mu \leq 31.41$
    B. $26.60 \leq \mu \leq 30.40$
    C. $25.94 \leq \mu \leq 31.06$
    D. $26.06 \leq \mu \leq 30.94$

Problem 24

Two different manufacturing processes are used to create a fiberglass composite. The two processes are compared by taking a random sample from each type and measuring density. The data are summarized below:

	Process 1	Process 2
Sample size	5	8
Sample mean (g/cc)	3.73	3.46
Sample std. dev. (g/cc)	0.23	0.21

What are the 90% confidence intervals for the difference between the mean densities from the two processes?

    A. $0.05 \leq \mu_1 - \mu_2 \leq 0.49$
    B. $0.10 \leq \mu_1 - \mu_2 \leq 0.44$
    C. $0.20 \leq \mu_1 - \mu_2 \leq 0.34$
    D. $0.25 \leq \mu_1 - \mu_2 \leq 0.29$

Probability & Statistics Topics on FE Civil Examination

Problem 25

Two different manufacturing processes are used to create a fiberglass composite. The two processes are compared by taking a random sample from each type and measuring density. The standard deviation for each manufacturing process is known. The data are summarized below:

	Process 1	Process 2
Sample size	5	8
Sample mean (g/cc)	3.73	3.46
Standard dev. σ (g/cc)	0.23	0.21

What are the 90% confidence intervals for the difference between the mean densities from the two processes?

A. $-0.02 \leq \mu_1 - \mu_2 \leq 0.56$
B. $0.03 \leq \mu_1 - \mu_2 \leq 0.51$
C. $0.27 \leq \mu_1 - \mu_2 \leq 0.41$
D. $0.25 \leq \mu_1 - \mu_2 \leq 0.36$

Problem 26

A clinic measures plasma cholesterol levels (mmol/L) of 10 patients. The results are 6.0, 6.6, 5.9, 7.0, 5.9, 5.8, 6.4, 6.2, 6.1 and 6.7. The sample mean is 6.26 mmol/L and sample standard deviation is 0.38 mmol/L
What are the 95% confidence intervals for the standard deviation of blood cholesterol levels of a population of patients large enough to be assumed to be normally distributed?

A. $0.07 \leq \sigma \leq 0.48$
B. $0.26 \leq \sigma \leq 0.69$
C. $0.06 \leq \sigma \leq 0.40$
D. $0.25 \leq \sigma \leq 0.63$

Problem 27

An architectural team designing a bridge is considering the following design alternatives:
   (a) The structural system can be one of three different types
   (b) The color scheme can be one of six different types
   (c) The bridge width can be either 4-lane or 6-lane.

How many different unique bridge designs can the team come up with?

A. 11
B. 36
C. 728
D. 8640

Probability & Statistics Topics on FE Civil Examination

Problem 28
A bridge has 12 lighting pedestals as part of its superstructure design. Each pedestal is capable of supporting one light-post. If 6 identical light posts are available at a certain stage of the project, how many unique lighting arrangements can be created?
- A. 72
- B. 256
- C. 924
- D. 665,280

Problem 29
A biased coin has a 53% probability of showing heads. If the random variable X represents the outcome of the coin toss and the coin is tossed 120 times, what is the standard deviation of the random variable X?
- A. 4.28
- B. 5.00
- C. 6.00
- D. 5.47

Problem 30
Test scores on a standardized test for all 8th graders in Baltimore are normally distributed with a mean = 77 and standard deviation = 6. What is the probability that a specific student will receive a grade of B (80 < score < 90)?
- A. 29%
- B. 34%
- C. 37%
- D. 41%

Problem 31
Which expression describes the region shaded with a checkered pattern?

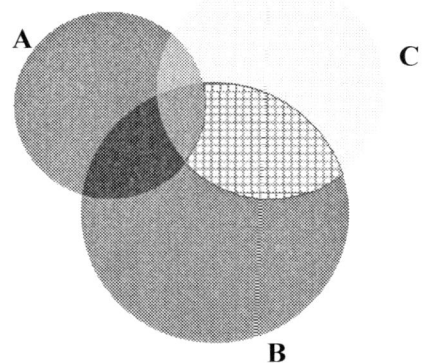

Probability & Statistics Topics on FE Civil Examination

A. $A^c \cap B \cap C^c$
B. $A \cup (B \cap C)^c$
C. $A^c \cap B \cap C$
D. $A^c \cap B \cup C$

Problem 32

A power plant is to be designed with a design life of 30 years. If the acceptable cumulative risk of failure due to seismic overload is 2%, what should be the return period of the design earthquake?

A. 30 years
B. 50 years
C. 500 years
D. 1500 years

Problem 33

Which of the following is the proper shape of a cumulative probability function for a normally distributed random variable?

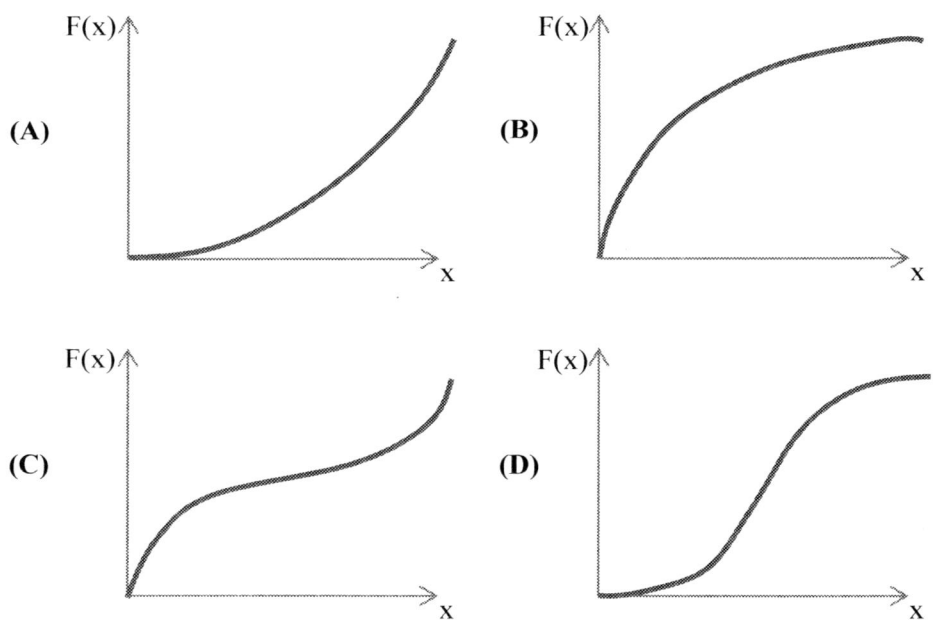

Probability & Statistics Topics on FE Civil Examination

Problem 34

At a pizzeria, there are 8 different toppings available. If doubling of toppings is not allowed, how many different types of 3 topping pizzas are possible?

- A. 56
- B. 336
- C. 672
- D. 6720

Problem 35

In a parlor game, a competitor throws a ball at a target. On each throw, the average person has a 15% probability of hitting the target. What is the probability that a person will be able to make at least 3 hits on 7 throws?

- A. 7%
- B. 5%
- C. 3%
- D. 1%

Probability & Statistics Solutions

Probability & Statistics Topics on FE Civil Examination

Solution 1
The sample variance is defined as:
$$s^2 = \frac{(X_i - \bar{X})^2}{n-1}$$
The sample mean is:
$$\bar{X} = \frac{\sum X_i}{n} = 24.943$$
The (absolute) deviations from the mean are:
0.343, 0.143, 0.043, 0.157, 0.257, 0.057, 0.057
Sum of the squares of the deviations = 0.237
Sample variance = 0.237 mm²/(7-1) = 0.0395 mm²

Answer is A

All of the permitted calculators do statistical computations such as sample mean, standard deviation etc. You should know how to use your calculator to quickly do what is otherwise a tedious calculation.

Solution 2
Pick any date of the year. Probability of a birthday being on that date = 1/365
Probability of a birthday being on any other date = 364/365
Probability that of 10 people, exactly two will have birthdays on that specific date:
$$P = C(10,2)\left(\frac{1}{365}\right)^2 \left(\frac{364}{365}\right)^8 = 0.00033$$
This can occur 365 ways (once for each date picked)
Therefore, probability of 2 out of 10 having a common birthday (any date) = 0.00033×365 = 0.12

Answer is C

Solution 3
Designating "taking the car" as C, "taking public transit" as T and "being late" as L
Probability of Joan taking the car = P(C) = 0.65
Probability of Joan taking public transit = P(T) = 0.35
Probability of Joan being late when she takes the car = P(L|C) = 0.40
Probability of Joan being late when she takes public transit = P(L|T) = 0.15

Probability that Joan took the car if she is late for work
$$P(C|L) = \frac{P(L|C)P(C)}{P(L|C)P(C) + P(L|T)P(T)} = \frac{0.4 \times 0.65}{0.4 \times 0.65 + 0.15 \times 0.35} = 0.832$$

Answer is D

Probability & Statistics Topics on FE Civil Examination

Solution 4

With a large sample (N > 30) we can assume that the heights are normally distributed.
Converting the value X = 100 cm to a Z value:

$$Z = \frac{X-\mu}{\sigma} = \frac{100-102}{1.56} = -1.282$$

Prob(Z < -1.282) = Prob(Z > +1.282)
F(-1.282) = R(1.282). See The FE Reference Handbook tables.
By interpolation from the table on p. 45
R(1.282) = 0.1

Answer is C

Also, note that the Z value of 1.282 corresponds to a specific (90th) percentile and therefore
F(+1.282) = 0.9

Solution 5

With a small sample (N < 30) we can assume that the probability distribution is the Student's t-distribution. Since we seek the 90% confidence interval, α = (1 – 0.9)/2 = 0.05. For degrees of freedom = N – 1 = 9 and α = 0.05, the t-value is 1.833

$$\frac{ts}{\sqrt{N}} = \frac{1.833 \times 1.56}{\sqrt{10}} = 0.9$$

90% confidence interval for the mean is:

$$\bar{X} - \frac{ts}{\sqrt{n}} \leq \mu \leq \bar{X} + \frac{ts}{\sqrt{n}}$$

$$102 - 0.9 \leq \mu \leq 102 + 0.9$$

$$101.1 \leq \mu \leq 102.9$$

Answer is C

Solution 6

	Business Owner	Students	Adult (Male)	Adult (Female)	Senior
Observed (o)	4	6	14	10	16
Expected (e)	10	10	10	10	10
o – e	-6	-4	+4	0	+6
(o-e)^2	36	16	16	0	36
(o-e)^2/e	3.6	1.6	1.6	0	3.6
χ^2	3.6	1.6	1.6	0	3.6

χ^2 = 3.6+1.6+1.6+0+3.6 = 10.4

Degrees of freedom: df = n – 1 = 4

Probability & Statistics Topics on FE Civil Examination

At the 95% level ($\alpha = 0.10$), the critical value from the Chi-square Distribution table is 7.78
Since the Chi-square value (10.4) is greater than the critical value (7.78), there IS significant difference between the groups.

Answer is A

Solution 7
This problem must be solved using the F-distribution tables.
Null hypothesis $\quad H_o: s_A^2 = s_B^2$
For the 5th grader sample, degrees of freedom: $v = 13-1 = 12$.
For the 4th grader sample, $v = 7-1 = 6$.
At the 95% confidence level ($\alpha = 0.05$), for $v_A = 12$, $v_B = 6$, $F_{0.05(12,6)}$ value = 4.00
$s_A^2 / s_B^2 = 3.24/2.23 = 1.45$
Since this value is less than the critical value (4.0), we cannot reject the null hypothesis. At this confidence level, there isn't a significant difference in the variances of the two groups.

Answer is D

Solution 8
Representing each range by its midpoint:

Speed (km/hr)	Frequency
43	12
49	19
55	41
61	21
67	7

The grouped mean is given by:
$$\bar{X} = \frac{\sum f_i X_i}{\sum f_i} = \frac{12 \times 43 + 19 \times 49 + 41 \times 55 + 21 \times 61 + 7 \times 67}{100} = 54.52 \; kmph$$

Answer is B

Solution 9
Representing each range by its midpoint:

Speed Range (km/hr)	Frequency
43	12
49	19
55	41
61	21
67	7

The grouped mean is given by:
$$\bar{X} = \frac{\sum f_i X_i}{\sum f_i} = \frac{12 \times 43 + 19 \times 49 + 41 \times 55 + 21 \times 61 + 7 \times 67}{100} = 54.52 \; kmph$$

The deviations from the mean are listed in the table below:

Speed (km/hr)	Frequency	Deviation
43	12	-11.52
49	19	-5.52
55	41	0.48
61	21	6.48
67	7	12.48

The variance is given by:
$$\sigma^2 = \frac{\sum f_i (X_i - \bar{X})^2}{\sum f_i}$$
$$= \frac{12 \times 11.52^2 + 19 \times 5.52^2 + 41 \times 0.48^2 + 21 \times 6.48^2 + 7 \times 12.48^2}{100}$$
$$= 41.53 \; (kmph)^2$$

Standard deviation σ = 6.44 kmph

Answer is D

Solution 10

Constructing a cumulative frequency column:

Speed Range (km/hr)	Frequency	Cumul. freq.
40 – 46	12	12
46 – 52	19	31
52 – 58	41	72
58 – 64	21	93
64 – 70	7	100

The median should be at a cumulative frequency of 50 (strictly speaking, it should be the average of the 50th and 51st observations), which falls in the range 52-58 kmph. The cumulative frequency corresponding to speed of 52 kmph is 31 and that corresponding to speed of 58 kmph is 72. Since the cumulative frequency of 50 is almost exactly halfway between these two values, the corresponding speed is midway between 52 and 58 kmph.

So, the median speed is 55 kmph.

Answer is B

Probability & Statistics Topics on FE Civil Examination

Solution 11
The expected value of a function g(x) is given by:
$$E[g(x)] = \int_{-\infty}^{\infty} f(x)g(x)dx$$
The probability density function can be expressed as:
f(x) = 0.05x + 0.2 for -4 < x < 0
f(x) = -0.033x + 0.2 for 0 < x < 6
Therefore, the expected value of y(x) = 2x² is calculated as:
$$E[y(x)] = \int_{-4}^{0} 2x^2(0.05x + 0.2)dx + \int_{0}^{6} 2x^2(-0.033x + 0.2)dx = 2.13 + 7.20 = 9.33$$
Answer is A

Solution 12
Defining p = probability of 'heads' = 0.53
and q = probability of 'tails' = 0.47
This is an example of binomial distribution.
Probability of 40 'heads' and 50 'tails' is calculated as:
$$C(90,40) \times 0.53^{40} \times 0.47^{50} = 0.02255$$
Answer is C

Solution 13
For each part in the sample, probability of being defective = 0.01; probability of being defect-free = 0.99.
Probability that 20 parts are defect free = 0.99^{20} = 0.818

Answer is A

Solution 14
n = 4; Σx = 6; Σy = 107; mean x = 1.5; mean y = 26.75
Σx² = 14
Σxy = 207

$$S_{xy} = \sum x_i y_i - \frac{1}{n}\sum x_i \sum y_i = 207 - \frac{6 \times 107}{4} = 46.5$$
$$S_{xx} = \sum x_i^2 - \frac{1}{n}\left(\sum x_i\right)^2 = 14 - \frac{6^2}{4} = 5$$

Slope: $\hat{b} = S_{xy}/S_{xx} = 46.5/5 = 9.3$

Intercept: $\hat{a} = \bar{y} - \hat{b}\bar{x} = 26.75 - 9.3 \times 1.5 = 12.8$

Answer is D

It is worthwhile to learn to do these statistical calculations on your calculator.

Probability & Statistics Topics on FE Civil Examination

Solution 15
Arrangements (order matters) of n objects when they appear in k groups, is calculated as
$$P(n; n_1, n_2, n_3, \cdots, n_k) = \frac{n!}{n_1! n_2! \cdots n_k!}$$
Therefore, with 20 objects (n = 20 balls) in three groups (k = 3 colors), the number of unique arrangements (permutations) is
$$\frac{20!}{10!\, 6!\, 4!} = 38{,}798{,}760$$

Answer is C

Solution 16
Variance is defined as:
$$\sigma^2 = \frac{\sum(X_i - \mu)^2}{N}$$
But, this can also be simplified to:
$$\sigma^2 = \frac{\sum X_i^2}{N} - \mu^2$$
Therefore, for the first group:
$\sum X_i = N\mu = 45 \times 32.5 = 1462.5$
$\sum X_i^2 = N(\sigma^2 + \mu^2) = 45 \times (2.1^2 + 32.5^2) = 47{,}729.7$
and for the second group:
$\sum X_i = N\mu = 55 \times 35.2 = 1936$
$\sum X_i^2 = N(\sigma^2 + \mu^2) = 55 \times (1.9^2 + 35.2^2) = 68{,}345.75$

Therefore, for the combined group of 100 kids:
$\sum X_i = 1462.5 + 1936 = 3398.5$
Mean = 3398.5/100 = 33.985
$\sum X_i^2 = 47{,}729.7 + 68{,}345.75 = 116{,}075.45$
Variance: $\sigma^2 = \frac{\sum X_i^2}{N} - \mu^2 = \frac{116{,}075.45}{100} - 33.985^2 = 5.774$

Answer is B

> The first definition of variance is in the handbook, but the alternate one is not. However, knowing it really helps for this problem.

Solution 17
C is a linear combination of two normally distributed random variables. Therefore, C is also normally distributed with parameters:
$$\mu_C = 45\mu_P + 12\mu_M = 45 \times 120 + 12 \times 230 = 8160$$
$$\sigma_C^2 = 45^2 \times \sigma_P^2 + 12^2 \times \sigma_M^2 = 45^2 \times 3.1^2 + 12^2 \times 6.5^2 = 25{,}544.3 \Rightarrow \sigma_C = 159.8$$
The Z value corresponding to C = 8400 is
$$Z = \frac{X - \mu}{\sigma} = \frac{8400 - 8160}{159.8} = 1.50$$
P(Z > 1.5) = 0.0668 (this is given by the R(x) function in the normal distribution table.

Probability & Statistics Topics on FE Civil Examination

Answer is D

Solution 18
The expected value of a random variable with finite number of discrete outcomes is:
$\mu = E[X] = \sum x_k f(x_k) = 1 \times 0.15 + 2 \times 0.20 + 3 \times 0.15 + 4 \times 0.20 + 5 \times 0.15 + 6 \times 0.15 = 3.45$
Answer is B

Solution 19
The inherent property of a probability density function is that the total area under the function is equal to 1.0. Since the base of this triangular p.d.f. is 8, the height must be 0.25. Therefore, the probability that -1 ≤ x ≤ 3 is equal to the area under the pdf between the limits x = -1 and x = +3.
By similar triangles, the ordinate at x = -1 is 1/3 x 0.25 = 0.0833 and the ordinate at x = +3 is 3/5 x 0.25 = 0.15
Area to the left of x = -1 is 0.04167
Area to the right of x = +3 is 0.225
Therefore are between x = -1 and x = +3 is 1.0 – 0.042 – 0.225 = 0.733
Answer is A

Solution 20
The word COMBINATIONS has 12 letters. However, three of these letters (I, O and N) are repeated (twice each). Therefore, number of unique **permutations** of the letters is:
$\frac{12!}{2!2!2!} = 59{,}875{,}200$
Answer is B

Solution 21
Let "C" signify ownership of a calculator and "M" signify ownership of a microscope.
P(C) = 0.63
P(C ∩ M) = 0.37
P(C ∩ M) = P(M|C)P(C)
P(M|C) = P(C ∩ M) ÷ P(C) = 0.37 ÷ 0.63 = 0.587

Answer is C

Solution 22
Since the population standard deviation σ is known and we seek the 90% confidence interval, α/2 = (1 – 0.9)/2 = 0.05. The corresponding Z value is 1.6449. The limits of the confidence interval are:
$$\bar{X} \pm Z_{\alpha/2} \frac{\sigma}{\sqrt{n}} = 28.5 \pm 1.6449 \times \frac{6.8}{\sqrt{21}} = 28.5 \pm 2.44$$

Therefore, confidence interval limits are:
$$26.06 \leq \mu \leq 30.94$$

Answer is D

Solution 23

Since the population standard deviation σ is not known and the sample size is small (less than 30), we should use the t-value instead of the Z-value. We seek the 90% confidence interval, α/2 = (1 – 0.9)/2 = 0.05. For dof ν = 20, the t-value is 1.725. The limits of the confidence interval are:

$$\bar{X} \pm t_{\alpha/2,\nu} \frac{s}{\sqrt{n}} = 28.5 \pm 1.725 \times \frac{6.8}{\sqrt{21}} = 28.5 \pm 2.56$$

Therefore, confidence interval limits are:
$$25.94 \leq \mu \leq 31.06$$

Answer is C

Solution 24

$n_1 = 5$; $S_1 = 0.23$; $\bar{Y}_1 = 3.73$
$n_2 = 8$; $S_2 = 0.21$; $\bar{Y}_1 = 3.46$
This is case B (standard deviations not known)
Degrees of freedom = $n_1 + n_2 - 2 = 11$
For 90% confidence, α/2 = 0.05
For α/2 = 0.05 and ν = 11, t = 1.796

$$t_{\alpha/2} \sqrt{\frac{\left(\frac{1}{n_1} + \frac{1}{n_2}\right)[(n_1 - 1)s_1^2 + (n_2 - 1)s_2^2]}{n_1 + n_2 - 2}}$$

For the given values, the term multiplying t is 0.12399 ≈ 0.124
The difference between the two sample means = 3.73 – 3.46 = 0.27
90% confidence interval for the difference between the means = 0.27 ± 1.796 x 0.124
$0.05 \leq \mu_1 - \mu_2 \leq 0.49$

Answer is A

Solution 25

$n_1 = 5$; $\sigma_1 = 0.23$; $\bar{Y}_1 = 3.73$
$n_2 = 8$; $\sigma_2 = 0.21$; $\bar{Y}_1 = 3.46$
This is case A (standard deviations known)

For 90% confidence, α/2 = 0.05
For α/2 = 0.05, Z = 1.6449

Probability & Statistics Topics on FE Civil Examination

$$Z_{\alpha/2}\sqrt{\frac{\sigma_1^2}{n_1}+\frac{\sigma_2^2}{n_2}} = 1.6449 \times \sqrt{\frac{0.23^2}{5}+\frac{0.21^2}{8}} = 0.294$$

The difference between the two sample means = 3.73 − 3.46 = 0.27
90% confidence interval for the difference between the means = 0.27 ± 0.294
-0.024 ≤ $\mu_1 - \mu_2$ ≤ 0.564

Answer is A

Solution 26
For dof = n − 1 = 10 − 1 = 9
For 95% confidence, $\alpha/2$ = 0.025, 1 − $\alpha/2$ = 0.975
For dof = 9, the Chi-square critical values are:
$$\chi^2_{0.975} = 2.70039 \text{ and } \chi^2_{0.025} = 19.0228$$
Confidence intervals for the variance:
$$\frac{(n-1)s^2}{\chi^2_{\alpha/2,n-1}} \leq \sigma^2 \leq \frac{(n-1)s^2}{\chi^2_{1-\alpha/2,n-1}}$$
$$\frac{9 \times 0.38^2}{19.0228} \leq \sigma^2 \leq \frac{9 \times 0.38^2}{2.70039}$$
$$0.068 \leq \sigma^2 \leq 0.481$$
$$0.261 \leq \sigma \leq 0.694$$

Answer is B

Solution 27
This problem is given solely to make the point that sometimes, it is as simple as 3 x 6 x 2 = 36 different combinations of these choices.
This is because we MUST choose a SINGLE structural system, a SINGLE color and a SINGLE roadway width as part of the design. This implies that we have a $^nC_1$ number of choices. Since $^nC_1$ = n, we have n choices for each independent aspect of the design.

Answer is B

Solution 28
Each lighting pedestal is in a unique position. Imagine them to be numbered 1 − 12. So, the question boils down to "how many different ways to choose 6 locations out of 12". Since the light-posts are identical, the order of the choice is immaterial. Thus, the answer is $^{12}C_6$ = 924

Answer is C

Solution 29

Probability & Statistics Topics on FE Civil Examination

As defined, the random variable X has a binomial distribution with parameters n = 120 and p = 0.53
The variance of a binomial distribution is:
$$\sigma^2 = np(1-p) = 120 \times 0.53 \times 0.47 = 29.9$$
Standard deviation: σ = 5.47

Answer is D

Solution 30
The standard normal (Z) values corresponding to X_1 = 80 and X_2 = 90 are:
$Z_1 = \frac{X_1 - \mu}{\sigma} = \frac{80-77}{6} = +0.5$ and
$Z_2 = \frac{X_2 - \mu}{\sigma} = \frac{90-77}{6} = +2.17$
F(+0.5) = 0.6915
F(+2.17) = 0.9848
Therefore, the probability that 0.5 < Z < 2.17 is 0.9848 – 0.6915 = 0.2933

Answer is A

Solution 31
The region shown belongs in the intersection of B and C. However, it excludes the region that is common to A, B and C. Therefore, it is part of the complement of A (A^c).

Answer is C

Solution 32
Let the annual probability (of occurrence) of the design earthquake (or greater) be p
Then, the probability of non-occurrence (in any given year) of the design earthquake = 1 – p
The probability of non-occurrence of the design earthquake for the entire 30-year life of the plant = $(1 - p)^{30}$
The probability of occurrence of the design earthquake during the entire 30-year life of the plant = $1 - (1 - p)^{30}$
Therefore, $1 - (1-p)^{30} = 0.02 \Rightarrow p = 0.000673$
The return period is defined as the inverse of the annual probability of occurrence:
$$N = \frac{1}{p} = \frac{1}{0.000673} = 1485 \; years$$

Answer is D

Solution 33
The probability density function for the normal distribution is symmetric about the mean and diminishes asymptotically to zero in the upper and lower tails. The cumulative probability function is the integral of the pdf, and therefore has small gradients (slope) at the lower and upper tails (corresponding to cumulative probability = 0 and 1 respectively).

Probability & Statistics Topics on FE Civil Examination

At the exact center, the pdf is peaked to the max value and therefore, the cumulative probability function has maximum slope). Only choice D fits all these criteria.
Answer is D

Solution 34
This is a case of combinations, since order of the toppings is immaterial. The number of 3 topping combinations (out of 8 available) is C(8,3)
$C(8,3) = \frac{8!}{5!3!} = 56$
Answer is A

Solution 35
This is an example of a binomial distribution. Each throw can be considered an independent experiment. Probability of success on each throw = 0.15. Probability of failure = 0.85
Probability of at least 3 hits = P(3) + P(4) + P(5) + P(6) + P(7)
However, it is easier to calculate as: 1 – P(0) – P(1) – P(2)
P(r ≥ 3) = 1 – P(0) – P(1) – P(2) = 1 – C(7,0)0.15^{0}0.85^7 – C(7,1)0.15^{1}0.85^6 – C(7,2)0.15^{2}0.85^5 = 1 – 0.32 – 0.396 – 0.21 = 0.07

Answer is A

Probability & Statistics Topics on FE Civil Examination

Computational Tools

Computational Tools Topics on FE Civil Examination   **4-6 problems**

Approximately 4% of exam

A. Spreadsheet computations
B. Structured programming (e.g., if-then, loops, macros)

Computational Tools Topics on FE Civil Examination

Problem 1
Convert the decimal number 23.75 to binary (base 2)
- A. 11011.111
- B. 11101.101
- C. 10111.111
- D. 10111.110

Problem 2

What is the decimal equivalent of the hexadecimal number 1A23F?

- A. 107511
- B. 107211
- C. 107071
- D. 107011

Problem 3

A fragment of a computer program is given below. What is the expression whose value is stored in the variable A at the end of the program?

```
INPUT X
A = 1
S = 1
FOR I = 1 TO 20
S = S*I
A = A + X^I/S
END
```

- A. $A = 1 + \frac{x}{1} + \frac{x^2}{2} + \cdots + \frac{x^{20}}{20}$
- B. $A = 1 + \frac{x}{1!} + \frac{x^2}{2!} + \cdots + \frac{x^{20}}{20!}$
- C. $A = 1 - \frac{x}{1} + \frac{x^2}{2} - \cdots + \frac{x^{20}}{20}$
- D. $A = 1 - \frac{x}{1!} + \frac{x^2}{2!} - \cdots + \frac{x^{20}}{20!}$

Computational Tools Topics on FE Civil Examination

Problem 4

In a spreadsheet, the following formula is entered into cell A2: =A1+2 and copied through the range A3:A10. The formula '= A$1^2+A1' is then typed into cell B1 and copied through the range B2:B10.

What is the value in cell B10?

	A	B	C	D
1	5			
2	=A1+2			
3				
4				
5				

- A. 23
- B. 48
- C. 462
- D. 552

Problem 5

An external hard drive contains 433.2 Mbytes of data. How much time is needed to transfer the data at an average transfer rate of 75 Mbps?

- A. 6.1 sec
- B. 46.2 sec
- C. 47.0 sec
- D. 48.5 sec

Problem 6

A computer's memory consists of the following hierarchy. For each component, the access time and hit rate is given. What is the average access time for this memory system?

Component	Capacity	Access Time	Hit Rate
Cache	2 MB	1 ns	95%
Main memory	2 GB	50 ns	90%
Hard Drive	500 GB	10 ms	100%

- A. 15.0 ns
- B. 15.0 μs
- C. 50.0 μs
- D. 9.0 ms

Problem 7

In a spreadsheet, cells A1 and B1 are initialized with values 2 and 6 respectively. The following formula is entered into cell A2: =A1+B$1 and copied through the range A3:A10. The formula '= A$1^2+A1' is then typed into cell B2 and copied through the range B3:B10.

What is the value in cell B10?

	A	B	C	D
1	2	6		
2	=A1+B$1	=A$1^2+A1		
3				
4				
5				

    A. 54
    B. 48
    C. 462
    D. 552

Problem 8

A fragment of a computer program is given below. What is the expression whose value is stored in the variable S at the end of the program?

```
S = 0
A = 2
FOR I = 1 TO 10
B = A^2
S = S+B
A = A+1
END
```

    A. 201
    B. 257
    C. 309
    D. 505

Computational Tools Topics on FE Civil Examination

Problem 9

A fragment of a computer program is given below. What is the value of variable B at the end of the program?

```
B = 0
N = 6
INPUT ARRAY X = {3, 1, 0, -2, 5, 7, 2, 0, 3, 5}
FOR I = 1 TO N
B = B + X(I)
END
B = B/N
```

    A. 2.40

    B. 2.33

    C. 14.0

    D. 24.0

Problem 10

In a spreadsheet, cell A1 contains the value 5. The following formula is entered into cell A2: =2*A1+7 and copied through the range A3:A10. The formula '= A2^2+$A1' is then typed into cell B2 and copied through the range B3:B10.

What is the value in cell B10?

	A	B	C	D
1	5			
2	=2*A1+7	=A$1^2+A1		
3				
4				
5				

    A. 37,668,906

    B. 37,667,128

    C. 37,666,452

    D. 37,665,834

Computational Tools Topics on FE Civil Examination

Problem 11

A fragment of a computer program is given below. What is the value of X(5) at the end of the program?

```
N = 10
INPUT ARRAY X = {3, 1, 0, -2, 5, 7, 2, 0, 3, 5}
FOR I = 1 TO N
TEMP = X(I)
FOR J = I+1 TO N
IF X(J) < X(I)
X(I) = X(J)
X(J) = TEMP
TEMP = X(I)
ELSE
CONTINUE
END
```

A. 0
B. 2
C. 3
D. 5

Problem 12

A fragment of a computer program is given below. What is the value of variable S at the end of the program?

```
S = 0
A = 4
B = 1.5
FOR I = 1 TO 10
T = A*B^(I-1)
S = S + T
END
```

A. 102.52
B. 153.77
C. 299.55
D. 453.32

Problem 13

In a spreadsheet, the values 5 and 8 are entered in cells C1 and D1 respectively. The formula =2*c$1+8*$d1 is then entered into cell A1. The contents of cell A1 are then copied to cell B7. What is the value in cell B7?

	A	B	C	D
1			5	8
2				
3				
4				
5				

- A. 12
- B. 16
- C. 56
- D. 74

Problem 14

Student exam scores are stored and grades are calculated in a spreadsheet. Columns B, C and D contain test scores from Tests 1, 2 and 3. Column E contains a factored score (out of 100). In column F, the following grade rule is to be applied:

   Total > 90   Grade = A
   90 > Total > 80   Grade = B
   80 > Total > 70   Grade = C
   70 > Total > 60   Grade = D
   60 > Total   Grade = F

What formula should be entered in cell F2 for the purpose of copying down through the range F3:F6?

	A	B	C	D	E	F
1		Test 1	Test 2	Test 3	Total	Grade
2	Adams					
3	Bray					
4	Carlos					
5	David					
6	Eugene					

- A. F2:=IF(E2>90,A,IF(E2>80,B,IF(E2>70,C,IF(E2>60,D,F))))
- B. F2: =IF(E2>90,"A",(IF(E2>80,"B",(IF(E2>70,"C",(IF(E2>60,"D","F")))))))
- C. F2: =IF(E2>90,A,(IF(E2>80,B,(IF(E2>70,C,(IF(E2>60,D,F)))))))
- D. F2: =IF(E2>90,'A',IF(E2>80,'B',IF(E2>70,'C',IF(E2>60,'D','F'))))

Problem 15

A fragment of a computer program is shown below. What is the value stored in variable N at the end of the code fragment?

- A. 3
- B. 5
- C. 7
- D. 9

```
L = 0
M = 0
N = 0
A = {4,5,6,2,-3,2,9,0,5,-2,7,5}
B = {1,7,-1,5,-3,6,2,3,1,8,3,2}
FOR I = 1 TO 7
  IF A(I)>B(I)
    L = L + 1
  ELSE IF A(I)== B(I)
    M = M + 1
  ELSE
    N = N + 1
END
```

Computational Tools Solutions

Computational Tools Topics on FE Civil Examination

Solution 1

Expressing 23 as the sum of powers of 2 (the base), we have:
$$23 = 1 \times 2^4 + 1 \times 2^2 + 1 \times 2^1 + 1 \times 2^0$$
Expressing 0.75 as the sum of powers of 2 (the base), we have:
$$0.75 = 1 \times 2^{-1} + 1 \times 2^{-2}$$
Therefore: $(23.75)_2 = 10111.11$

Answer is D

Solution 2

In the hexadecimal system, the symbol A has the decimal value 10 and F has the decimal value 15. Thus the number $(1A23F)_{16}$ has the decimal value equal to:

$$1 \times 16^4 + 10 \times 16^3 + 2 \times 16^2 + 3 \times 16^1 + 15 \times 16^0 = (107{,}071)_{10}$$

Answer is C

Solution 3

The line "S = S*I" builds the factorial function FACT(I). There is no sign switching from one term to the next.

Answer is B

Solution 4

The numbers in the range A1:A10 form an arithmetic series with a = 5 and d = 2. Cell A10 will contain the 10th term in the series = 5+9x2 = 23

The formula A$1^2 + A1 will get copied as A$1^2 +A10 from cell B1 into cell B10

Therefore, the entry in cell B10 will be 5^2 + 23 = 48

Answer is B

Solution 5

1 Mbyte = 2^{20} bytes = 8 x 2^{20} bits

75 Mbps = 75x10^6 bits/sec

Therefore, to transfer 433.2 Mbytes at 75 Mbps, the time needed is:

$$t = \frac{433.2 \times 8 \times 2^{20}}{75 \times 10^6} = 48.45 \ sec$$

Answer is D

Computational Tools Topics on FE Civil Examination

Solution 6

The hierarchy of access will be – first, the cache (with a hit rate of 95%), second, the main memory (with a hit rate of 90%) and finally, the hard drive (with a hit rate of 100%)

Thus, for N access attempts, first to cache, which has average access time = 1 ns. Total access time = N x 1 ns = N ns

However, since the cache has a 5% miss rate, 5% of N go to main memory, which has access time = 50 ns. Total access time = 0.05N x 50 ns = 2.5N ns

Further, since the main memory has 10% miss rate, 10% of 5% of N = 0.5% of N, access time = 10 ms = 10^7 ns. Total success time = 0.005N x 10^7 ns = 50,000N ns

TOTAL = N + 2.5N + 50,000N = 50,003.5N ns

Average access time = 50,003.5 ns = 50.0035 μs

Answer is C

Solution 7

Since the A column uses the formula A2=A1+B$1, it populates each cell in column A with the previous value incremented by the content of cell B1 (fixed cell addressing), which is 6. Thus, the A column develops as 2, 8, 14, 20, ..., 50, 56

Cell B10 would have the formula: B10 = A$1^2+A9.

A1 contains the value 2 and A9 has 50. Therefore, B10 will have the value 2^2 + 50 = 54

Answer is A

Solution 8

This is a classical algorithm for calculating the sum of a series. S is the series sum which is initialized to zero. The line S = S + B keeps adding 'B' terms, which in this case is A^2, starting with A = 2 and A being incremented by 1 every time. The length of the series is 10 terms.

Therefore, S will hold the sum: $S = 2^2 + 3^2 + 4^2 + \cdots + 11^2 = 505$

Solution 9

The code fragment above computes the sum of the first N (6) elements of the array X. In the last line, this sum is divided by N. Thus, at the end of the program, the variable B stores the average of the first 6 elements of the array X.

Computational Tools Topics on FE Civil Examination

The sum of the first 6 terms is 14. The average is 2.33

Answer is B

Solution 10

Since the A column uses the formula A2=2*A1+7, it populates each cell in column A with **double the previous value plus 7**. Thus, the A column develops as 5, 17, 41, 89, 185, 377, 761, 1529, 3065, 6137

Cell B2 has the formula: B2 = A2^2+$A1.

After copying, cell B10 would have the formula: A10^2+$A9. Thus, B10 will have the value 6137^2 + 3065 = 37,665,834

Answer is D

Solution 11

This is a classic example of an algorithm that sorts a set of numbers into ascending order. Starting with each number in the series, the program scans all the following numbers and if a smaller number is found, it is put near the beginning of the series. As a result, smaller numbers are moved to the front of series and larger numbers are pushed back. At the end of the program, the array X = {-2, 0, 0, 1, 2, 3, 3, 5, 5, 7}. The fifth element is 2.

Answer is B

Solution 12

This is a classic algorithm for calculating the sum of a geometric series. The first term of the series is A = 4 and the ratio between the successive terms is B = 1.5. The variable T stores the current value of the term of the series. The variable S stores the sum of first 10 terms in the series, by adding each value of T.

The sum of n terms in a geometric series is given by: $S_n = \frac{a(r^n-1)}{r-1} = \frac{4 \times (1.5^{10}-1)}{1.5-1} = 453.32$

Answer is D

Solution 13

In cell A1, the formula is "=2*C$1 + 8*$D1"

Upon copying it to cell B7, the formula becomes "=2*D$1 + 8*$D7"

Since cell D1 contains the value 8 and cell D7 has no entry, cell B7 will have the value 2x 8 = 16

Computational Tools Topics on FE Civil Examination

Answer is B

Solution 14

The proper structure of the IF-ELSE structure is that in choice B. Choice D also has the same structure, but alpha character values like letter grades should be in " ", not single quotes ' '

Answer is B

Solution 15

In this program, L, M and N are counters which are initialized to zero at the beginning of the program. Everytime an element of array A is found to be greater than the corresponding element of array B, counter L is incremented. Otherwise, for every insance where an element of array A is found to be equal to the corresponding element of array B, counter M is incremented. Failing these two tests means that an element of array A is found to be less than the corresponding element of array B, which is counted by counter N.

Thus, at the end of this code fragment, variable N will store the number of instances where an element of array A is found to be less than the corresponding element of array B. Because the loop counter I is equal to 7, only the first 7 pairs of A and B are compared. Out of the first 7, the number of instances where A(I) < B(I) is 3. If the entire data is scanned, N would be 5.

Answer is A

Ethics Topics on FE Civil Examination

Ethics and Professional Practice

Ethics and Professional Practice Topics on FE Civil Exam   4-6 problems
Approximately 4% of exam

A. Codes of ethics (professional and technical societies)
B. Professional liability
C. Licensure
D. Sustainability and sustainable design
E. Professional skills (e.g., public policy, management, and business)
F. Contracts and contract law

Ethics Topics on FE Civil Examination

Problem 1

You and your design group are competing for a multidisciplinary concept project. Your firm is the lead group in the design professional consortium formed to compete for the project. Your consortium has been selected to be the first to enter fee negotiations with the project owner. During negotiations, the amount you have to cut from your fee to be awarded the contract will require dropping one of the consortium members whose staff has special capabilities not found in the staff of the remaining consortium members.

Is your consortium response in the negotiations ethical?

   A. No, not if the owner is left with the impression that the consortium is still fully qualified to perform all the required tasks.
   B. Yes, if your remaining consortium members hire a few new, lower cost employees to do the special work originally intended to be provided by the consortium member dropped.
   C. No, because an engineer may not accept a contract to coordinate a project with other professional firms providing capabilities and services not under the engineer's direct control.
   D. Yes, if in accepting an assignment to coordinate a project, a single person will sign and seal all the documents in the entire consortium work.

Problem 2

Under what circumstances can a registered engineer sign and seal plans or documents he/she did not prepare?

   A. Under no circumstances.
   B. Registered engineers can coordinate projects that include segments that they are not competent in if a qualified registered engineer signs and seals plans or documents for those segments of the project.
   C. If the plans or documents were prepared by someone under the registered engineer's direct supervision and the registered engineer is an expert in the subject matter.
   D. When practicing in a state different than the one in which the engineer is registered.

Ethics Topics on FE Civil Examination

Problem 3

A registered engineer is retained as an expert witness by one of the parties in a civil case where the public safety is not involved. In investigating the technical data in the case, the engineer makes findings that are not favorable to the side of the party who retained her.

The engineer should:

    A. inform the party who retained her of the findings.
    B. inform the judge of the findings.
    C. inform the opposing party of the findings.
    D. say nothing about the findings until called to testify.

Problem 4

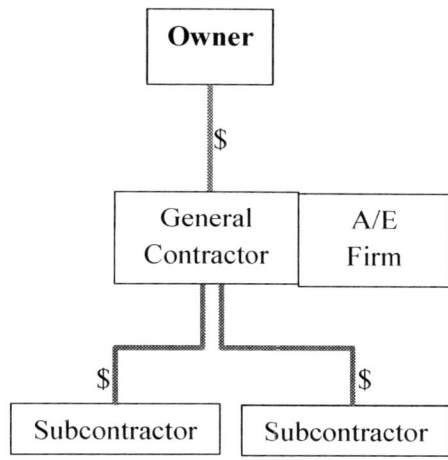

What kind of contractual relationship is shown in the diagram above?

    A. Traditional
    B. Design-Build
    C. Direct force
    D. Owner CM

Problem 5

You work for a multinational company that is venturing into a country where it has never done business. On one of the preliminary visits to one of the production facilities, you observe poor working conditions in the factory, compared to working conditions back in the home country. Upon inquiring, you are told that these conditions are the norm at all similar facilities. What is the course of action you should pursue?

    A. You should recommend to your supervisors that the contract must have language that ensures the same work conditions as prevalent in the home country.

83

Ethics Topics on FE Civil Examination

    B. You should ignore the working conditions and do nothing.
    C. You should recommend that all negotiations for the contract be discontinued.
    D. You should recommend that the contract be negotiated as it stands.

Problem 6

Which of the following statements is true about engineering licensure in the United States?

    A. A license to practice engineering (PE) in all of the United States is awarded upon passing a single national examination.
    B. After passing the PE examination in one state, an engineer can obtain a PE license in other states by filing a comity application.
    C. After passing the national PE examination in one state, additional examination may be required in order to receive a PE license in other states.
    D. Each state has additional examinations/requirements in addition to the national exam.

Problem 7

Which of the following could an engineer accept with the least likelihood of violating ethical standards?

    A. A pen set embossed with the name of an office supplies company.
    B. A fruit basket send by a previous client in appreciation of a previous job that was successfully completed.
    C. A trip to a resort where visiting engineers will attend technical seminars about products built by the sponsoring company.
    D. A $100 gift card from a company that manufactures bolts used for structural connections.

Problem 8

A professional engineer with long experience in hydrogeology reads a news report about a proposal seeking public funding for a dam. Based on her experience, she can identify several aspects of the proposed design that will pose severe environmental hazard. What is the most appropriate course of action that she should pursue?

    A. The engineer should write a letter to the editor urging lawmakers to cancel funding for the project.
    B. The engineer should do nothing because other qualified experts who know more specific information have taken, what must be, a good decision.
    C. The engineer should contact the project manager in charge of the proposal to seek more detailed information.
    D. The engineer should start a citizens' petition collecting signtures with the sole purpose of stalling funding for the project.

Ethics Topics on FE Civil Examination

Problem 9

Which of the following statements is true?
I. Ethical standards vary with time.
II. Ethical standards are the same as legal standards.
III. Proper ethical code is conditional on local culture.
   A. I and II
   B. I and III
   C. II and III
   D. I, II and III

Problem 10

An engineer has a full-time position as a structural engineer at an A&E firm. During the weekends, the engineer works on privately obtained consulting jobs. Occasionally, for the consuting job, the engineer uses a Structural Analysis and Design software which is licensed to his employer, to which has access using a remote VPN connection from home. This action is most probably unethical because:

   A. The engineer's employment contract prohibits misuse and misapppriation of the software license.
   B. The company has not given the engineer permission to use the software for outside contracts.
   C. The access gives the engineer an unfair economic advantage.
   D. The use of the software on private computers can make the software vulnerable to computer viruses and render it unoperational.

Problem 11

An engineer serves as the sole point of contact with a state agency accepting bids for an upcoming contract. The bid submitted by one of the contractors is accompanied by two Superbowl tickets. What is the most appropriate course of action for this engineer?

   A. Return the tickets and reject the bid.
   B. Accept the tickets and accept the bid.
   C. Report the company, return the tickets and accept the bid.
   D. Report the company, return the tickets reject the bid.

Ethics Topics on FE Civil Examination

Problem 12

While pursuing your professional duties as a professional engineer, you become aware of some instances of wilful disregard of rules of professional conduct (promulgated by the state society of professional engineers) by a colleague, who is also a professional engineer. The colleague in question is working on a project where you have no involvement. Which of the following is the most appropriate course of action on your part?

    A. Do nothing, because you have no responsibility in said project.
    B. Report the behavior to the project manager overseeing your colleague.
    C. Report the behavior to your direct supervisor and expect him to follow up.
    D. Report the behavior to the society of professional engineers.

Problem 13

A company designs, builds and sells prefabricated commercial buildings. During a recent heavy snowstorm, the roof of one of the buildings (designed and constructed by this company) failed, leading to significant damage to the buildings and its contents. Which of the following reasons is the most likely reason the building owner may not recover damages from the company?

    A. Insurance policy has an 'act of God' clause.
    B. Statute of limitations.
    C. The contents of the building are not covered by insurance policies.
    D. None of the above. The safety of the building and its contents are the legal responsibility of the company that designed the roof.

Problem 14

Following an airplane crash, the preliminary statement from the NTSB implies structural failure of the fuselage. You are a licensed structural engineer, specializing in the design of steel bridges and buildings. A local radio station wants to interview you to seek your opinion about the possible causes and ramifications of the failure. What should be your course of action?

    A. Agree to do the interview, since your expertise in structural engineering qualifies you to comment on the event.
    B. Agree to do the interview, but make it clear that your expertise is only with buildings and bridges and not aircraft.
    C. Decline the interview because your expertise is only with buildings and bridges and not aircraft.
    D. Decline the interview because the NTSB investigation prohibits you from expressing an opinion that might conflict with the official version.

Ethics and Professional Practice Solutions

Ethics Topics on FE Civil Examination

Solution 1

It is never ethical to accept a contract if you or the organization you are negotiating for cannot complete the work. Answer (A) does not tell us if the scope of the contract will be reduced so the consortium can complete the work without the eliminated partner, or if the consortium has some other way of completing the work without the special skills of the eliminated partner, so we can't really say that answer (A) is correct, but it is the best option provided.

Therefore, the answer is (A).

Solution 2

Answer (B) is a true statement, but it has nothing to do with the problem statement. Plans or documents prepared under the direct supervision of a registered engineer where the engineer is an expert, can be signed and sealed by the engineer assuming he or she has reviewed the plans or documents.

Answer is C

Solution 3

In this case, the engineer has only an obligation to her client until she is called to the stand, so she should report her findings to the party who retained her and that party will decide whether or not to call the engineer to testify.

Therefore, (A) is correct.

Solution 4

The relationship between a team of general contractor and A&E firm, which work in tandem, rather than in a hierarchy, indicates a design build contract.

Answer is B

Solution 5

Working conditions vary significantly from country to country. It is hasty to make a rash judgment of a culture that one doesn't understand. For this reason, option C is incorrect. On the other hand, to do nothing (option B) is not ethical either. Option D is basically the same as option B. The only viable alternative is A – while achieving 'the same' working conditions is an unrealistic objective, it is the ethical alternative.

Answer is A

Ethics Topics on FE Civil Examination

Solution 6

A is incorrect because of the word "all". Some states have additional requirements.

D is incorrect because of the word "each". Some states have additional requirements, not all.

B is incorrect because licensure by comity is not automatic. If the comity state has extra requirements, they must be satisfied, as stated in C

Answer is C

Solution 7

The dollar-value associated with a gift is immaterial. Therefore, A, C and D all fall in the same category. They are all gifts from a company with a 'vested interest'. Since the fruit basket gift is a gift based on a 'past' relationship and not to secure a future relationship, it seems the one least likely to violate ethical stadards.

Answer is B

Solution 8

B is incorrect because the engineer DOES have relevant experience and doing nothing is 'passing the buck'. Option D could be an ordinary citizen's response, but the engineer, based on education and experience, should do more. Option A can be an initial response, but C is more specific.

Answer is C

Solution 9

Ethical standards are not absolute in space and time. They are a function of social norms, which are in turn a function of the time and location. Also, ethical standards are based on moral standards and are often higher than legal standards. Therefore, I and III are true.

Answer is B.

Solution 10

Choices A, B and D could all be true, except that we have to make assumptions of facts that are not stated in the question.

Choice C is definitely true because the engineer has not paid for the license and therefore has lower overhead costs compared to other individuals/companies competing for the same contracts.

Answer is C

Ethics Topics on FE Civil Examination

Solution 11

The engineer must not accept the tickets. This rules out option B. Since no specific rules governing the bid process are stated, this cannot be the basis for rejecting the bid. This rules out options A and D. Option C mentions "report the company, return the tickets and accept the bid". This seems to be the clearest course of action. Making a formal report of the rickets inclusion with the bid seems to be governed by prudence (rather than ethics)

Answer is C

Solution 12

If the behavior violates rules of professional conduct set up by the state society of professional engineers, then you should report directly to that professional society.

Answer is D

Solution 13

Standard contracts provide protection against design and construction defects and claims arising out of them for only a limited time (statute of limitations). All other choices require us to make assumptions about the coverage provided by the policy.

Answer is B

Solution 14

You should decline to do the interview specifically because your area of expertise is not in aircraft design and even though you have general expertise in structural design, any opinion you express may be misinterpreted by the general public as the final word of an 'expert'.

If your training had been specifically in structural design of aircraft systems, unless you live in police state, you would have been perfectly within your rights to express your opinion, whether they agreed with the official statement or not.

Answer is C

Engineering Economics

Engineering Economics Topics on FE Civil Examination   4-6 problems
Approximately 4% of exam

A. Discounted cash flow (equivalence, PW, equiv annual worth, FW, rate of return)
B. Cost (e.g., incremental, average, sunk, estimating)
C. Analyses (e.g., breakeven, benefit-cost, life cycle)
D. Uncertainty (e.g., expected value and risk)

Engineering Economics Topics on FE Civil Examination

Problem 1
A contractor has the following options for a project lasting 18 months:

Option A:
　　Monthly rental of excavation equipment at $15,000 per month + operating costs $2,000/month

Option B:
　　Purchase equipment for $200,000
　　Maintenance costs $8,000/month
　　Resale value of equipment after 18 months = $120,000

Annual interest rate = 10%

The benefit:cost ratio option B (purchasing) is most nearly:
- A. 1.26
- B. 1.37
- C. 1.55
- D. 2.12

Problem 2
A piece of construction equipment has an initial cost of $45,000, annual maintenance cost of $2,000, useful life of 10 years and a salvage value of $6,000. If the nominal MARR is 8%, what is the present worth of all costs for owning the equipment?
- A. $ 55,640
- B. $ 59,000
- C. $ 61,200
- D. $ 71,000

Problem 3
A piece of construction equipment has an initial cost of $45,000, useful life of 10 years and a salvage value of $6,000. If straight line depreciation is used, what is the book value at the end of the seventh year?
- A. $ 13,500
- B. $ 17,700
- C. $ 11,300
- D. $ 6,000

Problem 4

A piece of construction equipment has an initial cost of $45,000 and a useful life of 10 years. If the ACRS method of depreciation is used, what is the book value at the end of the seventh year?

A. $ 11,500
B. $ 11,700
C. $ 8,800
D. $ 10,300

Problem 5

A piece of construction equipment has an initial cost of $45,000, useful life of 10 years and a salvage value of $6,000. If the 'sum of years digits' method of depreciation is used, what is the book value at the end of the seventh year?

A. $ 4,250
B. $ 6,150
C. $ 7,250
D. $ 8,350

Problem 6

A company invests $200,000 in a piece of equipment that manufactures a widget called X3P2. The useful life of the equipment is 10 years and the salvage value is $50,000. The cost for raw materials per piece of X3P2 is $3 and the sale price is $6.50. If annual overhead expenses are $20,000, how many widgets must the company manufacture annually to make a 20% profit? Use MARR = 6%

A. 15,000
B. 18,000
C. 20,000
D. 24,000

Problem 7

A company invests $200,000 in a piece of equipment that manufactures a widget called X3P2. The useful life of the equipment is 10 years and the salvage value is $50,000. The cost for raw materials per piece of X3P2 is $3 and the sale price is $4.50. If annual overhead expenses are $18,000 and the company manufactures 28,000 units annually, what is the rate of return on investment? Use MARR = 6%

A. 5.4%
B. 6.4%
C. 8.1%
D. 9.2%

Problem 8

A company invests $200,000 in a piece of equipment that manufactures a widget called X3P2. The useful life of the equipment is 10 years, at the end of which the salvage values is zero. If the annual overhead expenses are $12,000 and the company generates annual net revenue of $42,000, what is the rate of return on investment? Use MARR = 6%

A. 6.1%
B. 7.4%
C. 8.1%
D. 9.2%

Problem 9

Annual maintenance costs for a water treatment plant for a small community are $30,000 in year 2001 and expected to increase by $500 each year during 2002-2020. If the MARR is 6%, what is the present worth of all maintenance costs during the period 2001-2020?

A. $695,000
B. $623,450
C. $511,050
D. $387,700

Problem 10

An investment fund is declared at a nominal annual interest rate of 7%. What is the effective annual yield if compounding is performed every two weeks?

A. 7.24%
B. 7.18%
C. 7.10%
D. 6.89%

Problem 11

The current purchase price of a piece of capital equipment is $150,000. The equipment has a useful life of 10 years and a salvage value of $20,000. If MARR is 8% and inflation is 2%, what should be the annual investment over the life of the equipment to offset the replacement cost?

A. $9,333
B. $15,333
C. $23,333
D. $25,333

Problem 12
A company purchases some capital equipment for $250,000. The equipment has a useful life of 10 years and a salvage value of $20,000. Straight line depreciation is used. Annual revenue generated from items manufactured by the equipment are $55,000 and annual expenses for raw materials and maintenance is $11,000. The company pays 35% corporate taxes on net profits. What is the annual profit after taxes?
- A. $7,350
- B. $23,000
- C. $36,650
- D. $44,000

Problem 13
A 9% bond with a face value of $100,000 is offered on January 1, 2010. Maturity date for the bond is Dec. 31, 2014. The bond pays interest every six months – on June 30 and December 31. If the current MARR is 10%, what is the present worth of the bond?
- A. $93,350
- B. $97,040
- C. $98,150
- D. $100,000

Problem 14
A dam will have initial cost of $15 million, annual maintenance cost of $75,000 and major maintenance every 5 years of $300,000. If the MARR is 8% per year, what is the capitalized cost of the dam?
- A. $15,976,615
- B. $16,231,165
- C. $16,576,875
- D. $17,123,145

Problem 15
A local municipality is contemplating the feasibility of repairing a bridge. The estimated useful life of the bridge is 20 years. The MARR is 6%. The relevant cost estimates are shown below. All costs are shown in thousands of dollars.

	Existing	Repair
Initial cost	0	50
Annual cost		
Years 1 – 10	8	3
Years 11 – 20	11	4
Salvage value	5	20

The benefit:cost ratio of making repairs is most nearly:

A. 1.15
B. 1.21
C. 1.32
D. 1.45

Problem 16

An asphalt paving surfacing alternative is being evaluated using the present worth for future expenditures over an expected 40 yr life. The initial cost of the asphalt surface is $700,000. It will require overlays at several intervals during the expected life. The cost of the future overlays will be $252,000 at 10 yr from construction, $332,000 at 17 yr, $420,000 at 23 yr, $530,000 at 29 yr, and $671,000 in 35 yr. The inflation rate is set at 4% annually for the analysis. What is the present worth of the asphalt alternative?

A. $1,551,000
B. $1,672,000
C. $1,711,000
D. $1,824,000

Problem 17

A local municipality must make a determination about the feasibility of repairing a bridge. The estimated useful life of the bridge is 25 years. The MARR is 7%. The relevant cost estimates are shown below. All costs are shown in thousands of dollars. If the decision is taken to repair the bridge, the present worth of all expenses is most nearly:

A. $222,945
B. $241,364
C. $258,771
D. $267,981

	Existing	Repair
Initial cost	0	160
Annual cost		
Years 1 – 10	20	5
Years 11 – 25	25	8
Salvage value	0	50

Problem 18

Sidewalks for a community must be reconstructed and maintained. There are two options in the choice of material – concrete and brick. Costs for both alternatives are shown below. The MARR is 7%. All costs are shown in thousands of dollars. The difference in EUAC between the two options is most nearly:

A) EUAC for concrete is less by $2,200
B) EUAC for concrete is less by $4,700

C) EUAC for concrete is more by $2,200
D) EUAC for concrete is more by $4,700

	Concrete	Brick
Initial cost	140	100
Annual maintenance	12	8
Useful life (yrs)	14	9

Problem 19

For a community, it is estimated that a population's water consumption will double over the next 20 years. The cost of expanding the existing water supply system will be compared to a phased program of expansion. Immediate development would cost $420,000 with annual maintenance costs of $40,000. A phased program would involve an initial investment of $200,000 and an estimated expenditure of 650,000 in 10 years. Annual maintenance cost under the phased program is estimated to be $20,000. Assuming a *period of service = 20 years* for each system and MARR = 7%, calculate the benefit cost ratio of the phased program relative to the single investment program.

A. 1.56
B. 1.78
C. 1.92
D. 2.11

Problem 20

For a community, it is estimated that a population's water consumption will double over the next 20 years. The cost of expanding the existing water supply system will be compared to a phased program of expansion. Immediate development would cost $420,000 with annual maintenance costs of $40,000. A phased program would involve an initial investment of $200,000 and an estimated expenditure of 650,000 in 10 years. Annual maintenance cost under the phased program is estimated to be $20,000. Assuming a *perpetual period of service* for each system and MARR = 7%, calculate the cost ratio of the phased program relative to the single investment program.

A. 0.67
B. 0.82
C. 0.89
D. 0.93

Problem 21

After purchasing a gravel pit and crushing equipment, the contractor is considering an alternative plan to improve the operation of the pit. The alternative plan will produce an equal amount of crushed rock and equal revenue. Assume a minimum acceptable rate of return of 10%

	Present Plan	Alternative Plan
Initial cost ($)		25,000
Salvage value ($)		5,000
Annual cost ($)	150,000	145,000
Life in years	-	5

The benefit-cost ratio of the alternative plan, when compared to the present plan, is most nearly:

- A) 0.7
- B) 0.9
- C) 1.0
- D) 1.1

Problem 22

A small town needs to choose one of two options for its water supply needs of its population. Assume average daily consumption = 125 gpcd. The options are presented below:

Option A: Purchase water from a neighboring county
Average distance from source = 20 miles
Distribution cost = $23/million gallons/mile
Water treatment cost = $560/ million gallons

or

Option B: Build its own water treatment & distribution system
Initial Cost = $12 million
Annual maintenance cost = $50,000
User costs = $200/million gallons
Design life = 30 years
The minimum acceptable rate of return = 6%

What is most nearly the population for which option B becomes economically feasible?

- A) 15,000
- B) 20,000
- C) 25,000
- D) 30,000

Engineering Economics Solutions

Solution 1
Monthly interest rate = 10/12 = 0.833%

For this interest rate and n = 18 months,

$$(A/P, 0.00833, 18) = \frac{i(1+i)^n}{(1+i)^n - 1} = \frac{0.00833 \times 1.00833^{18}}{1.00833^{18} - 1} = 0.0601$$

$$(A/F, 0.00833, 18) = \frac{i}{(1+i)^n - 1} = \frac{0.00833}{1.00833^{18} - 1} = 0.0517$$

The costs (of purchasing relative to renting) are:

$200,000 (P). This can be converted to an annuity:

A = 200,000x0.0601 = + 12,020

- 120,000 (F) considered as a negative cost. This can be converted to an annuity:

A = -120,000x0.0517 = - 6,204

Monthly benefit (purchasing relative to renting) is:

$15k +2k – 8k = $9k

Benefit cost ratio: $B/C = \frac{9{,}000}{12{,}020 - 6{,}204} = 1.55$

Answer is C

> Answer (A) would be obtained by considering the resale value as a benefit, but it SHOULD be considered as a negative cost.

Solution 2
Converting the annuity to a present worth:

$$2000 \left(\frac{P}{A}, 10 \text{ yrs}, 8\%\right) = 2000 \times 6.7101 = 13420$$

Converting the salvage to a present worth:

$$6000 \left(\frac{P}{F}, 10 \text{ yrs}, 8\%\right) = 6000 \times 0.4632 = 2779$$

Total present worth of all costs = 45,000 + 13,420 – 2,779 = 55,641

Since these are all COSTS, the present worth should actually be – $55,641

Answer is A

Solution 3
Depreciation = initial cost – salvage value = $39,000

Annual depreciation = $39,000/10 = $3,900

At the end of 7 years, book value = initial cost – total depreciation to date = $45,000 – 7x3,900 = $17,700

Answer is B

Solution 4
Built into the ACRS depreciation schedule given in the handbook, the total percentage value remaining after year 7 = 6.6 + 6.5 + 6.5 + 3.3 = 22.9%

Therefore, book value after end of year 7 = 0.229x45,000 = $10,305

Answer is D

Solution 5

According to the 'sum of years digits' method, since the sum of integers 1 to 10 (years digits) = 55, the depreciation fractions (years 1 to 10) are:

$$\frac{10}{55}, \frac{9}{55}, \frac{8}{55}, \frac{7}{55}, \frac{6}{55}, \frac{5}{55}, \frac{4}{55}, \frac{3}{55}, \frac{2}{55}, \frac{1}{55}$$

Therefore, at the end of year 7, the fraction remaining (book value) is

$$\frac{3}{55} + \frac{2}{55} + \frac{1}{55} = \frac{6}{55}$$

Book value: $BV = \frac{6}{55} \times (45000 - 6000) = 4254.55$

Answer is A

Solution 6

Let us convert all quantities to annual basis.

The initial investment can be converted to an annuity: $A_1 = 200{,}000 \left(\frac{A}{P}, 6\%, 10 \text{ yrs}\right) = 27{,}180$

The salvage value can be converted to an annuity: $A_2 = 50{,}000 \left(\frac{A}{F}, 6\%, 10 \text{ yrs}\right) = 3795$

Let's say the company needs to make x items/year. Since revenue = 120% of expenses:

$$6.5x = 1.2(3x + 20000 + 27180 - 3795)$$

Solving this, x = 17,952

Answer is B

Solution 7

Let us convert all quantities to annual basis.

Annual profit: A = (4.5 – 3.0)x28,000 = 1.5x28,000 = 42,000

For what rate of interest are expenses = revenue (BREAK EVEN CONDITION)?

$$200{,}000 \left(\frac{A}{P}, i, 10 \text{ yrs}\right) - 50{,}000 \left(\frac{A}{F}, i, 10 \text{ yrs}\right) + 18{,}000 - 42{,}000 = 0$$

By trial and error:

For i = 5%, LHS = 200000x0.1296-50000x0.0796-24000=-2060

For i = 6%, LHS = 200000x0.1359-50000x0.0759-24000=-615

For i = 8%, LHS = 200000x0.149-50000x0.069-24000=2350

Therefore, the interest rate for which present worth = 0 is close to and slightly greater than 6%. Exact solution (unnecessary for multiple choice exam) is 6.42%

Answer is B

Solution 8

This is a much simpler version of the previous problem (because of no salvage)

Initial investment, P = 200,000
Net annual return, A = 42,000 − 12,000 = 30,000
A/P = 30,000/200,000 = 0.150
For what rate of interest is A/P = 0.150 for n = 10 yrs?
By trial and error:
For i = 6%, A/P = 0.1359
For i = 8%, A/P = 0.1490
Therefore, the interest rate for which present worth = 0 is slightly greater than 8%.
Exact solution (unnecessary for multiple choice exam) is 8.15%

Answer is C

Solution 9

This is an example of a gradient series (arithmetic progression). The payment series is 30k, 30.5k, 31k ...
This can be decomposed into an annuity of 30k and a gradient series 0, 0.5k, 1k ...
The present worth of all payments is:

$$P = 30,000 \times \left(\frac{P}{A}, 6\%, 20 \ yrs\right) + 500 \times \left(\frac{P}{G}, 6\%, 20 \ yrs\right) = 30,000 \times 11.4699 + 500 \times 87.2304 = \$387,712$$

Answer is D

Solution 10

Since 1 year = 52 weeks, there are 52/2 = 26 compounding periods in the year.
The nominal interest rate per compounding period = 7/26 = 0.2692%
The annual compounding factor F/P is:

$$\left(\frac{F}{P}, 0.2692\%, 26 \ periods\right) = 1.002692^{26} = 1.0724$$

Therefore, the effective annual interest rate is 7.24%

Answer is A

Solution 11

The effective interest rate, including inflation is:
$$d = i + f + if = 0.08 + 0.02 + 0.08 \times 0.02 = 0.1016$$

Future worth of 150k: $F = 150,000 \left(\frac{F}{P}, 10.16\%, 10 \ yrs\right) = 150,000 \times 1.1016^{10} = 394,757$

Salvage value = 20,000
Therefore, the future sum that needs to be provided for = 394,757 − 20,000 = $374,757

$$\left(\frac{A}{F}, 10.16\%, 10 \ yrs\right) = \frac{i}{(1+i)^n - 1} = \frac{0.1016}{1.1016^{10} - 1} = 0.06227$$

The annuity A = 0.06227×374,757 = $23,334.50

Answer is C

Solution 12

The difference between initial cost and salvage value = $230,000. This amount is to be written off equally per year. Therefore annual depreciation = $23,000
Annual gross profits (before taxes) = 55,000 – 11,000 = $44,000
Deducting annual depreciation (as a loss), taxable profits (before taxes) = 44k – 23k = 21k
Taxes = 0.35x21k = $7,350
Therefore, annual profits after taxes = 44k – 7.35k = 36.65k

Answer is C

Solution 13

The bond has a maturity period of 5 years. It generates income of ½ x 0.09 x 100,000 = $4,500 every 6 months for 5 years (10 bi-annual installments).

MARR = 10% per year is equivalent to 4.88% every 6 months. Since $1.0488^2 = 1.10$

The present worth of this income stream is:

$$4{,}500 \times \left(\frac{P}{A}, i = 4.88\%, n = 10\right) = 4{,}500 \times 7.767 = 34{,}951$$

Face value on maturity = 100,000, whose present value is

$$100{,}000 \times \left(\frac{P}{F}, i = 10\%, n = 5\right) = 100{,}000 \times 0.6209 = 62{,}090$$

Present worth of bond = $97041
The difference $2959 is called the discount

Answer is B

Solution 14

The initial cost is already a present worth and therefore does not need any adjustment. The (perpetual) annual maintenance cost of $70,000 can be converted to a present worth using:

$$P = \frac{A}{i} = \frac{75{,}000}{0.08} = 937{,}500$$

The major maintenance which occurs once every 5 years can be converted to an infinite annuity by:

$$300{,}000 \times \left(\frac{A}{F}, 8\%, 5\ yrs\right) = 300{,}000 \times 0.1705 = 51{,}150$$

This (perpetual) annuity can then be converted to a present value using:

$$P = \frac{A}{i} = \frac{51{,}150}{0.08} = 639{,}375$$

Total capitalized cost = 15,000,000 + 937,500 + 639,375 = $16,576,875

Answer is C

Solution 15

The repair option has the following:

Initial cost = $50,000

Years 1-10: Savings in annual maintenance = $5,000

Years 11-20: Savings in annual maintenance = $7,000

This can be expressed as a 20 year annuity of $7k MINUS a 10 year annuity of $2k

Benefit (converted to present value) is:

$$7k\left(\frac{P}{A}, 20\ yrs, 6\%\right) - 2k\left(\frac{P}{A}, 10\ yrs, 6\%\right) = 7,000 \times 11.4699 - 2,000 \times 7.3601$$
$$= 65,569.10$$

Extra salvage ($15,000) converted to present worth:

$$15k\left(\frac{P}{F}, 20\ yrs, 6\%\right) = 15,000 \times 0.3118 = 4677$$

Benefit cost ratio: $B/C = \frac{65569.10}{50000 - 4677} = 1.45$

Answer is D

> Note: an alternative calculation that may appeal to some is to count the salvage value as a benefit, which results in a benefit:cost ratio given by: $\frac{B}{C} = \frac{65569 + 4877}{50000} = 1.41$. However, this approach is not recommended. The salvage value should be considered as a negative cost (cost offset), as in the first calculation.

Solution 16

The present worth is given by:

$$PW = 700,000 + 252,000 \times \left(\frac{P}{F}, 10\ yrs, 4\%\right) + 332,000 \times \left(\frac{P}{F}, 17\ yrs, 4\%\right) + 420,000$$
$$\times \left(\frac{P}{F}, 23\ yrs, 4\%\right) + 530,000 \times \left(\frac{P}{F}, 10\ yrs, 4\%\right) + 671,000$$
$$\times \left(\frac{P}{F}, 10\ yrs, 4\%\right) = 1,551,0000$$

Present worth of all expenses = $1,551,000

Answer is A

Solution 17

Convert everything to *present worth*

The cost of repairs (relative to the 'do-nothing' option) = $160,000

The 1-10 year annuity of $5,000 has a present worth of 5,000 x (P/A, 10 years, 7%) = 5,000 x 7.0236 = 35,118

The 11-25 year annuity of $8,000 is a shifted annuity, whose origin is at year 10.

Engineering Economics Topics on FE Civil Examination

This has a present worth of 8,000 x (P/A, 15 years, 7%) x (P/F, 10 years, 7%) = 8,000 x 9.1079 x 0.5083 = 37,036.

The value of the shifted annuity could also have been calculated as:
8,000 x (P/A, 25 years, 7%) − 3,000 x (P/A, 10 years, 7%) = 8,000 x 11.6536 − 3,000 x 7.0236
= 72,158 (which is essentially identical to 35,118 + 37,036

The salvage value (negative cost) is a future value, which has a present worth given by
−50,000 x (P/F, 25 years, 7%) = −50,000 x 0.1842 = − 9,210

The present worth of all expenses = 160,000 + 35,118 + 37,036 − 9,210 = $222,944

Answer is A

Solution 18
EUAC for concrete (convert everything to *annuity*) = 12,000 + 140,000 x (A/P, 14 years, 7%)
= 12,000 + 140,000 x 0.1143 = $28,002
EUAC for brick = 8,000 + 100,000 x (A/P, 9 years, 7%) = 8,000 + 100,000 x 0.1535 = $23,350
EUAC for concrete is more by $4,652

Answer is D

Solution 19
The cash flow line for options 1 & 2 may be drawn as

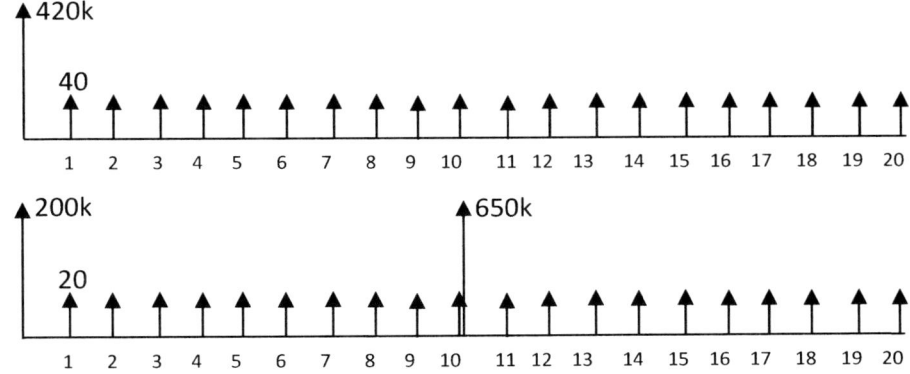

The costs and benefits of option 2 relative to option 1 may be sketched as:

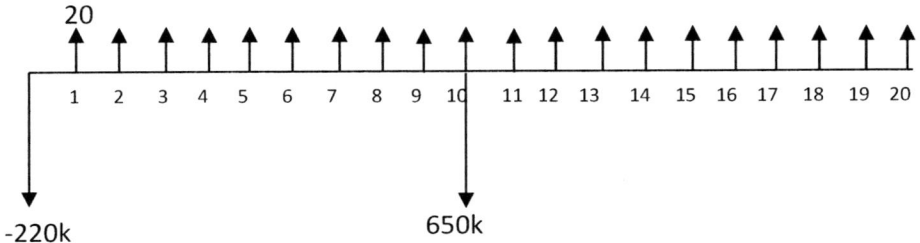

Now, the net cost of option 2 (relative to option 1) is (in terms of present worth):
$$-220 + 650\left(\frac{P}{F}, 10\ years, 7\%\right) = -220 + 650 \times 0.5083 = 110.395$$
The relative benefit of option 2 (relative to option 1) is given by:
$$20\left(\frac{P}{A}, 20\ years, 7\%\right) = 20 \times 10.5940 = 211.88$$

Benefit/Cost ratio = 211.88/110.395 = 1.92

Answer is C

Solution 20
For a perpetual annuity, capitalized cost = A/i
Present worth of Plan A (single capital investment) in thousands of dollars:
420 + 40 ÷ 0.07 = 991.43
Present worth of Plan B (two-stage capital investment) in thousands of dollars:
200 + 650(P/F, 10 years, 7%) + 20 ÷ 0.07 = 200 + 650x0.5083 + 20 ÷ 0.07 = 816.109
Cost ratio (Plan B relative to Plan A) = 816.109 ÷ 991.43 = 0.823

Answer is B

Solution 21
Initial Cost of Plan B (relative to plan A) = $25,000. This can be converted to an annuity using:
25,000 x (A/P,10%,5 yrs) = 25000 x 0.2638 = $6,595
Annual benefit of plan B (relative to plan A) = 150,000 – 145,000 = $5,000
Additional salvage value of plan B (relative to plan A) = $5,000. This is to be considered as a negative cost (cost offset) and can be converted to an annuity using:
5,000 x (A/F,10%,5 yrs) = 5000 x 0.1638 = $819
Benefit:Cost ratio = 5000/(6595 – 819) = 0.87

Solution 22
Assuming population = P
Annual consumption = 125 x 365 x P gallons = 0.0456P million gallons

Engineering Economics Topics on FE Civil Examination

OptionA: Cost = (560+23x20)x0.0456P = 46.51P
Option B: Converting all costs to annual cost
Initial Cost = $12 million x (A/P,30 yrs,6%) = $12 \times 10^6 \times 0.0726$ = 871,200
Annual maintenance cost = $50,000
User costs = $200/million gallons = 200x0.0456P = 9.12P
46.51P = 921,200 + 9.12P
P = 24,638

Answer is C

Statics Topics on FE Civil Examination

Statics

Statics Topics on FE Civil Examination   **7–11 problems**
Approximately 7% of exam

A. Resultants of force systems
B. Equivalent force systems
C. Equilibrium of rigid bodies
D. Frames and trusses
E. Centroid of area
F. Area moments of inertia
G. Static friction

Statics Topics on FE Civil Examination

Problem 1
A 5 kg block on a 35° incline is acted upon by a horizontal force F as shown. What is the minimum force required to keep the block in static equilibrium?

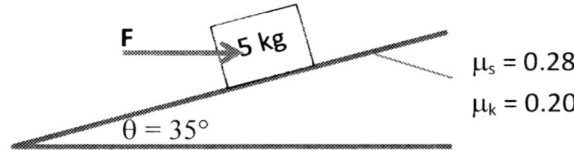

A. 12.2 N
B. 17.2 N
C. 46.2 N
D. 81.2 N

Problem 2
What is the force in the highlighted member of the truss shown below?

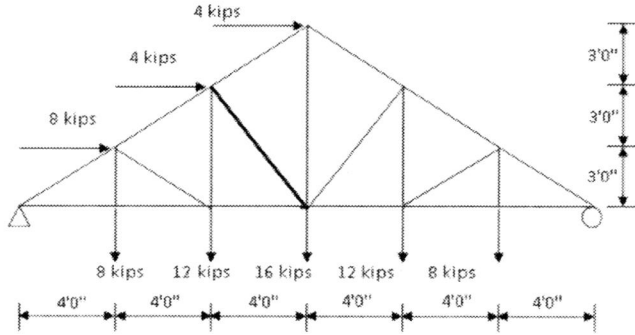

A. 17.6 kips compression
B. 17.6 kips tension
C. 23.8 kips compression
D. 23.8 kips tension

Problem 3
A force F = 500 N acts along line AB as shown. What is the component of the force along line AC? Coordinates are in meters.

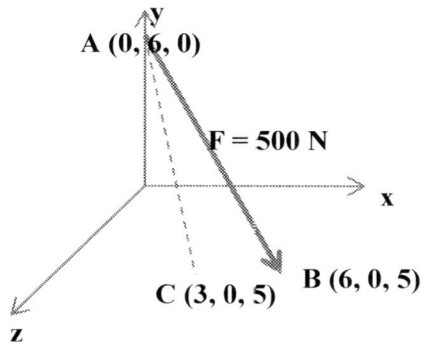

A. 356 N
B. 482 N
C. 246 N
D. 470 N

Problem 4
A force F = 500 N acts along line AB as shown. What is the moment of the force about point C? Coordinates are in meters.

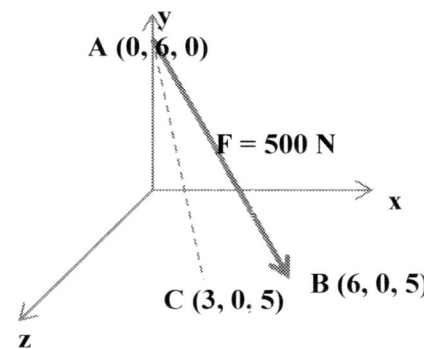

A. 870 N-m
B. 980 N-m
C. 1190 N-m
D. 1340 N-m

Problem 5

A doorway frame consists of two 1.8 m high uprights capped with a semi-circular arch as shown. That is the height of the centroid of the frame above the ground?

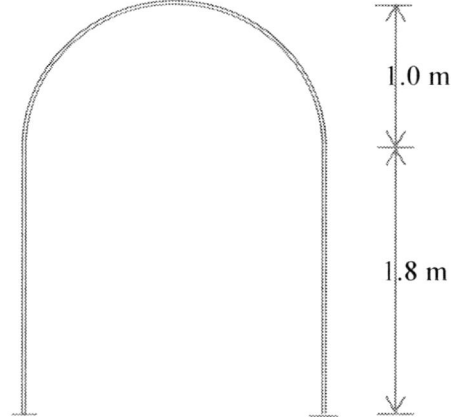

- A. 1.23 m
- B. 1.40 m
- C. 1.52 m
- D. 1.69 m

Problem 6

What is the moment of inertia I_{xx} (x-x axis indicated on figure) of the flanged section shown below? All dimensions are mm.

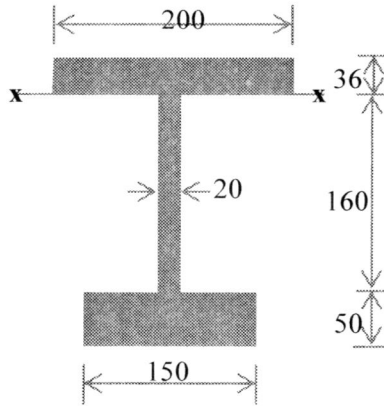

- A. 2.89×10^8 mm^4
- B. 6.54×10^7 mm^4
- C. 1.52×10^7 mm^4
- D. 9.17×10^6 mm^4

Problem 7

A fixed and a movable pulley are used to support a load 120 kg as shown. If the pulleys are assumed to be massless & frictionless, what is the force F necessary for static equilibrium?

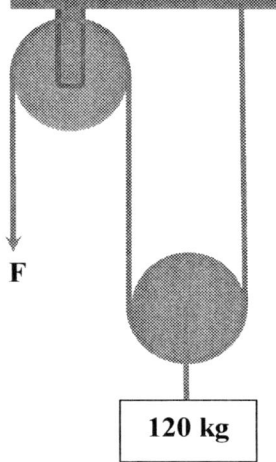

A. 60 N
B. 120 N
C. 590 N
D. 1180 N

Problem 8

A fixed and a movable pulley are used to support a load 120 kg as shown. If the pulleys are assumed to be massless and the coefficient of friction between the rope and the pulleys is 0.10, what is the *minimum* force **F** necessary for static equilibrium?

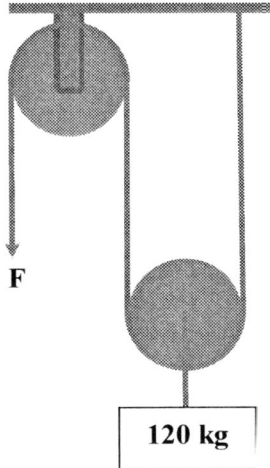

A. 360 N
B. 430 N
C. 590 N
D. 806 N

Problem 9
Which of the following statements is true about the truss shown below?

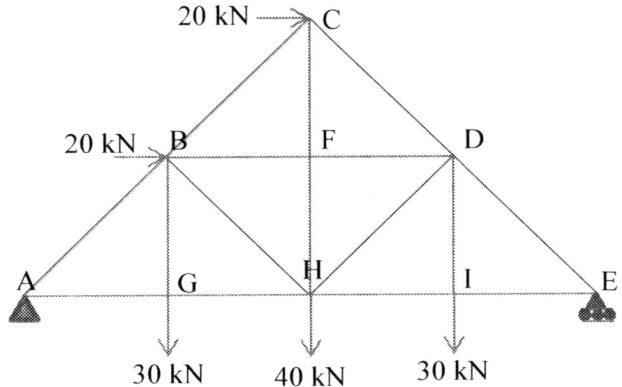

A. Truss is unstable
B. Truss is statically determinate, stable
C. Truss is statically indeterminate, indeterminacy is external
D. Truss is statically indeterminate, indeterminacy is internal

Problem 10
For the truss shown below, what is the force in member GD?

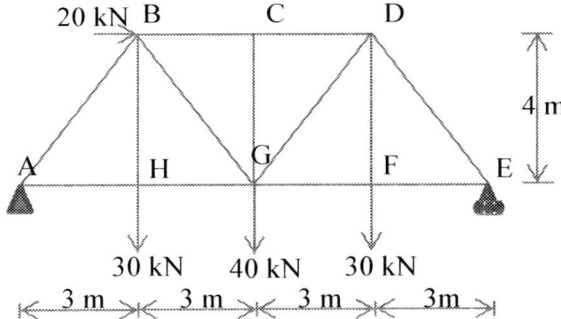

A. 71 kN (tension)
B. 71 kN (compression)
C. 33 kN (tension)
D. 33 kN (compression)

Problem 11

For the three-hinged frame show below, what is the reaction force at the support A? The crown C is hinged.

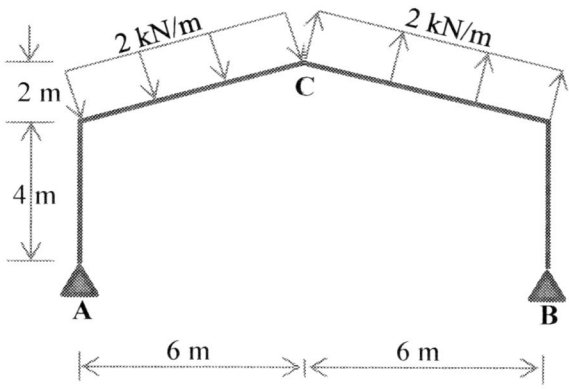

A. 2.67 kN
B. 3.33 kN
C. 4.0 kN
D. 4.8 kN

Problem 12

A square thread screw-jack with mean thread diameter = 34 mm and pitch = 8 mm is used to lift a load F = 40 kN. If the coefficient of friction is 0.16, what is the torque necessary to lift the load?

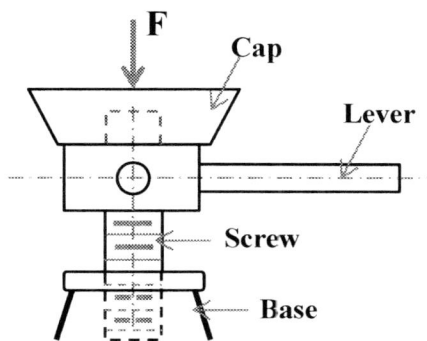

A. 120 N-m
B. 160 N-m
C. 200 N-m
D. 480 N-m

Problem 13

A piece of sheet metal is shown below. All dimensions are in mm. The center of the semicircular hole is 60 mm to the right of the origin. What are the coordinates of the centroid?

    A. x = 58, y = 94
    B. x = 67, y = 108
    C. x = 58, y = 69
    D. x = 65, y = 84

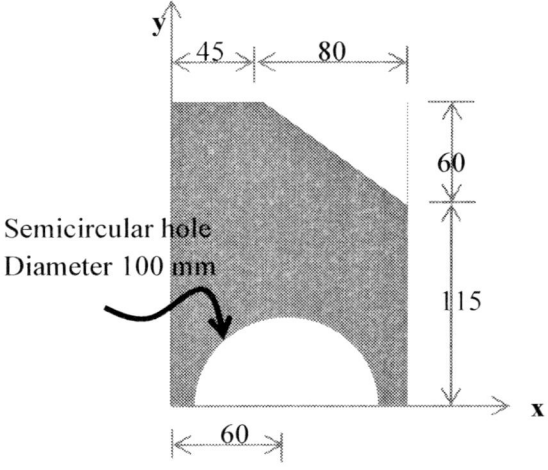

Problem 14

A system of steel cables supports the loads as shown. What is the force **F** necessary to keep the system in static equilibrium?

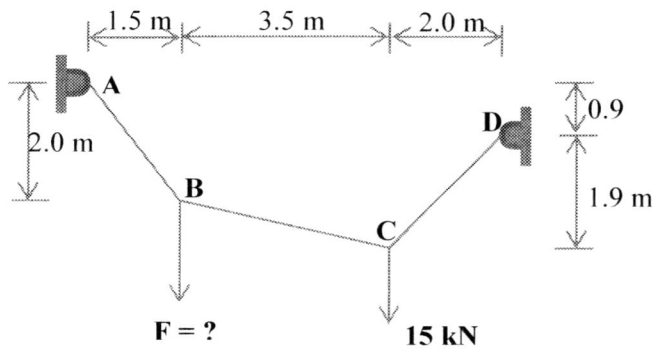

    A. F = 12 kN
    B. F = 13 kN
    C. F = 14 kN
    D. F = 15 kN

Problem 15

A frame ABCDE is supported by a hinge at A and roller support at D as shown. If the 30 kN force at C and the distributed load over DE is to be replaced by a vertical (acting upward) force of 12 kN at C, while maintaining the same reaction at support D, what is the additional moment that must be applied at C?

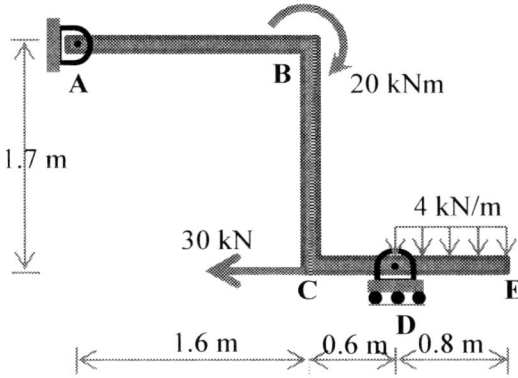

A. M = 40.12 kNm clockwise
B. M = 40.12 kNm anticlockwise
C. M = 78.52 kNm clockwise
D. M = 78.52 kNm anticlockwise

Problem 16

A rope is wrapped around a cylindrical capstan of diameter 20 cm as shown. The point of tangency of the rope is P located at coordinates (10, 0, 40)^{cm} as shown. The far end of the rope is Q(10, 20, 45)^{cm} where a tension T = 18 kN is applied. What is the torque about the axis of the capstan?

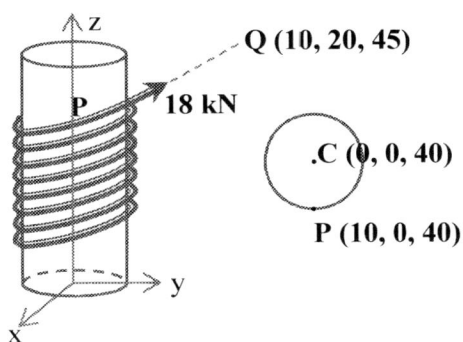

A. 1.53 kNm
B. 1.75 kNm
C. 2.30 kNm
D. 3.53 kNm

Problem 17

A cable wrapped around a movable pulley and a fixed pulley is used to lift a load as shown. If all pulleys are massless and frictionless, what is the mechanical advantage of the pulley system?

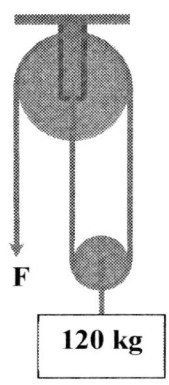

A. 1.0
B. 1.5
C. 2.0
D. 3.0

Problem 18

An elevated water tank is supported by 4 tower legs as shown. The empty tank weighs 6 kips and the full tank weighs 300 kips. The resultant wind force of 120 kips acts at a height of 65 ft as shown. Each tower leg is supported by an isolated square footing.

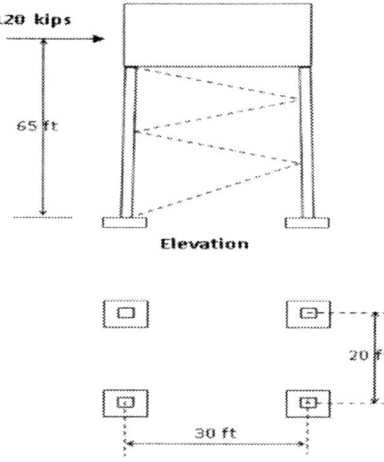

The maximum design uplift force (kips) for designing anchor bolts for each footing is most nearly:
    A. 65 kips
    B. 130 kips
    C. 73.5 kips
    D. 128.5 kips

Statics Topics on FE Civil Examination

Problem 19

A beam is supported by a hinged support at the left and by an inclined roller on the right as shown below. What is the reaction at the hinge?

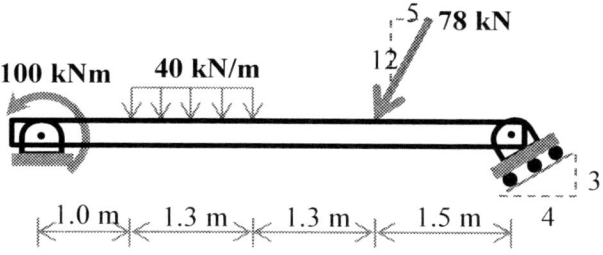

A. $R_B = 60$ kN
B. $R_B = 72$ kN
C. $R_B = 84$ kN
D. $R_B = 100$ kN

Problem 20

The tower truss shown below has frictionless hinges at each node. A vertical load acts at node A. For the load shown, how many zero-force members does the structure have?
A. 3
B. 4
C. 5
D. 6

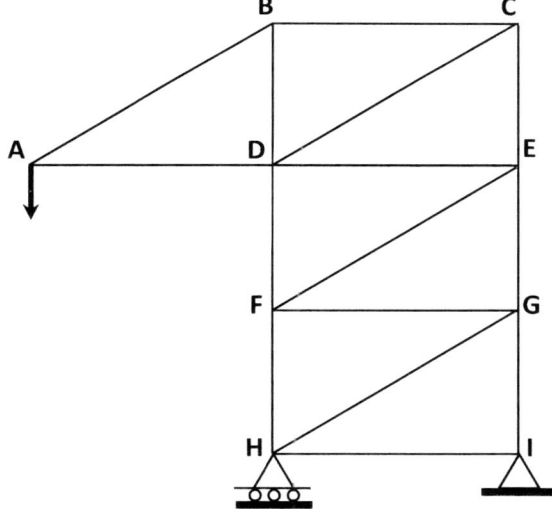

Problem 21

A 3-hinged arch bridge ABC (hinged supports at A & C; internal hinge at B) carries a uniformly distributed deck load 20 kN/m. What is the horizontal thrust reaction at A?

A. $H_A = 52.5$ kN (to the left)
B. $H_A = 52.5$ kN (to the right)
C. $H_A = 72.5$ kN (to the left)
D. $H_A = 72.5$ kN (to the right)

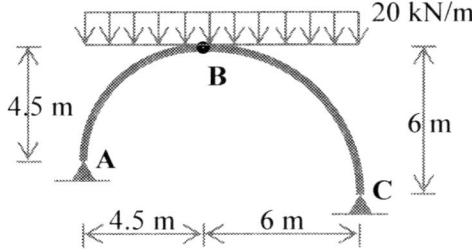

Problem 22

A simply supported beam is shown below. What is the reaction at the roller support at B?

A. $B_y = 11.28$ kN
B. $B_y = 11.97$ kN
C. $B_y = 7.92$ kN
D. $B_y = 9.03$ kN

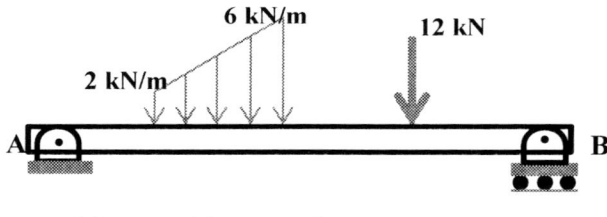

Problem 23

A truss is loaded as shown. What is the force in member DE?

A. 28 kN (tension)
B. 28 kN (compression)
C. 37 kN (tension)
D. 37 kN (compression)

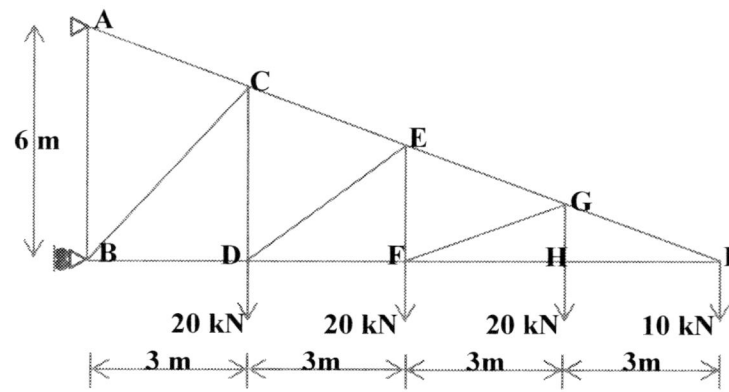

Problem 24

What is the moment of inertia I_z of the shape shown below? All dimensions are in mm.

A. 2.7×10^8 mm^4
B. 4.0×10^8 mm^4
C. 5.4×10^8 mm^4
D. 9.9×10^8 mm^4

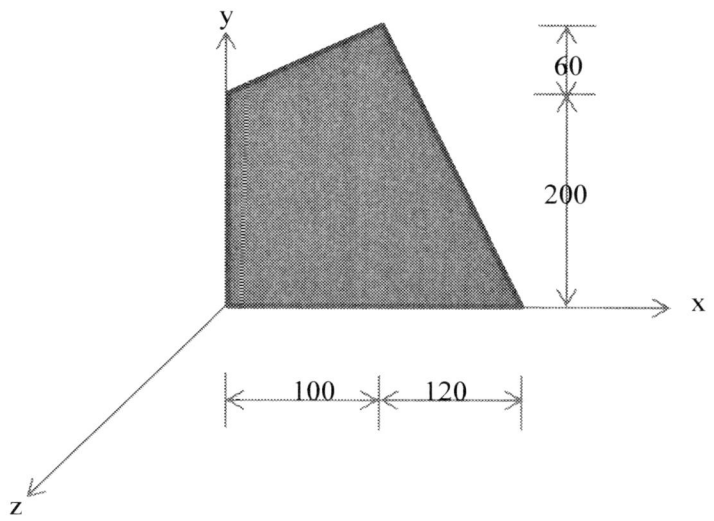

Problem 25

What is the area of the region bounded by the parabola $3(y - 3)^2 = 4(x - 2)$, the line y = 2 and the line x = 5, as shown shaded in the figure below?

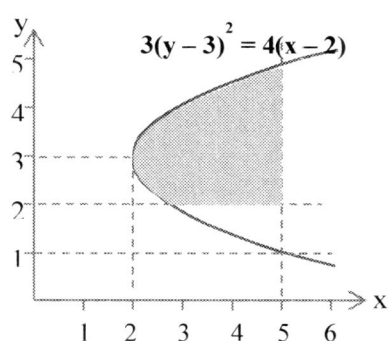

A. 4.35
B. 5.75
C. 6.25
D. 6.75

Problem 26

Find the moment of inertia I_x of the shaded area bounded by the curve $y = x^3$, the x-axis and the lines $x = 2$ and $x = 4$ as shown.

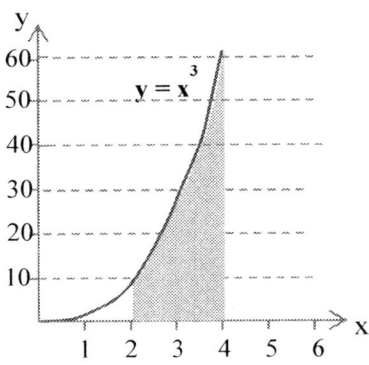

A. 8,730
B. 16,145
C. 34,918
D. 36,129

Problem 27

A frame ABCDE is supported by a hinge at A and roller support at D as shown. The frame is subject to the following loads: a clockwise couple on joint B, a 30 kN force at C and a uniformly distributed load over DE. What is the vertical reaction at D?

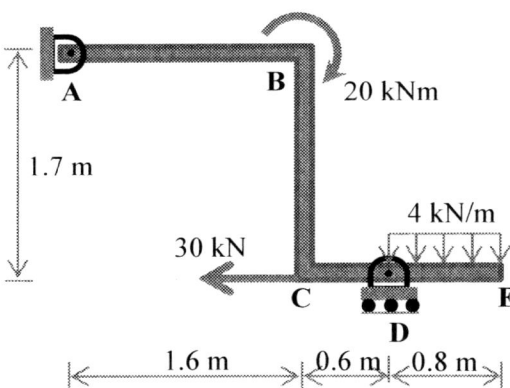

A. 22.8 kN
B. 27 kN
C. 36 kN
D. 41.3 kN

Problem 28

A rectangular plate ABCD is acted upon by the forces indicated below. What is the resultant moment about the center of the plate?

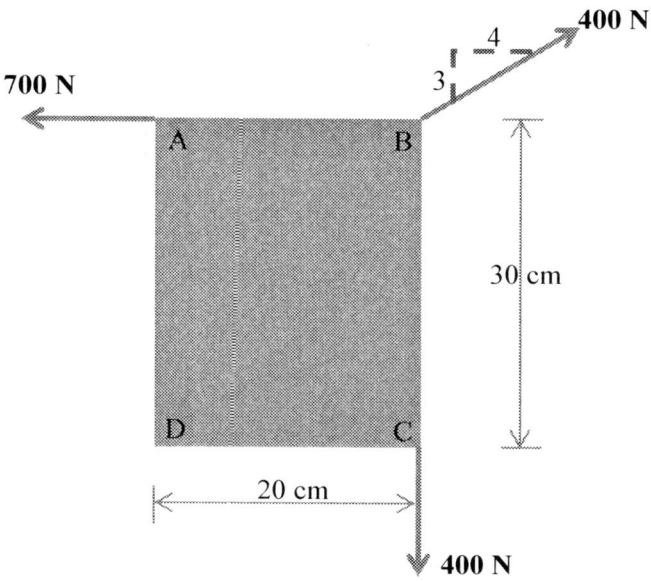

A. 37 Nm
B. 41 Nm
C. 57 Nm
D. 62 Nm

Problem 29

What is the product of of inertia I_{xy} for the shape shown below? All dimensions are in mm.

A. 1.87×10^7 mm^4
B. 2.15×10^7 mm^4
C. 2.85×10^7 mm^4
D. 3.21×10^7 mm^4

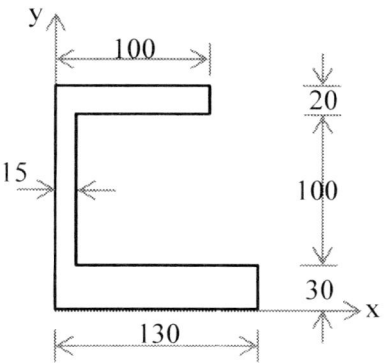

Statics Topics on FE Civil Examination

Statics Solutions

Solution 1

The free body diagram of the block, resolving forces along, and perpendicular to the incline, is shown. The minimum force will prevent it from sliding DOWNSLOPE.

> Note that if the question had asked for the maximum force F (for static equilibrium), we would solve for the condition just before the block starts sliding UPSLOPE. This decision will affect the choice of the friction force, which always opposes incipient motion.

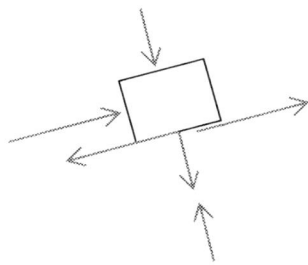

$F_y = N - F \sin 35 - 40.1 = 0 \Rightarrow N = F \sin 35 + 40.1$

$F_x = F \cos 35 - 28.1 + \mu N = 0 \Rightarrow F \cos 35 - 28.1 + 0.28(F \sin 35 + 40.1) = 0 \Rightarrow F = 17.22\ N$

Answer is B

Solution 2

Reactions at the hinge support can be found by taking moments about the roller support. This yields $A_y = 24.5\ k$

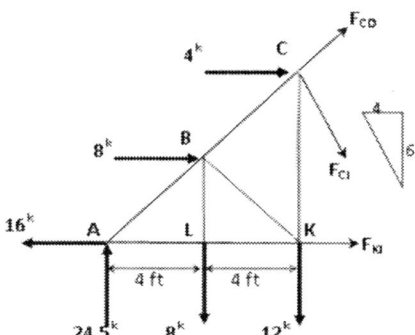

Taking moments about A (so that the intersecting forces F_{CD} and F_{KJ} are not involved):

$$\frac{4}{\sqrt{52}} F_{CJ} \times 6 + \frac{6}{\sqrt{52}} F_{CJ} \times 8 + 8 \times 3 + 4 \times 6 + 8 \times 4 + 12 \times 8 = 0$$

F_{CJ} = - 17.63 kips

Answer is A

Statics Topics on FE Civil Examination

> Note that if the end-game (of taking moments about A) is seen ahead of time, then it is obvious that the vertical reaction at A will not be necessary and therefore one can avoid that calculation.

Solution 3
AB = 6**i** − 6**j** + 5**k**
Magnitude of AB: $|AB| = \sqrt{6^2 + 6^2 + 5^2} = 9.85$
Unit vector u_{AB} = AB/|AB| = 0.61**i** − 0.61**j** + 0.51**k**
Force **F** = 500 (0.61**i** − 0.61**j** + 0.51**k**) = 305**i** − 305**j** + 254**k**
AC = 3**i** − 6**j** + 5**k**
Magnitude of AC: $|AC| = \sqrt{3^2 + 6^2 + 5^2} = 8.37$
Unit Vector u_{AC} = AC/|AC| = 0.36**i** − 0.72**j** + 0.60**k**
Component along AC = **F** · **u**$_{AC}$ = 481.8 N
Answer is B

Solution 4
AB = 6**i** − 6**j** + 5**k**
Magnitude of AB: $|AB| = \sqrt{6^2 + 6^2 + 5^2} = 9.85$
Unit Vector u_{AB} = AB/|AB| = 0.61**i** − 0.61**j** + 0.51**k**
Force **F** = 500 (0.61**i** − 0.61**j** + 0.51**k**) = 305**i** − 305**j** + 254**k**
CB = 3**i**
M$_c$ = **r** x **F** = 3**i** x (305**i** − 305**j** + 254**k**) = − 915 **k** − 762 **j**
Magnitude of M$_c$ = 1190.7 N-m
Answer is C

> The moment arm can be taken as either CA or CB. CB has the more convenient form (to perform the cross-product)

CA = −3**i** + 6**j** − 5**k**
CB = 3**i**

Solution 5
Ignoring the thickness of the frame, it can be idealized as 3 lines: (1) the left upright, (2) the arch and (3) the right upright. Lengths and centroid heights (measured from the ground) are summarized below:

Line	Length L (m)	Centroid height Y (m)	LY
1	1.8	0.9	1.62
2	3.14	2.22	6.99
3	1.8	0.9	1.62
	6.74		10.23

Statics Topics on FE Civil Examination

$$\bar{Y} = \frac{\sum L_i Y_i}{\sum L_i} = 1.52$$

Answer is C

Solution 6
Using parallel axis theorem, the total moment of inertia is calculated as the sum of I_{xx} for each of the 3 rectangles (listed from top to bottom)

$$I_{xx1} = \frac{1}{12} \times 200 \times 36^3 + 7200 \times 18^2 = 3.11 \times 10^6$$

$$I_{xx2} = \frac{1}{12} \times 20 \times 160^3 + 3200 \times (-80)^2 = 2.73 \times 10^7$$

$$I_{xx3} = \frac{1}{12} \times 150 \times 50^3 + 7500 \times (-185)^2 = 2.58 \times 10^8$$

Total I_{xx} = 2.89x10^8 mm^4

Answer is A

> For a rectangle:
> $$I_{xx} = \frac{1}{12} bh^3 + Ad^2$$

Solution 7
Since a single continuous cable has constant cable tension, we have two cable segments (around the movable pulley) supporting the load W = 120x9.81 = 1177.2 N. Therefore, tension in cable = 1177.2 ÷ 2 = 588.6 N.

From the equilibrium of the fixed pulley, the force F is equal to the cable tension.

Answer is C

Solution 8
The friction between each pulley and the rope (angle of contact = 180° = 3.142 rad). Since the MINIMUM force F is asked for, we must solve for the case $F_3 > F_2 > F_1$

$$\frac{F_3}{F_2} = \frac{F_2}{F_1} = e^{\mu\theta} = e^{0.1 \times 3.142} = 1.37$$

From the free body diagram of the movable pulley, $F_3 + F_2 = 2.37 F_2 = 1177.2 \rightarrow F_2 = 496.7$ N

Statics Topics on FE Civil Examination

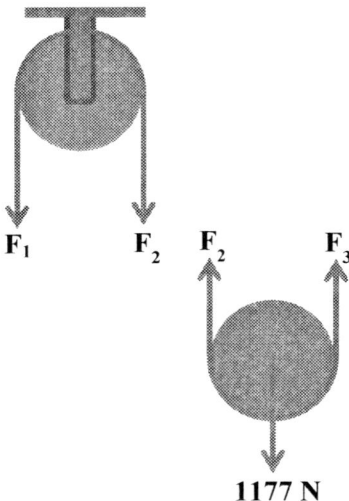

$F_2 = 1.37\ F_1 \rightarrow F_1 = 362.6$ N

Answer is A

Solution 9
For the truss, shown:
Number of members, M = 16
Number of joints, J = 9
Number of external reactions, R = 3
M + R = 19
2J = 18
Therefore, the truss is statically indeterminate (first order). The three external reactions can be found from using the three equilibrium equations applied to the entire structure. Therefore, the source of indeterminacy is not external, it's internal.

Answer is D

Solution 10
Taking moments about A:
$$M_A = 20 \times 4 + 30 \times 3 + 40 \times 6 + 30 \times 9 - 12E_y = 0$$
E_y = 56.67 kN

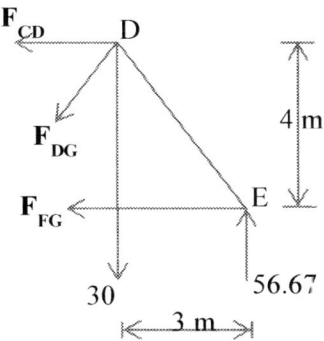

$$F_y = -F_{DG} \times \frac{4}{5} - 30 + 56.67 = 0 \Rightarrow F_{DG} = 33.33 \ kN$$

Answer is C

Solution 11

The hypotenuse length of the gable roof is √(2²+6²) = 6.325 m

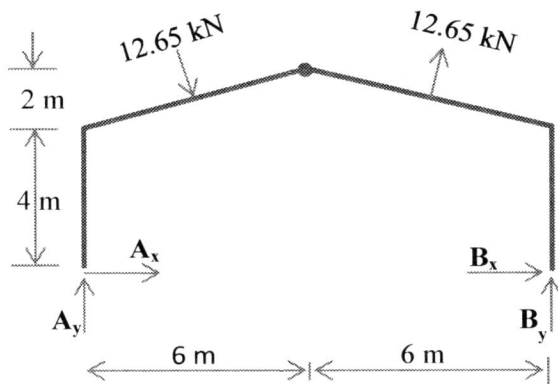

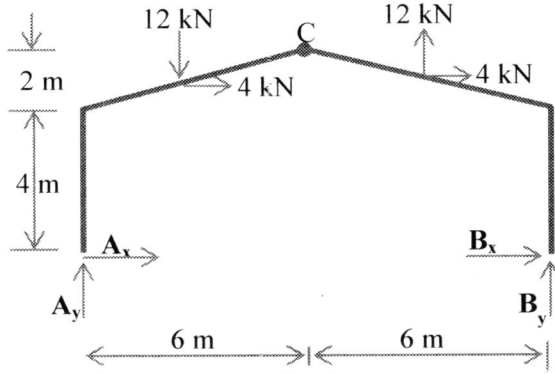

Taking moments about B (whole structure):
$$M_B = 12 \times 3 + 4 \times 5 - 12 \times 9 + 4 \times 5 + 12A_y = 0 \Rightarrow A_y = 2.67 \ kN$$
Taking moments about C (left half of structure):
$$M_{C,left} = -12 \times 3 - 4 \times 1 - 6A_x + 6A_y = 0 \Rightarrow A_x = -4 \ kN$$

Total reaction at A: $R_A = \sqrt{A_x^2 + A_y^2} = \sqrt{4^2 + 2.67^2} = 4.81\ kN$

Answer is D

Solution 12
The axial load F = 40000 N

With a pitch of 8 mm and a diameter of 34 mm, it means that the thread advances 8 mm over a circumference of πD = 34π

Pitch angle: $\tan \alpha = \frac{p}{\pi D} = \frac{8}{34\pi} = 0.075 \Rightarrow \alpha = 4.28°$

Coefficient of friction μ = 0.16
Friction angle: $\phi = \tan^{-1} 0.16 = 9.09°$

To lift the load, the positive angle should be used.

Torque: $M = Pr \tan(\alpha + \phi) = 40{,}000 \times \frac{0.034}{2} \times \tan(4.28 + 9.09) = 161.6\ Nm$

Answer is B

Solution 13
The three component shapes are marked 1, 2 and 3. Their properties are listed in the table.

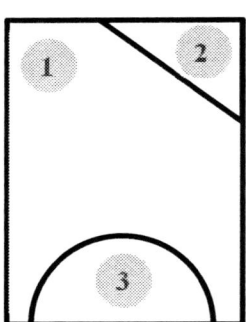

Shape	Area	X	Y
1	21,875	62.5	87.5
2	2,400	98.33	155
3	3,927	60	21.22

Coordinates of the centroid:
$$x_c = \frac{\sum x_i A_i}{\sum A_i} = \frac{62.5 \times 21875 - 98.33 \times 2400 - 60 \times 3927}{21875 - 2400 - 3927} = 57.6$$
$$y_c = \frac{\sum y_i A_i}{\sum A_i} = \frac{87.5 \times 21875 - 155 \times 2400 - 21.22 \times 3927}{21875 - 2400 - 3927} = 93.8$$

Answer is A

STRATEGY: Since the y-coordinate values are unique in all 4 choices, just solving for y_c is sufficient.

Solution 14

At node C, the free body diagram is

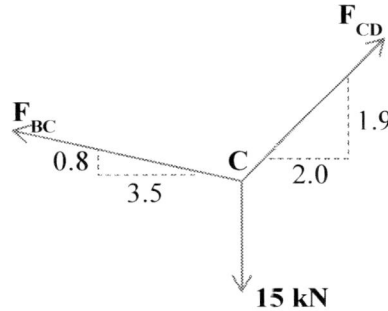

$$F_x = 0 \Rightarrow F_{BC} \frac{35}{35.9} = F_{CD} \frac{20}{27.6} \Rightarrow F_{CD} = 1.345 F_{BC}$$
$$F_y = 0 \Rightarrow F_{BC} \frac{8}{35.9} + F_{CD} \frac{19}{27.6} = 15 \Rightarrow 0.2228 F_{BC} + 0.6884 F_{CD} =$$
$$= 0.2228 F_{BC} + 0.6884 \times 1.345 F_{BC} = 1.15 F_{BC} = 15 \Rightarrow F_{BC} = 13.06\ kN$$

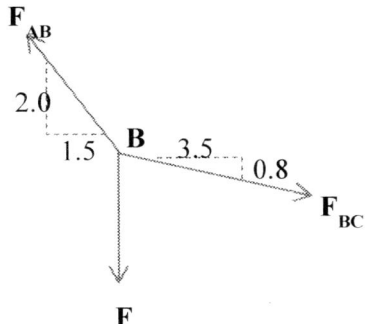

$$F_x = 0 \Rightarrow F_{BC} \frac{35}{35.9} = F_{AB} \frac{15}{25} \Rightarrow F_{AB} = 1.625 F_{BC} = 21.22\ kN$$
$$F_y = 0 \Rightarrow F = F_{BC} \frac{-8}{35.9} + F_{AB} \frac{20}{25} = -0.223 \times 13.06 + 0.8 \times 21.22 = 14.06\ kN$$

Answer is C

Statics Topics on FE Civil Examination

Alternate solution

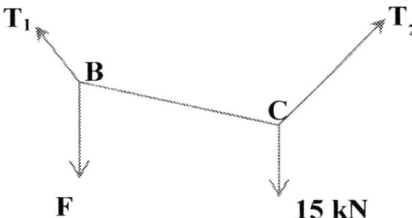

Taking moments about B:
$$\sum M_B = 15 \times 3.5 - T_2 \frac{19}{27.6} \times 3.5 - T_2 \frac{20}{27.6} \times 0.8 = 0 \Rightarrow T_2 = 17.56 \, kN$$

Taking moments about A:
$$\sum M_B = F \times 1.5 + 15 \times 5 - T_2 \frac{19}{27.6} \times 5 - T_2 \frac{20}{27.6} \times 2.8 = 0 \Rightarrow F = 14.06 \, kN$$

Solution 15

The question states "the 30 kN force at C and the distributed load over DE is to be replaced by a vertical (acting upward) force of 12 kN at C". This means that the couple at B is unaffected. Also, the vertical reaction at D is unchanged. These two items can therefore be excluded from the equivalence of the two systems. Since the reactions at A will certainly change, we take moments about A so that they are excluded from the calculations.

For the existing system, sum of moments about A:
$$M_{A,1} = 30 \times 1.7 + 0.8 \times 4 \times 2.6 = 59.32 \, kNm \, (clockwise)$$

For the new system, sum of moments about A:
$$M_{A,2} = 12 \times 1.6 = 19.2 \, kNm \, (anticlockwise)$$

Therefore, an additional couple M = 78.52 kNm clockwise must be added.

Answer is C

Solution 16

Vector PQ is: $\overline{PQ} = 20j + 5k$

Unit vector along PQ: $u_{PQ} = \frac{20j+5k}{\sqrt{20^2+5^2}} = 0.97j + 0.2425k$

Force vector: $\overline{F} = 18(0.97j + 0.2425k) = 17.46j + 4.37k$

Moment of force F about center (marked C on the section view): $M_C = r \times F = 10i \times (17.46j + 4.37k) = 174.6k - 43.7j$

The component of this moment along the axis of the cylinder (which happens to be the z axis) is calculated as the dot product of the moment and the unit vector along the axis (which is **k**)

Therefore, the torque about the axis, T = 174.6 kN-cm = 1.746 kNm

Answer is B

Solution 17

Since the cable-pulley contact is frictionless, the tension in the cable is constant. The FBD of the 120 kg mass is shown below.

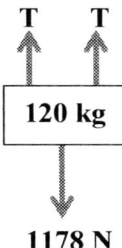

For static equilibrium, T = 589 N. This is equal to the force F that must be exerted as effort.
Mechanical advantage = Load/Effort = 2

Answer is C

Solution 18

Since gravity forces counteract uplift, we must consider the empty tank case here. The weight of 6 kips is carried equally by each leg. Therefore, the compression at each footing = 1.5 kips.
The lateral force creates an overturning moment = 120k x 65 ft = 7800 k-ft on the horizontal plane at the top of the footings. This overturning moment is shared equally by two couples (4 legs in two pairs). Therefore, each resisting couple = 3900 k-ft.
Since the lever arm on each couple is 30 ft, the force at each footing = 3900 ÷ 30 = 130 kips. This is an added compression under the legs on the far side (right) of the tower and an uplift under the legs on the near side (left).
Therefore, the near side legs experience a 'net' uplift of 130 – 1.5 = 128.5 kips

Answer is D

Solution 19

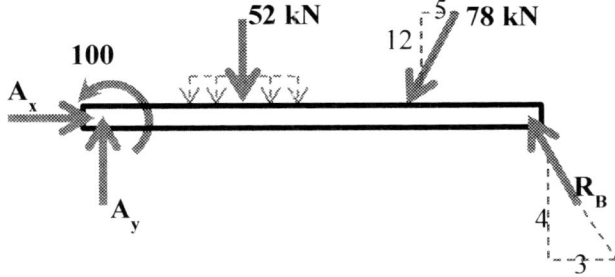

Taking moments about A:

$$\sum M_A = 5.1 \times \frac{4}{5} R_B + 100 - 52 \times 1.65 - \frac{12}{13} \times 78 \times 3.6 = 0 \Rightarrow R_B = 60.0 \, kN$$

Statics Topics on FE Civil Examination

For horizontal equilibrium:
$$\sum F_x = A_x - \frac{5}{13} \times 78 - \frac{3}{5} \times 60 = 0 \Rightarrow A_x = 66 \ kN$$

For vertical equilibrium, $A_y + 0.8R_B = 52 + 72 = 124$
Therefore, $A_y = 76$ kN

Reaction at the hinge: $R_A = \sqrt{A_x^2 + A_y^2} = \sqrt{66^2 + 76^2} = 100.7 \ kN$

Answer is D

Solution 20

- Since the load is vertical, the only horizontal reaction (at node I) is zero.
- Without the horizontal reaction I_x at node I, there are three forces (ONLY TWO LINES OF ACTION) in equilibrium (F_{HI}, F_{GI} and I_y), of which F_{HI} acts alone along its line of action. **Therefore F_{HI} must be zero.**
- With F_{HI} = zero, at node H, there are three forces (ONLY TWO LINES OF ACTION) in equilibrium (F_{FH}, F_{HG} and H_y), of which F_{HG} acts alone along its line of action. **Therefore F_{HG} must be zero.**
- With F_{HG} = zero, at node G, there are three forces (ONLY TWO LINES OF ACTION) in equilibrium (F_{EG}, F_{FG} and F_{GI}), of which F_{FG} acts alone along its line of action. **Therefore F_{FG} must be zero.**
- With F_{FG} = zero, at node F, there are three forces (ONLY TWO LINES OF ACTION) in equilibrium (F_{DF}, F_{FE} and F_{FH}), of which F_{FE} acts alone along its line of action. **Therefore F_{FE} must be zero.**
- With F_{FE} = zero, at node E, there are three forces (ONLY TWO LINES OF ACTION) in equilibrium (F_{DE}, F_{CE} and F_{EG}), of which F_{DE} acts alone along its line of action. **Therefore F_{DE} must be zero.**

Note: Beyond this point, the condition of ONLY TWO LINES OF ACTION is not satisfied at any of the nodes A, B, C, D. Thus, there are 5 zero force members - **F_{HI}, F_{HG}, F_{FG}, F_{FE} and F_{DE}**
Answer is C

Solution 21
Taking moments about C (for the entire structure):
$$M_C = 20 \times 10.5 \times 5.25 - 1.5H_A - 10.5V_A = 0$$

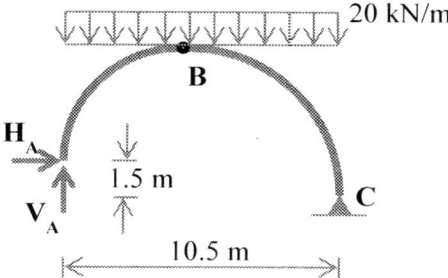

Taking moments about B (for the left half of the structure):
$$M_B = 20 \times 4.5 \times 2.25 + 4.5H_A - 4.5V_A = 0$$

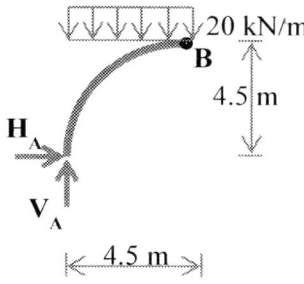

The equations are:
$$1.5H_A + 10.5V_A = 20 \times 10.5 \times 5.25 \Rightarrow H_A + 7V_A = 735$$
$$4.5H_A - 4.5V_A = -202.5 \Rightarrow H_A - V_A = -45$$

Solving these two equations, $H_A = 52.5$; $V_A = 97.5$

Answer is B

Solution 22

Replacing each distributed load as a resultant acting at the centroid, we have the following FBD

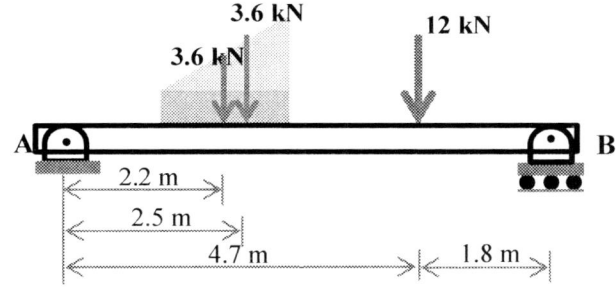

Now, taking moments about A:
$$\sum M_A = 3.6 \times 2.2 + 3.6 \times 2.5 + 12 \times 4.7 - 6.5B_y = 0 \Rightarrow B_y = 11.28\ kN$$

Answer is A

Solution 23

For this structure, it is not necessary to calculate the support reactions, if one makes a vertical cut (say) through members CE, DE and DF and considers the substructure to the *right* of the section. This substructure would have the free body diagram shown below:

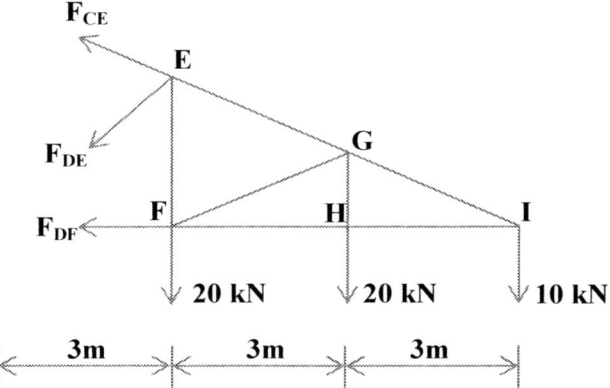

To eliminate the unwanted forces (F_{CE} and F_{DF}) from the equation, it is best to take moments about the point of intersection of these forces (point I). Since length EF is 3 m (half of truss height 6 m) and DF is 3 m, F_{DE} has 1:1 slope. Thus, the moment equilibrium equation is:

$$\sum M_I = 20 \times 3 + 20 \times 6 + \frac{1}{\sqrt{2}} F_{DE} \times 6 + \frac{1}{\sqrt{2}} F_{DE} \times 3 = 0 \Rightarrow 6.364 F_{DE} + 180 = 0$$
$$\Rightarrow F_{DE} = -28.3$$

Answer is B

Solution 24

The shape is subdivided into three known parts – (1) a triangle on top, (2) a rectangle and (3) a triangle on the right. Centroid locations for each shape are marked on the diagram below.

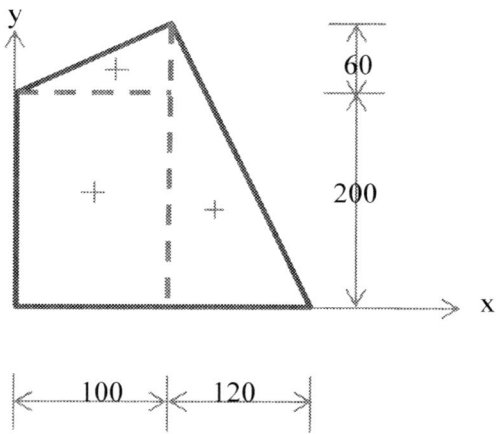

Using parallel axis theorem, the total moment of inertia I_{xx} is calculated as the sum of I_{xx} for each of the 3 component pieces (1 to 3)

$$I_{xx1} = \frac{1}{36} \times 100 \times 60^3 + 3000 \times 220^2 = 1.46 \times 10^8$$

$$I_{xx2} = \frac{1}{12} \times 100 \times 200^3 + 20000 \times 100^2 = 2.67 \times 10^8$$

$$I_{xx3} = \frac{1}{36} \times 120 \times 260^3 + 15600 \times 86.7^2 = 1.76 \times 10^8$$

Total I_{xx} = 5.89x10^8 mm^4

Using parallel axis theorem, the total moment of inertia I_{yy} is calculated as the sum of I_{yy} for each of the 3 component pieces (1 to 3)

$$I_{yy1} = \frac{1}{36} \times 60 \times 100^3 + 3000 \times 66.7^2 = 1.50 \times 10^7$$

$$I_{yy2} = \frac{1}{12} \times 200 \times 100^3 + 20000 \times 50^2 = 6.67 \times 10^7$$

$$I_{yy3} = \frac{1}{36} \times 260 \times 120^3 + 15600 \times 140^2 = 3.18 \times 10^8$$

Total I_{yy} = 4.00x10^8 mm^4

Therefore, $I_z = I_x + I_y$ = 9.89 x10^8 mm^4

Answer is D

Solution 25
The region can be spanned using horizontal strips as shown below.

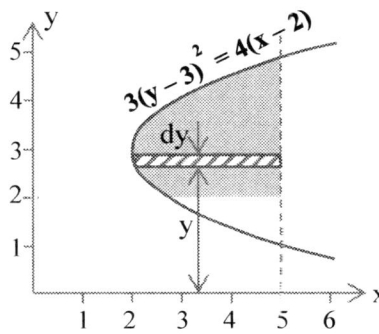

Rearranging the equation of the parabola gives:
$$x = 0.75y^2 - 4.5y + 8.75$$

Width of the shaded strip:
$$w = 5 - x = -0.75y^2 + 4.5y - 3.75$$

Area:

$$A = \int dA = \int_{2}^{5}(-0.75y^2 + 4.5y - 3.75)dy = -0.25y^3 + 2.25y^2 - 3.75y|_{2}^{5} = 6.75$$

Answer is D

Solution 26
Using vertical strip elements, since each element has the x-axis as its base, we can use the formula for the moment of inertia of a rectangle about its base (I = 1/3 bh³)

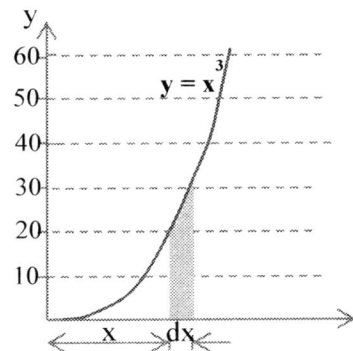

$$I_x = \int \tfrac{1}{3}y^3 dx = \tfrac{1}{3}\int_{2}^{4} x^9 dx = \tfrac{x^{10}}{30}\Big|_{2}^{4} = 34{,}918.4$$

Answer is C

Solution 27
Writing the sum of moments about A:
$$M_A = 20 + 30 \times 1.7 + 0.8 \times 4 \times 2.6 - 2.2D_y = 0$$
$$D_y = 36.05 \ kN$$

Therefore, the vertical reaction at D is 36.05 kN.

Answer is C

Solution 28
The solution of this problem is greatly simplified by noticing that the three forces intersect at B, Therefore, the moment can be calculated by using a single r vector – from the center of the plate to point B. This vector (cm) is:

$$r = 10i + 15j$$

The total resultant force (N) acting at B is:

$$F = -700i + 400\left(\tfrac{4}{5}i + \tfrac{3}{5}j\right) - 400j = -380i - 160j$$

Moment (N-cm) about center of plate:

Statics Topics on FE Civil Examination

$$M = r \times F = (10i + 15j) \times (-380i - 160j) = -1600k + 5700k = 4100k$$

Therefore, moment = 41 Nm

Answer is B

Solution 29

Dividing the shape into 3 component rectangles (as shown below), since the product of inertia of each rectangle about its own centroid is zero, the products of inertia about the x-y axes shown are given by:

$$I_{xy} = I_{x_c y_c} + A d_x^2 d_y^2 = 0 + A d_x^2 d_y^2$$

$(I_{xy})_1 = 2000 \times 50 \times 140 = 1.4 \times 10^7 \ mm^4$
$(I_{xy})_2 = 1500 \times 7.5 \times 80 = 9.0 \times 10^5 \ mm^4$
$(I_{xy})_3 = 3900 \times 65 \times 15 = 3.8 \times 10^6 \ mm^4$

$$I_{xy} = 1.87 \times 10^7 \ mm^4$$

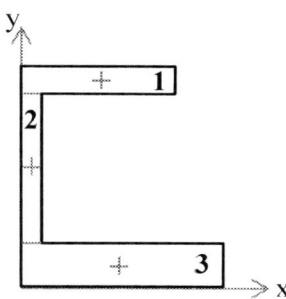

Answer is A

Dynamics

Dynamics Topics on FE Civil Examination 4-6 problems
Approximately 4% of exam

A. Kinematics (e.g., particles and rigid bodies)
B. Mass moments of inertia
C. Force acceleration (e.g., particles and rigid bodies)
D. Impulse momentum (e.g., particles and rigid bodies)
E. Work, energy, and power (e.g., particles and rigid bodies)

Dynamics Topics on FE Civil Examination

Problem 1
An airplane's path is tracked by radar using the distance r(t) and angular elevation θ(t) functions given below (r measured in km, θ measured in radians, t in seconds). At t = 5 seconds, what is the speed of the aircraft?

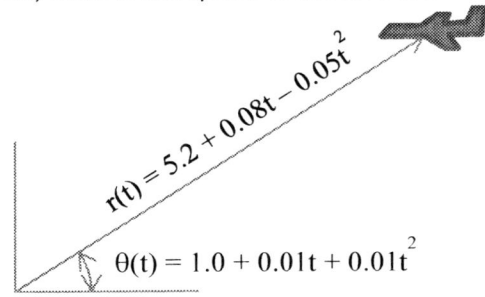

$r(t) = 5.2 + 0.08t - 0.05t^2$

$\theta(t) = 1.0 + 0.01t + 0.01t^2$

A. 1100 km/hr
B. 1300 km/hr
C. 1800 km/hr
D. 2300 km/hr

Problem 2
A turntable starts spinning from rest (at t = 0) and accelerates uniformly at 1 rad/s² to an angular speed of 120 rpm. How many revolutions does it take to reach maximum speed?

A. 11.5
B. 12.5
C. 13.5
D. 14.0

Problem 3
A cannon fires a shot from the top of a cliff as shown. The muzzle velocity V = 240 m/s and the angle α = 40°. What is the range (R) of the cannon?

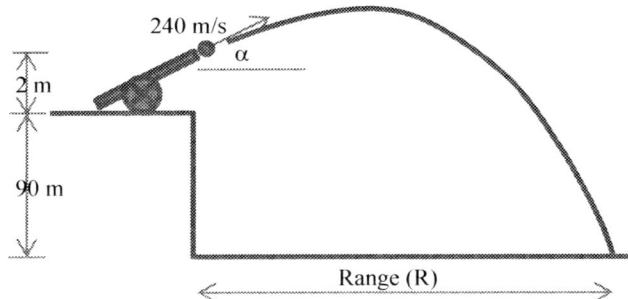

A. 4667 m
B. 5883 m
C. 6565 m
D. 7281 m

Dynamics Topics on FE Civil Examination

Problem 4

A pulley system consisting of a fixed and a movable pulley is loaded as shown. If the pulleys are assumed to be massless and frictionless, what is the vertical acceleration of the 60 kg mass?

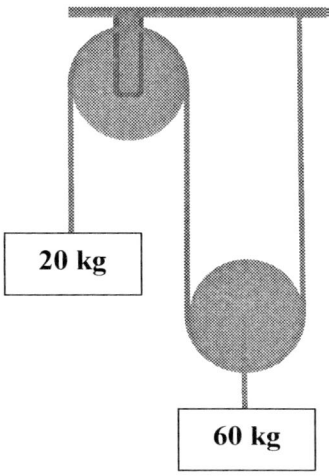

A. 2.2 m/s²
B. 2.4 m/s²
C. 2.6 m/s²
D. 2.8 m/s²

Problem 5

Two billiard balls (A: mass = 170 g and B: mass = 190 g) collide on a horizontal table after traveling along the dashed lines as shown). Velocities just before impact are indicated on the diagram. If the coefficient of restitution for the impact is 0.9, what are the velocities after impact?

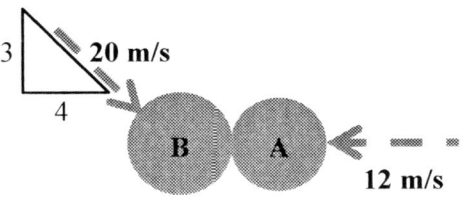

A. $v_A = 12.4i$ and $v_B = -9.1i - 12j$
B. $v_A = 16.1i$ and $v_B = -10.1i - 12j$
C. $v_A = 12.4i$ and $v_B = -9.1i - 12j$
D. $v_A = 16.1i$ and $v_B = -9.1i - 12j$

Dynamics Topics on FE Civil Examination

Problem 6

Two identical billiard balls (mass = 170 g) collide on a horizontal table after traveling along the dashed lines as shown). Velocities just before impact are indicated on the diagram. If the impact is considered to be perfectly elastic, what are the velocities after impact?

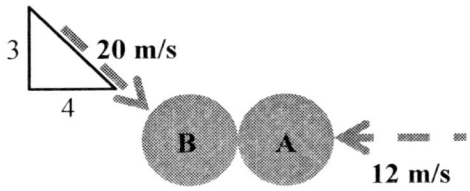

A. $v_A = -16i$ and $v_B = -12i + 12j$
B. $v_A = 16i$ and $v_B = -12i - 12j$
C. $v_A = 12i$ and $v_B = -9i - 12j$
D. $v_A = -12i$ and $v_B = -12i - 12j$

Problem 7

A 5 kg block travelling to the right has a velocity of 20 m/s when it is at a distance of 10 m from a mass-less bumper attached to a spring with spring constant k = 100 N/cm. The horizontal surface and the block have coefficient of static friction = 0.25 and kinetic friction = 0.20. What is the maximum compression of the spring?

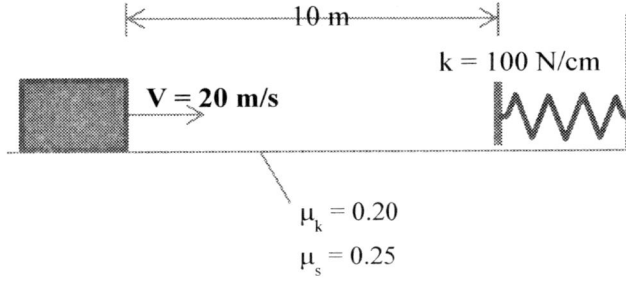

A. 44.7 cm
B. 42.5 cm
C. 90.0 cm
D. 32.6 cm

Problem 8

A car is travelling at the crest of a hill as shown below. At the crest, the hill has a radius of curvature = 240 m. If the tangential velocity = 120 km/hr and acceleration = 5 kmph/sec, what is the total acceleration?

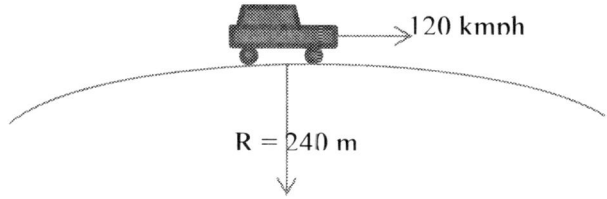

A. 1.39 m/s^2
B. 4.63 m/s^2
C. 4.83 m/s^2
D. 5.98 m/s^2

Problem 9

A metal bead (mass = 90 g) is released from rest at position A on a smooth circular guide rod (radius 35 cm) under the effect of a linear spring whose undeformed length is 25 cm. If there is no friction between the guide rod and the sliding mass, what is the velocity of the bead when it passes point B?

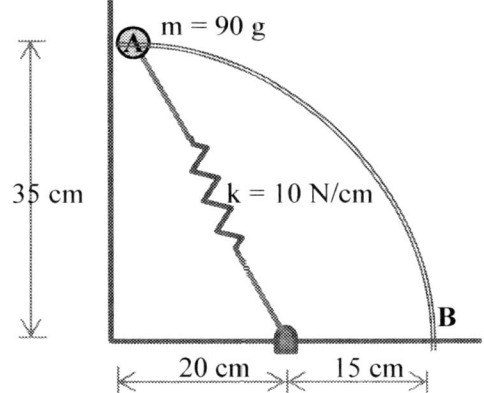

A. 9.5 m/s
B. 12.5 m/s
C. 16.8 m/s
D. Mass never reaches point B

Dynamics Topics on FE Civil Examination

Problem 10

A bullet with mass m = 90 g is fired into and gets embedded in a wooden block whose mass is M = 3 kg. The velocity of the bullet just before impact is 250 m/s. What is the distance traveled by the block before it comes to rest?

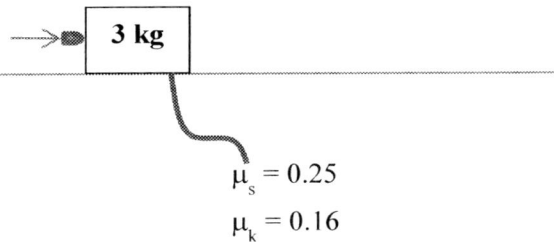

A. 17 m
B. 21 m
C. 8.5 m
D. 10.5 m

Problem 11

A force F of short duration acts on a stationary mass, m = 1.6 kg. The profile of force F is shown in the figure below. What is the velocity of the mass at t = 0.05 seconds?

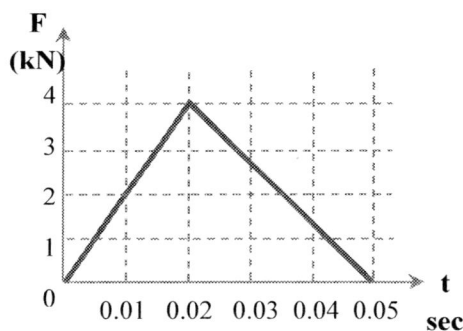

A. 125 m/s
B. 62.5 m/s
C. 31.3 m/s
D. 12.5 m/s

Problem 12

A prismatic rod with mass 5 kg is supported by a frictionless hinge at a distance 65 cm from the left end as shown. The rod is held static in the horizontal position as shown and released from rest. What is the acceleration of the left end of the rod upon being released?

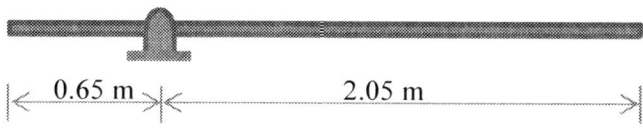

|← 0.65 m →|← 2.05 m →|

A. 0.64 m/s^2
B. 1.25 m/s^2
C. 4.06 m/s^2
D. 6.25 m/s^2

Problem 13

A spring-mass system is shown below. What is the natural period of vibration?

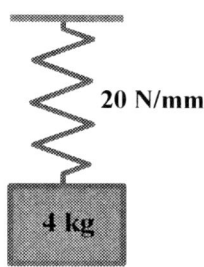

20 N/mm

4 kg

A. 0.04 sec
B. 0.09 sec
C. 1.79 sec
D. 11.25 sec

Problem 14

A steel rod (diameter = 12 mm, length = 40 cm, mass = 360 g) supports a cylindrical mass (mass = 4.7 kg, radius = 80 mm and height = 30 mm) at the bottom end as shown. The top end of the rod is fixed. What is the natural period of twisting oscillations?

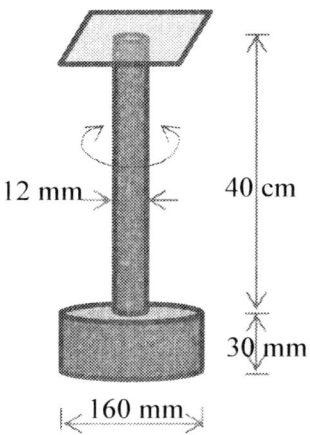

A. 0.64 sec
B. 0.50 sec
C. 0.38 sec
D. 0.12 sec

Problem 15

A fixed pulley having radius = 100 mm and mass = 10 kg supports a smooth cable which supports two masses – of 20 kg and 60 kg – as shown in the figure below. What is the acceleration of the 60 kg mass?

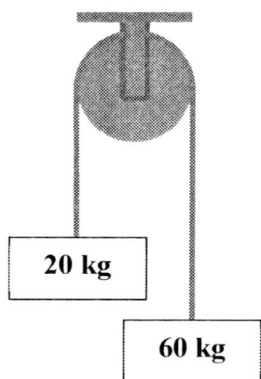

A. 4.32 m/s^2
B. 4.46 m/s^2
C. 4.62 m/s^2
D. 4.85 m/s^2

Problem 16

A rigid rod BD is hinged to the ends of rods AB and ED, which are in turn supported by hinged supports A and E, as shown in the figure below.

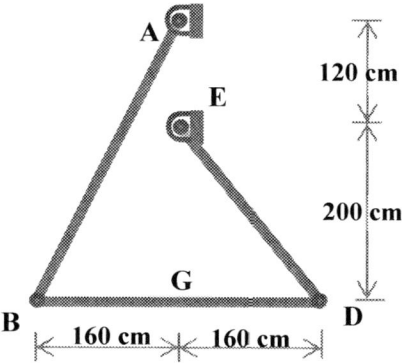

If the rod BD rotates clockwise by 4 rad/sec, what is the velocity of point G?

A. 996 cm/s
B. 932 cm/s
C. 824 cm/s
D. 786 cm/s

Problem 17

Two billiard balls (m_A = 170 g, m_B = 200 g) collide on a horizontal table after traveling along the dashed lines as shown). Velocities just before impact are indicated on the diagram. If the coefficient of restitution is 0.8, how much of the initial kinetic energy is lost due to the impact?

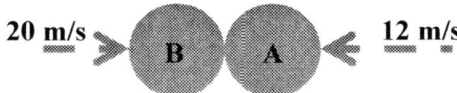

A. 20%
B. 32%
C. 0%
D. 26%

Dynamics Topics on FE Civil Examination

Problem 18

Two billiard balls (m_A = 170 g, m_B = 200 g) collide on a horizontal table after traveling along the dashed lines as shown). Velocities just before impact are indicated on the diagram. If the coefficient of restitution is 0.8, what is the impulse of the force acting on each ball?

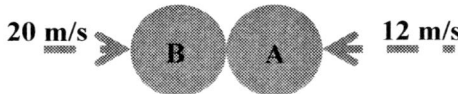

A. 2.7 Ns
B. 3.2 Ns
C. 4.4 Ns
D. 5.3 Ns

Problem 19

A metal disk of uniform thickness having mass = 3 kg is suspended from a frictionless pin as shown. If the force of 200 N acts as shown below, what is the instantaneous acceleration at the point of application of the force?

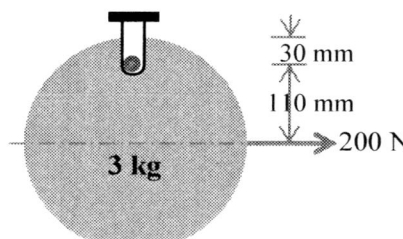

A. 40 m/s²
B. 50 m/s²
C. 60 m/s²
D. 70 m/s²

Problem 20

A metal disk of radius r = 140 mm rolls (without slipping) on a level surface with a forward velocity v = 3 m/s. What is the relative velocity of point A with respect to point B?

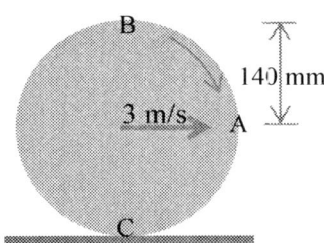

A. 3 m/s
B. 4.25 m/s
C. 6 m/s
D. 6.71 m/s

Problem 21

A 5 kg block on a 35° incline is acted upon by a horizontal force F = 200 N as shown. What is the acceleration (m/s^2) of the block?

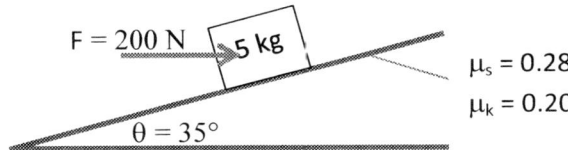

A. 11 m/s^2 up slope
B. 21 m/s^2 up slope
C. 11 m/s^2 down slope
D. 21 m/s^2 down slope

Dynamics Topics on FE Civil Examination

Dynamics Solutions

Solution 1

Using r-θ coordinates, the velocity vector is:
$$v(t) = \dot{r}e_r + r\dot{\theta}e_\theta = (0.08 - 0.1t)e_r + (5.2 + 0.08t - 0.05t^2)(0.01 + 0.02t)e_\theta$$

At t = 5, this becomes:
$$v(t) = -0.42e_r + 0.48e_\theta$$

Magnitude of the velocity vector: $V = \sqrt{0.42^2 + 0.48^2} = 0.638 \frac{km}{sec} = 2296 \frac{km}{hr}$

Answer is D

Solution 2

Final angular velocity: ω = 120 rev/min = 2 rev/sec = 4π rad/sec

For constant acceleration: $\omega_f^2 = \omega_0^2 + 2\alpha\theta \Rightarrow \theta = \frac{\omega_f^2 - \omega_0^2}{2\alpha} = \frac{12.57^2 - 0}{2 \times 1} = 79 \, rad = 12.6 \, revolutions$

Answer is B

Solution 3

This is a case of constant acceleration. Vertical acceleration = acceleration due to gravity
Let the origin be located at the tip of the muzzle and the vertical (y) axis be measured positive upward, as shown below.

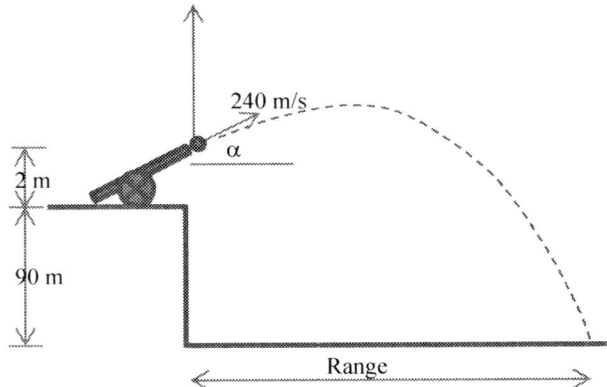

At t = 0, y = 0, v_y = 240 sin 40 = + 154.3 m/s
At the instant of hitting the ground, t = T, y = -92
With y-axis pointing up, a_y = -9.81 m/s²

$$s = v_0 t + \frac{1}{2}at^2$$

$-92 = 154.3T - 4.9T^2$
Solving this quadratic, T = 32 seconds

Dynamics Topics on FE Civil Examination

Since the horizontal velocity is constant (zero horizontal acceleration), $V_x = 240 \cos 40 = 183.9$ m/s

Range = 183.9 x 32 = 5883 m

Answer is B

Solution 4
Free body diagrams of the two blocks are shown below. Cable has constant tension T.

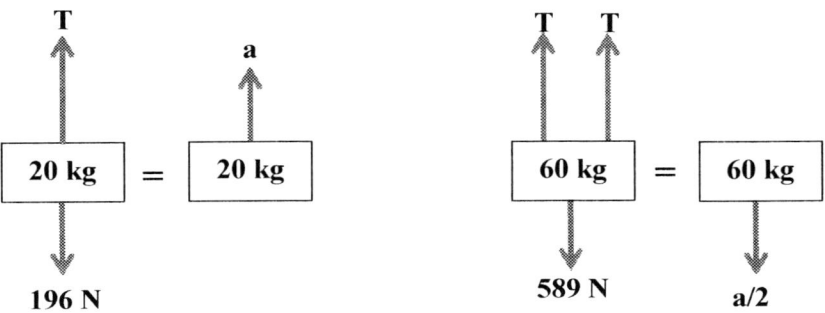

Let us assume that the 60 kg mass falls, causing the 20 kg mass to rise. Since for every unit displacement of the 20 kg mass, the shortening of the cable segment is compensated by the lengthening of TWO cable segments supporting mass of 60 kg, the corresponding displacement of the 60 kg mass is ½. For this reason, when the upward acceleration of the 20 kg mass is assumed to be 'a', the downward acceleration of the 60 kg mass is written as a/2. The dynamic equations of equilibrium for the two masses are:

$T - 196 = 20a$

$589 - 2T = 60 \times \frac{a}{2} = 30a$

Solving these two equations, a = + 2.81 m/s²

Answer is D

Solution 5
The velocities along and perpendicular to the line of impact are shown.

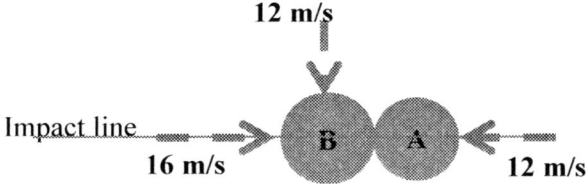

Conservation of momentum applies to both components:

Dynamics Topics on FE Civil Examination

$$190(16i - 12j) + 170(-12i) = 170(v_{Ax}i + v_{Ay}j) + 190(v_{Bx}i + v_{By}j)$$

Only the velocities along the line of impact are affected by the coefficient of restitution

$$0.9 = \frac{(v_B - v_A)_f}{(v_A - v_B)_i} = \frac{v_{Bx} - v_{Ax}}{-12 - 16} \Rightarrow v_{Ax} - v_{Bx} = 25.2$$

The conservation of momentum in x- direction:

$$190 \times 16 + 170 \times -12 = 170 v_{Ax} + 190 v_{Bx} = 1000$$

Solving these equations: $v_{Ax} = 16.1; \ v_{Bx} = -9.1$

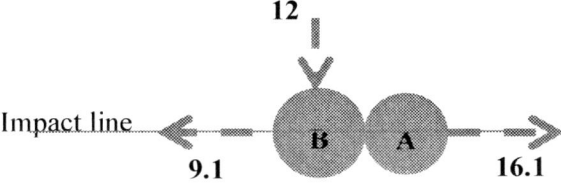

Alternatively, using the formula in the FERH,

$$v_{Ax} = \frac{190 \times 16 \times (1 + 0.9) + (170 - 0.9 \times 190) \times -12}{190 + 170} = 16.1$$

$$v_{Bx} = \frac{170 \times -12 \times (1 + 0.9) - (0.9 \times 170 - 190) \times 16}{190 + 170} = -9.1$$

The y-components of the velocity remain unchanged: $v_{Ay} = 0; \ v_{Bx} = -12$

Answer is D

Solution 6

When two identical objects (same mass) collide in a perfectly elastic impact (e = 1), the two masses 'trade' velocities along the line of impact. For this simple solution, BOTH conditions must exist.

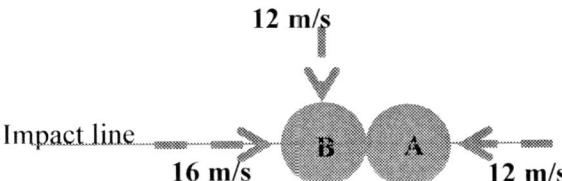

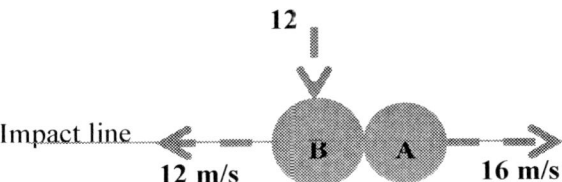

The velocities along and perpendicular to the line of impact are shown. Since BOTH conditions are met (identical mass AND elastic impact), the horizontal velocity components of A and B are exchanged.
Therefore, after impact, $v_{Ax} = 16$; $v_{Bx} = -12$

The y-components of the velocity remain unchanged: $v_{Ay} = 0$; $v_{Bx} = -12$

Answer is B

Solution 7
Assume that the maximum compression of the spring is X. At the instant of maximum compression, the velocity = 0. The normal force between the block and the ground is constant W = 49.0 N. Therefore, the (kinetic) friction force is constant at F_f = 0.2x49 = 9.8 N

Using the principle of work and energy, initial kinetic energy = elastic energy stored in spring + energy lost (work done) due to friction

$$\frac{1}{2} \times 5 \times 20^2 = \frac{1}{2} \times 10000 \times X^2 + 9.8 \times (10 + X)$$

Solving this quadratic, X = 0.424

Answer is B

Solution 8
V_t = 120 km/hr = 33.3 m/s
a_t = 5 kmph/sec = 1.39 m/s²

Normal acceleration: $a_n = \frac{v_t^2}{\rho} = \frac{33.3^2}{240} = 4.63 \frac{m}{s^2}$

The two components of acceleration are orthogonal. Therefore the magnitude of total acceleration is given by:
$a = \sqrt{1.39^2 + 4.63^2} = 4.83 \frac{m}{s^2}$

Answer is C

Solution 9
The stretched length of the spring (when the mass is at A) is given by: $l = \sqrt{20^2 + 35^2} = 40.3\ cm$
Therefore, at this position, the deformation of the spring is: Δ = 40.3 – 25 = 15.3 cm
Total energy in the system (using the horizontal line through B as the datum) when the mass is stationary at A:

$$E_A = 0.09 \times 9.81 \times 0.35 + \frac{1}{2} \times 10^3 \times 0.153^2 = 12\ Nm$$

Dynamics Topics on FE Civil Examination

When the mass is at B, the deformed length of the spring is 15 cm
Therefore, at this position, the deformation of the spring is: $\Delta = 15 - 25 = -10$ cm
Total energy in the system (using the horizontal line through B as the datum) when the mass is at B:

$$E_B = \frac{1}{2} \times 10^3 \times 0.1^2 + \frac{1}{2} \times 0.09 \times V^2 = 5 + 0.045V^2$$

Equating $E_A = E_B$ yields V = 12.47 m/s

Answer is B

Solution 10
Since the bullet gets lodged in the block (zero relative velocity after impact), this is a case of a plastic impact (e = 0). The two objects have a common velocity V after impact. Applying conservation of momentum, this is given by:

$$m_1 V_1 + m_2 V_2 = (m_1 + m_2)V$$

$$V = \frac{m_1 V_1 + m_2 V_2}{m_1 + m_2} = \frac{0.09 \times 250 + 3 \times 0}{0.09 + 3} = 7.28 \frac{m}{s}$$

The deceleration (due to friction) is $\mu_k g$ = 0.16x9.81 = 1.57 m/s²

With initial velocity V = 7.28 m/s and acceleration = - 1.57 m/s², the block-bullet combination will travel a distance d, calculated from kinematics equations for constant acceleration

$$d = \frac{V_f^2 - V_i^2}{2a} = \frac{0^2 - 7.28^2}{2 \times -1.57} = 16.9 \ m$$

Answer is A

Solution 11
The impulse of the force between t = 0 and t = 0.05 seconds is given by the integral
$I = \int F \, dt$
which is the area under the F-t curve.

$$I = \int F \, dt = \frac{1}{2} \times 4000 \times 0.05 = 100 \ Ns$$

According to the Impulse-Momentum principle:

$$\Delta(mv) = \int F \, dt = 100 \ Ns$$

Since the mass is stationary at t = 0, the velocity at t= 0.05 seconds is:
$V = \frac{100}{1.6} = 62.5 \frac{m}{s}$

Answer is B

Solution 12

The effective location of the weight (49 N) of the rod is at the midpoint, which is 0.7 m to the right of the hinge support. When the rod is released, this force has an unbalanced moment about the hinge. This moment is 49x0.7 = 34.3 Nm

The equation of dynamic equilibrium is:
$$M = I\alpha$$
where M is the resultant moment and I is the moment of inertia about the hinge.

The moment of inertia about the hinge is calculated using the Parallel axis theorem.
$$I = \frac{mL^2}{12} + md^2 = \frac{5 \times 2.7^2}{12} + 5 \times 0.7^2 = 5.49 \; kg \cdot m^2$$

Angular acceleration: $\alpha = \frac{M}{I} = \frac{34.3}{5.49} = 6.25 \frac{rad}{s^2}$

At t = 0, the velocity is still zero. So the centrifugal acceleration (which would act horizontally towards the hinge) is still zero.

At the left end, the acceleration is given by:
$$a = r\alpha = 0.65 \times 6.25 = 4.06 \frac{m}{s^2}$$

Answer is C

Solution 13

Spring stiffness = 20 N/mm = 20,000 N/m
From the handbook, the natural frequency:
$$\omega = \sqrt{\frac{k}{m}} = \sqrt{\frac{20{,}000}{4}} = 70.71 \; rad/sec$$

Period: $T = \frac{2\pi}{\omega} = \frac{2\pi}{70.71} = 0.09 \; sec$

Answer is B

Solution 14

Mass moment of inertia of the end mass: $I = \frac{MR^2}{2} = \frac{4.7 \times 0.08^2}{2} = 0.15 \; kgm^2$

Mass moment of inertia of the rod itself:
$$I = \frac{MR^2}{2} = \frac{0.36 \times 0.006^2}{2} = 6.5 \times 10^{-6} \; kgm^2 \; (negligible)$$

Polar moment of inertia of rod: $J = \frac{\pi R^4}{2} = \frac{\pi \times 0.006^4}{2} = 2.036 \times 10^{-9}$

Torsional stiffness of the rod: $k_t = \frac{GJ}{L} = \frac{80 \times 10^9 \times 2.036 \times 10^{-9}}{0.4} = 407.2$

Natural frequency:
$$\omega = \sqrt{\frac{k_t}{I}} = \sqrt{\frac{407.2}{0.15}} = 52.1 \; rad/sec$$

Period: $T = \frac{2\pi}{\omega} = \frac{2\pi}{52.1} = 0.12 \; sec$

Answer is D

Solution 15

Usually, when the pulley-cable friction can be neglected (smooth pulley), the tension in the cable is constant. However, in this case, the pulley mass is not negligible and the resulting inertia will lead to the tension in the two cable segments to be different. The free body diagrams of (1) the 20 kg mass, (2) the pulley and (3) the 60 kg mass are shown

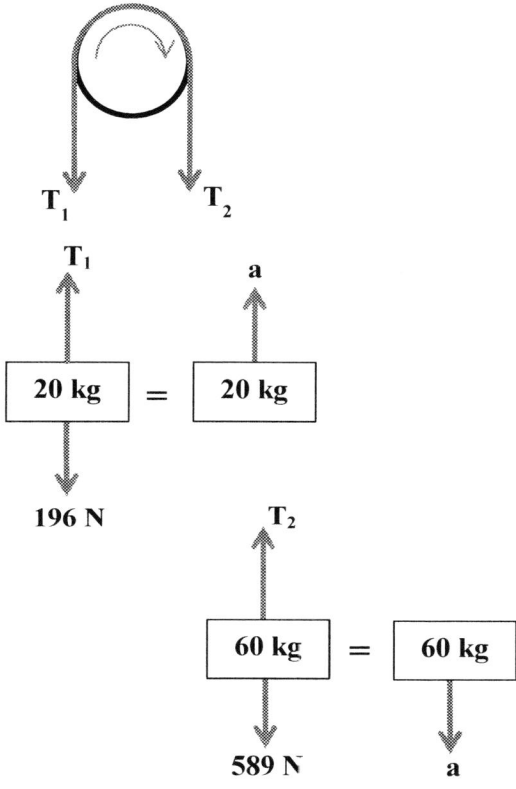

For mass 1: $\quad T_1 - 196 = 20a$ (1)

For the pulley: $\quad T_2 r - T_1 r = \frac{1}{2} M r^2 \alpha \Rightarrow T_2 - T_1 = \frac{1}{2} M r \alpha = \frac{1}{2} M a$ (2)

For mass 2: $\quad 589 - T_2 = 60a$ (3)

From equations (1) and (3), we get:
$$T_2 - T_1 = 589 - 60a - (196 + 20a) = 393 - 80a$$

Therefore:
$$393 - 80a = \frac{1}{2} M a$$
$$a = \frac{393}{80 + \frac{1}{2} \times 10} = 4.62 \ m/s^2$$

Answer is C

If the mass of the pulley were neglected, the acceleration of each mass would have been:
$$a = \frac{(60 - 20) \times 9.81}{60 + 20} = 4.91 \ m/s^2$$

Dynamics Topics on FE Civil Examination

Solution 16

Taking B as the origin, line BA can be described by the equation 2x − y = 0, and line DE by the equation 5x + 4y = 1600.

Since AB rotates about hinge A, the velocity vector v_B is perpendicular to AB. Similarly, since ED rotates about hinge E, the velocity vector v_D is perpendicular to ED. The radial lines AB and ED intersect at the point whose coordinates are obtained by solving the equations for AB and ED. This point has coordinates (123.1, 246.2) and is the instantaneous center of rotation of bar BD (since it is obtained from the intersection of the radial vectors at D and E)

Distance of point G(160, 0) from the ICR(123.1, 246.2) is 248.95 cm
Velocity of point G: $v_G = \omega r = 4 \times 248.95 = 995.8 \; cm/sec$

Answer is A

Solution 17

The velocities after impact are given by:

$$v'_A = \frac{m_B v_B(1 + 0.8) + (m_A - 0.8 m_B)v_A}{m_A + m_B} = \frac{200 \times 20 \times 1.8 + (170 - 0.8 \times 200) \times -12}{370}$$
$$= 19.14 \; m/s$$

$$v'_B = \frac{m_A v_A(1 + 0.8) - (0.8 m_A - m_B)v_B}{m_A + m_B} = \frac{170 \times -12 \times 1.8 - (0.8 \times 170 - 200) \times 20}{370}$$
$$= -6.46 \; m/s$$

Energy before impact: $E = \frac{1}{2} m_A v_A^2 + \frac{1}{2} m_B v_B^2 = \frac{1}{2} \times 0.17 \times 12^2 + \frac{1}{2} \times 0.2 \times 20^2 = 52.24 \; J$

Energy after impact: $E' = \frac{1}{2} m_A v'^2_A + \frac{1}{2} m_B v'^2_B = \frac{1}{2} \times 0.17 \times 19.14^2 + \frac{1}{2} \times 0.2 \times 6.46^2 = 35.3 \; J$

Energy loss = 16.94 J, which is 32.4% of the original 52.24 J

Answer is B

If the collision were perfectly elastic (e = 1), then no calculations would be necessary. Energy would have been conserved.

Solution 18

The velocity of ball A after impact is given by:

$$v'_A = \frac{m_B v_B(1 + 0.8) + (m_A - 0.8 m_B)v_A}{m_A + m_B} = \frac{1.8 \times 200 \times 20 + (170 - 0.8 \times 200) \times -12}{370}$$
$$= 19.14 \; m/s$$

The impulse acting on the ball = change in momentum.

Momentum of ball A before impact = 0.17x-12 = -2.04 Ns
Momentum of ball A after impact = 0.17x19.14 = 3.25 Ns
Impulse on each ball = change in momentum = 5.29 Ns

Answer is D

Solution 19
The (mass) moment of inertia of the disk about the axis through the hinge is calculated using the Parallel Axis Theorem. (The y and y_c axes come out of the plane)

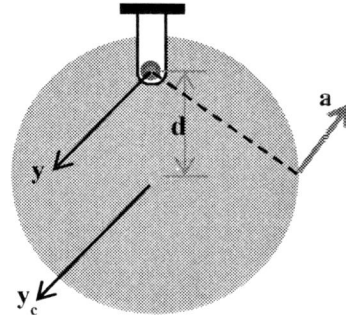

$$I_y = I_{y_c} + Md^2 = \frac{1}{2}MR^2 + Md^2 = \frac{1}{2}(3)(0.14^2) + (3)(0.11^2) = 0.0657 \ kg \cdot m^2$$

Moment about the hinge: M_y = 200x0.11 = 22 Nm

Angular acceleration: $\alpha = \frac{M_y}{I_y} = \frac{22}{0.0657} = 334.9 \ rad/s^2$

Radial distance from hinge to point of application of force: $r = \sqrt{0.11^2 + 0.14^2} = 0.178 \ m$

Linear acceleration: $a = r\alpha = 59.6 \ m/s^2$

Answer is C

Solution 20
At the instant shown, the bottom of the wheel (the point where it touches the ground) is the instantaneous center of rotation.

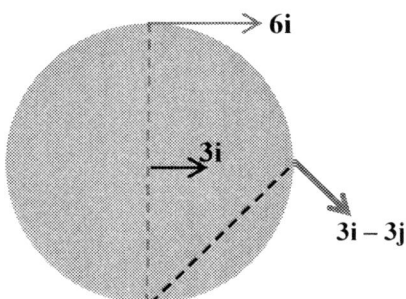

The velocity of the center of the disk is pure translation with horizontal velocity v = 3 m/s

Angular velocity: $\omega = \frac{V}{r} = \frac{3}{0.14} = 21.43 \ rad/sec$

Radial distance from this ICR to point B = 0.28 m

Velocity of B: $v_B = 21.43 \times 0.28 = 6\ m/s$
This velocity is horizontal. Therefore, it can be written as v_B = 6**i**
Radial distance from the ICR to point A = $\sqrt{(0.14^2 + 0.14^2)}$ = 0.198 m
Velocity of A: $v_A = 21.43 \times 0.198 = 4.24\ m/s$
This velocity is perpendicular to CA. Therefore, it can be written as v_A = 3**i** − 3**j**
Relative velocity: $v_{A|B} = v_A - v_B = 3\boldsymbol{i} - 3\boldsymbol{j} - 6\boldsymbol{i} = -3\boldsymbol{i} - 3\boldsymbol{j}$
Magnitude of $v_{B|A}$ = 4.24 m/s

Answer is B

Solution 21
The free body diagram of the block, resolving forces along, and perpendicular to the incline, is shown

```
              200 sin35
              = 114.7 N
                 ↓
200 cos 35   ┌─────┐
= 163.8 N →  │ 5 kg│
             └─────┘
                 ↓
  49 sin 35    49 cos 35
  = 28.1 N     = 40.1 N      F = 200 N
```

Since the up-plane force is more than the downplane component of the weight, the block will have a tendency to move upstream. Therefore, the *friction force will act down-plane.*
The total normal force perpendicular to the plane = 114.7 + 40.1 = 154.8 N
Friction force (with motion) = 0.2x154.8 = 30.96 N
Unbalanced up-plane force = 163.8 − 28.1 − 30.96 = 104.74 N
Acceleration = 104.74/5 = 20.95 m/s^2

Answer is B

Note: If the down-plane forces had been dominant, causing the block to slide DOWN the incline, then everything would be unchanged except the friction force, which would act up-plane.

Mechanics of Materials

Mechanics of Materials Topics on FE Civil Examination   7–11 problems
Approximately 7% of exam

A. Shear and moment diagrams
B. Stresses and strains (e.g., axial, torsion, bending, shear, thermal)
C. Deformations (e.g., axial, torsion, bending, thermal)
D. Combined stresses
E. Principal stresses
F. Mohr's circle
G. Column analysis (e.g., buckling, boundary conditions)
H. Composite sections
I. Elastic and plastic deformations
J. Stress-strain diagrams

Problem 1
A steel tensile coupon cut from 5 mm thick sheet, is subject to a tensile force as shown below. What is the axial strain in the narrowed (20 mm wide) test section?

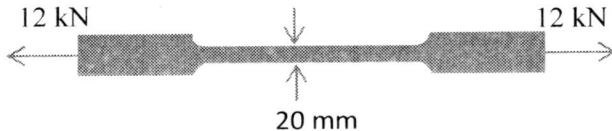

A. 100 με
B. 200 με
C. 600 με
D. 1,200 με

Problem 2
A steel tensile coupon cut from 5 mm thick sheet, is subject to a tensile force as shown below. What is the altered width (20 mm dimension)?

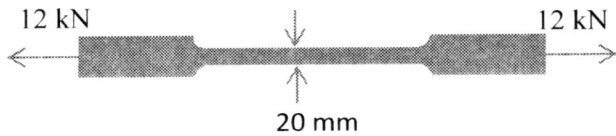

A. 20.0036 mm
B. 19.9964 mm
C. 20.0120 mm
D. 19.9880 mm

Problem 3
A hollow circular steel shaft (O.D. 40 mm, I.D. 32 mm) is subject to a torque T = 400 Nm. What is the twist angle per unit length?
  A. 2.4 degrees/meter
  B. 1.9 degrees/meter
  C. 2.8 degrees/meter
  D. 3.2 degrees/meter

Problem 4
For the beam shown below, what is the bending moment at point P?

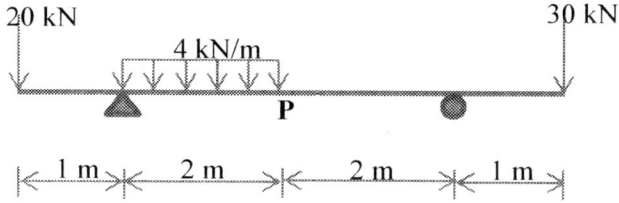

A. -16 kNm
B. -20 kNm
C. -21 kNm
D. -30 kNm

Problem 5
The section shown below is used as the cross-section of a beam which has a maximum bending moment M = 256 kNm (causing convexity on the bottom surface). All section dimensions are mm

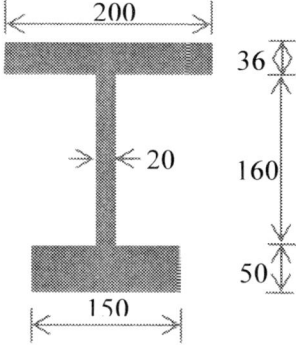

What is the maximum bending stress in the beam?
A. 170 MPa (compressive)
B. 170 MPa (tensile)
C. 200 MPa (compressive)
D. 200 MPa (tensile)

Problem 6

For the state of stress shown below (all stress in MPa), what is the maximum compressive normal stress?

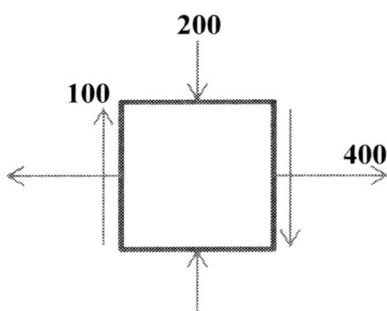

A. 216 MPa
B. 300 MPa
C. 416 MPa
D. 482 MPa

Problem 7

For the state of stress shown below (all stress in MPa), what is the value of the von Mises stress?

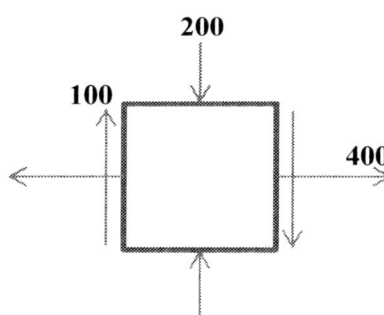

A. 215 MPa
B. 300 MPa
C. 415 MPa
D. 550 MPa

Problem 8

Several steel samples are tested in a cyclic tensile test to failure. The plot below shows the peak tensile stress at failure as a function of the number of cycles of loading. According to the modified Goodman theory, if a steel specimen is subjected to a mean tensile stress of 400 MPa, what is the magnitude of stress fluctuations above this mean that will cause failure?

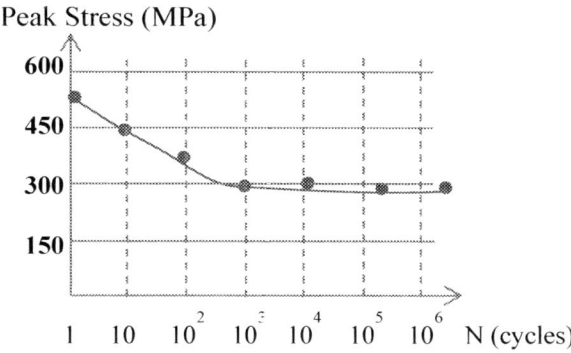

A. 60 MPa
B. 70 MPa
C. 80 MPa
D. 90 MPa

Problem 9

For the beam loaded as shown below, which is a correct shape for the bending moment diagram?

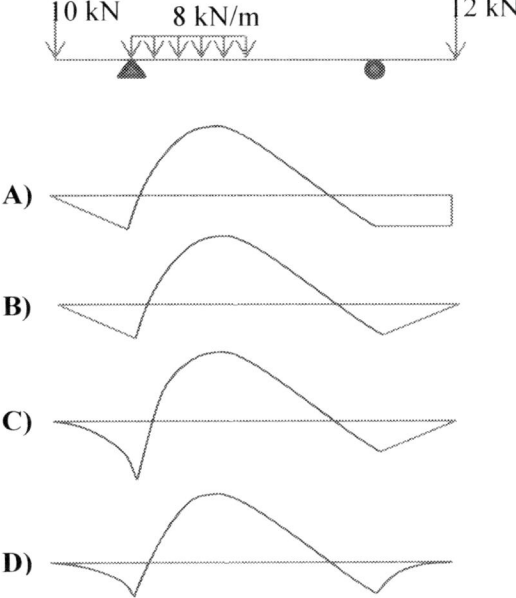

Problem 10

The results of a tensile test of a prismatic metal specimen are summarized in the curve below. What is most nearly the modulus of elasticity of the specimen?

A. 190 GPa
B. 230 GPa
C. 250 GPa
D. 300 GPa

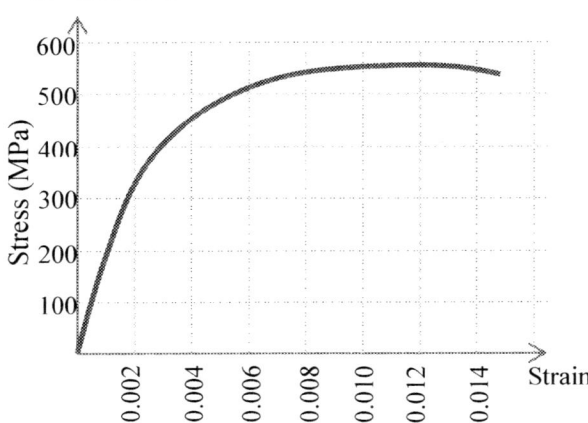

Problem 11

The results of a tensile test of a prismatic metal specimen are summarized in the curve below. What is most nearly the yield stress of the specimen?

A. 325 MPa
B. 375 MPa
C. 425 MPa
D. 475 MPa

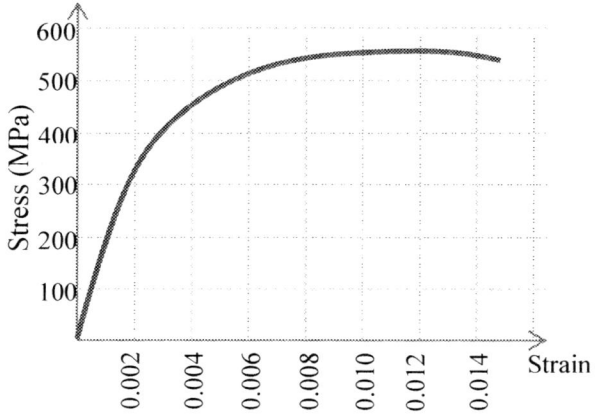

Problem 12

For the 3D steel element shown below, assume that all loads are uniformly distributed on the faces of the element. What is the deformed length in the z-direction?

A. 75.15 mm
B. 74.92 mm
C. 75.08 mm
D. 75.04 mm

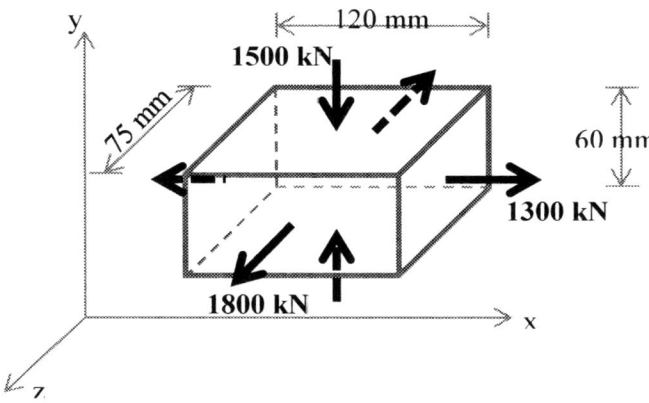

Problem 13

A steel pipe having O.D. = 100 mm and wall thickness = 5 mm carries water at a pressure = 300 kPa. What is the circumferential stress in the pipe?

A. 1.43 MPa
B. 1.89 MPa
C. 2.53 MPa
D. 2.85 MPa

Problem 14

A steel beam is loaded with two point loads as shown below. What is the deflection at midspan?

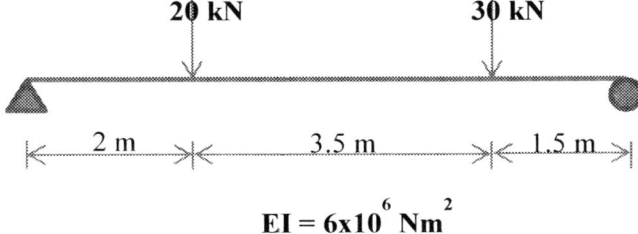

$EI = 6 \times 10^6 \ Nm^2$

A. 40 mm
B. 34 mm
C. 22 mm
D. 18 mm

Problem 15

A simply supported beam is loaded with a couple at the right support as shown. What is the maximum deflection?

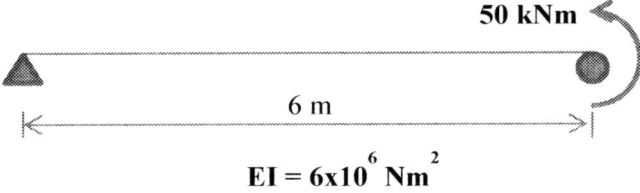

$EI = 6 \times 10^6 \, Nm^2$

A. 23 mm
B. 21 mm
C. 19 mm
D. 17 mm

Problem 16

A composite rod is constructed by fusing a steel sleeve onto a brass core as shown. Mechanical and thermal properties of brass and steel are shown in the table below:

	Steel	Brass
E (GPa)	205	110
ν	0.3	0.32
α (/°C)	11.7×10^{-6}	20.5×10^{-6}

If the assembly is stress free at 20°C and then heated to 150°C, what is the stress in the brass core?

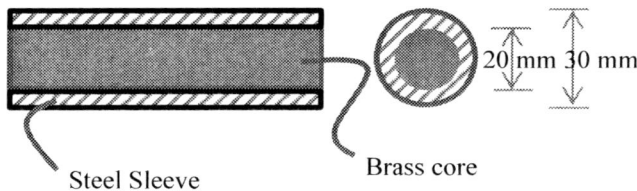

A. 103 MPa
B. 89 MPa
C. 75 MPa
D. 66 MPa

Problem 17
A hollow steel shaft (I.D. = 20 mm; O.D. = 30 mm) is subjected to a torsional moment M = 200 N-m. If the length of the shaft is 50 cm, what is the twist angle?

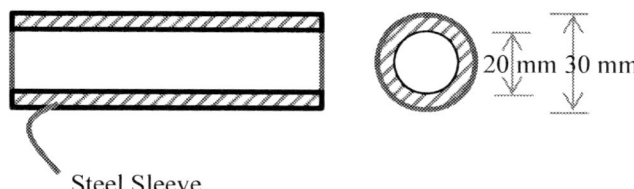

Steel Sleeve

A. 1.12°
B. 0.85°
C. 0.62°
D. 0.32°

Problem 18
A rectangular timber column (E = 10 GPa) has a 100 mm x 200 mm cross section and length L = 4 m. The bottom of the column is restrained against rotation and lateral translation while the top is only restrained against lateral translation? What is the critical buckling load of the column?

A. 210 kN
B. 420 kN
C. 630 kN
D. 840 kN

Problem 19
The section shown below is used as the cross-section of a beam which has a maximum shear force V = 50 kN. All section dimensions are mm

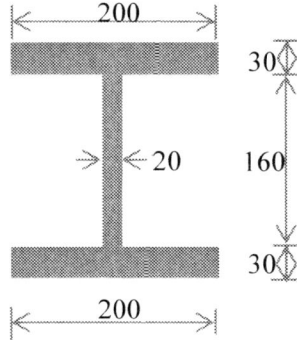

What is the maximum shear stress in the beam?

A. 32 MPa
B. 27 MPa
C. 22 MPa
D. 15 MPa

Problem 20
A hollow steel shaft has the cross section shown below. If the maximum torsional moment experienced by the section is 100 Nm, what is the maximum shear stress?

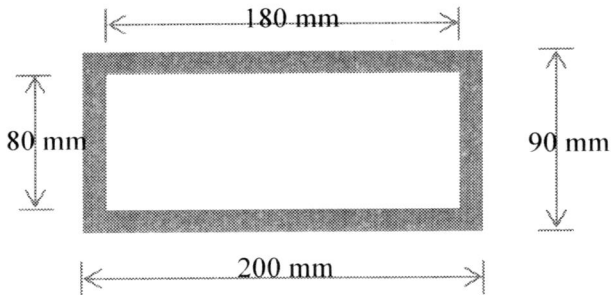

A. 0.62 MPa
B. 1.24 MPa
C. 2.78 MPa
D. 5.56 MPa

Problem 21
At a particular point on a beam subject to transverse loads, the following stresses have been measured.

Bending stress σ_{xx} = 28.5 ksi (tension)

σ_{yy} = 0

τ_{xy} = 14.8 ksi

The steel used for the beam has the following ultimate stresses:

σ_{ult} = 45 ksi (tension)

τ_{ult} = 30 ksi

The factor of safety based on stress is most nearly:

A. FS = 2.75
B. FS = 1.46
C. FS = 1.29
D. FS = 1.18

Problem 22
A hot-rolled circular steel rod is tested in a rotating beam test to determine its endurance limit. The tensile strength of the steel is 600 MPa. What is the percent increase in the endurance limit by machining the surface?
A. 12% increase
B. 18% increase
C. 24% increase
D. 42% increase

Problem 23

A steel rod of diameter 20 mm is fixed at the left end as shown. At a temperature of 20°C, a gap of 0.1 mm exists between the right end of the rod and a rigid wall. If the temperature of the rod is raised to 120°C, what is the stress in the rod?

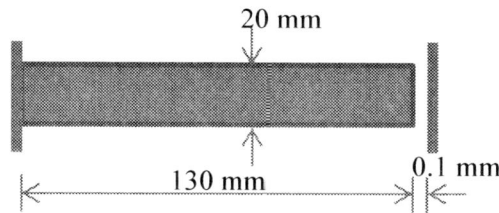

A. σ = 20 MPa
B. σ = 40 MPa
C. σ = 80 MPa
D. σ = 160 MPa

Problem 24

A steel pipe having O.D. = 100 mm and wall thickness = 5 mm carries water at a pressure = 300 kPa. What is the circumferential stress in the pipe, using the thick walled theory?

A. 1.43 MPa
B. 1.89 MPa
C. 2.53 MPa
D. 2.85 MPa

Problem 25

Several steel samples are tested in a cyclic tensile test to failure. The results are:
Yield stress = 420 MPa
Fatigue strength = 280 MPa
If a steel specimen is subjected to a mean stress level of 350 MPa, what is the maximum stress fluctuation above this mean that will cause fatigue failure according to the Soderberg theory?

A. 45 MPa
B. 55 MPa
C. 65 MPa
D. 75 MPa

Problem 26

A block of elastic material is subjected to a vertical load P = 200 kN, as shown below. The left face of the block is fused to a rigid surface, while the load P is distributed evenly over the right face as shown. The elastic properties of the material are: Modulus of elasticity = 4 GPa, Poisson's ratio = 0.28. What are the minimum values of dimensions 'a' and 'b' if the maximum allowable shear stress is 30 MPa and the maximum downward deflection of the loaded face is 1mm?

A. a = 45 mm; b = 70 mm
B. a = 35 mm; b = 70 mm
C. a = 55 mm; b = 85 mm
D. a = 35 mm; b = 85 mm

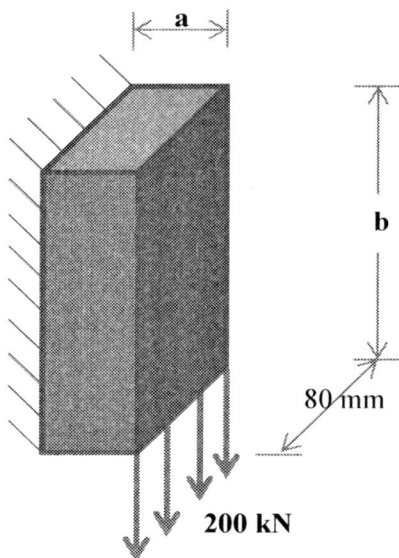

Problem 27

A rectangular timber beam is reinforced with a 20 mm thick steel plate as shown. If the bending moment, M acting on the beam section is 40 kNm, what is the maximum bending stress in the steel plate? Use E_{wood} = 10 GPa

A. 3 MPa
B. 30 MPa
C. 40 MPa
D. 60 MPa

Mechanics of Materials Topics on FE Civil Examination

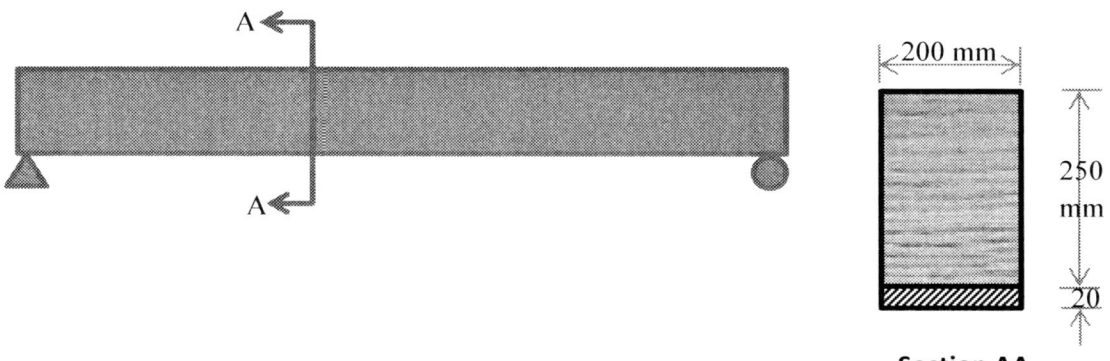

Section AA

Problem 28

A 20 ft beam carries a load that decreases linearly from a maximum of 400 lbf/ft at its left support to 0 lbf/ft at the midspan of the beam. Measured from the left support, the point at which the shear is zero is most nearly:

A. 14.1 ft
B. 5.9 ft
C. 4.1 ft
D. 3.2 ft

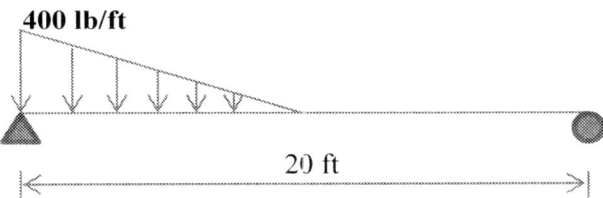

Problem 29

A 16 ft cantilever beam carries a linearly varying distributed load as shown. The beam is made of steel and the moment of inertia of the prismatic section is 1200 in^4. What is the maximum deflection?

A. 0.10 in
B. 0.15 in
C. 0.20 in
D. 0.25 in

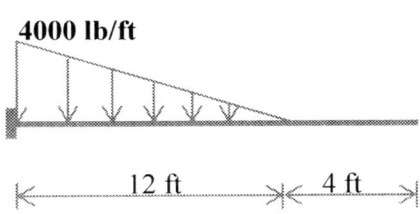

Mechanics of Materials Topics on FE Civil Examination

Problem 30

A symmetric I-shaped section (shown below on the left) has the properties indicated (I_{xx} = 540 in⁴; A = 26 in²). The section is then reinforced with a rectangular plate (8 inch wide x 1 inch thick) as shown on the right. What is the percent increase in the (centroidal) moment of inertia of the section as a result of adding the plate?

    A. 32%
    B. 45%
    C. 67%
    D. 88%

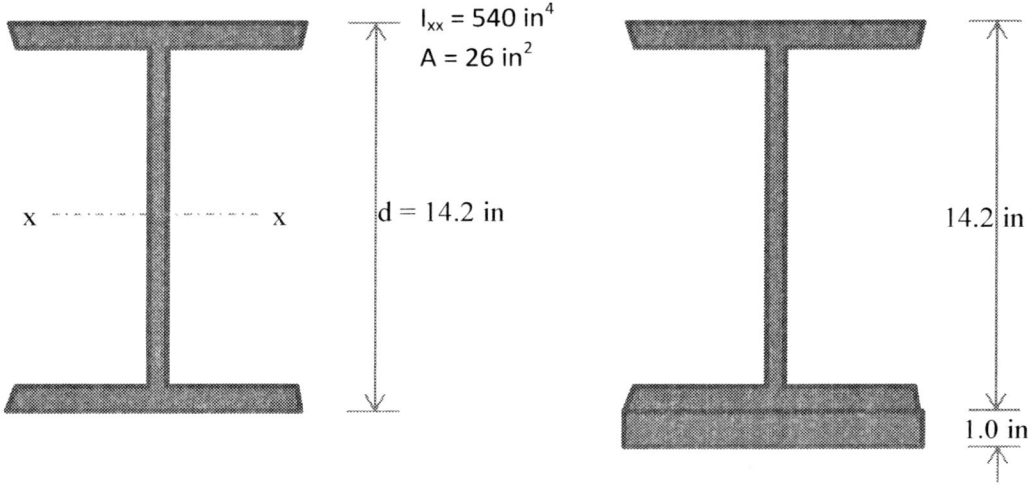

Mechanics of Materials Solutions

Solution 1
Cross sectional area: A = 20x5 = 100 mm² = 1x10⁻⁴ m²
Axial stress: $\sigma = \frac{P}{A} = \frac{12,000}{1\times10^{-4}} = 1.2 \times 10^8 Pa = 120\ MPa$
Axial Strain: $\varepsilon = \frac{\sigma}{E} = \frac{1.2\times10^8}{2\times10^{11}} = 6 \times 10^{-4} = 600\ \mu\varepsilon$
Answer is C

Solution 2
Cross sectional area: A = 20x5 = 100 mm² = 1x10⁻⁴ m²
Axial stress: $\sigma = \frac{P}{A} = \frac{12,000}{1\times10^{-4}} = 1.2 \times 10^8 Pa = 120\ MPa$
Axial Strain: $\varepsilon = \frac{\sigma}{E} = \frac{1.2\times10^8}{2\times10^{11}} = 6 \times 10^{-4} = 600\ \mu\varepsilon$
Poisson's ratio ν = 0.3 (for steel). Therefore, transverse strain in the other two directions is given by:
$\varepsilon_{lateral}$ = –0.3x600 με = –180 με = – 0.00018
Therefore, the new width = 20x(1 – 0.00018) = 19.9964 mm

Answer is B

Solution 3
Twist angle for a circular shaft is given by:
$$\phi = \frac{TL}{GJ}$$
Polar moment of inertia: $J = \frac{\pi a^4}{2} = \frac{\pi(0.02^4 - 0.016^4)}{2} = 1.484 \times 10^{-7}\ m^4$
Twist angle per unit length:
$$\frac{\phi}{L} = \frac{T}{GJ} = \frac{400}{80 \times 10^9 \times 1.484 \times 10^{-7}} = 0.0337\ \frac{rad}{m}$$
Twist angle per unit length = 1.93° per m.

Answer is B

Solution 4
Designating the supports as A (left) and B right) and taking moments about A:
$$M_A = -20 \times 1 + 8 \times 1 - 4B_y + 30 \times 5 = 0$$
Vertical reaction at B: B_y = 34.5 kN. Therefore, A_y = 58 – 34.5 = 23.5 kN

The shear diagram is shown below.

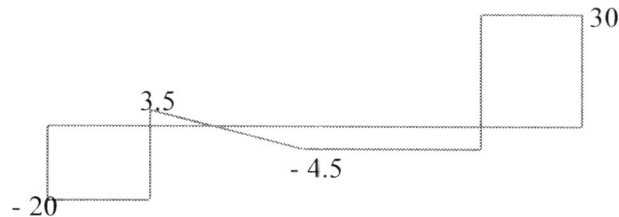

The distance over which the downward sloping part of the diagram drops to zero is calculated as 3.5 kN/4 kN/m = 0.875 m

The areas under the different parts of the shear diagram are shown below.

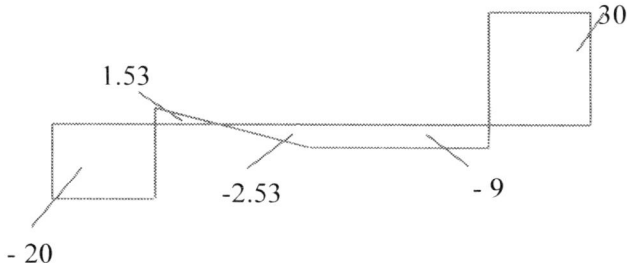

Bending moment at P = −20 + 1.53 − 2.53 = −21 kNm

Answer is C

Solution 5

The centroid is calculated as the weighted average of the centroid coordinates for the 3 rectangles.

$$\bar{y} = \frac{228 \times 7200 + 130 \times 3200 + 25 \times 7500}{7200 + 3200 + 7500} = 125.4 \; mm$$

Total depth is 246 mm and distance from bottom fiber to centroid is 125.4. Therefore, distance to top fiber is 120.6. Thus, the bottom fiber is furthest from the neutral axis. Using parallel axis theorem, the total moment of inertia is calculated as the sum of I_{xx} for each of the 3 rectangles (listed from top to bottom)

$I_{xx1} = \frac{1}{12} \times 200 \times 36^3 + 7200 \times 102.6^2 = 7.66 \times 10^7$

$I_{xx2} = \frac{1}{12} \times 20 \times 160^3 + 3200 \times 4.6^2 = 6.89 \times 10^6$

$I_{xx3} = \frac{1}{12} \times 150 \times 50^3 + 7500 \times 100.4^2 = 7.72 \times 10^7$

Total I_{xx} = 1.61x10^8 mm^4 = 1.61x10^{-4} m^4

Maximum bending stress (at bottom fiber) is:

$$\sigma = \frac{Mc}{I} = \frac{256 \times 10^3 \times 0.1254}{1.61 \times 10^{-4}} = 1.99 \times 10^8$$

Thus the max bending stress is 199 MPa (tensile because curvature is convex on bottom fiber)

Answer is D

Solution 6
The stress state can be summarized:

$\sigma_{xx} = +400$

$\sigma_{yy} = -200$

$\tau_{xy} = -100$

The principal stresses are given by:

$$\sigma_{1,2} = \frac{\sigma_{xx} + \sigma_{yy}}{2} + \sqrt{\left(\frac{\sigma_{xx} - \sigma_{yy}}{2}\right)^2 + \tau_{xy}^2}$$

$$= \frac{400 - 200}{2} \pm \sqrt{\left(\frac{400 - \{-200\}}{2}\right)^2 + (-100)^2} = 100 \pm 316$$

$$= -216, 416$$

Answer is A

Solution 7
The stress state can be summarized:

$\sigma_{xx} = +400$

$\sigma_{yy} = -200$

$\tau_{xy} = -100$

The von Mises stress is given by:

$$\sigma' = \sqrt{\sigma_x^2 - \sigma_x \sigma_y + \sigma_y^2 + 3\tau_{xy}^2} = \sqrt{400^2 - 400 \times -200 + (-200)^2 + 3 \times (-100)^2}$$

$$= 556.8 \; MPa$$

Answer is D

Solution 8
From the plot, S_{ut} = 530 MPa and S_e = 300 MPa

σ_m = 400 MPa

According to the modified Goodman theory, fracture occurs when:

$$\frac{\sigma_m}{S_{ut}} + \frac{\sigma_a}{S_e} > 1$$

$$\frac{400}{530} + \frac{\sigma_a}{300} > 1 \Rightarrow \sigma_a > 73.6 \; MPa$$

Therefore, fluctuating stress cannot exceed 73.6 MPa.

Answer is B

Solution 9

The loaded beam has 4 segments – (1) from the free left end to the pinned support, (2) from the pinned support to the end of the uniform load, (3) from the end of the uniform load to the roller support and (4) from the roller support to the free right end.
Over these 4 segments, the distributed load function is (1) zero, (2 constant, (3) zero and (4) zero respectively. The bending moment function is two polynomial orders higher than the load function.

Therefore, the bending moment function segments should be (1) linear, (2) quadratic, (3) liner and (4) linear respectively.

Answer is B

Solution 10

The modulus of elasticity is calculated as the slope of the initial tangent of the curve. This is approximately:

$$E = \frac{\Delta\sigma}{\Delta\varepsilon} = \frac{380 \times 10^6}{0.002} = 1.9 \times 10^{11} = 190 \, GPa$$

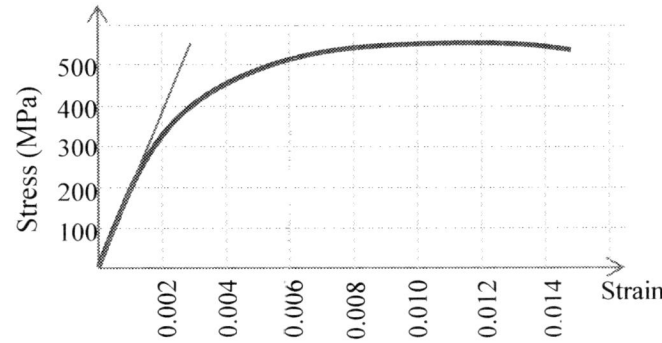

Answer is A

Solution 11

The yield stress is estimated using the 0.2% offset rule. From a strain = 0.002, a line is drawn parallel to the initial tangent of the curve. This is shown on the figure below. The intersection of this line with the curve is nominally taken to be the yield point.
Yield Stress: σ_y = 470 MPa

Mechanics of Materials Topics on FE Civil Examination

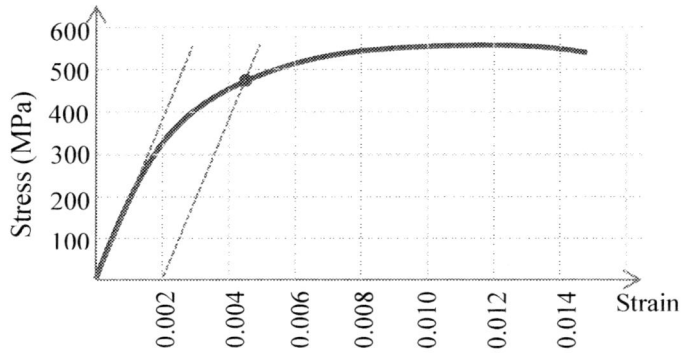

Answer is D

Solution 12

Steel: E = 200 GPa; ν = 0.3

The normal stresses in the three orthogonal directions are:

$$\sigma_{xx} = +\frac{1300 \times 10^3}{0.075 \times 0.06} = +289 \, MPa$$

$$\sigma_{yy} = -\frac{1500 \times 10^3}{0.075 \times 0.12} = -167 \, MPa$$

$$\sigma_{zz} = +\frac{1800 \times 10^3}{0.12 \times 0.06} = +250 \, MPa$$

The normal strain in the z direction is:

$$\varepsilon_{zz} = +\frac{\sigma_{zz}}{E} - \nu\left(\frac{\sigma_{xx}}{E} + \frac{\sigma_{yy}}{E}\right) = \frac{250 \times 10^6 - 0.3 \times (289 - 167) \times 10^6}{200 \times 10^9} = 1.067 \times 10^{-3}$$

Deformed length of the 75 mm edge:
$$L' = 75(1 + 1.067 \times 10^{-3}) = 75.08 \, mm$$

Answer is C

Solution 13

Internal diameter: $D_i = D_o - 2t = 100 - 10 = 90 \, mm$

Mean diameter = 95 mm; mean radius = 47.5 mm

Wall thickness = 5 mm ≈ $0.1 r_m$

According to the thin-walled theory:

Hoop stress: $\sigma_t = \frac{P_i r}{t} = \frac{3 \times 10^5 \times 0.0475}{0.005} = 2.85 \times 10^6 \, Pa = 2.85 \, MPa$

Answer is D

Solution 14

For a simple span carrying a point load, the following equation is given in the handbook:

$$\delta = -\frac{Pbx}{6EIL}[L^2 - b^2 - x^2] \quad \text{for x < a}$$

For the 20 kN load, using the origin at the right support, use P = 20,000, a = 5, b = 2, L = 7, x = 3.5.

$$\delta_{20} = -\frac{2 \times 10^4 \times 2 \times 3.5}{6EI \times 7}[7^2 - 2^2 - 3.5^2] = -\frac{109{,}167}{EI}$$

For the 30 kN load, using the origin at the right support, P = 30,000, a = 5.5, b = 1.5, L = 7, x = 3.5.

$$\delta_{30} = -\frac{3 \times 10^4 \times 1.5 \times 3.5}{6EI \times 7}[7^2 - 1.5^2 - 3.5^2] = -\frac{129{,}375}{EI}$$

Total deflection: $\delta = \frac{238{,}542}{EI} = \frac{238{,}542}{6 \times 10^6} = 0.0398 \, m = 39.8 \, mm$

Answer is A

Solution 15
This is one of the standard cases.
$$y_{max} = -\frac{M_o L^2}{\sqrt{243} EI} = -\frac{50{,}000 \times 6^2}{\sqrt{243} \times 6 \times 10^6} = -0.0192 \, m = -19.2 \, mm$$
Answer is C

The following is to instruct how to proceed if it were not a standard load case listed in the handbook. The bending moment diagram can be constructed by observation.

50 kNm

Therefore, the bending moment function is the straight line: $M(x) = 8{,}333x$
Using the moment-curvature relationship:
$$\frac{d^2y}{dx^2} = \frac{M(x)}{EI} = \frac{8333x}{6 \times 10^6} = 1.389 \times 10^{-3}x$$
$$\frac{dy}{dx} = 6.944 \times 10^{-4} x^2 + c_1$$
$$y = 2.315 \times 10^{-4} x^3 + c_1 x + c_2$$

Using boundary conditions:
At x = 0, y = 0 → $c_2 = 0$
At x = 6, y = 0 → $c_1 = -8.333 \times 10^{-3}$
$$y = 2.315 \times 10^{-4} x^3 - 8.333 \times 10^{-3} x$$
Deflection maximum when dy/dx = 0 → x = 3.464 m
At x = 3.46, deflection: y = - 1.92x10⁻² m = - 19.2 mm

Solution 16

Since the coefficient of thermal expansion for brass is more than that of the steel, the brass core is under compression and the steel sleeve is under tension. These two forces must be equal and opposite. Also, since the materials are fused, they must deform equally.

$$A_{brass} = \frac{\pi}{4} 0.02^2 = 3.14 \times 10^{-4}$$

$$A_{steel} = \frac{\pi}{4}(0.03^2 - 0.02^2) = 3.93 \times 10^{-4}$$

For brass, total elongation = sum of thermal expansion + compression shortening is:

$$\Delta L_B = +\alpha L \Delta T - \frac{PL}{AE} = 20.5 \times 10^{-6} \times L \times 130 - \frac{PL}{3.14 \times 10^{-4} \times 110 \times 10^9}$$
$$= L(2.67 \times 10^{-3} - 2.895 \times 10^{-8} P)$$

For steel, total elongation = sum of thermal expansion + tension lengthening is:

$$\Delta L_S = +\alpha L \Delta T + \frac{PL}{AE} = 11.7 \times 10^{-6} \times L \times 130 + \frac{PL}{3.93 \times 10^{-4} \times 205 \times 10^9}$$
$$= L(1.52 \times 10^{-3} + 1.241 \times 10^{-8} P)$$

Equating $\Delta L_B = \Delta L_S$

P = 27, 804 N

Stress in brass core: $\sigma_B = \frac{P}{A} = \frac{27805}{3.14 \times 10^{-4}} = 88.6 \ MPa$

Answer is B

Solution 17

For steel, modulus of rigidity G = 80 GPa

The polar moment of inertia of the shaft is:

$$J = \frac{\pi}{32}(0.03^4 - 0.02^4) = 6.38 \times 10^{-8}$$

$$\phi = \frac{TL}{GJ} = \frac{200 \times 0.5}{80 \times 10^9 \times 6.38 \times 10^{-8}} = 0.0196 \ rad = 1.12°$$

Answer is A

Solution 18

Buckling occurs about the weaker axis (i.e. the one with the smaller moment of inertia):
The weak-axis moment of inertia of the cross-section is calculated as: $I = 1/12 \times 0.2 \times 0.1^3 = 1.667 \times 10^{-5} m^4$

From the Civil Engineering section, the K value for the given condition (case b) is 0.7

Euler's buckling load: $P_E = \frac{\pi^2 EI}{(KL)^2} = \frac{\pi^2 \times 10 \times 10^9 \times 1.667 \times 10^{-5}}{(0.7 \times 4)^2} = 209{,}812 \ N$

Answer is A

Solution 19

The centroid is at mid-height (by observation of symmetry)
Using parallel axis theorem, the total moment of inertia is calculated as the sum of I_{xx} for each of the 3 rectangles (listed from top to bottom)

$$I_{xx1} = I_{xx3} = \frac{1}{12} \times 200 \times 30^3 + 6000 \times 95^2 = 5.46 \times 10^7$$

$$I_{xx2} = \frac{1}{12} \times 20 \times 160^3 + 3200 \times 0^2 = 6.83 \times 10^6$$

Total $I_{xx} = 2I_{xx1} + I_{xx2} = 1.16 \times 10^8$ mm^4 = 1.16×10^{-4} m^4

First moment of the half section about the neutral axis: $Q = 30 \times 200 \times 95 + 80 \times 20 \times 40 = 6.83 \times 10^5$ $mm^3 = 6.83 \times 10^{-4}$ m^3

Maximum shear stress occurs at the centroid:

$$\tau = \frac{VQ}{Ib} = \frac{50 \times 10^3 \times 6.83 \times 10^{-4}}{1.16 \times 10^{-4} \times 0.02} = 1.47 \times 10^7$$

Thus the max shear stress is 14.7 MPa

Answer is D

Note: For an I-shaped (flanged) section – symmetric or not – a good approximation for the maximum shear stress is V/A$_{web}$, which in this case, would yield:

$$\tau_{max} \approx \frac{V}{A_{web}} = \frac{50,000}{0.02 \times 0.16} = 1.56 \times 10^7$$

which is a fairly good approximation for the exact value of 14.7 MPa (6% error) with a lot less work.

Solution 20

For a thin-walled section, A$_m$ is the total area enclosed by the wall centerline. This area is shown shaded below.

$A_m = 0.19 \times 0.085 = 0.01615$ m^2

Wall thickness t = 5 mm for the longer wall segments (thinnest wall develops largest shear stress)

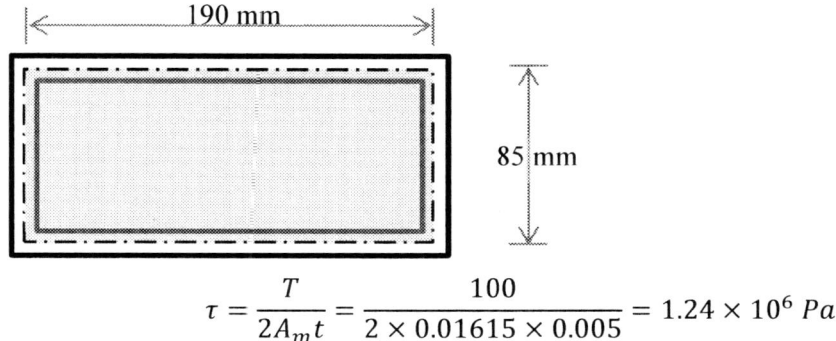

$$\tau = \frac{T}{2A_m t} = \frac{100}{2 \times 0.01615 \times 0.005} = 1.24 \times 10^6 \ Pa$$

Answer is B

Solution 21

The maximum bending stress is given by:
$$\sigma_{max} = \frac{\sigma_{xx} + \sigma_{yy}}{2} + \sqrt{\left(\frac{\sigma_{xx} - \sigma_{yy}}{2}\right)^2 + \tau_{xy}^2}$$

With $\sigma_{yy} = 0$, this becomes:
$$\sigma_{max} = \frac{\sigma_{xx}}{2} + \sqrt{\frac{\sigma_{xx}^2}{4} + \tau_{xy}^2} = \frac{28.5}{2} + \sqrt{\frac{28.5^2}{4} + 14.8^2} = 34.8$$

The maximum shear stress is given by:
$$\tau_{max} = \sqrt{\frac{\sigma_{xx}^2}{4} + \tau_{xy}^2} = \sqrt{\frac{28.5^2}{4} + 14.8^2} = 20.6$$

Factor of safety based on normal stress:
$$FS = \frac{\sigma_{ult}}{\sigma_{max}} = \frac{45}{34.8} = 1.29$$

Factor of safety based on shear stress:
$$FS = \frac{\tau_{ult}}{\tau_{max}} = \frac{30}{20.6} = 1.46$$

Overall factor of safety = 1.29

Answer is C

Solution 22

With all other factors remaining unchanged, the surface factor k_a is given by:
$$k_a = a S_{ut}^b$$
For hot-rolled steel, a = 57.7, b = - 0.718
Therefore,
$$k_a = 57.7 \times 600^{-0.718} = 0.584$$
For a machined surface, a = 4.51, b = -0.265
Therefore,
$$k_a = 4.51 \times 600^{-0.265} = 0.828$$

Therefore, the relative increase (going from hot-rolled to machined) is 0.828/0.584 = 1.42, which is a 42% increase in endurance limit.

Answer is D

Solution 23

The (unrestricted) thermal elongation of the rod would be:
$$\Delta L = L\alpha\Delta T = 130 \times 11.7 \times 10^{-6} \times 100 = +0.152 \, mm$$
This implies that the 0.1 mm gap will close. As a result, the rod will experience a compression reaction at each wall. Shortening of rod due to compression load

Mechanics of Materials Topics on FE Civil Examination

$$\Delta L = -\frac{PL}{AE}$$

The cross sectional area: $A = \pi r^2 = \pi \times 0.01^2 = 3.14 \times 10^{-4}$

The net length change of the rod is:

$$\Delta L = +1.52 \times 10^{-4} - \frac{P \times 0.1301}{A \times 200 \times 10^9} = 1 \times 10^{-4}$$

$0.52 \times 10^{-4} = \frac{P}{A} \times 6.5 \times 10^{-13}$

Stress: $\sigma = \frac{P}{A} = \frac{0.52 \times 10^{-4}}{6.5 \times 10^{-13}} = 7.99 \times 10^7 \, Pa = 79.9 \, MPa$

Answer is C

Solution 24

Internal diameter: $D_i = D_o - 2t = 100 - 10 = 90 \, mm$

Outer radius = 50 mm, inner radius = 45 mm

Hoop stress: $\sigma_t = P_i \left(\frac{r_o^2 + r_i^2}{r_o^2 - r_i^2}\right) = 3 \times 10^5 \times \frac{0.05^2 + 0.045^2}{0.05^2 - 0.045^2} = 2.86 \times 10^6 \, Pa = 2.86 \, MPa$

Answer is D

Compare this answer to that in problem 13, which uses the thin-walled approximation yielding the answer 2.85 MPa (0.35% error)

Solution 25

From the data, S_y = 420 MPa and S_e = 280 MPa

σ_m = 350 MPa

According to the Soderberg theory, fatigue failure occurs when:

$$\frac{\sigma_m}{S_y} + \frac{\sigma_a}{S_e} > 1$$

$$\frac{350}{420} + \frac{\sigma_a}{280} > 1 \Rightarrow \sigma_a > 46.7 \, MPa$$

Therefore, fluctuating stress cannot exceed 46.7 MPa.

Answer is A

Solution 26

The modulus of rigidity (shear modulus), G is given by: $G = \frac{E}{2(1+v)} = \frac{4}{2(1+0.28)} = 1.56 \, GPa$

Shear stress: $\tau = \frac{P}{A} = \frac{200 \times 10^3}{0.08 \times b} \leq 30 \times 10^6 \Rightarrow b \geq 0.084 \, m = 84 \, mm$

Shear strain: $\gamma = \frac{\delta}{a}$

Modulus of rigidity:

$$G = \frac{\tau}{\gamma} = \frac{P/0.08b}{\delta/a} = \frac{Pa}{0.08b\delta} \Rightarrow \delta = \frac{Pa}{0.08bG} \leq 0.001 \Rightarrow a \leq \frac{0.001 \times 0.08 \times b \times 1.56 \times 10^9}{200 \times 10^3} \leq 0.624b$$

Thus, edge 'b' must be at least 84 mm and thickness 'a' must be at least 0.624 times b

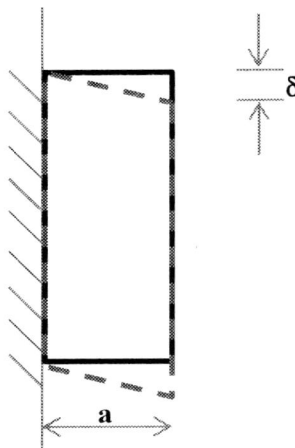

Answer is C (only one to meet BOTH criteria)

Solution 27

E_{steel} = 200 GPa

E_{wood} = 10 GPa

Modular ratio, n = E_{steel}/E_{wood} = 200/10 = 20

Replace 200 mm wide steel plate with equivalent wood plate 200x20 = 4000 mm wide

Centroid height (measured from bottom edge) of equivalent wood section is given by:

$$\bar{y} = \frac{4000 \times 20 \times 10 + 200 \times 250 \times 145}{4000 \times 20 + 200 \times 250} = 61.92 \; mm = 0.062 \; m$$

Moment of inertia of equivalent wood section about this centroid is calculated using parallel axis theorem, the total moment of inertia is calculated as the sum of I_{xx} for the 2 rectangles (listed from bottom to top)

$$I_{xx1} = \frac{1}{12} \times 4000 \times 20^3 + 80000 \times (61.92 - 10)^2 = 2.183 \times 10^8$$

$$I_{xx2} = \frac{1}{12} \times 200 \times 250^3 + 50000 \times (61.92 - 145)^2 = 6.055 \times 10^8$$

Total I_{xx} = 8.24x10^8 mm^4 = 8.24x10^{-4} m^4

Bending stress in steel (bottom edge at distance 6.92 mm from NA): $\sigma = n\frac{Mc}{I} = \frac{20 \times 40000 \times 0.062}{8.24 \times 10^{-4}} = 6 \times 10^7 Pa = 60\ MPa$

Answer is D

Solution 28

The first step is to calculate the support reactions. The resultant force of the distributed load is ½ x 400 x 10 = 2000 lb. The effective location of this resultant is at a distance x = 1/3 x 10 = 3.33 ft from the left support. The reaction at the left support is therefore 16.67/20 x 2000 = 1667 lb

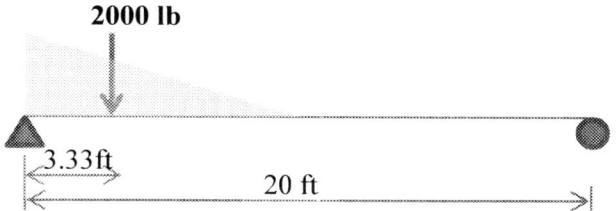

For the segment 0 < x < 10, the load function w(x) is the linear function: $w(x) = 400 - 40x$

$$\frac{dV}{dx} = -w(x) \Rightarrow V(x) = -\int w(x)dx = 20x^2 - 400x + c$$

Since, at x = 0, the value of the shear force V(0) = reaction 1667, the constant c = 1667

Therefore, the complete shear function $V(x) = 20x^2 - 400x + 1667$

Setting this equal to zero, we get (by solving the quadratic), x = 5.92 ft

Answer is B

Solution 29

According to standard load case (cantilever no. 6) in the FE Reference Handbook, the deflection at x = 12 ft is given by:

$$\Delta_{12} = \frac{w_o L^4}{30EI} = \frac{4000 \times 12^4}{30EI} = \frac{2{,}764{,}800}{EI}$$

And the slope at the same location is given by:

$$\theta_{12} = \frac{w_o L^3}{24EI} = \frac{4000 \times 12^3}{24EI} = \frac{288{,}000}{EI}$$

Since the portion from x = 12 to x = 16 is not loaded, it will not bend further. This section of the beam will remain straight (at the same slope as at x = 12).

Therefore, the maximum deflection (at x = 16) is given by:

$$\Delta_{16} = \Delta_{12} + 4 \times \theta_{12} = \frac{2764800 + 4 \times 288000}{EI} = \frac{39,16,800}{EI}$$

In calculating the numerical values of this deflection, one has to pay attention to the units embedded in the constant in the numerator. They are lb (force) and ft (length). Therefore, the product EI must be also expressed in lb-ft²

$$EI = 29 \times 10^6 \frac{lb}{in^2} \times \left(\frac{12\ in}{ft}\right)^2 \times 1200\ in^4 \times \left(\frac{ft}{12\ in}\right)^4 = 2.417 \times 10^8\ lbft^2$$

Therefore, deflection: $\Delta_{16} = \frac{3,916,800}{2.417 \times 10^8} = 0.0162\ ft = 0.194\ in$

Answer is C

Solution 30

First, the centroid of the reinforced section has to be found. Measuring distances (y) from the bottom edge of the plate:

Shape	Area A (in²)	Centroid Y (in)	AY
Plate	8	0.5	4.0
I-section	26	8.1	210.6
	34		214.6

$$\bar{Y} = \frac{\Sigma A_i Y_i}{\Sigma A_i} = \frac{214.6}{34} = 6.31$$

Using parallel axis theorem, the total moment of inertia is calculated as the sum of I_{xx} for each of the 2 shapes (listed from top to bottom)

$$I_{xx1} = \frac{1}{12} \times 8 \times 1^3 + 8 \times (0.5 - 6.31)^2 = 270.72\ in^4$$

$$I_{xx2} = 540 + 26 \times (8.1 - 6.31)^2 = 623.31\ in^4$$

Total I_{xx} = 894.03 in⁴
This represents a 66% increase

Answer is C

Materials

Materials Topics on FE Civil Examination   **4-6 problems**

Approximately 4% of exam

A. Mix design (e.g., concrete and asphalt)
B. Test methods and specifications (e.g., steel, concrete, aggregates, asphalt, wood)
C. Physical and mechanical properties of concrete, ferrous and nonferrous metals, masonry, wood, engineered materials (e.g., FRP, laminated lumber, wood/plastic composites), and asphalt

Materials Topics on FE Civil Examination

Problem 1

Which of the following statements about heat treatment of metals is NOT true?

- A. Annealing increases ductility
- B. Cold working increases ductility
- C. Rate of cooling affects yield strength
- D. Quenching of steel can change the phase composition

Problem 2

The largest internal crack in a silicon carbide ceramic is 30 μm. The fracture toughness of the ceramic is 3.75 MPa-m$^{1/2}$. What is the peak stress that this material can withstand?

- A. 546 MPa
- B. 496 MPa
- C. 386 MPa
- D. 350 MPa

Problem 3

A Kevlar composite material contains 60% by volume of Kevlar 49 fibers with a tensile modulus of elasticity = 190 GPa. The epoxy matrix has a tensile modulus of elasticity = 4 GPa. If stressed under iso-stress conditions, what is the effective modulus of elasticity of the composite?

- A. 54 GPa
- B. 25 GPa
- C. 115 GPa
- D. 10 GPa

Problem 4

A Kevlar composite material contains 60% by volume of Kevlar 49 fibers with a tensile modulus of elasticity = 190 GPa. The epoxy matrix has a tensile modulus of elasticity = 4 GPa. If stressed under iso-strain conditions, what is the effective modulus of elasticity of the composite?

- A. 54 GPa
- B. 25 GPa
- C. 115 GPa
- D. 10 GPa

Materials Topics on FE Civil Examination

Problem 5

If the ASTM grain size for a crystal lattice is 11, what is the expected number of grains that will be observed in a surface area 1 cm²?

- A. 0.8 million
- B. 1.6 million
- C. 3.2 million
- D. 6.4 million

Problem 6

An iron-carbon alloy containing 2% carbon is taken from a temperature of 1200°C to 800°C goes through what kind of reaction?

- A. Eutectic
- B. Eutectoid
- C. Peritectic
- D. Peritectoid

Problem 7

An iron alloy contains 2.2% carbon. What is the composition of the alloy at a temperature T = 1200°C?

- A. γ-iron 80%, liquid 20%
- B. γ-iron 20%, liquid 80%
- C. δ-iron 70%, liquid 30%
- D. δ-iron 30%, liquid 70%

Problem 8

At a temperature of 300°C the diffusion coefficient (D) and activation energy (Q_d) for copper in silicon are:

$$D_{300} = 7.8 \times 10^{-11} m^2/s$$

$$Q_d = 41.5 \, kJ/mol$$

What is the diffusion coefficient at a temperature T = 400°C?

- A. 2.13×10^{-11} m²/s
- B. 2.85×10^{-10} m²/s
- C. 7.12×10^{-10} m²/s
- D. 2.05×10^{-9} m²/s

Materials Topics on FE Civil Examination

Problem 9

Fresh charcoal made from a living tree contains Carbon-14 which will give a radioactive count of 13.60 disintegrations per minute per gram of carbon. A piece of charcoal found gave 1.04 disintegrations per minute per gram of carbon. Carbon-14 has a half-life of 5730 years. What is the age of the charcoal?

- A. 5020 years
- B. 11,045 years
- C. 17,550 years
- D. 21,250 years

Problem 10

The Brinell hardness number (BHN) for a steel specimen is 150. What is the approximate value of the tensile strength?

- A. 415 MPa
- B. 470 MPa
- C. 525 MPa
- D. 570 MPa

Problem 11

Which of the following statements about Portland cement concrete is NOT true?

- A. Air entrainment reduces strength
- B. Air entrainment reduces durability
- C. Water content affects strength
- D. Hydration is an exothermic reaction

Problem 12

Which of the following statements is not true?

- A. Amorphous solids do not have well-defined melting points
- B. Crystalline solids have a specific atomic arrangement.
- C. Internal planes within a crystal lattice are orthogonal
- D. Amorphous solids are formed from cooling of liquids

Materials Topics on FE Civil Examination

Problem 13

A plain concrete cylinder beam (cross-section: 6 inch width x 8 inch depth) is tested as shown. If the load P that causes cracking in the beam is 1600 lb, what is the tensile strength of the concrete?

A. 350 psi
B. 450 psi
C. 550 psi
D. 650 psi

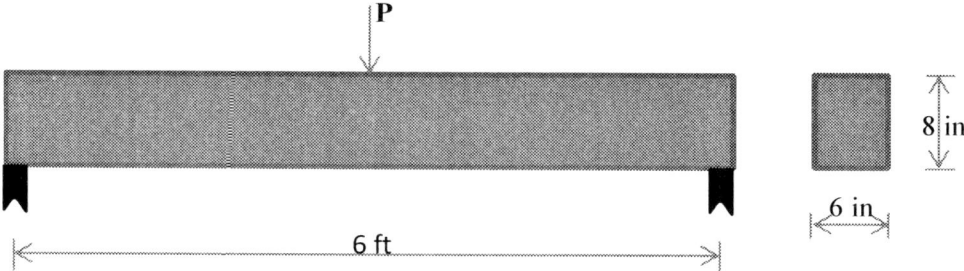

Problem 14

Concrete test cylinders (6 inch x 12 inch) are tested as part of quality control measures for a project. Results from compression tests are summarized in the table below. What is the mean compressive strength predicted by this sample?

A. 3200 psi
B. 3300 psi
C. 3400 psi
D. 3500 psi

Sample	1	2	3	4	5	6	7	8	9
Load at failure (lb)	88,500	91,235	90,886	91,214	89,055	90,765	90,882	89,561	91,238

Problem 15

A concrete mix has proportions 1:1.6:2.6 (cement: sand: coarse aggregate) by weight. The following specifications are given:

Cement	specific gravity = 3.15
	94 lbs per sack
Sand	specific gravity = 2.62 (SSD)
Coarse aggregate	specific gravity = 2.65 (SSD)
Added water	5.8 gal per sack cement
Air	3% (by volume)

The quantity of cement (lb/yd^3) is most nearly:

A) 630
B) 650
C) 670
D) 690

Materials Topics on FE Civil Examination

Materials Solutions

Materials Topics on FE Civil Examination

Solution 1

Annealing can improve ductility, soften material, relieve internal stresses and refines the structure by making it more homogeneous. A is true.

Cold working increases the dislocation density of the metal, thereby inhibiting further slip by dislocation movement. Thus, cold working decreased ductility. B is false.

Rate of cooling affects grain size and this has an impact on yield strength. C is true

Rapid cooling (quenching) can affect the final phase composition of steel. D is true.

Answer is B

Solution 2

For an interior crack, y = 1

Crack length 2a = 30x10⁻⁶ m → a = 1.5x10⁻⁵ m

Maximum stress: $\sigma = \frac{1}{\sqrt{\pi a}} \frac{K_I}{y} = \frac{1}{\sqrt{\pi \times 1.5 \times 10^{-5}}} \times \frac{3.75}{1.0} = 546 \, MPa$

Answer is A

Solution 3

Under *iso-stress* conditions, the effective modulus of elasticity is given by the harmonic average of the component values.

$$E_m = \frac{1}{\frac{f_A}{E_A} + \frac{f_B}{E_B}} = \frac{1}{\frac{0.6}{190} + \frac{0.4}{4}} = 9.69 \, GPa$$

Answer is D

Solution 4

Under *iso-strain* conditions, the effective modulus of elasticity is given by the arithmetic average of the component values.

$$E_m = f_A E_A + f_B E_B = 0.6 \times 190 + 0.4 \times 4 = 115.6 \, GPa$$

Answer is C

Solution 5

$$N_{0.0645} = 2^{11-1} = 1024$$

Actual area = 1 cm² = 100 mm²

Therefore, total number of grains: $N_{actual} = 1024 \times \frac{100}{0.0645} = 1.59 \times 10^6$

Answer is B

Materials Topics on FE Civil Examination

Solution 6

At 2% carbon, at 1200°C the alloy is γ + liquid

At 2% carbon, at 800°C the alloy is γ + carbide

This is a **peritectic reaction**

Answer is C

Solution 7

On the Fe_3C phase diagram, if a horizontal line is drawn at T = 1200°C, the point corresponding to 2.2% carbon lies in the γ+Liquid region. The boundary of pure γ-iron occurs at 1.8% carbon, while the boundary of liquid state occurs at 3.7% carbon. Therefore, at 2.2% carbon, the lever rule fractions are 0.4/1.9 = 0.21 and 1.5/1.9 = 0.79

Thus, the alloy is 79% γ-iron and 21% in liquid state

Answer is A

Solution 8

Diffusion coefficient is given by:

$$D_T = D_o e^{-\frac{Q_d}{RT}}$$

$$D_{300} = D_o e^{-\frac{41500}{8.314 \times 573}} = 1.647 \times 10^{-4} \times D_o$$

Equating this to the given value $D_{300} = 7.8 \times 10^{-11}$, we get D_o = 4.736 x 10^{-7}

$$D_{400} = D_o e^{-\frac{41500}{8.314 \times 673}} = 4.736 \times 10^{-7} \times 6.1 \times 10^{-4} = 2.85 \times 10^{-10}$$

Answer is B

Solution 9

N_o = 13.6

N = 1.04

τ = half-life = 5730 years

$$N = N_o e^{-0.693 t/\tau}$$

$$t = \frac{\tau}{0.693} \ln\left(\frac{N_o}{N}\right) = \frac{5730}{0.693} \ln\left(\frac{13.6}{1.04}\right) = 21{,}256.8$$

Answer is D

Solution 10

For steels there is a correlation between the BHN and the tensile strength.

TS (MPa) ≈ 3.5BHN

Therefore, tensile strength ≈ 3.5 x 150 = 525 MPa

Answer is C

Solution 11

Entrainment of air introduces air bubbles in the concrete matrix, which allows the concrete to expand and contract without cracking. Therefore, air entrainment improves durability. (B) is false

Answer is B

Solution 12

Crystalline structures have a specific arrangement of atoms forming a lattice, which is characterized by the presence of facets and internal planes. However, these planes can form various angles, not just 90 degrees. C is false. All other statements are true

Answer is C

Solution 13

The maximum moment due to load P = 1600 lb occurs at the bottom edge of the beam at midspan.

$$M = \frac{PL}{4} = \frac{1600 \times 6}{4} = 2400 \; lb \cdot ft = 28800 \; lb \cdot in$$

Section modulus of the beam: $S = \frac{bh^2}{6} = \frac{6 \times 8^2}{6} = 64 \; in^3$

Maximum bending stress: $\sigma = \frac{M}{S} = \frac{28800}{64} = 450 \; psi$

Answer is B

Solution 14

The average failure load = ΣP/N = 722,571/9 = 90,321 lb

Compressive strength (average): $\sigma = \frac{P}{A} = \frac{90321}{\pi(3)^2} = 3194.5 \; psi$

Answer is A

Solution 15

Assume 1 sack cement: W = 94 lb. $V = 94/(3.15 \times 62.4) = 0.478$ ft^3

Sand: W = 1.6 x 94 = 150.4 lb. $V = 150.4/(2.62 \times 62.4) = 0.920$ ft^3

Coarse: W = 2.6 x 94 = 244.4 lb. $V = 244.4/(2.65 \times 62.4) = 1.478$ ft^3

Added water: $V = 5.8$ gal $= 5.8/7.48 = 0.775$ ft^3

Total volume of components = 3.651 ft^3

The components above represent 97% of total volume, since air = 3% by volume.

Therefore, total volume = 3.651÷0.97 = 3.764 ft^3

The quantity of cement = 94 lb/3.764 ft^3 = 24.97 lb/ft^3 = 674 lb/yd^3

Answer is C

Fluid Mechanics

Fluid Mechanics Topics on FE Civil Examination 4–6 problems
Approximately 4% of exam

A. Flow measurement
B. Fluid properties
C. Fluid statics
D. Energy, impulse, and momentum equations

Problem 1

A 10 cm x 10 cm plate is adjacent to a fixed wall with a 2mm thick layer of fluid in the intervening space. The viscosity of the fluid is 1.2 Ns/m^2.

What is the force required to impart a velocity of 2 m/s to the moving plate?

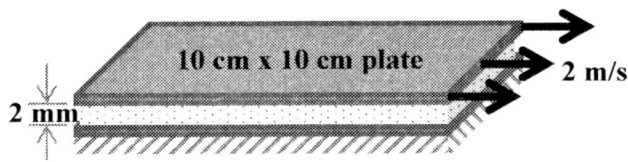

- A. 8 N
- B. 12 N
- C. 16 N
- D. 128 N

Problem 2

An orifice meter (orifice diameter = 50 mm) is inserted in a 10 cm diameter cast iron pipe carrying water at 15°C. The pressure difference across the meter is 1.5 atm. The orifice coefficient is 0.72. The discharge (L/min) through the pipe is most nearly?

- A. 650 L/min
- B. 1050 L/min
- C. 1500 L/min
- D. 2350 L/min

Problem 3

A mercury manometer is connected to a pressure tap in the side of a conduit flowing full with water. What is the gage pressure in the conduit?
- A. 136 kPa
- B. 1.2 kPa
- C. 16 kPa
- D. 35 kPa

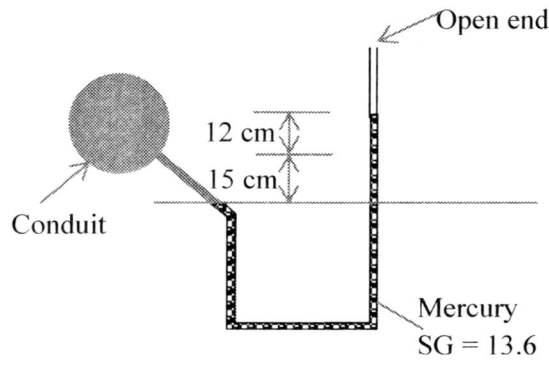

Fluid Mechanics Topics on FE Civil Examination

Problem ?

A 4 m deep water reservoir is regulated by a hinged gate which is rectangular in shape. The dimensions of the gate are: height = 5 m, width (perpendicular to the plane of the diagram) = 8 m. The gate is hinged at the top and restrained by a single clip at the bottom as shown. In the condition shown, what is the force on the clip?

    A. 335 kN
    B. 456 kN
    C. 532 kN
    D. 628 kN

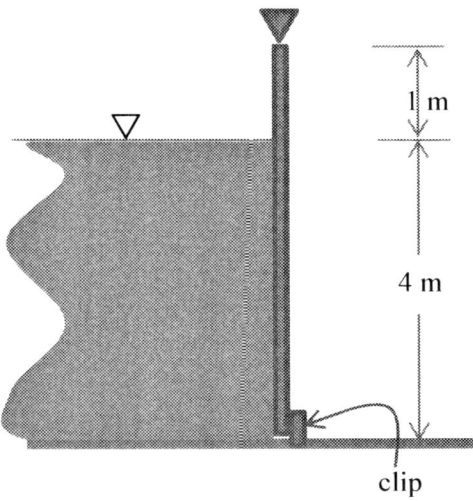

Problem ?

A pump is to be selected to deliver water at the rate of 0.1 m^3/s. If the efficiency of the pump is 85% and the necessary total lift (head) is 65 m, what is the required power rating of the pump?

    A. 75 kW
    B. 64 kW
    C. 38 kW
    D. 32 kW

Fluid Mechanics Topics on FE Civil Examination

Problem ?

A tank contains water to a fixed elevation as shown. A rounded orifice with diameter = 1 cm exists with its centerline 2.1 m below the water surface. What is the flow rate through the nozzle?

- A. 0.1 L/min
- B. 0.5 L/min
- C. 7.2 L/min
- D. 30 L/min

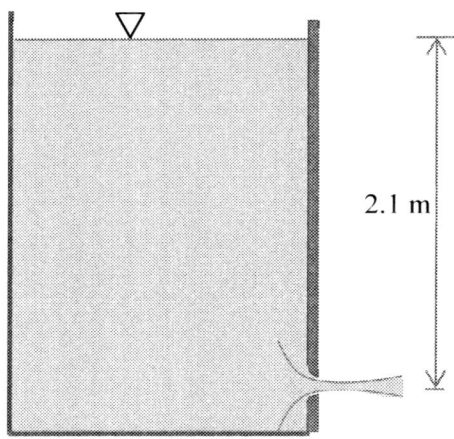

Problem ?

A water jet of diameter 1 cm and a flow rate Q = 1 L/sec is deflected by a fixed plate as shown. The velocity of the deflected jet is 6 m/s. What is the force on the plate?

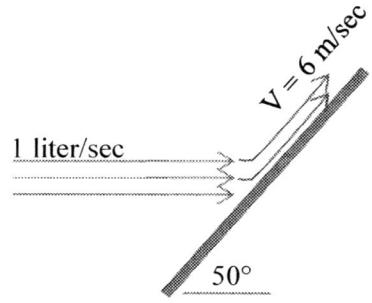

- A. 10 N
- B. 15 N
- C. 20 N
- D. 25 N

Fluid Mechanics Topics on FE Civil Examination

Problem ?

A 30 cm diameter cast iron pipe conveys water at 20°C at the rate of 0.2m³/sec. What is the head loss due to friction according to the Darcy Weisbach model?

    A. 6 m per 1000 m of pipe
    B. 16 m per 1000 m of pipe
    C. 26 m per 1000 m of pipe
    D. 36 m per 1000 m of pipe

Problem ?

A sphere of diameter 20 cm is completely submerged in sea water (SG = 1.08, μ = 0.001 Pa-s). If the water flows with a horizontal velocity V = 0.5 m/s, what is the drag force?

    A. 8.5 N
    B. 4.25 N
    C. 17.0 N
    D. 85.0 N

Problem 1?

A prismatic object is neutrally buoyant 20 cm below the free surface as shown. The object has plan dimensions 1 m x 1m and is 50 cm deep. Fluids 1 and 2 are immiscible. What is the weight of the object?

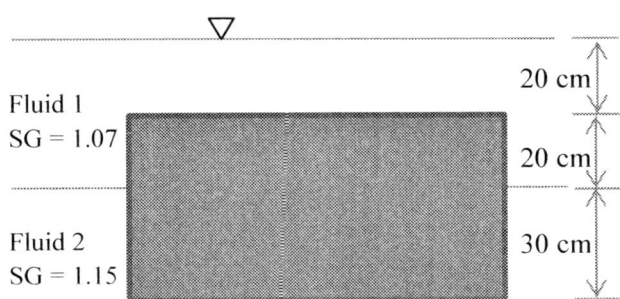

    A. 2812 N
    B. 3625 N
    C. 4350 N
    D. 5500 N

Problem 11

A glass capillary tube (diameter 1 mm) is inserted into an open reservoir of a liquid. The surface tension of the liquid is 85 dynes/cm. The diagram shows a magnified view of the liquid inside the tube.

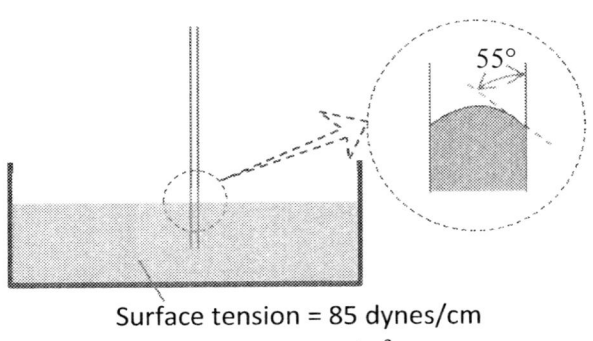

Surface tension = 85 dynes/cm
Density = 10,000 kg/m^3

Which of the following is true?

A. Liquid rises 2 mm in the tube
B. Liquid falls 2 mm in the tube
C. Liquid rises 4 mm in the tube
D. Liquid falls 4 mm in the tube

Problem 12

A reducer is placed at the location of a transition where water flows from a 150 mm diameter pipe to a 100 mm diameter. If the velocity at the upstream end of the pipe is 4.5 m/s, what is the velocity at the downstream end?

A. 2.0 m/s
B. 3.0 m/s
C. 6.8 m/s
D. 10.1 m/s

Fluid Mechanics Topics on FE Civil Examination

Problem 13

Water at temperature of 10°C flows through a 150 mm diameter galvanized iron pipe. The average flow velocity is 4 m/s. What is the Reynolds number?

- A. 3.4×10^5
- B. 4.6×10^5
- C. 3.4×10^6
- D. 4.6×10^6

Problem 14

Water at temperature of 10°C flows through a 150 mm diameter galvanized iron pipe. The average flow velocity is 4 m/s. What is the pressure loss due to friction across a 100 m length of this pipe?

- A. 3 m
- B. 9 m
- C. 11 m
- D. 16 m

Problem 15

The lift coefficient for an airfoil is zero for an angle of attack = -6°. If the coefficient of lift at an angle of attack = 5° is 1.0, what is the coefficient of lift when the angle of attack is 10°?

- A. 2.20
- B. 2.04
- C. 1.83
- D. 1.45

Problem 16

The elevation of the hydraulic grade line at a point along a water supply pipeline is 329 m above sea level. The elevation of the invert of the 600 mm diameter pipe is 249 m above sea level. If the flow rate is 0.2 m³/s, what is the fluid pressure at this location?

- A. 8.0×10^4 Pa
- B. 7.8×10^5 Pa
- C. 8.1×10^5 Pa
- D. 8.4×10^6 Pa

Fluid Mechanics Topics on FE Civil Examination

Problem 1

The elevation of the hydraulic grade line at a point along a water supply pipeline is 329 m above sea level. The elevation of the invert of the 600 mm diameter pipe is 249 m above sea level. If the flow rate is 1.0 m³/s, what is the elevation of the EGL at this location?

- A. 329.64 m above sea level
- B. 329.32 m above sea level
- C. 328.71 m above sea level
- D. 328.45 m above sea level

Problem 1

A Venturi meter with throat diameter = 100 mm is inserted in a 300 mm diameter cast iron pipe carrying water at 15°C. The pressure difference across the meter is 1.5 atm. The velocity coefficient of the meter is 0.90. The discharge (L/min) through the pipe is most nearly?

- A. 1230 L/min
- B. 5050 L/min
- C. 7400 L/min
- D. 8240 L/min

Problem 1

A Pitot tube is inserted into a 15 cm diameter pipe conveying water at a temperature of 14°C. The water rises in the Pitot tube to a height of 200 mm above the centerline as shown in the figure. What is the flow rate?
- A. 3.5 L/s
- B. 12 L/s
- C. 21 L/s
- D. 83 L/s

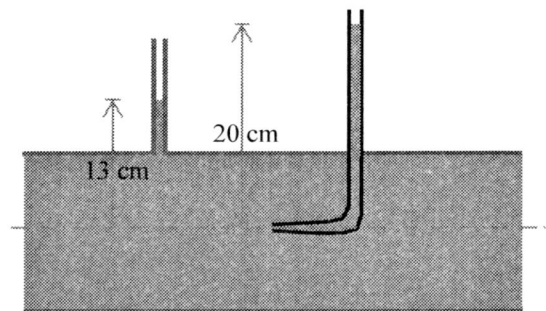

Fluid Mechanics Topics on FE Civil Examination

Problem 20

A rectangular plate is submerged under water as shown. The width of the plate (perpendicular to the drawing plane) is 4 m. What is the resultant force acting on the upper surface of the plate?

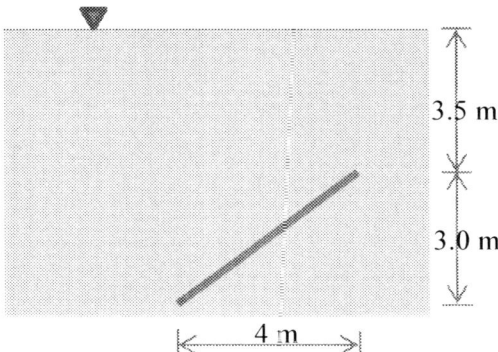

A. 1,265,300 N
B. 1,125,100 N
C. 1,030,400 N
D. 980,000 N

Problem 21

A 50 mm diameter steel pipe carries a flow rate Q = 120 L/min of a fluid with the following properties:

Viscosity = 300 cP
Density = 2400 kg/m^3

What is the maximum flow velocity in the pipe?

A. 2.00 L/s
B. 1.50 L/s
C. 1.28 L/s
D. 1.00 L/s

Problem 22

The deformation response of a fluid to applied shear stress is represented by the curve below. Which of the following statements is true?

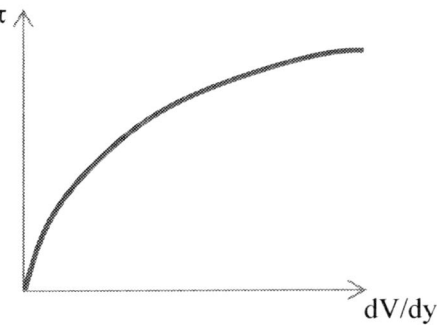

A. The fluid is Newtonian
B. The fluid is a pseudo-plastic fluid
C. The fluid is a dilatant fluid
D. The viscosity of the fluid is constant

Problem 23

A pseudo-plastic fluid's viscosity characteristics are described by the equation:

$$\tau = K \left(\frac{dV}{dy}\right)^n$$

where K = 0.3 Pa.s$^{0.8}$ and n = 0.8. The density of the fluid is 950 kg/m³

If a 50 mm diameter pipe conveys a flow rate Q = 0.012 m³/s of this fluid, what is the Reynolds number?

A. 970
B. 1450
C. 2300
D. 3650

Fluid Mechanics Topics on FE Civil Examination

Problem 2☐

A 150 mm diameter pipe conveys water at a flow rate $Q = 0.2$ m³/s from a reservoir using a sharp edged exit as shown below. What is the head loss at the point where the water leaves the reservoir?

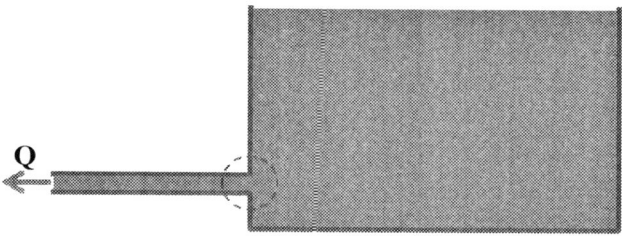

A. 3.3 m
B. 6.5 m
C. 13.0 m
D. 26.0 m

Problem 2☐

A pipe carries a flow rate $Q = 1$ m³/s into node A of a pipeline network. At node A, the flow splits into three pipes (numbered 1, 2 and 3) which then reconnect at node B as in the diagram below. Length, diameter and approx. values of friction factor are given. What fraction of the influent flow rate passes through pipe no. 2?

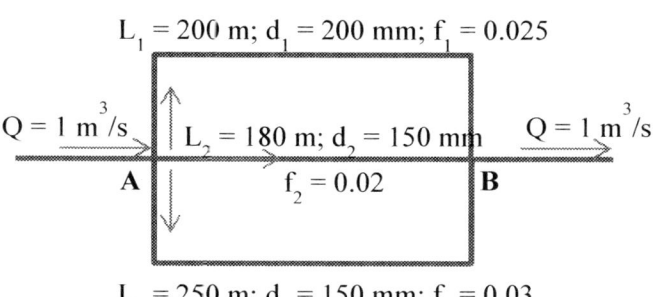

A. 20%
B. 25%
C. 30%
D. 35%

Fluid Mechanics Topics on FE Civil Examination

Problem 2?

A filter bed is 2 m deep and is packed with spherical rocks with diameter 40 mm. The porosity of the filter bed is 35%, If water at 15°C trickles through the filter at a vertical velocity of 20 mm/sec, what is the pressure loss through the filter?

- A. 121 Pa
- B. 402 Pa
- C. 572 Pa
- D. 1023 Pa

Problem 2?

A scaled model of a building has a 1:50 geometric scale. The properties of air under field conditions are: density ρ = 1.28 kg/m³ and viscosity μ = 1.7x10^{-5} Pa-sec. The model is to be tested in a water tunnel and the water properties are: density ρ = 1000 kg/m³ and viscosity μ = 0.001 Pa-sec.

If Reynolds number similarity is desired, what is the velocity scale?

- A. 2.1
- B. 3.8
- C. 5.2
- D. 6.9

Problem 2?

What is the drag coefficient for a flat plate 2 m wide x 5 m long x 1 cm thick immersed in water flowing with velocity V = 6 m/s. Assume water temperature = 10°C?

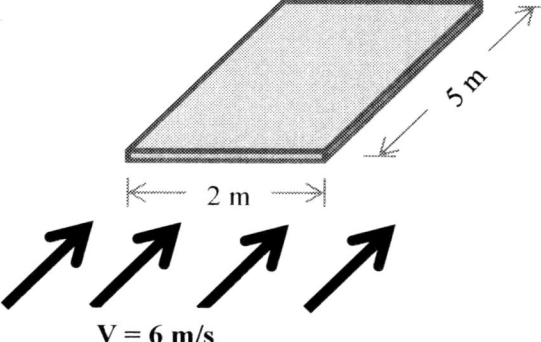

- A. 0.0027
- B. 0.0034
- C. 0.0043
- D. 0.031

Fluid Mechanics Topics on FE Civil Examination

Problem 2

A skydiver weighing 80kg uses a parachute with a projected diameter of 6 m as shown below. The drag coefficient of the parachute (while falling vertically) is 1.4. If the average air density is 1.24 kg/m^3, what is the terminal velocity of the skydiver when dropping vertically?

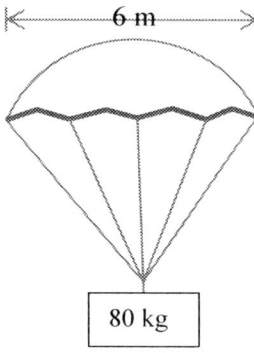

A. 14 kmph
B. 20 kmph
C. 28 kmph
D. 40 kmph

Fluid Mechanics Solutions

Fluid Mechanics Topics on FE Civil Examination

Problem 1

The velocity gradient through the thickness of the fluid: $\frac{dV}{dy} = \frac{V}{t} = \frac{2}{0.002} = 1000\ s^{-1}$

Shear stress: $\tau = \mu \frac{dV}{dy} = 1.2 \times 1000\ s^{-1} = 1200\ \frac{N}{m^2}$

Force: $F = \tau A = 1200 \times 0.1 \times 0.1 = 12\ N$

Answer is B

Problem 2

Flow rate of an orifice meter is given by:

$$Q = CA_o \sqrt{2g\left(\frac{p_1}{\gamma} + z_1 - \frac{p_2}{\gamma} - z_2\right)}$$

Ignoring the elevation difference between the two pressure taps at 1 and 2, we get

$$Q = CA_o \sqrt{2g\left(\frac{p_1 - p_2}{\gamma}\right)} = CA_o \sqrt{2\left(\frac{p_1 - p_2}{\rho}\right)}$$

1.0 atm = 1.013x10⁵ Pa

$$Q = 0.72 \times \pi \times 0.025^2 \sqrt{2\left(\frac{1.5 \times 1.013 \times 10^5}{1000}\right)}$$

Q = 0.02464 m³/s = 24.64 L/s = 1478.7 L/min

Answer is C

Problem 3

Since the mercury columns are balanced below the line marked 'datum', the pressure on either side of that line must be equal.

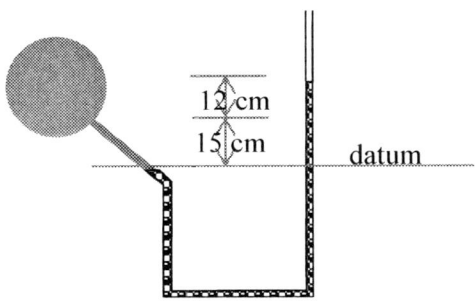

On the left, the pressure is due to the pressure in the conduit + a 15 cm tall column of water.

$$p_{left} = p_{conduit} + 1000 \times 9.81 \times 0.15$$

On the right, the pressure is due to the atmospheric pressure + a 27 cm tall column of mercury.

$$p_{right} = p_{atm} + 1000 \times 13.6 \times 9.81 \times 0.27$$

Equating the two pressures, we get:

$$p_{conduit} - p_{atm} = 1000 \times 13.6 \times 9.81 \times 0.27 - 1000 \times 9.81 \times 0.15 = 34550.8 \; Pa$$

Answer is D

Problem 2

The hydrostatic pressure against the lower 4 m of the gate is triangular, as shown. The centroid of the gate is at a depth of 2 m. The resultant force is calculated as the pressure at the centroid of the gate x area of the gate = (1000 x 9.81 x 2) x (4 x 8) = 627,840 N

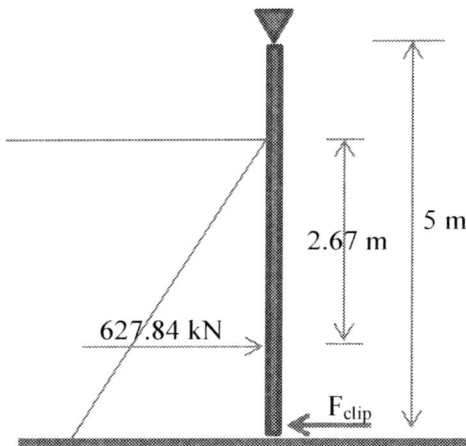

The effective location of this force is 2/3 x 4 = 2.67 m below water surface (3.67 m below hinge)

Taking moments about the hinge:

$$F_{clip} \times 5 = 627.84 \times 2.67 \Rightarrow F_{clip} = 335 \; kN$$

Answer is A

Fluid Mechanics Topics on FE Civil Examination

Solution

The pump power equation is:

$$P = \frac{\rho g Q H}{\eta} = \frac{1000 \times 9.81 \times 0.1 \times 65}{0.85} = 75{,}018 \; W$$

Answer is A

Solution

For a jet discharging feely into the atmosphere:

$$Q = C A_o \sqrt{2gh}$$

For a rounded orifice, the discharge coefficient C = 0.98

Orifice area; $A_o = \pi r^2 = \pi \times 0.005^2 = 7.854 \times 10^{-5} \; m^2$

$$Q = 0.98 \times 7.854 \times 10^{-5} \sqrt{2 \times 9.81 \times 2.1} = 4.94 \times 10^{-4} \frac{m^3}{s} = 0.494 \frac{L}{s} = 29.6 \; L/min$$

Answer is D

Solution

Flow rate, Q = 1 L/sec = 0.001 m³/s

Approach velocity: $V = Q/A = \frac{0.001}{\pi/4 \times 0.01^2} = 12.73 \; m/s$

After impacting the plate, V_x = 6 cos 50 = 3.86 m/s and V_y = 4.60 m/s

Applying conservation of momentum in x and y directions respectively:

$$\sum F_x = \Delta(\rho Q V)_x = 1000 \times 0.001 \times (3.86 - 12.73) = -8.88 \; N$$

$$\sum F_y = \Delta(\rho Q V)_y = 1000 \times 0.001 \times (4.6 - 0) = 4.6 \; N$$

The forces calculated above are forces acting ON the fluid.

Force acting on the plate = + 8.88 – 4.6

Resultant force on plate: $F = \sqrt{8.88^2 + 4.6^2} = 10 \; N$

Answer is A

Solution

Fluid Mechanics Topics on FE Civil Examination

At a temperature of 20°C, the kinematic viscosity of water is $v = 1.003 \times 10^{-6}$ m²/s

Velocity: $V = \dfrac{Q}{A} = \dfrac{0.2}{\pi/4(0.3)^2} = 2.83 \dfrac{m}{s}$

Reynolds number: $Re = \dfrac{VD}{v} = \dfrac{2.83 \times 0.3}{1.003 \times 10^{-6}} = 8.4 \times 10^5$

For C.I. pipe, absolute roughness: e = 0.25 mm

Relative roughness: e/D = 0.25/300 = 0.00083

For Re = 8.4x10⁵ and e/D = 0.00083, friction factor f = 0.019

Head loss due to friction over 1 m length of pipe: $h_f = f \dfrac{L}{D} \dfrac{V^2}{2g} = 0.019 \times \dfrac{1}{0.3} \times \dfrac{2.83^2}{2 \times 9.81} = 0.0258\ m$

This head loss can be expressed as 25.8 m per 1000 m of pipe length.

Answer is C

Problem 9

Dynamic viscosity of water is μ = 0.001 Pa-s

Density ρ = 1.08x1000 = 1080 kg/m³

Reynolds number: $Re = \dfrac{\rho VD}{\mu} = \dfrac{1080 \times 0.5 \times 0.2}{0.001} = 1.08 \times 10^5$

For Re = 1.08x10⁵, drag coefficient C_D = 1.0 (for a sphere)

Drag force: $F_D = \dfrac{1}{2} \rho V^2 A C_D = \dfrac{1}{2} \times 1080 \times 0.5^2 \times \pi \times 0.1^2 \times 1.0 = 4.24\ N$

Answer is B

Problem 10

According to Archimedes Principle, an object floats when the buoyant force (which is the weight of the displaced liquid) is equal to the weight of the object.

$$W = \rho_1 V_1 g + \rho_2 V_1 g = (1070 \times 0.2 + 1150 \times 0.3) \times 9.81 = 5484\ N$$

Answer is D

Problem 11

The angle β is the angle between the wetted tube and the tangent to the surface. Therefore, β =125°

Fluid Mechanics Topics on FE Civil Examination

σ = 85 dynes/cm = 85x10⁻⁵ N/cm = 85x10⁻³ N/m

$$h = \frac{4\sigma \cos \beta}{\rho g d} = \frac{4 \times 0.085 \times \cos 125}{10000 \times 9.81 \times 1 \times 10^{-3}} = -0.002$$

Thus, the liquid experiences a capillary DROP of 2 mm.

Answer is B

Problem 12

The continuity equation states:

$$\rho V A = constant$$

Since water is essentially incompressible, this reduces to:

$$VA = constant$$

Therefore: $\frac{V_1}{V_2} = \frac{A_2}{A_1} = \left(\frac{D_2}{D_1}\right)^2 = \left(\frac{100}{150}\right)^2 = \frac{4}{9}$

Therefore, velocity in the smaller pipe = 9/4 x velocity in larger pipe = 9/4 x 4.5 = 10.1 m/s

Answer is D

Problem 13

The kinematic viscosity of water at 10°C is ν = 1.306x10⁻⁶ m²/s

Reynolds no: $Re = \frac{VD}{\nu} = \frac{4 \times 0.15}{1.306 \times 10^{-6}} = 4.6 \times 10^5$

Answer is B

Problem 14

The kinematic viscosity of water at 10°C is ν = 1.306x10⁻⁶ m²/s

Reynolds no: $Re = \frac{VD}{\nu} = \frac{4 \times 0.15}{1.306 \times 10^{-6}} = 4.6 \times 10^5$

For galvanized iron pipe, absolute roughness e = 0.15 mm. Relative roughness e/D = 0.15/150 = 0.0010

For Re = 4.6x10⁵ and e/D = 0.001, f = 0.02

Head loss: $h_f = f \frac{L}{D} \frac{V^2}{2g} = \frac{0.02 \times 100 \times 4^2}{0.15 \times 2 \times 9.81} = 10.87\ m$

Answer is C

Fluid Mechanics Topics on FE Civil Examination

Solution 1:

The coefficient of lift is given by:
$$C_L = 2\pi k \sin(\alpha + \beta)$$

The angle β = 6° (negative of the angle for zero lift)

When α = 5°,
$$C_L = 2\pi k \sin(5 + 6) = 1.2k = 1.0$$

Therefore k = 0.833

When α = 10°,
$$C_L = 2\pi k \sin(10 + 6) = 1.732k = 1.44$$

Answer is D

Solution 1:

The HGL elevation is defined as: $\frac{p}{\rho g} + z$

The elevation of the pipe centerline = 249 + 0.3 = 249.3 m above sea level

Therefore, the pressure head: p/ρg = 329 − 249.3 = 79.7 m

Pressure: $p = 79.7 \times 1000 \times 9.81 = 7.82 \times 10^5 Pa$

Answer is B

Solution 1:

The HGL elevation is defined as: $\frac{p}{\rho g} + z$

The EGL elevation is defined as: $\frac{p}{\rho g} + z + \frac{V^2}{2g}$

The flow velocity: $V = \frac{Q}{A} = \frac{1.0}{\frac{\pi}{4} \times 0.6^2} = 3.54 \frac{m}{s}$

EGL elevation: $\left(\frac{p}{\rho g} + z\right) + \frac{V^2}{2g} = 329 + \frac{3.54^2}{2 \times 9.81} = 329.64\ m$

Answer is A

Fluid Mechanics Topics on FE Civil Examination

Solution 12

Elevation difference between the two pressure taps at 1 and 2: $z_2 - z_1 = \frac{D_1 - D_2}{2} = \frac{0.3 - 0.1}{2} = 0.1$

Diameter ratio: $D_2/D_1 = 0.333$

Area ratio: $A_2/A_1 = 0.111$

1.5 atm = $1.5 \times 1.013 \times 10^5 = 1.52 \times 10^5$ Pa

Flow rate of the Venturi meter is given by:

$$Q = \frac{C_v A_2}{\sqrt{1 - (A_2/A_1)^2}} \sqrt{2g\left(\frac{p_1}{\gamma} + z_1 - \frac{p_2}{\gamma} - z_2\right)}$$

we get

$$Q = \frac{0.9 \times \frac{\pi}{4}(0.1)^2}{\sqrt{1 - 0.111^2}} \sqrt{2 \times 9.81 \times \left(\frac{1.52 \times 10^5}{9810} - 0.1\right)} = 0.1236 \frac{m^3}{s}$$

Q = 0.1236 m³/s = 123.6 L/s = 7416.6 L/min

Answer is C

Solution 13

The 13 cm head is equivalent to the static pressure head p/γ at the centerline of the pipe

The 20 cm head is equivalent to the dynamic pressure head p/γ +V²/2g at the centerline of the pipe

Therefore, the velocity head: $\frac{V^2}{2g} = 20 - 13 = 7\ cm$

Velocity: $V = \sqrt{2 \times 9.81 \times 0.07} = 1.172 \frac{m}{s}$

Flow rate: $Q = VA = 1.172 \times \frac{\pi}{4} \times 0.15^2 = 0.0207 \frac{m^3}{s} = 20.7\ L/sec$

Answer is C

Solution 2

Pressure at the top of the plate: $p_1 = \rho g z_1 = 1000 \times 9.81 \times 3.5 = 34{,}335\ Pa$

Pressure at the top of the plate: $p_2 = \rho g z_2 = 1000 \times 9.81 \times 6.5 = 63{,}765\ Pa$

Vertical projection of plate area: $A_v = 3 \times 4 = 12\ m^2$

Volume of trapezoidal column of fluid above plate: $V_f = \frac{3.5+6.5}{2} \times 4 \times 4 = 80 \ m^3$

Total force on plate: $\underline{F} = [34,335 \times 12 + (63765 - 34335) \times 12/2]\underline{i} + [80 \times 9810]\underline{j} = 5.89 \times 10^5 \underline{i} + 7.85 \times 10^5 \underline{j}$

Magnitude of force F: $|F| = \sqrt{(5.89 \times 10^5)^2 + (7.85 \times 10^5)^2} = 9.81 \times 10^5 \ N$

Note that even though this solution is worked out according to the FE handbook, it is much easier to remember that the resultant force on the plate is the product of the pressure at the centroid multiplied by the total area of the plate. Since the depth of the centroid is 5.0 m, this would directly yield: $|F| = p_c A = (1000 \times 9.81 \times 5) \times (5 \times 4) = 9.81 \times 10^5 \ N$

Answer is D

Problem 21

Flow rate: Q = 120 L/min = 0.12 m³/min = 2x10⁻³ m³/s

Area of flow: $A = \frac{\pi D^2}{4} = \frac{\pi \times 0.05^2}{4} = 1.96 \times 10^{-3}$

Average flow velocity: $V = \frac{Q}{A} = \frac{2 \times 10^{-3}}{1.96 \times 10^{-3}} = 1 \frac{m}{s}$

Dynamic viscosity: μ = 300 cP = 0.3 Pa-s

Reynolds number: $\frac{\rho V D}{\mu} = \frac{2400 \times 1.0 \times 0.05}{0.3} = 400$

Since the Reynolds number is much less than 2000, the flow is laminar. For laminar flow in a circular pipe, velocity profile is parabolic and maximum velocity $v_{max} = 2v_{ave} = 2.0$ m/s

Answer is A

Problem 22

The plot of shear stress vs velocity gradient is nonlinear. That means that the fluid is non-Newtonian and therefore has variable 'viscosity'. This rules out (A) and (D). The curvature of the plot (convex on top) indicates that the power law index, n < 1. This means that the fluid is pseudo-plastic.

Answer is B

Problem 23

Cross-sectional area: $A = \frac{\pi D^2}{4} = \frac{\pi (0.05)^2}{4} = 1.96 \times 10^{-3} \ m^2$

Velocity: $V = \frac{Q}{A} = \frac{0.012}{1.96 \times 10^{-3}} = 6.11 \frac{m}{s}$

Reynolds number: $Re = \dfrac{V^{2-n} D^n \rho}{K\left(\dfrac{3n+1}{4n}\right)^n 8^{n-1}} = \dfrac{6.11^{1.2} \times 0.05^{0.8} \times 950}{0.3 \times \left(\dfrac{3.4}{3.2}\right)^{0.8} \times 8^{-0.2}} = 3652$

Answer is D

Solution 2:

Cross-sectional area: $A = \dfrac{\pi D^2}{4} = \dfrac{\pi (0.15)^2}{4} = 1.77 \times 10^{-2}\ m^2$

Velocity: $V = \dfrac{Q}{A} = \dfrac{0.2}{1.77 \times 10^{-2}} = 11.32\ \dfrac{m}{s}$

For a sharp entrance (into pipe), minor loss coefficient C = 0.5

Head loss: $h = C \dfrac{V^2}{2g} = 0.5 \times \dfrac{11.32^2}{2 \times 9.81} = 3.3\ m$

Answer is A

Solution 2:

Since the head loss in each pipe must be equal and Darcy Weisbach formula for friction loss is given by:

$$h_f = f \dfrac{L}{D} \dfrac{V^2}{2g}$$

Head loss h_f is proportional to fLV^2/D

However, since for a circular pipe: $V = \dfrac{Q}{A} = \dfrac{Q}{\pi D^2/4}$

$$h_f \propto \dfrac{fLV^2}{D} \propto \dfrac{fLQ^2}{D^5}$$

Since the head loss in each pipe segment is equal,

$$\dfrac{f_1 L_1 Q_1^2}{D_1^5} = \dfrac{f_2 L_2 Q_2^2}{D_2^5} = \dfrac{f_3 L_3 Q_3^2}{D_3^5}$$

$$\dfrac{0.025 \times 200 \times Q_1^2}{200^5} = \dfrac{0.02 \times 180 \times Q_2^2}{150^5} = \dfrac{0.03 \times 250 \times Q_3^2}{150^5}$$

This yields:
$$1.563 Q_1^2 = 4.741 Q_2^2 = 0.988 Q_3^2$$

If we take the square root:
$$1.25 Q_1 = 2.18 Q_2 = 0.99 Q_3$$

Fluid Mechanics Topics on FE Civil Examination

Therefore $Q_1 = 1.74Q_2$ and $Q_3 = 2.20Q_2$

Total flow $Q = Q_1 + Q_2 + Q_3 = 4.94Q_2$

Therefore, $Q_2 = 0.20Q$

Answer is A

Problem 2

For water at 15°C, $\rho = 999.1$ kg/m³; $\mu = 0.001139$ Pa.s

For perfectly spherical particles ($\Phi_s = 1$), the pressure gradient according to the Ergun equation is the sum of the viscous and the inertial effects:

$$\frac{\Delta p}{L} = \frac{150 v_o \mu (1-\varepsilon)^2}{\Phi_s^2 D_p^2 \varepsilon^3} + \frac{1.75 \rho v_o^2 (1-\varepsilon)}{\Phi_s D_p \varepsilon^3}$$

$$\frac{\Delta p}{L} = \frac{150 \times 0.02 \times 0.001139 \times 0.65^2}{1 \times 0.04^2 \times 0.35^3} + \frac{1.75 \times 999.1 \times 0.02^2 \times 0.65}{1 \times 0.04 \times 0.35^3}$$

$$\frac{\Delta p}{L} = 21.0 + 265.1 = 286.1$$

Therefore, for the 2 m depth of the filter, total pressure loss = 286×2 = 572 Pa

Answer is C

Problem 2

Reynolds number is: $Re = \frac{\rho V L}{\mu}$

For dynamic similarity, $Re_m = Re_p$

$$\frac{\rho_m V_m L_m}{\mu_m} = \frac{\rho_p V_p L_p}{\mu_p} \Rightarrow \frac{V_m}{V_p} = \frac{\rho_p L_p}{\rho_m L_m} \frac{\mu_m}{\mu_p} = \frac{1.28}{1000} \times \frac{50}{1} \times \frac{0.001}{1.7 \times 10^{-5}} = 3.765$$

Answer is B

Problem 2

The kinematic viscosity of water at T = 10°C is $n = 1.306 \times 10^{-6}$ m²/s.

Reynolds number: $Re = \frac{VL}{\nu} = \frac{6 \times 5}{1.306 \times 10^{-6}} = 2.3 \times 10^7$

According to the handbook: $C_D = \frac{0.031}{Re^{1/7}} = 0.00275$

Answer is A

Fluid Mechanics Topics on FE Civil Examination

Problem 2:

The projected area (on horizontal plane) of the parachute is: $A = \pi R^2 = \pi \times 3^2 = 28.27\ m^2$

The drag force (upward) is given by:

$$F_D = \frac{1}{2}\rho V^2 C_D A = \frac{1}{2} \times 1.24 \times V^2 \times 1.4 \times 28.3 = 24.54 V^2$$

The weight of the skydiver is W = 80x9.81 = 785 N

For terminal velocity (zero acceleration), these two forces must be equal.

$24.54 V^2 = 785 \Rightarrow V = 5.66\frac{m}{s} = 20.4\ kmph$

Answer is B

Hydraulics & Hydrologic Systems Topics on FE Civil Examination

Hydraulics and Hydrologic Systems

Hydraulics & Hydrologic Systems Topics   **8-12 problems**
Approximately 8% of Exam

A. Basic hydrology (e.g., infiltration, rainfall, runoff, detention, flood flows, watersheds)
B. Basic hydraulics (e.g., Manning equation, Bernoulli theorem, open-channel flow, pipe flow)
C. Pumping systems (water and wastewater)
D. Water distribution systems
E. Reservoirs (e.g., dams, routing, spillways)
F. Groundwater (e.g., flow, wells, drawdown)
G. Storm sewer collection systems

Problem 1

A trapezoidal open channel with bottom width = 10 ft and side slopes 2H:1V conveys water at a uniform depth of 5 ft. If Manning's roughness coefficient = 0.014 and the longitudinal slope of the channel bottom is 0.4%, what is the flow rate?

A. 755 ft^3/s
B. 960 ft^3/s
C. 1420 ft^3/s
D. 1730 ft^3/s

Problem 2

A 36 inch diameter concrete pipe with a longitudinal slope = 0.3% conveys flow rate 20 MGD. Assume n = 0.013 (constant with depth). The depth of flow (inches) is most nearly:

A. 22 inches
B. 24 inches
C. 26 inches
D. 28 inches

Problem 3

A concrete pipe (Manning's n = 0.013) conveys a peak flow rate = 30 ft^3/s. The elevation difference between the ends of the pipe is 8 ft and the length of the pipe is 2000 ft. The required diameter (inches) is most nearly:

A. 28 in
B. 30 in
C. 32 in
D. 34 in

Hydraulics & Hydrologic Systems Topics on FE Civil Examination

Problem 4

The 1 hour unit hydrograph of excess precipitation is described by the following data:

Time (hrs)	0.0	1.0	2.0	3.0	4.0	5.0
Discharge Q (cfs/inch)	0	40	90	60	20	0

A storm produces the following pattern of excess precipitation – 1.2 inches of excess precipitation during the first hour followed by 0.6 inches during second hour and 0.4 inches during the third hour. The stream discharge at the end of the fourth hour is most nearly:
  A. 126 ft³/s
  B. 110 ft³/s
  C. 96 ft³/s
  D. 88 ft³/s

Problem 5

A trapezoidal channel has a longitudinal slope of 0.5% and sides at 1V:3H slopes as shown. Manning's n is given as 0.020. If the depth of flowing water is 2 feet, the velocity is most nearly
  A) 3.5 fps
  B) 3.8 fps
  C) 5.6 fps
  D) 6.8 fps

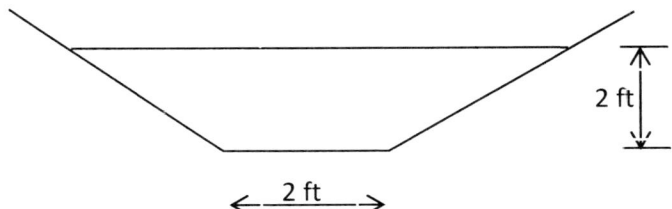

Problem 6

The pump is used to deliver water through the system shown in the figure.

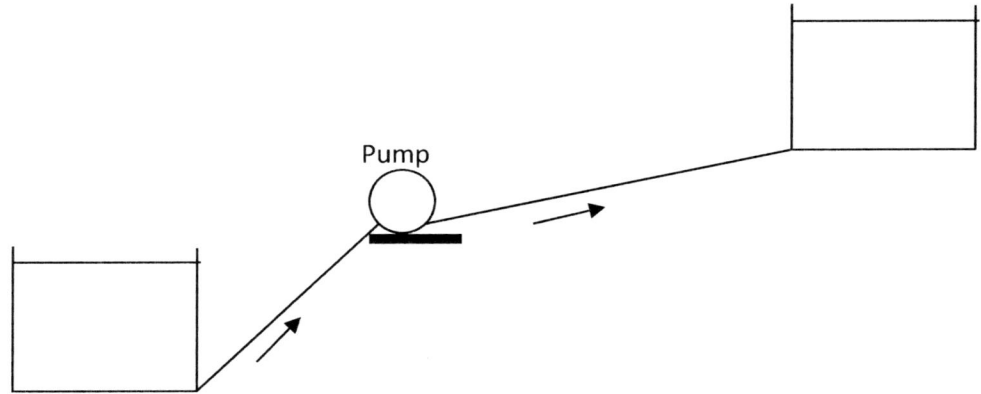

Which of the following will reduce the tendency for pump cavitation?
  I.   Increasing the discharge pipe diameter.
  II. Lowering the pump elevation.
  III. Increasing the suction pipe diameter.

A) II and III only
B) II only
C) I and II only
D) I, II and III

Problem 7

A rectangular open channel of width = 10 ft has a critical velocity = 15 ft/s. The flow rate at this critical velocity is most nearly:

A) 800 ft³/s
B) 1000 ft³/s
C) 1200 ft³/s
D) 1400 ft³/s

Problem 8

A rectangular channel conveys a flow rate = 20 ft³/s. The Manning's n = 0.015 and the longitudinal slope is 0.2%. If the channel is most efficient, the flow area is most nearly

A) 1.6 ft²
B) 2.6 ft²
C) 5.2 ft²
D) 7.8 ft²

Problem 9

A 48 inch diameter concrete pipe (n = 0.015) conveys water at a depth of 18 inches. If the longitudinal depth of the pipe is 0.6%, what is the flow rate?

A) 22
B) 28
C) 34
D) 39

Problem 10

A storm drain inlet is being designed for a 2.4 acre parking lot. The rainfall intensity is 4.2 in/hr and the rational runoff coefficient is 0.95. The peak discharge (ft^3/sec) is most nearly:

A) 8
B) 10
C) 12
D) 14

Problem 11

An orifice meter (orifice diameter = 2 inches) is inserted in a 4 inch diameter cast iron pipe carrying water at 15°C. The pressure difference across the meter is 1.5 atm. The orifice coefficient is 0.72. The discharge (gal/min) through the pipe is most nearly:

A) 250
B) 400
C) 1600
D) 2200

Problem 12

The 1-hour unit hydrograph of excess precipitation is shown in the table below.

Time (hr)	0	1	2	3	4	5
Discharge Q (cfs/inch)	0	35	75	105	40	0

A 2 hour storm produces 1.7 inches of runoff during the first hour followed by 0.8 inches of runoff during second hour. The peak discharge (ft^3/sec) due to this storm is most nearly:

A) 210
B) 239
C) 263
D) 287

Problem 13

A rain gage at a weather station records the following rainfall depths during a storm event. The peak intensity of rainfall (in/hr) during the storm is most nearly:

A. 0.6
B. 2.0
C. 3.2
D. 3.6

Time (min)	Depth (inches)
0	0.0
10	0.2
20	0.5
30	0.9
40	1.5
50	1.8
60	2.0

Problem 14

A rectangular channel is 15 feet wide and conveys a flow rate = 120,000 gal/min. The flow is conveyed down a spillway, at the bottom of which the depth of flow is 15 inches. What is the Froude number at the bottom of the spillway?

A. 2.3
B. 3.4
C. 4.8
D. 5.6

Hydraulics & Hydrologic Systems Topics on FE Civil Examination

Problem 15

A watershed (area = 370 acres) is subdivided into 5 distinct land use classifications, as shown in the table below. Using the NRCS method, the net runoff (inches) from a 20-year storm with gross rainfall = 5.6 inches is most nearly:
- A. 1.6 inches
- B. 2.2 inches
- C. 2.9 inches
- D. 3.6 inches

Region	Area (acres)	Land use	Soil type	Time for overland flow (min)	Curve number	Rational runoff coefficient
A	80	Lawns: fair condition	B	30	69	0.4
B	80	Forest	C	45	45	0.2
C	50	Paved	B	15	98	0.9
D	90	Residential: 4 lots/acre	D	25	87	0.6
E	70	Forest	A	45	35	0.2

Problem 16

A watershed (area = 370 acres) is subdivided into 5 distinct land use classifications, as shown in the table below. Storm runoff data have been abstracted into a set of intensity-duration-frequency curves. Using the Rational Method, the runoff discharge (ft^3/sec) from a 20-year storm with gross rainfall = 5.6 inches is most nearly:
- A. 510 cfs
- B. 543 cfs
- C. 574 cfs
- D. 608 cfs

Region	Area (acres)	Land use	Soil type	Time for overland flow (min)	Curve number	Rational runoff coefficient
A	80	Lawns: fair condition	B	30	69	0.4
B	80	Forest	C	45	45	0.2
C	50	Paved	B	15	98	0.9
D	90	Residential: 4 lots/acre	D	25	87	0.6
E	70	Forest	A	45	35	0.2

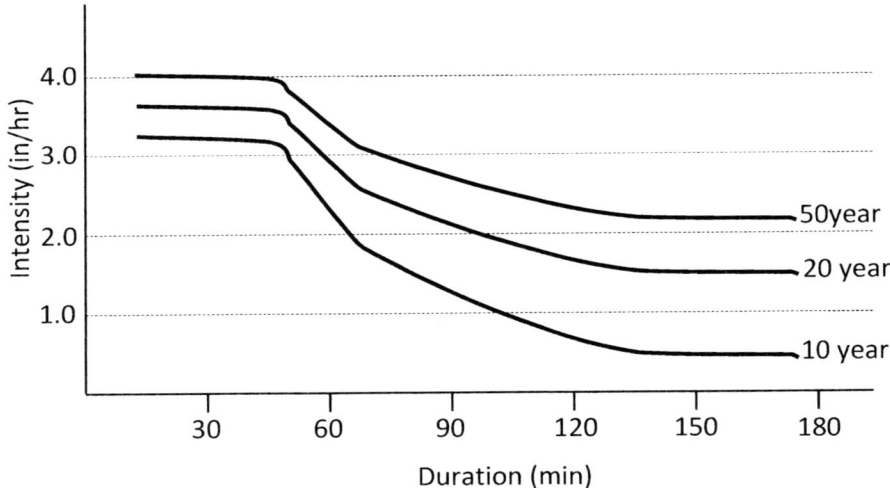

Problem 17

A symmetric triangular channel with sideslopes 1V:3H conveys a flow rate 10 cfs. If the longitudinal slope is 0.5% and Manning's n = 0.015, the critical velocity in the channel (ft/sec) is most nearly:

A. 6.12 ft/sec
B. 4.65 ft/sec
C. 3.87 ft/sec
D. 2.85 ft/sec

Problem 18

A rectangular 10 foot wide channel has 5 feet deep water flowing through. If the Froude number is 0.8, then the flow (ft^3/s) is most nearly

A) 500
B) 600
C) 700
D) 800

Problem 19

An undeveloped subdivision has a composite curve number = 63. Following development (construction of buildings and paving of roads), the composite curve number is 76. If the gross rainfall in the design storm is 5 inches, what is the percent increase in the runoff depth due to development?

A) 35%
B) 42%
C) 53%
D) 67%

Problem 20

The minimum specific energy in a rectangular open channel is 9 ft. The critical velocity is most nearly:

- A) 8.7 ft/sec
- B) 12.3 ft/sec
- C) 14.0 ft/sec
- D) 15.4 ft/sec

Problem 21

The flow rate in a circular conduit (diameter = 3 ft) is 35 ft^3/s. The conduit is brick-lined and laid on a slope of 0.5%. Assume Manning's n = 0.014 (constant). The depth of flow (inches) in the pipe is most nearly:

- A) 21
- B) 24
- C) 27
- D) 30

Problem 22

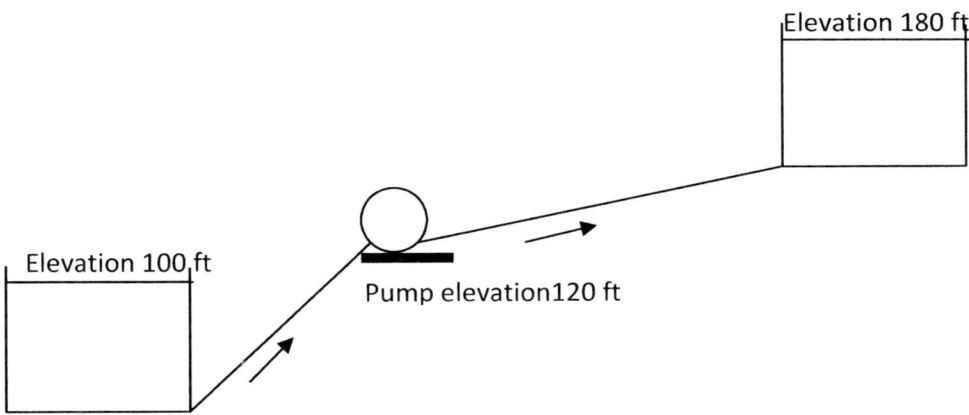

The pump located at an elevation of 120 ft is used to pump a flow Q = 3000 gal/min from a reservoir with surface elevation 100 ft to another reservoir with surface elevation 180 ft. The approximate efficiency of the pump is 85%. The characteristics of the pipe system are given below:

Suction line: 800 ft length, 18 inch diameter, C = 100
Discharge line: 2500 ft length, 12 inch diameter, C = 100

The brake horsepower of the pump is most nearly
- A) 83
- B) 102
- C) 122
- D) 145

Problem 23

A 12 inch pipe (cast iron, Hazen Williams C = 120) serves as the outfall from a large reservoir whose water surface elevation is 145 ft. The longitudinal slope of the pipe is 0.01 ft/ft. The bottom of the reservoir is at elevation 125 ft and the outfall of the pipe is at elevation 95 ft. Kinematic viscosity of water is 1.217×10^{-5} ft²/sec. The flow rate (gpm) in the pipe is most nearly:

- A) 500
- B) 1000
- C) 1500
- D) 2500

Problem 24

A buried pipe culvert has an elliptical cross section as shown. What is the hydraulic diameter when the culvert is flowing full?
- A. 0.29 m
- B. 0.58 m
- C. 0.87 m
- D. 1.15 m

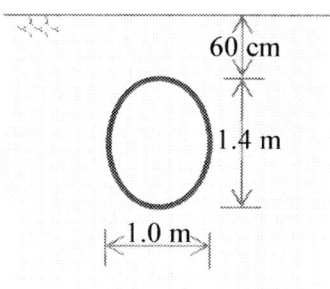

Problem 25

The parking lot shown below is graded such that the concrete pavement slopes towards the 400 ft long gutter in the center of the lot. Rain falling on the parking lot drains to the gutter. The gutter flow drains into a storm sewer inlet at one end. Only runoff from the parking lot enters this storm sewer inlet. Adjacent land drains elsewhere. For a significant rainfall event, the mean sheet flow velocity across the concrete parking lot is estimated to be 0.5 ft/sec. The estimated mean flow velocity in the gutter is 2.0 ft/sec. What is the time of concentration for the sewer inlet?

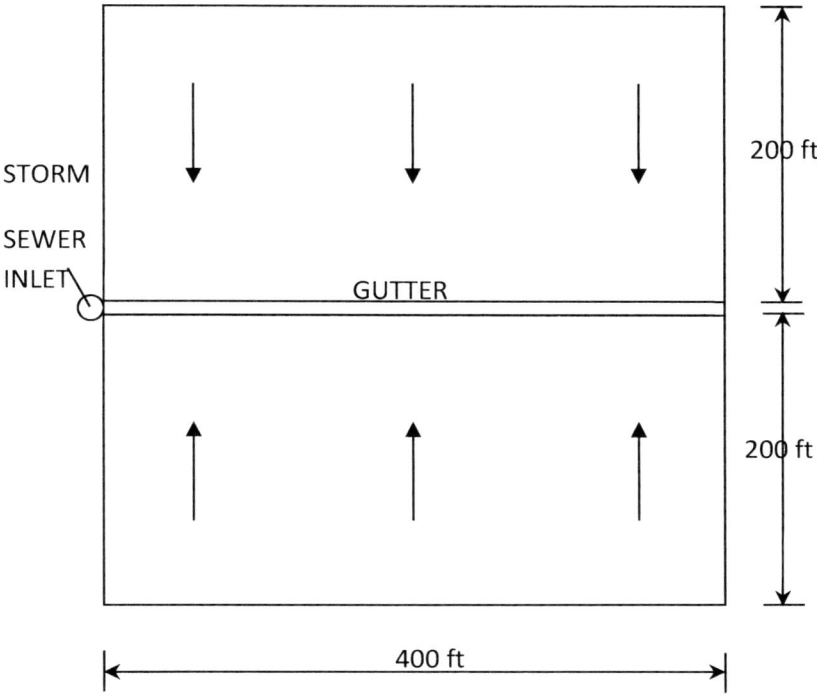

A. 8 minutes
B. 10 minutes
C. 12 minutes
D. 14 minutes

Problem 26

A trapezoidal channel has a longitudinal slope of 0.5% and sides at 1V:3H slopes as shown. Manning's n is given as 0.020. If the depth of flowing water is 2 m, the velocity is most nearly?

Hydraulics & Hydrologic Systems Topics on FE Civil Examination

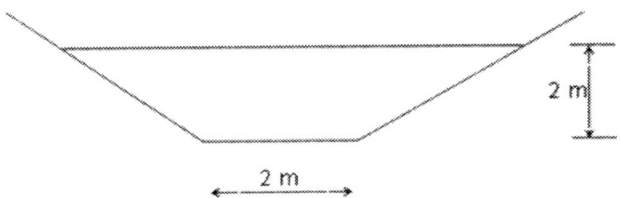

A. 15.2 m/s
B. 12.0 m/s
C. 4.1 m/s
D. 3.2 m/s

Problem 27

Water flows at a depth of 36 cm in a 45 cm diameter pipe laid on a longitudinal slope of 0.6%. The Hazen Williams coefficient is 100. What is the flow rate?

A. 0.07 m³/s
B. 0.12 m³/s
C. 0.26 m³/s
D. 0.90 m³/s

Problem 28

A reservoir empties through a rectangular weir of width 3 m as shown. The contractions are suppressed. The elevation of the bottom of the weir is 120.5 m above sea level. If the elevation of the reservoir free surface immediately behind the weir is 124.7 m above sea level, what is the discharge through the weir?

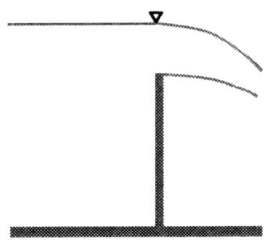 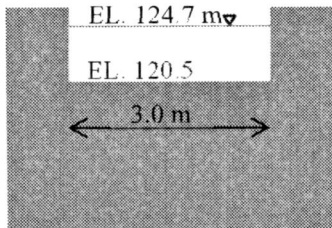

A. 86.0 m³/s
B. 78.5 m³/s
C. 63.2 m³/s
D. 47.5 m³/s

Problem 29

Water is pumped from a confined aquifer using a vertical, screened well (diameter = 9 inches) penetrating fully into the aquifer as shown below. The aquifer has a transmissivity = 50,000 ft²/day. The steady-state pumping rate is 1.3 ft³/sec. The initial piezometric surface and the drawdown cone are shown on the fgure. If the elevation of the piezometric surface at the edge of the well is 55 ft, what is the elevation at a radial distance of 100 ft?

- A. 56 ft
- B. 57 ft
- C. 58 ft
- D. 59 ft

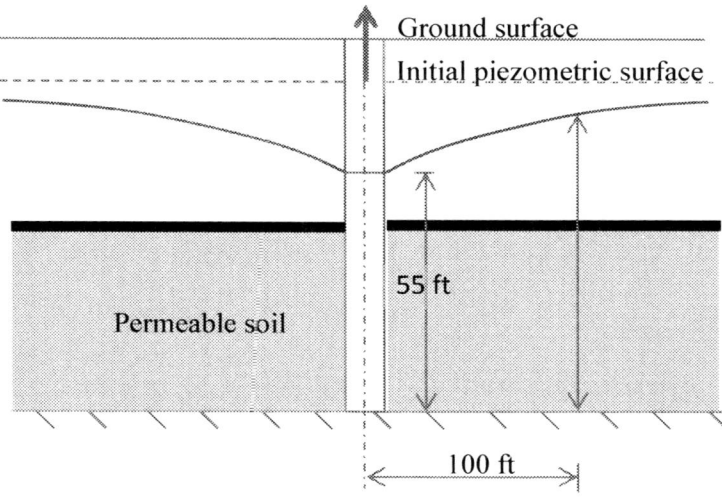

Problem 30

What is the discharge through a 90° V-notch weir if the water surface behind the weir is 45 cm above the bottom of the weir?

- A. 105 L/s
- B. 125 L/s
- C. 175 L/s
- D. 190 L/s

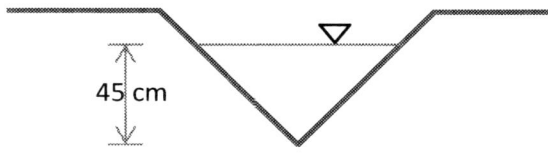

Problem 31

A 350 acre watershed is subdivided into 4 subcategories (A-D) by land use and land cover as shown in the table below. What is the expected runoff volume from the watershed following a storm with gross rainfall = 3.6 inches?

- A. 43,200 yd³

B. 58,800 yd³
C. 65,100 yd³
D. 70,000 yd³

Region	Area (ac)	CN
A	120	63
B	80	89
C	110	79
D	40	55

Problem 32

A well is sunk through the entire thickness (80 ft) of a sandy aquifer as shown. The bottom of the aquifer is bounded by a layer of impermeable clay. The steady state discharge from the pumped well is 185 ft³/hr. Observation wells 1 and 2 are drilled at radial distances 30 ft and 180 ft respectively. The drawdown cone is shown as a dashed line. The permeability of the sandy soil (ft/s) is most nearly:

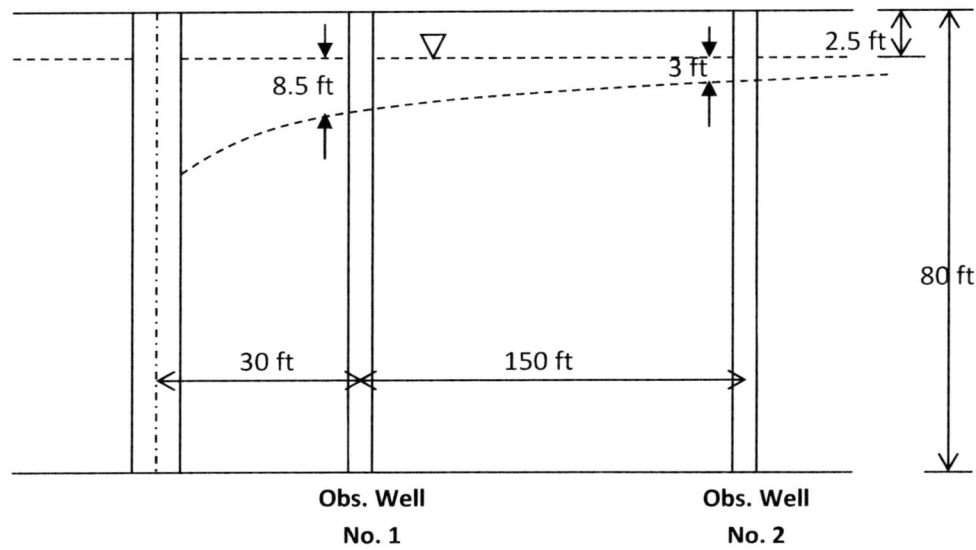

A) 4.0×10^{-5} ft/sec
B) 3.0×10^{-5} ft/sec
C) 2.0×10^{-5} ft/sec
D) 1.0×10^{-5} ft/sec

Problem 33

Seepage takes place vertically through a sand bed under the influence of a hydraulic head difference of 20 ft. The sand bed has the following properties:

Thickness = 35 ft
Sand unit weight = 120 lb/ft³

Sand moisture content = 18%
Hydraulic conductivity = 4.0 x 10^{-4} in/sec
Void ratio = 0.40

What is the seepage velocity of water through the voids in the sand bed?

A. 1.9 in/hr
B. 2.8 in/hr
C. 4.1 in/hr
D. 6.5 in/hr

Problem 34

Water flows in a circular conduit under gravitational forces. The longitudinal slope of the conduit is 1% and the value of Manning's n = 0.015 (constant with depth). If the diameter of the conduit is 48 inches, what is the depth of flow for which the flow rate conveyed by the conduit is maximum?

A. 42 inches
B. 44 inches
C. 46 inches
D. 48 inches

Problem 35

The table below shows flow data for an open channel with an irregular cross section. At which depth is the channel conveying flow at critical depth?

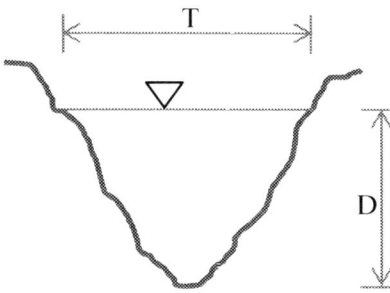

A. 2 ft
B. 4 ft
C. 6 ft
D. 8 ft

Depth D (ft)	Width T (ft)	Area A (ft²)	Flow rate Q (ft³/sec)
2.0	3.52	4.12	52
4.0	4.95	6.75	108
6.0	7.10	12.90	265
8.0	10.34	36.22	430

Hydraulics and Hydrologic Systems Solutions

Hydraulics & Hydrologic Systems Topics on FE Civil Examination

Solution 1

For depth = 5 ft and side slope = 2:1, the horizontal flare on each side = 10 ft, resulting in a top width = 30 ft.
The area of flow = 100 ft²

Wetted perimeter: $P = 10 + 2 \times 5\sqrt{5} = 32.36\ ft$

Hydraulic radius: $R_h = \frac{A}{P} = \frac{100}{32.36} = 3.09\ ft$

Velocity: $V = \frac{1.486}{n} R^{2/3} S^{1/2} = \frac{1.486 \times 3.09^{2/3} \times 0.004^{1/2}}{0.014} = 14.24\ fps$

Flow rate: $Q = VA = 1424\ cfs$

Answer is C

Solution 2

This is an unknown depth of flow problem. It is best solved using the Hydraulic Elements figure on page 162 of the FE Reference Handbook

Flow rate: Q = 20 MGD = 20 x 1.5472 = 31 cfs

For a pipe flowing full:
Flow area: $A = \frac{\pi D^2}{4}$
Wetted perimeter: $P = \pi D$
Hydraulic radius: $R_h = \frac{A}{P} = \frac{D}{4}$

Flow rate: $Q_f = VA = \left(\frac{1.486}{n}\left(\frac{D}{4}\right)^{2/3} S^{1/2}\right)\left(\frac{\pi D^2}{4}\right) = \frac{0.4632}{n} D^{8/3} S^{1/2} = \frac{0.4632 \times 3^{8/3} \times 0.003^{1/2}}{0.013} =$ 36.5 cfs

Flow ratio: $\frac{Q}{Q_f} = \frac{31}{36.5} = 0.85$

Assuming n = 0.013 to be constant with depth, d/D = 0.68, leading to d = 24.5 inches

Answer is B

Solution 3

For concrete pipe, Manning's n = 0.013
Longitudinal slope S = 8/2000 = 0.004
Peak flow rate = 30 ft³/s
Flow rate conveyed by circular pipe flowing full (based on Chezy-Manning formula):
Flow area: $A = \frac{\pi D^2}{4}$

Wetted perimeter: $P = \pi D$

Hydraulic radius: $R_h = \frac{A}{P} = \frac{D}{4}$

Flow rate (flowing full): $Q_f = VA = \left(\frac{1.486}{n} R^{2/3} S^{1/2}\right)\left(\frac{\pi D^2}{4}\right) = \frac{0.4632}{n} D^{8/3} S^{1/2}$

Required diameter: $D = \left[\frac{nQ_f}{0.4632 \times \sqrt{S}}\right]^{3/8} = \left[\frac{0.013 \times 30}{0.4632 \times \sqrt{0.004}}\right]^{3/8} = 2.64\ ft = 31.7\ in$

Answer is C

Solution 4

The effect of the first hour should use a lag time of 4 hrs (ordinate = 20)
The effect of the second hour should use a lag time of 3 hrs (ordinate = 60)
The effect of the third hour should use a lag time of 2 hrs (ordinate = 90)
Therefore the effect of a pattern shown in the figure is 1.2x20 + 0.6x60 + 0.4x90 = 96 cfs

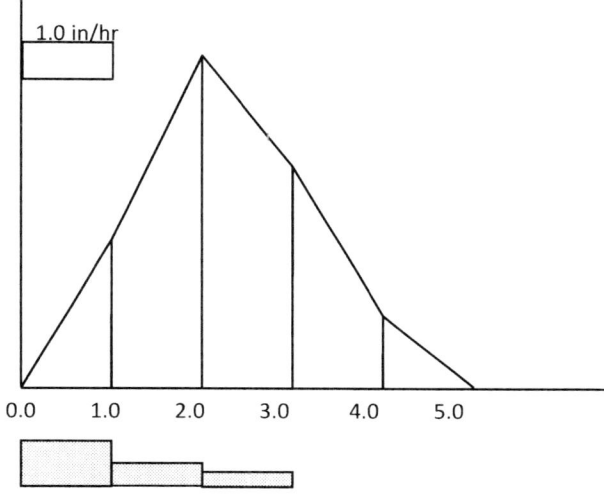

Answer is C

Solution 5

For depth = 2 ft and side slope = 3:1, the horizontal flare on each side = 6 ft, resulting in a top width = 14 ft.

The area of flow = ½ x (2+14) x 2 = 16 ft²

Wetted perimeter: $P = 2 + 2 \times 2\sqrt{10} = 14.65\ ft$

Hydraulic radius: $R_h = \frac{A}{P} = \frac{16}{14.65} = 1.09\ ft$

Velocity: $V = \frac{1.486}{n} R^{2/3} S^{1/2} = \frac{1.486 \times 1.09^{2/3} \times 0.005^{1/2}}{0.020} = 5.56\ fps$

Answer is C

Solution 6

Lowering the pump increases the available suction head, thereby reducing cavitation potential. Increasing the suction pipe diameter lowers the velocity in the suction line (for a particular flow rate), which in turn lowers the friction loss in the suction line, thereby increasing the available suction head. Increasing the discharge pipe diameter has no effect on the available suction head. Choices II and III are correct.

Answer is A

Solution 7

Since Fr = 1 (critical flow):

$$Fr = \frac{V_c}{\sqrt{gd_c}} = 1 \Rightarrow V_c = \sqrt{gd_c} = 15 \Rightarrow d_c = \frac{15^2}{32.2} = 6.99$$

Flow area = 69.9 ft². Flow rate = 69.9 x 15 = 1048 ft³/s

Answer is B

Solution 8

For a rectangular channel configured to be most efficient, depth = half the width.
Let depth = d; width = 2d; Flow area = 2d²; Wetted perimeter = 4d; Hydraulic radius = d/2

$$Q = VA = \left[\frac{1.486}{0.015} \times \left(\frac{d}{2}\right)^{2/3} \times 0.002^{1/2}\right] \times 2d^2 = 5.582 \times d^{8/3} = 20 \Rightarrow d = 1.614\ ft$$

Flow area = 2d² = 5.21 sq. ft.

Answer is C

Solution 9

n = 0.015
S = 0.006
Using the hydraulic elements chart on page 162:
Flow rate conveyed by circular pipe flowing full (based on Chezy-Manning formula):

Flow area: $A = \frac{\pi D^2}{4}$

Wetted perimeter: $P = \pi D$

Hydraulic radius: $R_h = \frac{A}{P} = \frac{D}{4}$

Flow rate: $Q_f = VA = \left(\frac{1.486}{n}\left(\frac{D}{4}\right)^{2/3} S^{1/2}\right)\left(\frac{\pi D^2}{4}\right) = \frac{0.4632}{n} D^{8/3} S^{1/2} = \frac{0.4632}{0.015} \times 4^{8/3} \times 0.006^{1/2} = 96.4\ cfs$

Depth ratio: d/D = 18/48 = 0.375. For this depth ratio, the flow ratio Q/Q_f = 0.29

Therefore, Q = 0.29×96.4 = 27.96 cfs

Answer is B

Solution 10
Area, A = 2.4 acre = 2.4 × 43560 = 104,544 ft²
Rational coefficient, C = 0.95
Intensity, i = 4.2 in/hr = 9.72 × 10⁻⁵ ft/sec
The peak discharge: $Q = CiA = 0.95 \times 9.72 \times 10^{-5} \times 104544 = 9.65\ ft^3/s$
Alternatively, $Q = CiA = 0.95 \times 4.2 \times 2.4 = 9.576\ acre \cdot in/hr = 9.65\ ft^3/s$

Answer is B

Solution 11
The flow rate through an orifice meter is given by:

$$Q = CA_o\sqrt{2gH} = CA_o\sqrt{2g\left(\frac{P_1 - P_2}{\gamma}\right)} = CA_o\sqrt{2\left(\frac{P_1 - P_2}{\rho}\right)}$$

Recognizing that 1 atm = 33.9 ft H₂O, we can use the first expression (H = 1.5×33.9 = 50.85 ft)

$$Q = CA_o\sqrt{2gH} = 0.72 \times \frac{\pi}{4} \times \left(\frac{2}{12}\right)^2 \sqrt{2 \times 32.2 \times 50.85} = 0.9\ cfs = 403\ gpm$$

Answer is B

Solution 12
The 1-hour unit hydrograph is used to construct the runoff contribution of the first hour and the second hour (staggered)

Time (hr)	0	1	2	3	4	5
Discharge Q (cfs/inch)	0	35	75	105	40	0

Time (hr)	0	1	2	3	4	5	6
Hour 1	0	59.5	127.5	178.5	68	0	
Hour 2		0	28	60	84	32	0
Total	0	59.5	155.5	238.5	152	32	0

Hydraulics & Hydrologic Systems Topics on FE Civil Examination

Max discharge = 238.5 cfs

Answer is B

Solution 13
The intensity during each period should be calculated from the incremental depth of precipitation during that period.

Time interval (min)	Depth (inches)
0 – 10	0.2
10 – 20	0.3
20 – 30	0.4
30 – 40	0.6
40 – 50	0.3
50 – 60	0.2

Peak intensity occurs during 30 – 40 min interval.
Intensity = 0.6 in/10 min = 3.6 in/hr

Answer is D

Solution 14
Q = 120,000 gpm = 120,000÷448.8 = 268 ft³/s
At the bottom of the spillway, width b = 15 ft, depth d = 15 inches = 1.25 ft
Velocity, V = Q/bd = 268/(15x1.25) = 14.3 ft/sec
For a rectangular channel, hydraulic depth = actual depth = 15 inches = 1.25 ft

Froude number: $Fr = \dfrac{V}{\sqrt{gd_h}} = \dfrac{14.3}{\sqrt{32.2 \times 1.25}} = 2.25$

Answer is A

Solution 15

Using the NRCS approach, we can calculate the runoff depth based on the composite curve number for the watershed, which is given by:

$$\overline{CN} = \dfrac{\sum CN_i A_i}{\sum A_i} = \dfrac{69 \times 80 + 45 \times 80 + 98 \times 50 + 87 \times 90 + 35 \times 70}{370} = 66$$

For CN = 66 and a gross rainfall P_g = 5.6 inches,

$$S = \dfrac{1000}{CN} - 10 = \dfrac{1000}{66} - 10 = 5.15$$

Hydraulics & Hydrologic Systems Topics on FE Civil Examination

$$Q = \frac{(P_g - 0.2S)^2}{P_g + 0.8S} = \frac{(5.6 - 0.2 \times 5.15)^2}{5.6 + 0.8 \times 5.15} = 2.15 \text{ in}$$

Runoff depth = 2.15 inches

Answer is B

Solution 16

Time of concentration = longest of all overland flow times = 45 min
From the i-d-f curves, for a 20-year storm, with duration = 45 minutes, we get intensity I = 3.7 in/hr.

Using the Rational Method (usually not used for areas larger than about 100 acres):

The composite Rational C coefficient is given by:
$$\bar{C} = \frac{\sum C_i A_i}{\sum A_i} = \frac{0.4 \times 80 + 0.2 \times 80 + 0.9 \times 50 + 0.6 \times 90 + 0.2 \times 70}{370} = 0.44$$

Rational method runoff discharge: $Q = CIA = 0.44 \times 3.7 \times 370 = 603 \frac{ac \cdot in}{hr} \cong 608 \text{ } cfs$

Answer is D

Solution 17
The longitudinal slope (S) and the channel roughness (n) DO NOT determine the *critical* flow parameters (such as depth or velocity). Therefore, for the question asked, they are unnecessary. However, they would be required data for the calculation of the *normal* depth.

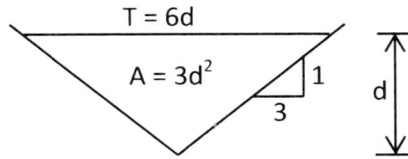

For a triangular channel with side slopes 3H:1V, the top width is given by: T = 6d and area A = 3d²

For critical flow, Q²T = A³g (page 163 of handbook)

$$10^2 \times 6d = (3d^2)^3 \times 32.2 \Rightarrow 600d = 869.4 \times d^6 \Rightarrow d = 0.929 \text{ } ft$$

Area of flow: $A = 3d^2 = 3 \times 0.929^2 = 2.586 \text{ } ft^2$

The corresponding critical velocity is given by: $V = \frac{Q}{A} = \frac{10}{2.586} = 3.87\ fps$

Answer is C

Solution 18

For a rectangular channel, hydraulic depth = actual depth = 5 ft

Froude number: $Fr = \frac{V}{\sqrt{gd_h}} = \frac{V}{\sqrt{32.2 \times 5}} = 0.8$

Therefore, velocity, V = 10.15 fps

Flow rate = Vbd = 10.15x10x5 = 507.5 ft³/s

Answer is A

Solution 19

Pre-development: CN = 63, gross rainfall P_g = 5.0 inches,

$$S = \frac{1000}{CN} - 10 = \frac{1000}{63} - 10 = 5.87$$

$$Q = \frac{(P_g - 0.2S)^2}{P_g + 0.8S} = \frac{(5.0 - 0.2 \times 5.87)^2}{5.0 + 0.8 \times 5.87} = 1.51\ in$$

Post-development: CN = 76, gross rainfall P_g = 5.0 inches,

$$S = \frac{1000}{CN} - 10 = \frac{1000}{76} - 10 = 3.16$$

$$Q = \frac{(P_g - 0.2S)^2}{P_g + 0.8S} = \frac{(5.0 - 0.2 \times 3.16)^2}{5.0 + 0.8 \times 3.16} = 2.53\ in$$

This represents a 67.5% increase

Answer is D

Solution 20

Minimum specific energy occurs for critical flow conditions. The critical depth $d_c = (q^2/g)^{1/3}$

At this depth, the critical velocity is given by

$$V_c = \frac{q}{d_c} = \sqrt{gd_c}$$

And the total specific energy is given by:

$$E_c = d_c + \frac{V_c^2}{2g} = \left(\frac{q^2}{g}\right)^{1/3} + \frac{(q/d_c)^2}{2g} = \left(\frac{q^2}{g}\right)^{1/3} + \frac{q^2}{2gd_c^2} = \left(\frac{q^2}{g}\right)^{1/3} + \frac{q^2 g^{2/3}}{2gq^{4/3}}$$

$$= \frac{3}{2}\left(\frac{q^2}{g}\right)^{1/3} = \frac{3}{2}d_c$$

Hydraulics & Hydrologic Systems Topics on FE Civil Examination

> Note: This (E_c = 1.5 d_c) is a result worth remembering. It is not explicitly given in the handbook.

Thus, if the minimum specific energy = 9 ft, the critical depth = 6 ft. The flow per unit width is: $q = \sqrt{gd_c^3} = \sqrt{32.2 \times 6^3} = 83.4 \; ft^2/s$

The critical velocity is given by $V_c = \frac{q}{d_c} = \frac{83.4}{6} = 13.9 \; ft/s$

Answer is C

Solution 21
Q = 35 ft³/sec
D = 3 ft
n = 0.014
S = 0.005

For pipe flowing full: $Q_f = VA = \left(\frac{1.486}{n} R^{2/3} S^{1/2}\right)\left(\frac{\pi D^2}{4}\right) = \frac{0.4632}{n} D^{8/3} S^{1/2} = \frac{0.4632}{0.014} \times 3^{8/3} \times 0.005^{1/2} = 43.9 \; cfs$

Q/Q$_f$ = 35/43.9 = 0.8. The corresponding depth ratio d/D (from the chart) is 0.68 (broken line for n constant with depth)

The depth of flow = 0.68 x 36 = 24 inches
Answer is B

Solution 22
Flow rate: Q = 3000 gal/min = 6.68 cfs
Suction line: 800 ft length, 18 inch diameter, C = 100
Discharge line: 2500 ft length, 12 inch diameter, C = 100
Pressure loss (psi): $P = \frac{4.52 \times Q^{1.85} \times L}{C^{1.85} \times D^{4.87}} = \frac{4.52 \times 3000^{1.85} \times 800}{100^{1.85} \times 18^{4.87}} + \frac{4.52 \times 3000^{1.85} \times 2500}{100^{1.85} \times 12^{4.87}} = 35.4 \; psi$
Since 1 atm = 14.7 psi = 33.9 ft of water, the 35.4 psi pressure loss is equivalent to head loss (friction) = 81.6 ft

Total dynamic head = static head + head loss = (180 − 100) + 81.6 = 161.6 ft

The fluid power = 62.4 × 6.68 × 161.6 = 67,360 $lb - \frac{ft}{sec}$ = 122.5 hp

Brake horsepower = 122.5/0.85 = 144 hp

Answer is D

Solution 23

The slope of the pipe is 0.01. Height difference between two ends of the pipe = 30 ft.

Therefore the length of the pipe = 30 ÷ 0.01 = 3000 ft
Hazen Williams C = 120

If flow velocity is V (ft/sec), head loss due to friction is given by

$$h_f = \frac{3.022 \times V^{1.85} \times 3000}{120^{1.85} \times 1^{1.165}} = 1.29 V^{1.85}$$

Bernoulli's equation applied between free surface at reservoir and free flow at the outfall:

$$145 + \frac{p_{atm}}{\gamma} + 0 - 1.29 V^{1.85} = 95 + \frac{p_{atm}}{\gamma} + \frac{V^2}{2g}$$

Solving approximately (trial and error): V = 7.15 ft/sec

Flow rate = 7.15 x π/4 x 1^2 = 5.62 cfs = 2516 gpm

Note that if it is recognized that the $V^2/2g$ term is much smaller than the $1.29V^{1.85}$ term, the solution of the equation is a lot simpler (though approximate)

$$50 \approx 1.29 V^{1.85} \Rightarrow V \approx 7.22 \; ft/sec$$

Answer is D

Solution 24

Area of ellipse: $A = \pi a b = \pi \times 0.7 \times 0.5 = 1.1 \; m^2$

Approximate perimeter: $P = 2\pi \sqrt{\frac{a^2 + b^2}{2}} = 2\pi \sqrt{\frac{0.7^2 + 0.5^2}{2}} = 3.82 \; m$

The hydraulic radius is defined as:

$$R_H = \frac{Flow\;area}{Wetted\;perimeter} = \frac{1.1}{3.82} = 0.288 \; m$$

The hydraulic diameter is defined as:

$$D_H = 4 R_H = 4 \times 0.288 = 1.15 \; m$$

Answer is D

Hydraulics & Hydrologic Systems Topics on FE Civil Examination

Solution 25

Time of concentration = time for sheet flow + time for channel flow = 200/0.5 + 400/2.0 = 600 sec = 10 min

Answer is B

Solution 26

Top width: T = 2 + 3x2x2 = 14 m

Area: $A = \frac{1}{2}(2 + 14) \times 2 = 16 \; m^2$

Wetted perimeter: $P = 2\sqrt{10} \times 2 = 12.65 \; m$

Hydraulic radius: $R_h = \frac{A}{P} = \frac{16}{12.65} = 1.265 \; m$

According to Manning's equation, velocity:

$$V = \frac{1}{n} R_h^{2/3} S^{1/2} = \frac{1}{0.02} \times 1.265^{2/3} \times 0.005^{1/2} = 4.14 \frac{m}{s}$$

Answer is C

Solution 27

The depth-to-diameter ratio d/D = 36/45 = 0.8
For this d/D, hydraulic radius ratio R/R_f = 1.22
For pipe flowing full, hydraulic radius $R_f = \pi R^2/2\pi R = R/2 = D/4$ = 11.25 cm.
Therefore, actual hydraulic radius = 1.22x11.25 = 13.73 cm = 0.137 m
For this d/D, the area ratio A/A_f = 0.86
Actual area = 0.86x πR^2 = 1688.6 cm^2 = 0.169 m^2
Hazen-Williams equation for velocity:

$$v = 0.849 C R_H^{0.63} S^{0.54} = 1.53 \frac{m}{s}$$

Flow rate: $Q = vA = 1.53 \times 0.169 = 0.259 \frac{m^3}{s}$

Answer is C

Solution 28

Weir head H = 124.7 − 120.5 = 4.2 m
Free discharge (for suppressed weir):

$$Q = CLH^{3/2} = 1.84 \times 3 \times 4.2^{3/2} = 47.5 \frac{m^3}{s}$$

Answer is D

Hydraulics & Hydrologic Systems Topics on FE Civil Examination

Solution 29

Flow rate, Q = 1.3 ft³/s

Transmissivity, T = 50,000 ft²/day = 0.579 ft²/s

At the edge of the well, r_1 = 4.5 in = 0.375 ft. Radial distance at point of interest, r_2 = 100 ft.

For a confined aquifer:

$$Q = \frac{2\pi T(h_2 - h_1)}{\ln(r_2/r_1)} \Rightarrow h_2 - h_1 = \frac{Q}{2\pi T} \ln(r_2/r_1) = \frac{1.3}{2\pi \times 0.579} \ln(100/0.375) = 2.0 \, ft$$

Height of piezometric surface at r_2 = 100 ft is h_2 = 55 + 2 = 57 ft

Answer is B

Solution 30

For a 90-degree V-notch weir (SI version): $Q = 1.40 H^{5/2} = 1.40 \times 0.45^{5/2} = 0.19 \frac{m^3}{s} = 190 \, L/s$

Answer is D

Solution 31

The composite curve number is given by: $\overline{CN} = \frac{\sum CN_i A_i}{\sum CN_i} = \frac{63 \times 120 + 89 \times 80 + 79 \times 110 + 55 \times 40}{120 + 80 + 110 + 40} = 73$

Maximum basin retention: $S = \frac{1000}{CN} - 10 = \frac{1000}{73} - 10 = 3.69$

Runoff depth: $Q = \frac{(P - 0.2S)^2}{P + 0.8S} = \frac{(3.6 - 0.2 \times 3.69)^2}{3.6 + 0.8 \times 3.69} = 1.25 \, in$

On the watershed area = 350 acres = 1.5246x10⁷ ft², runoff volume: $V = QA = \frac{1.25 \times 1.5246 \times 10^7}{12} = 1.59 \times 10^6 \, ft^3 = 58,820 \, yd^3$

Answer is B

Solution 32

Water elevation (above bottom of aquifer) at wells 1 & 2 are 74.5 ft and 69 ft respectively.

$$Q = \frac{\pi K(y_1^2 - y_2^2)}{\ln(r_1/r_2)} \Rightarrow K = \frac{Q \ln(r_1/r_2)}{\pi(y_1^2 - y_2^2)} = \frac{185 \times \ln(180/30)}{\pi(74.5^2 - 69^2)} = 0.816 \frac{ft}{hr} = 3.8 \times 10^{-5} \, ft/s$$

Answer is A

Hydraulics & Hydrologic Systems Topics on FE Civil Examination

Solution 33

Porosity of the soil: $n = \dfrac{e}{1+e} = \dfrac{0.4}{1.4} = 0.29$

Seepage velocity is given by: $v = \dfrac{K}{n}\dfrac{dh}{dx} = \dfrac{4\times 10^{-4}}{0.29} \times \dfrac{20}{35} = 7.9 \times 10^{-4}\,\dfrac{in}{s} = 2.84\ in/hr$

Answer is B

Solution 34

From the hydraulic elements graph in the handbook, for constant n, the Q/Q_f curve has a maximum value (1.08) for a depth ratio d/D = 0.92

Therefore, under gravity forces, this pipe will transmit maximum (8% more than when flowing full) flow rate when the depth of flow d = 0.92D = 44.2 inches

Answer is B

Solution 35

For a channel of arbitrary cross section, at critical depth, the following relationship must hold:

$$A^3 g = Q^2 T \Rightarrow \dfrac{Q^2 T}{A^3} = g$$

Thus, if evaluate the parameter Q^2T/A^3 for each flow condition, the one which is closest to the value of g is at critical depth.

For D = 2 ft, Q^2T/A^3 = 136.1
For D = 4 ft, Q^2T/A^3 = 187.7
For D = 6 ft, Q^2T/A^3 = 32.3
For D = 8 ft, Q^2T/A^3 = 40.2

Thus, critical flow occurs at depth = 6 ft

Answer is C

Hydraulics & Hydrologic Systems Topics on FE Civil Examination

Structural Analysis Topics on FE Civil Examination

Structural Analysis

Structural Analysis Topics on FE Civil Examination**6-9 problems**
Approximately 6% of exam

A. Analysis of forces in statically determinant beams, trusses, and frames
B. Deflection of statically determinant beams, trusses, and frames
C. Structural determinacy and stability analysis of beams, trusses, and frames
D. Loads and load paths (e.g., dead, live, lateral, influence lines and moving loads, tributary areas)
E. Elementary statically indeterminate structures

Problem 1
For the simple truss shown below, the force in member AH is most nearly

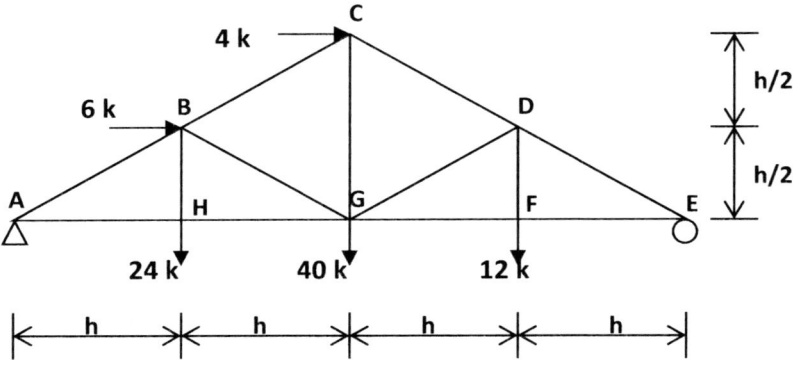

A) 89 kips (compression)
B) 89 kips (tension)
C) 79 kips (tension)
D) 79 kips (compression)

Problem 2
A plane truss is shown below. The total support reaction at A is most nearly:
  A) 24.5 kips
  B) 26.6 kips
  C) 29.3 kips
  D) 32.8 kips

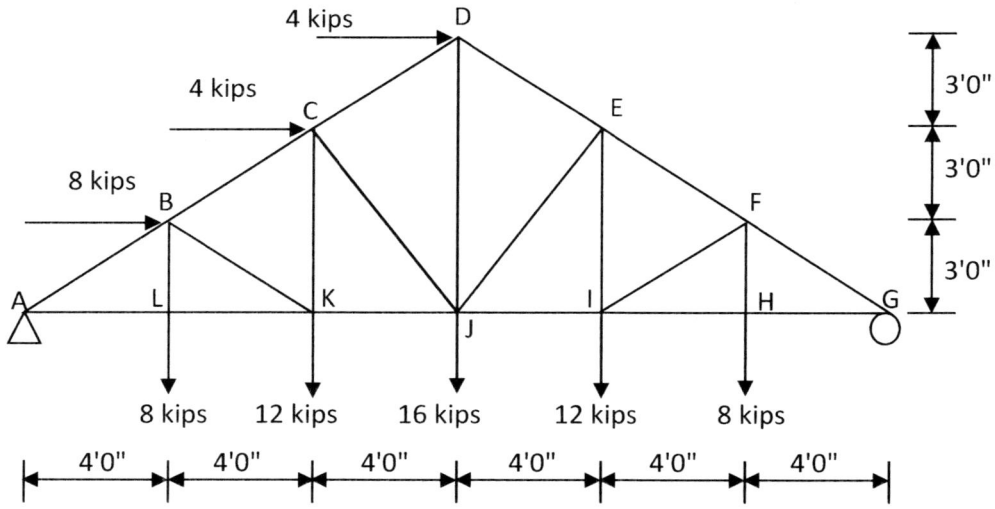

Problem 3

A truss is shown below. The axial force (kips) in the highlighted member (CJ) is most nearly:
- A) 31.2 kips (compression)
- B) 31.2 kips (tension)
- C) 17.6 kips (tension)
- D) 17.6 kips (compression)

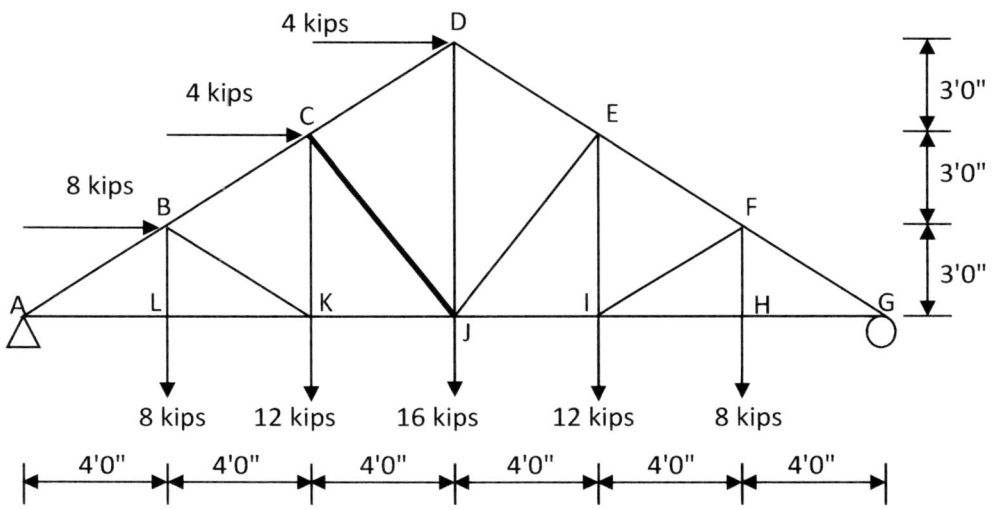

Problem 4

A system of regularly spaced rectangular timber beams supports a floor as shown. Assume modulus of elasticity of the timber = 1.5×10^6 psi. Beams are 2 inch x 10 inch (1.5"x9.25" dressed size) Beams have a simple span = 18 ft.

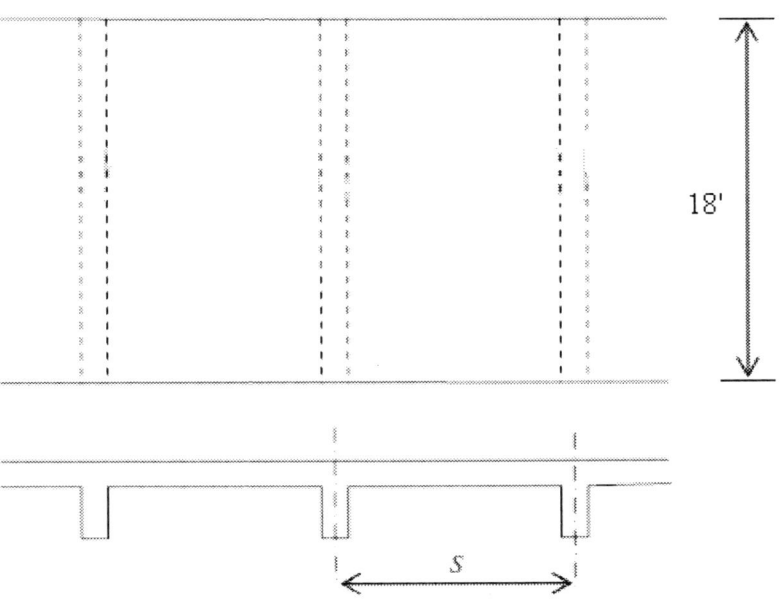

The floor load is 55 psf. If the maximum deflection of the beams is L/240, the allowable spacing between beams is most nearly:
- A. 2.5 feet
- B. 2.0 feet
- C. 1.5 feet
- D. 1.0 feet

Problem 5

An elevated water tank is supported by 4 tower legs as shown. The empty tank weighs 6 kips and the full tank weighs 300 kips. The resultant wind force of 120 kips acts at a height of 65 ft as shown. Each tower leg is supported by an isolated square footing. The maximum design uplift force (kips) for designing anchor bolts for each footing is most nearly:
- A. 128.5
- B. 130.0
- C. 231.5
- D. 245.0

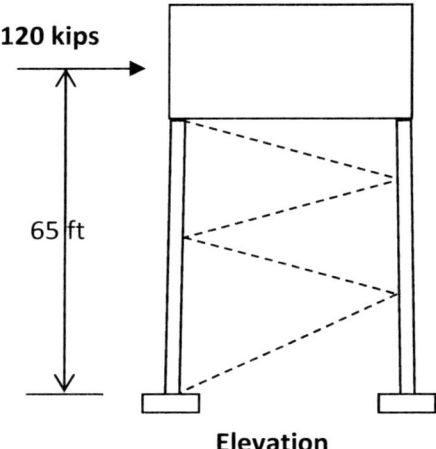

Elevation

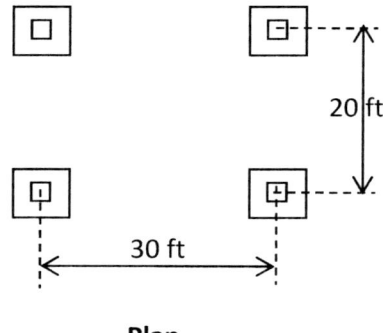

Plan

Structural Analysis Topics on FE Civil Examination

Problem 6

A temporary warning sign is constructed at a worksite by using a 14 in diameter bucket filled with ballast so as to serve as a counterweight (see figure). If the maximum (3 second gust) wind pressure is 55 psf (ignore the wind pressure on the bucket), the minimum required weight (lbs) of the counterweight is most nearly:

    A. 435
    B. 565
    C. 612
    D. 659

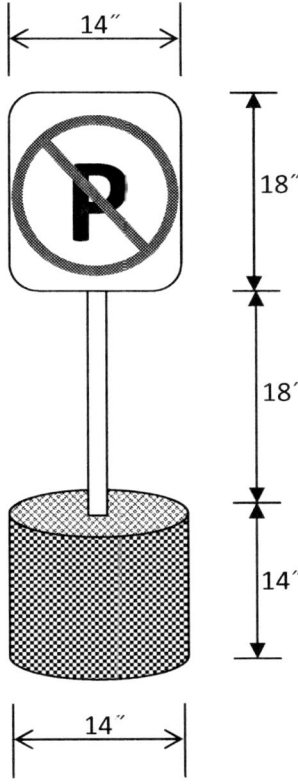

Problem 7

A steel angle is anchored to a wall as shown. Longitudinal spacing between anchor bolts is 18 inches. The heel of the angle is continuously supported by timber blocking (height = 1 inch, thickness = 0.5 inch). The angle supports a wall panel centered at a horizontal distance of 4 inches from the heel of the angle. The shear in anchor bolts (lbs) is most nearly:

    A. 56 lb
    B. 90 lb
    C. 135 lb
    D. 255 lb

Structural Analysis Topics on FE Civil Examination

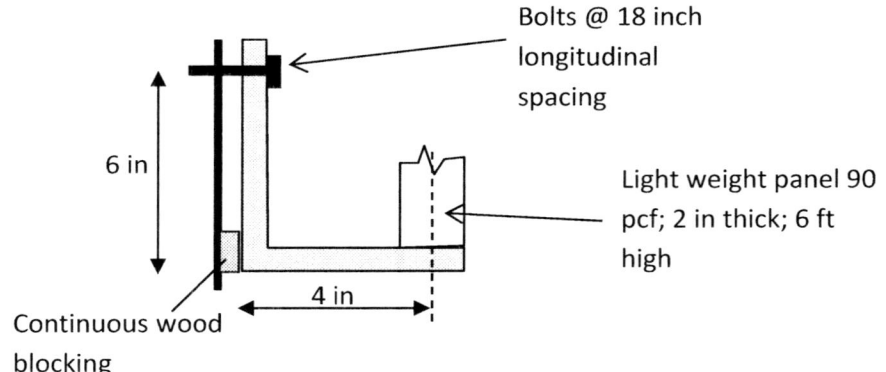

Problem 8
A steel beam supports a 6 inch lightweight concrete masonry wall (unit weight = 85 lb/ft³). The wall is 10 ft high and 12 ft long. The load on the beam (lb/ft) is most nearly:
- A) 850 lb/ft
- B) 425 lb/ft
- C) 5100 lb/ft
- D) 510 lb/ft

Problem 9
A crate weighing 900 lb is being lifted by 4 cables attached to the corners as shown. The attachment point for the cables (O) is 8 ft directly above the center of gravity of the load. The tension in each cable is most nearly:
- A. 225 lb
- B. 270 lb
- C. 312 lb
- D. 348 lb

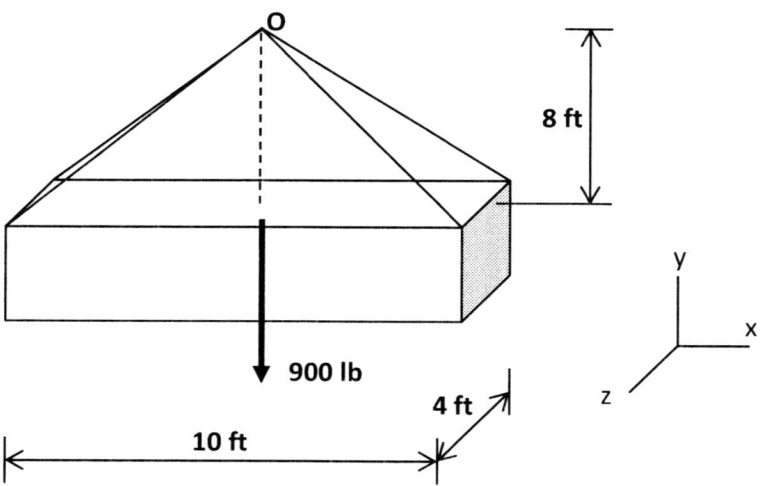

Problem 10

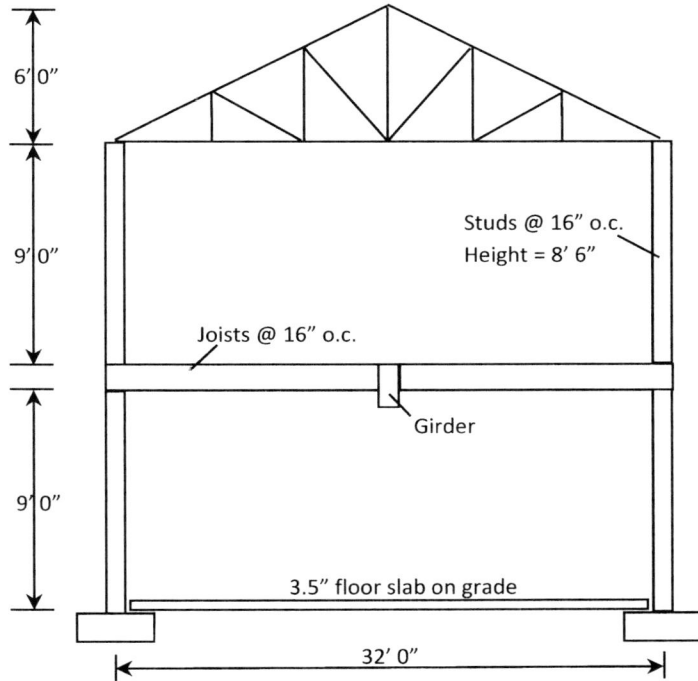

The following service loads apply to the timber framed bearing wall building shown in transverse section:
    Floor DL = 8 psf
    Roof DL = 10 psf (on horizontal projection)
    Floor LL = 40 psf
    Roof LL = 20 psf (on horizontal projection)
    Wall DL = 7 psf
    Wind pressure on stud walls = 25 psf

The service gravity load applied to each wall footing (lb/ft), is most nearly:
    (A) 764
    (B) 934
    (C) 1000
    (D) 1400

Problem 11

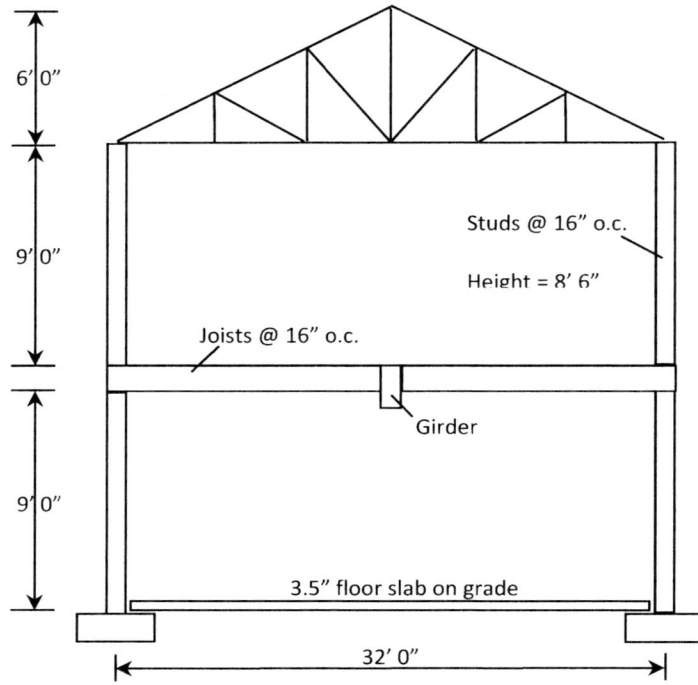

The following service loads apply to the timber framed bearing wall building shown in transverse section:
   Floor DL = 8 psf
   Roof DL = 10 psf (on horizontal projection)
   Floor LL = 40 psf
   Roof LL = 20 psf (on horizontal projection)
   Wall DL = 7 psf
   Wind pressure on stud walls = 25 psf

The service wind load moment which must be resisted by each wall stud is most nearly:
   (A) 225 lb-ft
   (B) 300 lb-ft
   (C) 900 lb-ft
   (D) 1200 lb-ft

Problem 12

A two-member truss is loaded with a vertical load of 20 kips at node B as shown. The cross-sections of the members AB and BC are: 2 in² for AB, 3 in² for BC. Modulus of elasticity E = 29000 ksi for both members. What is the vertical deflection at B?

- A. 0.1 in
- B. 0.15 in
- C. 0.2 in
- D. 0.25 in

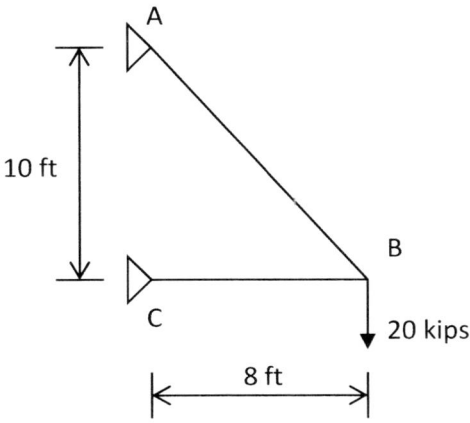

Problem 13

For the cable system shown, find the tension in cables AB and BC.

- A. T_{AB} = 12.8 k; T_{BC} = 18.8 k
- B. T_{AB} = 15.8 k; T_{BC} = 21.2 k
- C. T_{AB} = 21.2 k; T_{BC} = 16.8 k
- D. T_{AB} = 15.8 k; T_{BC} = 24.8 k

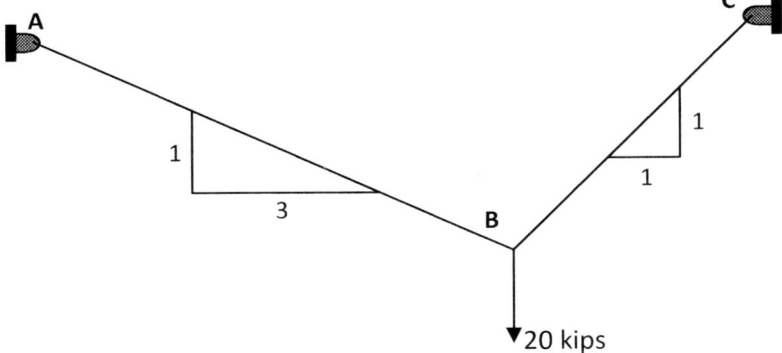

Structural Analysis Topics on FE Civil Examination

Problem 14

Computer analysis of a beam ABC shown below results in the following joint moments:

M_{AB} = 0.552 k-ft (counterclockwise)

M_{BA} = 5.645 k-ft (clockwise)

M_{BC} = 5.645 k-ft (counterclockwise)

M_{CB} = 0

The vertical reaction at B is most nearly:
- A. 3.67 kips
- B. 6.20 kips
- C. 8.12 kips
- D. 9.86 kips

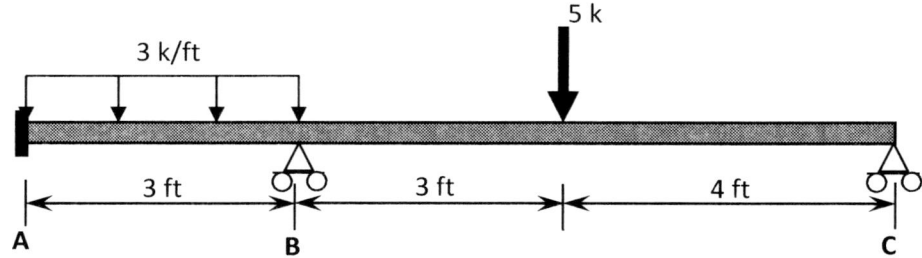

Problem 15

What is the vertical reaction at A for the beam shown below?
- A. 37 kips
- B. 39 kips
- C. 41 kips
- D. 43 kips

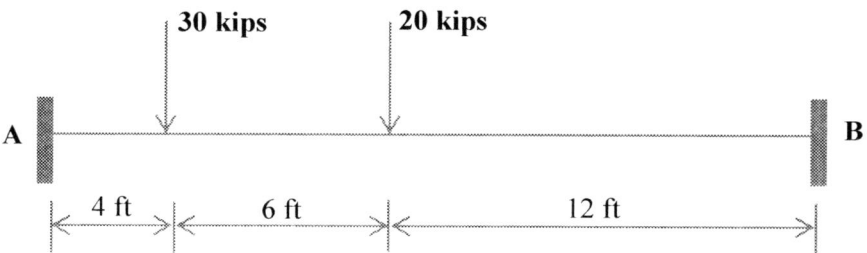

Problem 16
A 3-axle truck has the axle loads as shown below. What is the maximum bending moment produced by this truck as it travels across a 120 ft span simple span bridge?
    A. 1460 k-ft
    B. 1575 k-ft
    C. 1720 k-ft
    D. 1800 k-ft

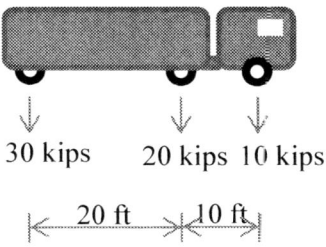

Problem 17
A truss carries a vertical 50 kN load at midspan as shown. The member forces (tension positive) have been calculated and are shown. All members are made of steel and have the following properties:
    Area = 3000 mm^2
    Moment of Inertia = 3×10^6 mm^4
What is the vertical deflection at the point of loading?
    A. 5.7 mm
    B. 8.3 mm
    C. 11.1 mm
    D. 15.8 mm

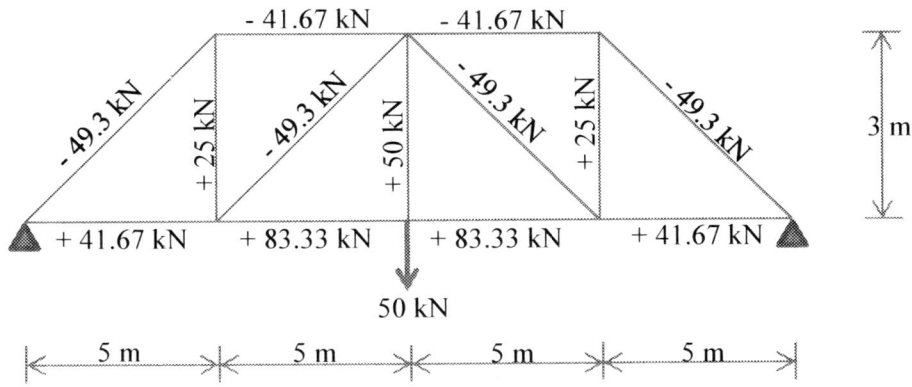

Structural Analysis Topics on FE Civil Examination

Problem 18

For the beam shown, identify the qualitative shapes of the shear force and bending moment diagrams

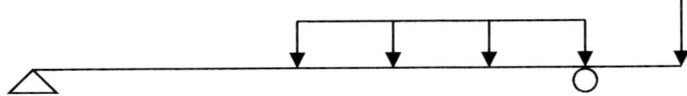

Problem 19

Draw the shear and bending moment diagrams for the beam shown below. The beam has an internal hinge at 6 ft from the left support.

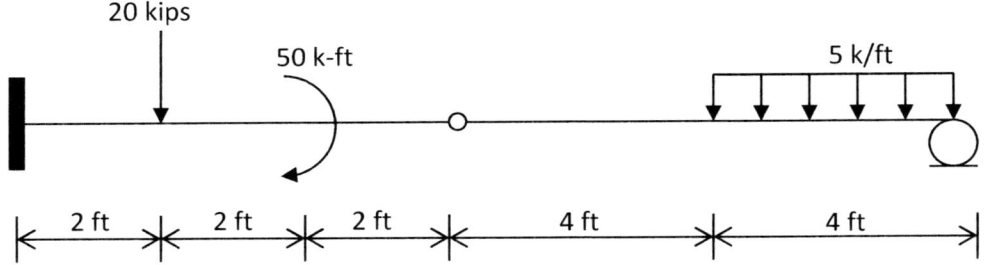

Problem 20

For the beam shown, identify the qualitative shapes of the shear force and bending moment diagrams

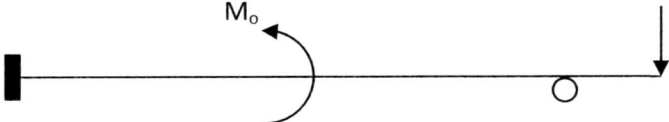

Problem 21

The beam shown below is a propped cantilever with an internal hinge at B. The loads are:
   Uniformly distributed dead load = 2 kips/ft
   Uniformly distributed live load = 1.4 kips/ft
   Single concentrated live load = 10 kips.

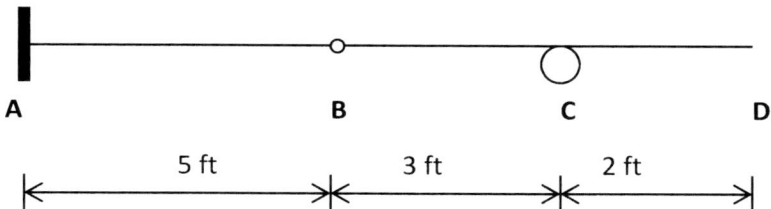

The maximum vertical reaction at A is most nearly:
   A. 21.8 kips
   B. 28.6 kips
   C. 30.8 kips
   D. 32.0 kips

Problem 22

A prismatic beam is fixed at one end and supported by a hinge at the other end, as shown below. What happens to the bending stiffness of the beam is the span is doubled and the moment of inertia is tripled?
   A. Bending stiffness increases by a factor of 6.0
   B. Bending stiffness increases by a factor of 1.5
   C. Bending stiffness decreases by a factor of 3.0
   D. Bending stiffness decreases by a factor of 1.5

Problem 23

A two dimensional frame has 8 joints, of which 5 are rigid and 3 are moment-free. The frame has 8 members and is supported by two fixed supports. Which of the following statements is true?
   A. The frame is stable and statically determinate
   B. The frame is stable and statically indeterminate to the second degree
   C. The frame is stable and statically indeterminate to the third degree
   D. The frame is unstable

Structural Analysis Topics on FE Civil Examination

Problem 24

The nominal live load for a four-story commercial building is 80 psf. The vertical load resisting system consists of flat plate floor slabs supported by a grid of columns spaced 25 ft in one plan direction and 20 ft in the other plan direction. What is the service live load for a first floor interior column, reduced according to ASCE-7 guidelines? Ignore roof live loads.

    A. 48.0 kips
    B. 53.3 kips
    C. 60.0 kips
    D. 120 kips

Problem 25

Which of the following statements are true?

1. Trusses consist of members that are assumed to be pinned together at their ends.
2. Truss members generally develop axial loads.
3. Truss members are rigidly connected at the joints.
4. The force system in a 2D truss is typically concurrent and coplanar.
5. Frame members develop bending moments, but not shear and axial forces.
6. A frame is generally a rigid structure.
7. Moments cannot be transmitted from one member to another in a frame.

    A. 1, 2, 5 and 6
    B. 1, 3, 6 and 7
    C. 1, 2 and 6
    D. 1, 2 and 7

Problem 26

Calculate the maximum possible uplift due to live load at support A for the beam shown below. The live load is uniformly distributed w = 4 kips/ft. Partial live load placement is permitted. Internal hinges exist at B and D.

    A. 7 kips
    B. 12 kips
    C. 14 kips
    D. 22 kips

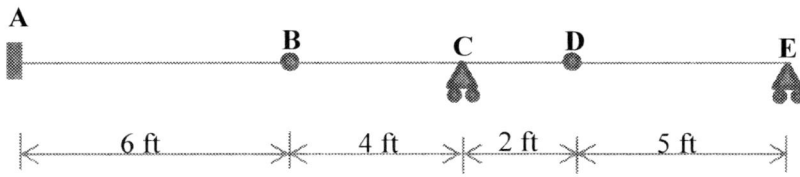

Problem 27

For the cantilever beam shown below, the distributed load varies linearly. What is the maximum deflection for the beam? The modulus of elasticity of the beam is 29×10^6 lb/in^2 and the moment of inertia is 1200 in^4.

A. 0.25 in
B. 0.55 in
C. 0.75 in
D. 1.15 in

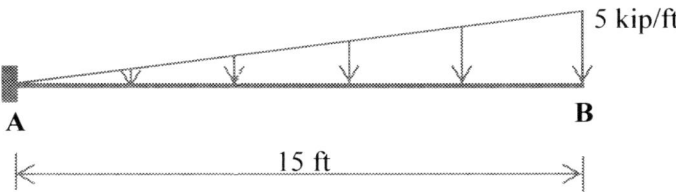

Problem 28

A 3-axle truck has the axle loads as shown below. What is the maximum shear force produced by this truck as it travels across a 120 ft span simple span bridge?
A. 46.50 k
B. 49.33 k
C. 53.17 k
D. 58.22 k

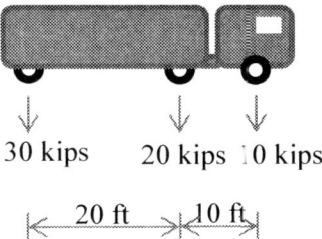

Structural Analysis Solutions

Structural Analysis Topics on FE Civil Examination

Solution 1

The vertical reaction at the roller E can be calculated by taking moments about A (since E_y produces a *counterlockwise* moment about A, we find the *net clockwise moment about A* and divide it by the moment arm (distance between G and A_y)

$$E_y = \frac{6\frac{h}{2} + 4h + 24h + 40 \times 2h + 12 \times 3h}{4h} = 36.75\ k$$

Reactions: A_x = -10 kips, A_y = 39.25 kips

Method of joints at A yields: F_{AH} = 89.5 kips (tension)

Note: For a node such as A, where 3 forces intersect, the polygon of forces is a triangle. Therefore, the force triangle will be similar to the geometric triangle. The free body diagram at node A is shown below.

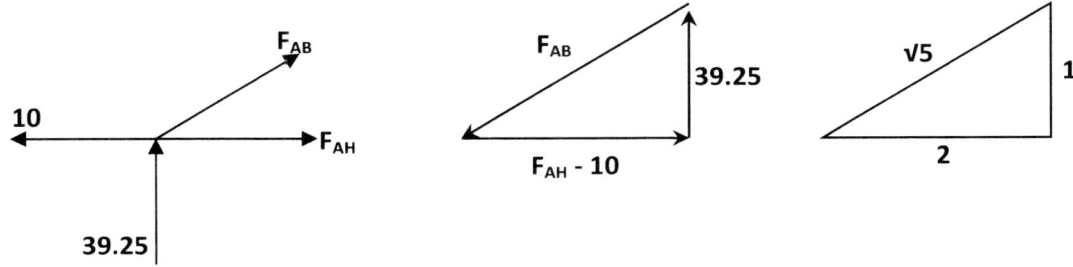

This leads to the following similarity relations:

$$\frac{F_{AH} - 10}{2} = \frac{39.25}{1} = \frac{F_{AB}}{\sqrt{5}}$$

leading to F_{AH} = 89.5 (tension)

Answer is B

Solution 2

The vertical reaction at A can be calculated by taking moments about G (since A_y produces a *clockwise* moment about G, we find the *net counterclockwise moment about G* and divide it by the moment arm (distance between G and A_y)

$$A_y = \frac{-8 \times 3 - 4 \times 6 - 4 \times 9 + 8 \times 4 + 12 \times 8 + 16 \times 12 + 12 \times 16 + 8 \times 20}{24} = 24.5\ k$$

> A short cut, using the lever rule, may be described as: The vertical load is symmetric; therefore, it will create equal (upward) reactions at both supports = 56/2 = 28 kips. The clockwise overturning moment (8x3+4x6+4x9=84 kip-ft) will be resisted by a couple (downward reaction at A and upward reaction at G) made up of equal and opposite forces = 84÷24 = 3.5 kips. Therefore the vertical reaction at A = 28 − 3.5 = 24.5 kips.

Structural Analysis Topics on FE Civil Examination

The horizontal reaction at A = total horizontal force on truss = 16 kips

Therefore, total reaction at hinge A: $R_A = \sqrt{A_x^2 + A_y^2} = \sqrt{16^2 + 24.5^2} = 29.3 \; kips$

Answer is C

Solution 3

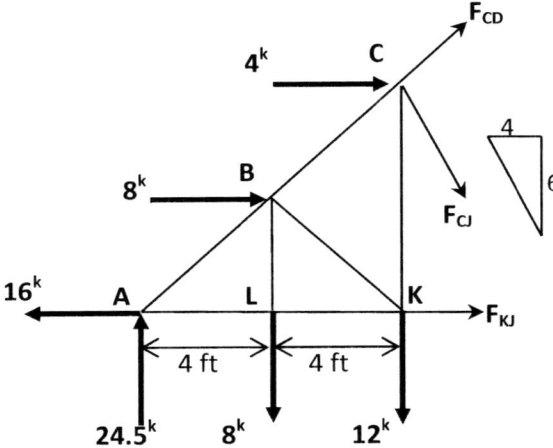

Taking moments about A (so that the intersecting forces F_{CD} and F_{KJ} are not involved):

$$\frac{4}{\sqrt{52}} F_{CJ} \times 6 + \frac{6}{\sqrt{52}} F_{CJ} \times 8 + 8 \times 3 + 4 \times 6 + 8 \times 4 + 12 \times 8 = 0 \Rightarrow F_{CJ} = -17.63 \; kips$$

Note that if the end-game (of taking moments about A) is seen ahead of time, then it is obvious that the vertical reaction at A will not be necessary and therefore one can avoid that calculation.

Answer is D

Solution 4
For a simply supported beam with uniformly distributed load, the maximum (elastic) deflection is given by

$$\Delta_{max} = \frac{5wL^4}{384EI}$$

Therefore,

$$\Delta_{max} = \frac{5wL^4}{384EI} \leq \frac{L}{240} \Rightarrow w \leq \frac{384EI}{1200L^3}$$

Moment of inertia of the dressed timber beam:

Structural Analysis Topics on FE Civil Examination

$$I = \frac{1}{12}bh^3 = \frac{1.5 \times 9.25^3}{12} = 98.93 \, in^4$$

$$w \leq \frac{384EI}{1200L^3} = \frac{384 \times 1.5 \times 10^6 \times 98.93}{1200 \times 216^3} = 4.71 \frac{lb}{in} = 56.54 \frac{lb}{ft}$$

Maximum spacing S = 56.54 plf ÷ 55 psf = 1.03 ft. **Use joists at 12 in spacing.**

Answer is D

Solution 5
Since gravity forces counteract uplift, we must consider the empty tank case here. The weight of 6 kips is carried equally by each leg. Therefore, the compression at each footing = 1.5 kips.

The lateral force creates an overturning moment = 120k x 65 ft = 7800 k-ft on the horizontal plane at the top of the footings. This overturning moment is shared equally by two couples (4 legs in two pairs). Therefore, each resisting couple = 3900 k-ft.

Since the lever arm on each couple is 30 ft, the force at each footing = 3900 ÷ 30 = 130 kips. This is an added compression under the legs on the far side (right) of the tower and an uplift under the legs on the near side (left).

Therefore, the near side legs experience a 'net' uplift of 130 – 1.5 = 128.5 kips

Answer is A

Solution 6
The solution will assume that the critical condition is overturning due to wind gusts.

Resultant wind force on the sign = 14 x 18 x 55 / 144 = 96.25 lb

Overturning moment about the tipping heel = 96.25 x 41 = 3946.3 lb-in

Stabilizing moment = W$_{bucket}$ x 7 in = 3946.3. Therefore W$_{bucket}$ = 563.8 lb.

Answer is B

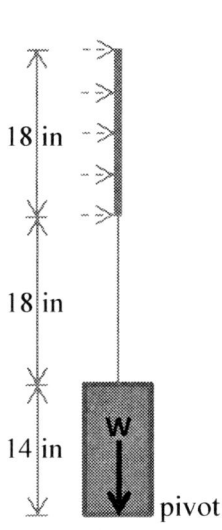

277

Structural Analysis Topics on FE Civil Examination

Solution 7
Considering a 18 in long strip of the angle (load incident on ONE bolt), the weight of the wall panel = 90 x 2/12 x 6 x 18/12 = 135 lb

Shear in anchor bolts is represented by A_y = 135 lb

Answer is C

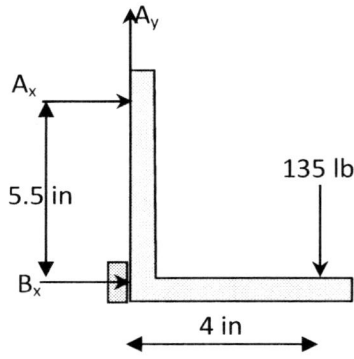

Solution 8
The load on the beam = 85 x 6/12 x 10 = 425 lb/ft

Answer is B

Solution 9
Even though the problem is 3-dimensional, we can take advantage of the symmetry in the problem. All cables carry equal load. The length of each cable is given by:

$$L = \sqrt{5^2 + 8^2 + 2^2} = 9.64 \; ft$$

The vertical component of each cable tension can therefore be written:
$$T_y = T\frac{8}{9.64} = 0.83T$$

Therefore, the equation of vertical equilibrium is:
$$4T_y - 900 = 0 \Rightarrow 4 \times 0.83T = 900 \Rightarrow T = 271 \; lb$$

Answer is B

Solution 10

The roof load is incident on 32 ft (horizontal projection). Each wall carries half of that (16 ft tributary width).
Total load from roof x 16 ft = 30x16 = 480 lb/ft

The floor load is incident on 32 ft (horizontal projection). Each 16 foot wide half is carried equally by the girder and one wall. Therefore, the girder receives load from 16 ft wide strip and each wall receives load from an 8 ft floor width.
Total load from floor x 8 ft = 48x8 = 384 lb/ft
Self weight of wall = 7 x 18 = 126 lb/ft
Total load to footing = 990 lb/ft

Answer is C

Solution 11
Wall stud spacing = 16 in
Uniform load on wall stud = 16/12 x 25 = 33.33 lb/ft
Wind load moment = $wL^2/8$ = 33.33x8.5²/8 = 301 ft-lb

Answer is B

Solution 12
Solve for truss member forces using equilibrium of joint B
F_{AB} = + 25.6 k (T)
F_{BC} = − 16.0 k (C)

Create the Virtual Load (consistent with desired deflection)

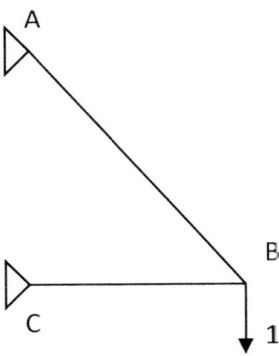

Calculate the member forces due to virtual load (NOTE: in this case, the real load and the virtual load look similar, so we can use scaling)
f_{AB} = + 1.28 (T)
f_{BC} = − 0.80 (C)

$$\Delta = \sum \frac{FfL}{AE} = \frac{25.6 \times 1.28 \times (12.81 \times 12)}{2 \times 29000} + \frac{-16 \times -0.8 \times (8 \times 12)}{3 \times 29000} = 0.1 \ in$$

NOTE: The positive sign of the answer indicates that this deflection is in the same sense as the assumed unit load (downward)

Answer is A

Solution 13

The free body diagram of joint B is shown below. Since this FBD has two unknowns, the two equations of equilibrium may be used to solve for them.

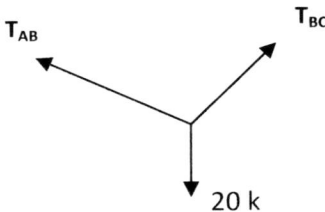

$$\sum F_x = -T_{AB}\frac{3}{\sqrt{10}} + T_{BC}\frac{1}{\sqrt{2}} = 0 \Rightarrow T_{AB} = 0.745 T_{BC}$$

$$\sum F_y = T_{AB}\frac{1}{\sqrt{10}} + T_{BC}\frac{1}{\sqrt{2}} = 20 \Rightarrow \left(0.745\frac{1}{\sqrt{10}} + \frac{1}{\sqrt{2}}\right)T_{BC} = 20 \Rightarrow T_{BC} = 21.21\ k;\ T_{AB} = 15.81\ k$$

Answer is B

Solution 14

Knowledge of the nodal moments M_{AB}, M_{BA}, M_{BC} etc. allows the 'decoupling' of the individual spans, as shown below.

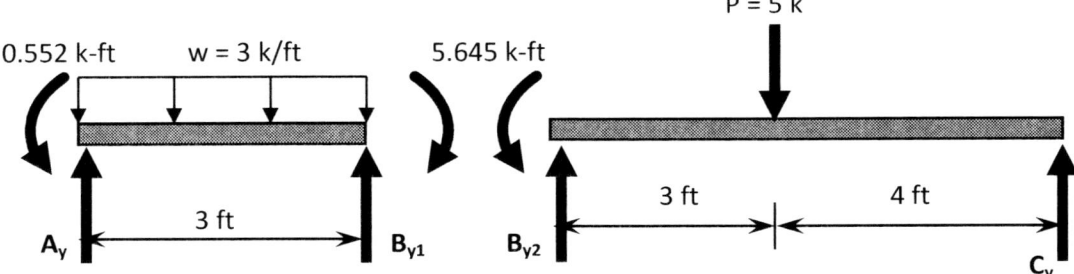

For the left substructure, the following are the two equilibrium equations:

$$\sum F_y = A_y - 9 + B_{y1} = 0$$

$$\sum M_A = 0.552 - 9 \times 1.5 - 5.645 + 3B_{y1} = 0 \Rightarrow B_{y1} = 6.198\ k$$

For the right substructure, the following are the two equilibrium equations:

Structural Analysis Topics on FE Civil Examination

$$\sum F_y = B_{y2} - 5 + C_y = 0$$

$$\sum M_C = 5.645 + 5 \times 4 - 7B_{y2} = 0 \Rightarrow B_{y2} = 3.664\ k$$

Therefore, the total vertical reaction at B is $B_y = B_{y1} + B_{y2} = 6.198 + 3.664 = 9.862$ kips

Answer is D

Solution 15

The total fixed end moment at end A is given by: $FEM_{AB} = \frac{30 \times 4 \times 18^2}{22^2} + \frac{20 \times 10 \times 12^2}{22^2} = 139.8\ kft$

The total fixed end moment at end B is given by: $FEM_{BA} = \frac{30 \times 18 \times 4^2}{22^2} + \frac{20 \times 12 \times 10^2}{22^2} = 67.4\ kft$

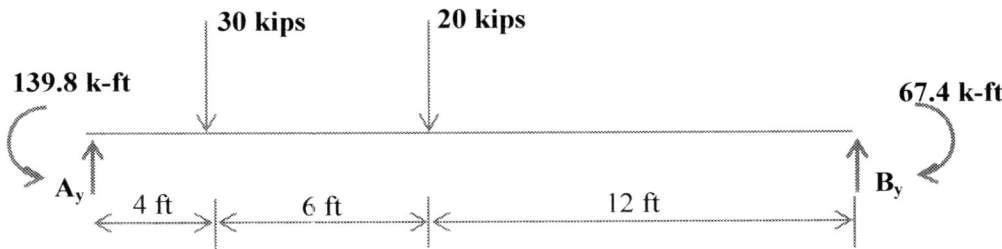

Taking moments about B: $M_B = 0 \Rightarrow 67.4 - 20 \times 12 - 30 \times 18 - 139.8 + 22A_y = 0$

Vertical reaction at A: $A_y = 38.75$ kips

Answer is B

Solution 16

The centroid of the wheel group is located at a distance x (from the rear axle) given by:

$$\bar{x} = \frac{20 \times 20 + 10 \times 30}{60} = 11.67\ ft$$

Positioning the vehicle such that the distance between wheel 2 and this resultant (8.33 ft) is bisected by the midpoint (x = 60) of the beam, wheel 2 is located at x = 64.17 ft, wheel 3 at x = 44.17 ft and wheel 1 at x = 74.17 ft. This is shown below.

Structural Analysis Topics on FE Civil Examination

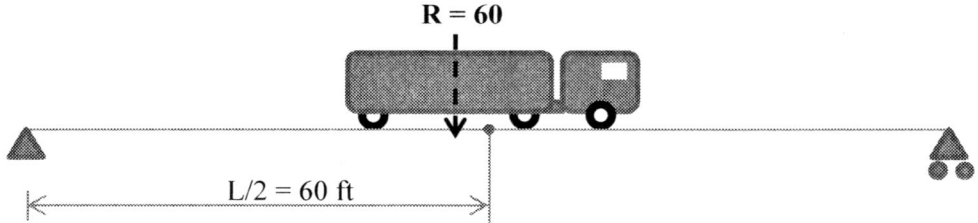

For this load placement, the reaction at left support is calculated as:

$$R_1 = \frac{30 \times 75.83}{120} + \frac{20 \times 55.83}{120} + \frac{10 \times 45.83}{120} = 32.08 \; kips$$

The shear diagram is shown below:

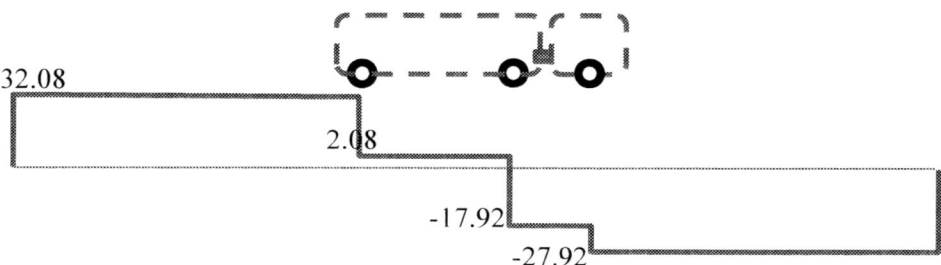

For this load placement, the maximum bending moment (under wheel 2) is calculated as:

$$M_{max} = 32.08 \times 44.17 + 2.08 \times 20 = 1458.6 \; kip-ft$$

Answer is A

Solution 17
According to the method of virtual work, the deflection at a point of truss is given by:

$\Delta = \sum \frac{FfL}{AE}$

Since all the members have the same cross sectional area (A) and modulus of elasticity (E), this can be simplified to:

$\Delta = \frac{\sum FfL}{AE}$

Since the question asks for vertical deflection at the load point, the unit lpad case a vertical load of 1 at the same point as the 50 KN load. Therefore, the forced (f) produced by the unit load can be obtained by scaling.

Structural Analysis Topics on FE Civil Examination

There are six 5 m long (horizontal) members, three 3 m long (vertical) members and four 5.83 m long (diagonal) members.

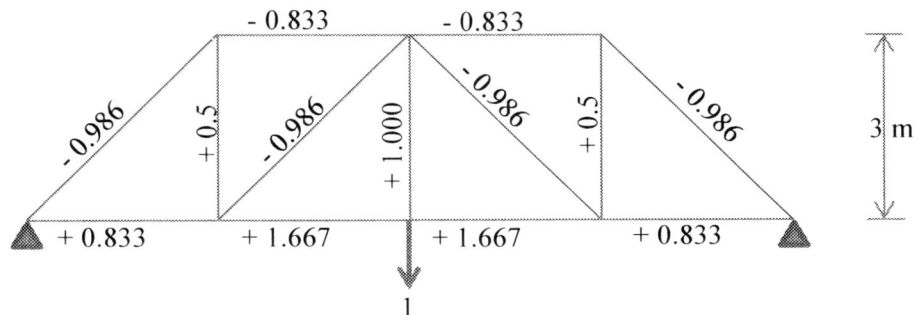

$$\Delta = \frac{\sum FfL}{AE} =$$
$$\frac{(-41.67 \times -0.833 \times 2 + 41.67 \times 0.833 \times 2 + 83.3 \times 1.667 \times 2) \times 5 + (25 \times 0.5 \times 2 + 50 \times 1) \times 3 + -49.3 \times -0.986 \times 4 \times 5.83}{AE} =$$
$$\frac{3442}{AE}$$

$A = 3000 \text{ mm}^2 = 3 \times 10^{-6} \text{ m}^4$
$E = 200 \text{ GPa} = 2 \times 10^{-1} \text{ N/m}^2$
$AE = 6 \times 10^5 \text{ Nm}^2$

Deflection: $\Delta = \frac{3442}{AE} = 0.0057 \, m = 5.7 \, mm$

Answer is A

Solution 18

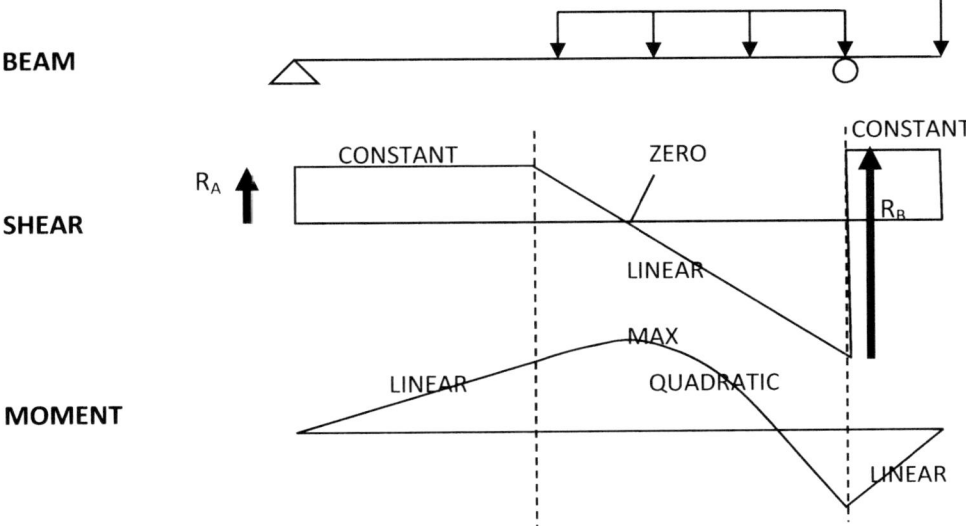

Solution 19

Structural Analysis Topics on FE Civil Examination

It is convenient to separate the structure at the hinge B and start solving from the simple span BC (both ends moment-free)

Reactions: By lever rule: $C_y = ¾ \times 20 = 15$ kips   & $B_y = ¼ \times 20 = 5$ kips
$A_y = 20 + 5 = 25$ kips
$M_A = 20 \times 2 + 50 + 5 \times 6 = 120$ kip-ft counterclockwise

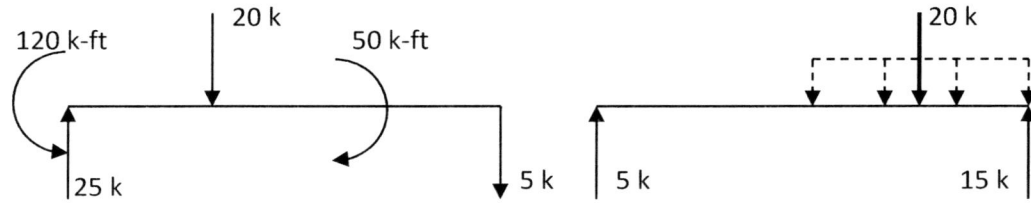

Shear Force diagram

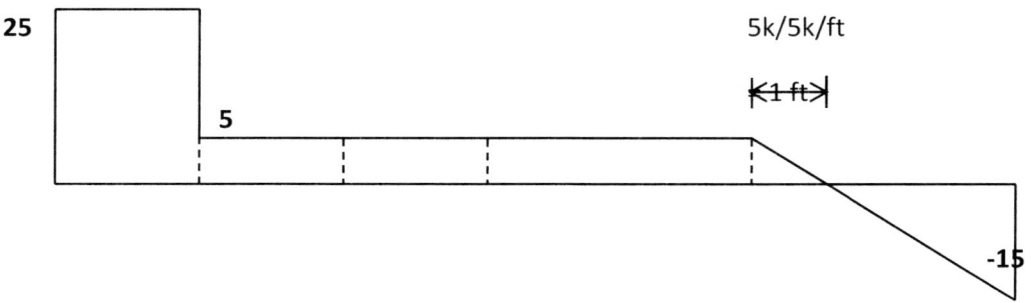

Bending Moment diagram

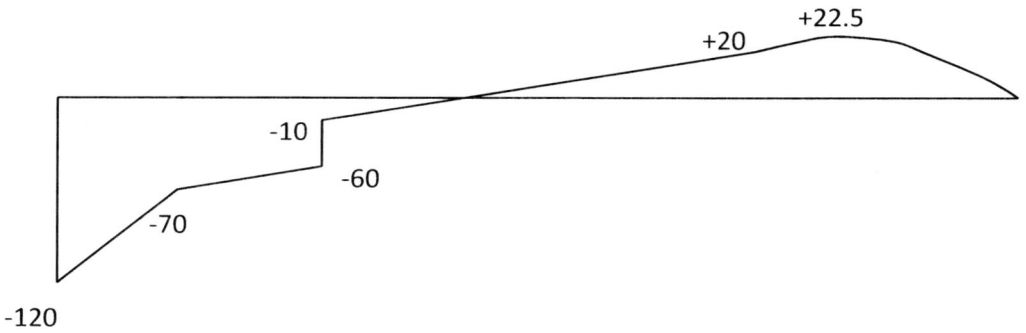

Solution 20

Structural Analysis Topics on FE Civil Examination

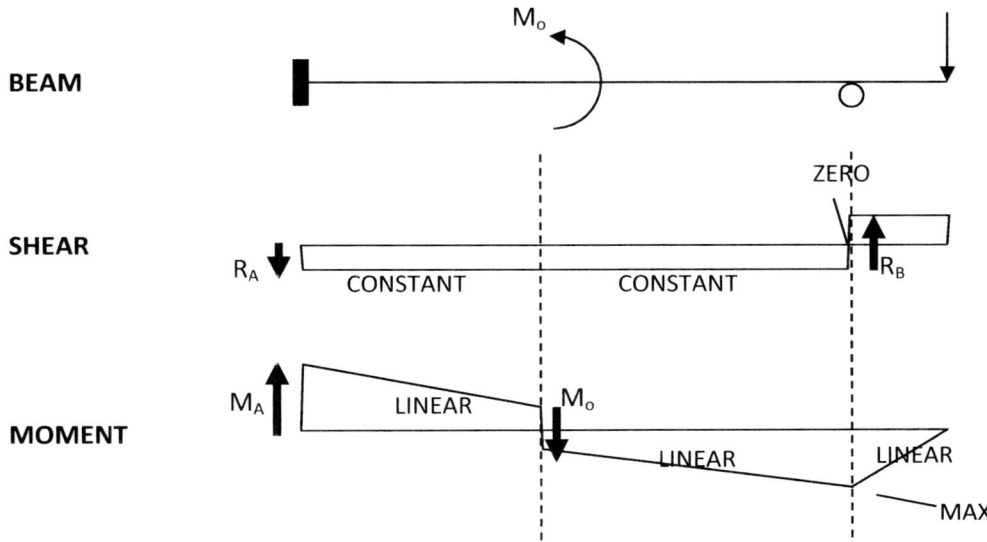

Solution 21
By the Müller-Breslau principle, first remove the vertical constraint while maintaining the other two constraints, and then apply a unit upward deflection to the beam at A (not be accompanied by any horizontal translation or rotation of the beam at A). The resulting deflected shape is given by the broken line in the figure below.

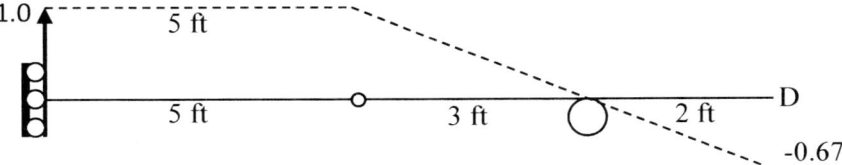

Thus, the *shape* of the influence line diagram for vertical reaction at A is as shown above. When the unit load is directly above the support A, the vertical reaction at A is equal to 1.0, the scaling factor for the above diagram is 1.0/1.0 = 1.0. By similar triangles, the value at D = − 0.67

Placing the dead load over the entire beam (no choice), live load over AC (to maximize positive contribution) and the point load anywhere along AB, the total vertical reaction A_y is:

$$A_y = 2 \times \left(1 \times \frac{5+8}{2} - \frac{1}{2} \times 2 \times 0.67\right) + 1.4 \times \left(1 \times \frac{5+8}{2}\right) + 10 \times 1 = 30.77 \; kips$$

Solution 22
Bending stiffness of the original beam is 4EI/L
Bending stiffness of the new beam is 4E(3I)/(2L) = 6EI/L

This means that the bending stiffness increases by a factor of 6/4 = 1.5

Structural Analysis Topics on FE Civil Examination

Answer is B

Solution 23

Number of members, m = 8
Number of reactions, r = 6 (in 2D, each fixed support has three reactions)
Number of joints, j = 8
Number of conditions equations (internal hinges), c = 3

3m+r = 30 represents the number of unknowns inherent in the structure
3j + c = 27 represents the number of equilibrium equations available

Structure is statically indeterminate to the third degree (30 – 27 = 3)

Answer is C

Solution 24

For a first floor column, load accumulates from 3 stories (2nd – 4th floors). The total area tributary to an interior column on this level = 3 x 25 x 20 = 1500 ft²

According to ASCE-7 guidelines, the nominal live load can be reduced to:

$$L_{reduced} = L_{nominal}\left(0.25 + \frac{15}{\sqrt{K_{LL}A_T}}\right) = 80\left(0.25 + \frac{15}{\sqrt{4 \times 1500}}\right) = 35.5\ psf$$

This reduced live load is subject to a lower limit of $0.4L_{nominal}$ = 32 psf

Therefore, the service live load used for the design of this column should be 35.5 psf

Total design load for the column = 35.5x1500 = 53,250 lb = 53.3 kips

Answer is B

Solution 25

Statements 3, 4, 5 and 7 are false as explained below:

3 is false because joints in an ideal truss are assumed to be pinned (moment-released) joints.

4 is false because the forces on a 2D truss are coplanar, but not necessarily concurrent (passing through a common point)

5 is false because frame members in general develop all three internal loads – axial force, shear force amd bending moment

Structural Analysis Topics on FE Civil Examination

7 is false because frame members are generally rigidly connected to each other and therefore, moments ARE stransmitted frommone member to the next.

Answer is C

Solution 26

Using the principle of Muller-Breslau (release vertical constraint at A, apply unit displacement, draw displaced shape), the influence diagram for vertical reaction at A (A_y) is

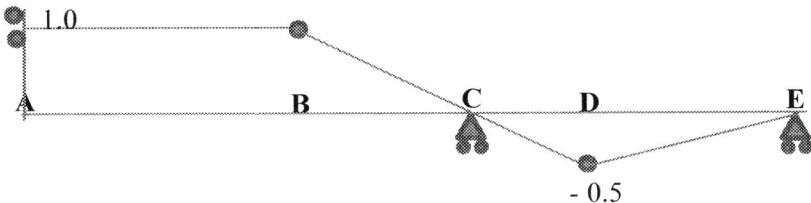

Therefore, to maximize uplift (negative reaction) at A, one must place the live load over CDE (where the influence diagram is negative). The resulting A_y is:

$$A_y = 4 \times \frac{1}{2} \times -0.5 \times 7 = -7 \; kips$$

Solution 27

This load case is not one of the standard cases in the Mechanics of materials section of the FE Handbook (pages 81-82). It must be derived from first principles. Since the load is defined using a single function, the method of successive integrations is not too bad.

The load function is: $w(x) = \frac{x}{3}$

Integrating this: $V(x) = -\int w(x)dx = -\frac{x^2}{6} + c_1$

At x = 0, the shear force is equal to the vertical reaction at A, A_y = 37.5 kips. Therefore constant c_1 = 37.5 k

$$V(x) = -\frac{x^2}{6} + 37.5$$

Integrating this: $M(x) = \int V(x)dx = -\frac{x^3}{18} + 37.5x + c_2$

At x = 0, the bending moment = reaction moment at A, M_A = - 375 kips. Therefore constant c_2 = - 375 k.ft

$$M(x) = -\frac{x^3}{18} + 37.5x - 375$$

Moment-curvature relationship: $y'' = \frac{M}{EI} = \frac{-\frac{x^3}{18}+37.5x-375}{EI}$

Integrating this twice: $y = \frac{-\frac{x^5}{360}+\frac{37.5x^3}{6}-\frac{375x^2}{2}+c_3 x+c_4}{EI}$

Since at x = 0, y = y' = 0 → $c_3 = c_4 = 0$

Deflection at x = 15 ft is calculated as: $y = \dfrac{-\dfrac{15^5}{360} + \dfrac{37.5 \times 15^3}{6} - \dfrac{375 \times 15^2}{2}}{EI} = -\dfrac{23203}{EI}$

EI = 29x10⁶x1200 lb.in² = 2.417x10⁵ kip-ft²

Deflection at x = 15 is dmax = 0.096 ft = 1.15 in

Answer is D

Solution 28

Positioning the vehicle such that the heaviest wheel is immediately adjacent to a support creates the maximum reaction and therefore maximum shear force in the beam.

The reaction at the left support:

$$A_y = 30 + \frac{20 \times 100}{120} + \frac{10 \times 90}{120} = 54.17 \; kips$$

Answer is C

Structural Analysis Topics on FE Civil Examination

Structural Design

Structural Design Topics on FE Civil Examination 6-9 problems
Approximately 6% of Exam

A. Design of steel components (e.g., codes and design philosophies, beams, columns, beam-columns, tension members, connections)
B. Design of reinforced concrete components (e.g., codes and design philosophies, beams, slabs, columns, walls, footings)

Problem 1
Find the plastic moment capacity of the built-up section shown below. Use F_y = 36 ksi

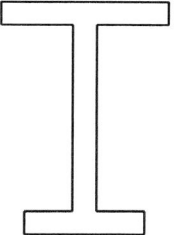

Top Flange Width = 12 inch
Bottom Flange Width = 10 inch
Top Flange thickness = 1 in
Bottom Flange thickness = 2 in
Web depth = 18 inch
Web thickness = ¾ inch

A. 975 kip-ft
B. 1050 kip-ft
C. 1125 kip-ft
D. 1200 kip-ft

Problem 2
A36 steel (F_y = 36 ksi, F_u = 58 ksi) is used for a truss. What is the minimum gross area needed for member BC? Assume effective net area = 0.75A_g. Loads shown are factored loads.

A. 13 in^2
B. 15 in^2
C. 17 in^2
D. 19 in^2

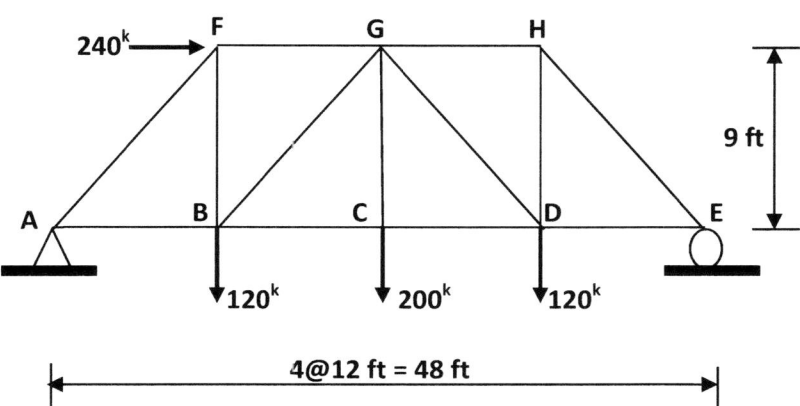

Structural Design Topics on FE Civil Examination

Problem 3 (LRFD)

A C10x30 is used as a tension member as shown. Bolts are ¾ inch diameter A325 high strength bolts. F_y = 36 ksi, F_u = 58 ksi. Geometric properties of the channel are:

d = 10.0 in
A = 8.82 in^2
b_f = 3.03 in
t_f = 0.436 in
t_w = 0.673 in

The design strength of the member is most nearly:
A) 195 kips
B) 275 kips
C) 315 kips
D) 355 kips

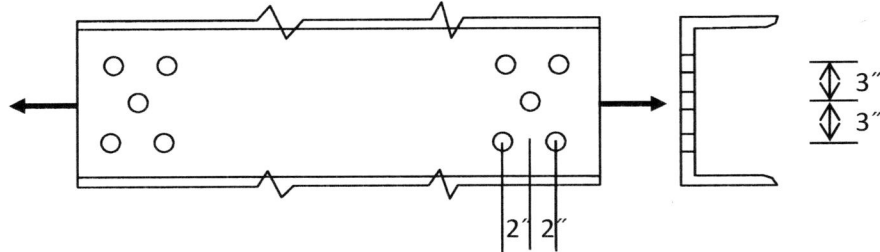

Problem 4 (LRFD)

A W16x67 beam has a simple span = 30 ft and carries a uniformly distributed load over the entire span. Steel grade is A992 grade 50. The compression flange of the beam has lateral support at the supports and at midspan only. Ignore C_b. The maximum factored load (kip/ft) the beam can carry is most nearly:
A) 2.75
B) 3.75
C) 4.50
D) 5.15

Problem 5 (LRFD)

A steel column (F_y = 50 ksi) has effective length = 20 ft. Find the smallest satisfactory W12 section that can support an axial load of 200 kips dead load + 215 kips live load.
A) W12x58
B) W12x53
C) W12x72
D) W12x65

Structural Design Topics on FE Civil Examination

Problem 6 (LRFD)

What is most nearly the axial **design capacity** of a W18x71 tension member based on the yield and fracture limit states? Assume $A_e = 0.75A_g$. Use $F_y = 42$ ksi and $F_u = 60$ ksi.

A. 700 kips
B. 784 kips
C. 868 kips
D. 933 kips

Problem 7 (LRFD)

A simply supported steel girder has a span L = 48 ft and has beams framing into it at quarter points as shown. The outer beams transfer equal vertical reactions P = 120 kips and the inner beam transfers a reaction of 240 kips to the girder. What is the most appropriate bending coefficient (C_b) to be used for the design of the girder?

A. 1.00
B. 1.15
C. 1.20
D. 1.32

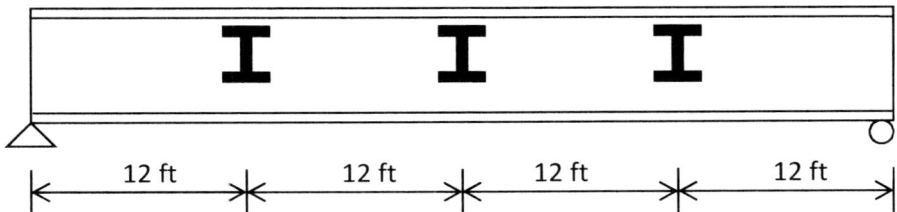

Problem 8 (LRFD)

What is the **nominal compression load capacity** of a W12x50 column whose governing slenderness ratio = 90? Use $F_y = 38$ ksi and $F_u = 55$ ksi.

A. 356 kips
B. 376 kips
C. 396 kips
D. 416 kips

Problem 9

What is the design load for a steel column whose service loads (axial) are as shown below?

$P_D = 100$ k, $P_L = 250$ k, $P_W = 180$ k

A. 256 k
B. 520 k
C. 533 k
D. 658 k

Structural Design Topics on FE Civil Examination

Problem 10
A simply supported steel beam carries a factored load (uniformly distributed) = 4.8 kip/ft over a span L = 24 ft. The compression flange has continuous lateral support. What is the lightest W- section which is satisfactory? Use F_y = 40 ksi

    A. W10x100
    B. W12x79
    C. W21x55
    D. W21x48

Problem 11
What is the lightest W-section for a beam with an ultimate design moment M_u = 400 k-ft. The beam has a span of 30 ft and its compression flange is laterally braced at midspan. Assume C_b = 1.0 and F_y = 50 ksi.

    A. W21x55
    B. W18x65
    C. W10x77
    D. W21x62

Problem 12
For the unbraced steel building frame shown in the figure, the numbers represent I/L ratios (in^4/ft) of the beams and columns. What is the effective length factor (K) for an interior column on the second floor (indicated in bold type)? Ignore inelastic behavior.

    A. 0.64
    B. 1.10
    C. 0.90
    D. 1.80

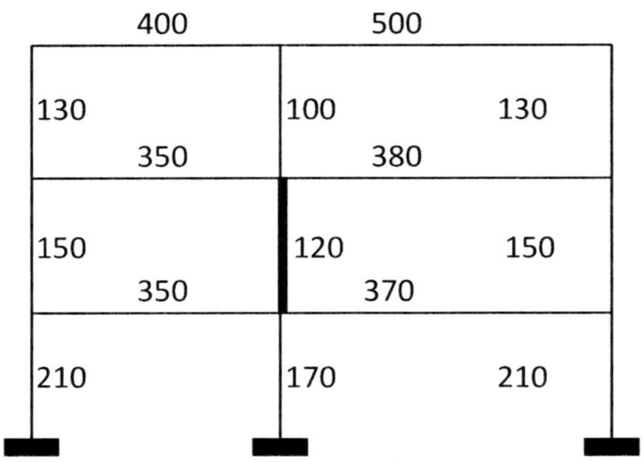

Problem 13

Find the governing net area for the tension member shown below.

A. 4.69 in²
B. 4.88 in²
C. 5.03 in²
D. 5.31 in²

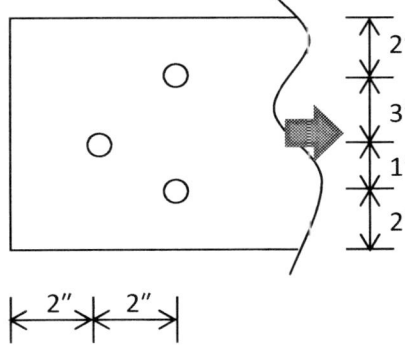

Plate thickness ¾ inch
Bolt diameter ¾ inch

Problem 14

A W10x39 section is used for a column of height 22 ft. The weak axis of the column is braced laterally at a height of 12 ft as shown. What is the governing slenderness ratio of the column? Both top and bottom ends of the column are restrained against translation and rotation.

Assume F_y = 50 ksi and F_u = 65 ksi

A. 66
B. 58
C. 46
D. 40

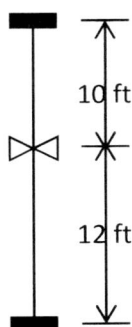

Structural Design Topics on FE Civil Examination

Problem 15 (LRFD)

For the beam shown below, the compression flange has continuous lateral support. Select the lightest W-section that will safely support the load. Use $F_y = 50$ ksi

    A. W21x55
    B. W24x55
    C. W18x60
    D. W21x50

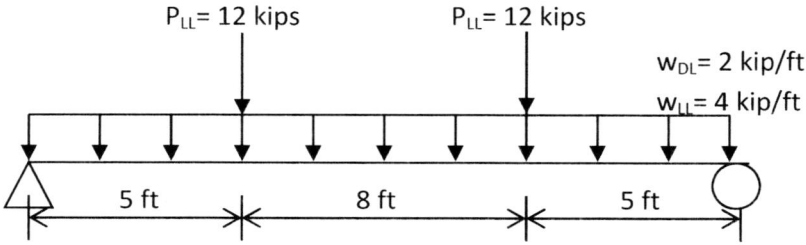

Problem 16

A 16″ x 20″ reinforced concrete ($f_c' = 4000$ psi, $f_y = 60000$ psi) column is subjected to the following loads.

$P_D = 300$ kips (concentric)
$P_L = 180$ kips (eccentric; e = 4 inches)

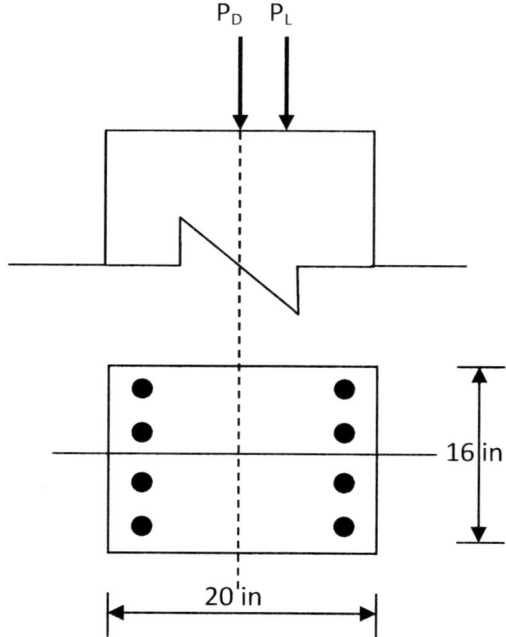

The required area of steel (in²) is most nearly:
- A. 3.2 in²
- B. 4.6 in²
- C. 5.8 in²
- D. 7.2 in²

Problem 17

A circular concrete column supports a 300 kips dead load and a 350 kip live load. All loads are concentric. The longitudinal reinforcement is laterally confined by a continuous spiral. The compressive strength of the concrete is 4000 psi and the yield stress of the reinforcement steel is 60 ksi. If the maximum (permitted by ACI) reinforcement is used, the required (minimum) cross sectional area of the column (in²) is most nearly

- A) 130
- B) 150
- C) 200
- D) 230

Problem 18

A reinforced concrete (f_c' = 4 ksi, f_y = 60 ksi) beam is simply supported over a span L = 25 ft. The width of the rectangular section is 15 inches and depth is 24 inches. The tensile reinforcement is 4 no. 10 bars. Shear reinforcement is in the form of no. 4 U-shaped stirrups. What is the tensile strain in the steel?

- A. 0.0055
- B. 0.0061
- C. 0.0067
- D. 0.0082

Problem 19

A short reinforced concrete column has an 18 inch x 18 inch cross section. It is reinforced with two lines of reinforcement bars with a total of 12 No. 10 bars, as shown The service level axial loads are: P_{DL} = 220 kips, P_{LL} = 400 kips. (Assume f_c' = 4000 psi, f_y = 60,000 psi).

What is the maximum permitted eccentricity of the load?

- A. 1.8 inches
- B. 2.5 inches
- C. 3.1 inches
- D. 3.7 inches

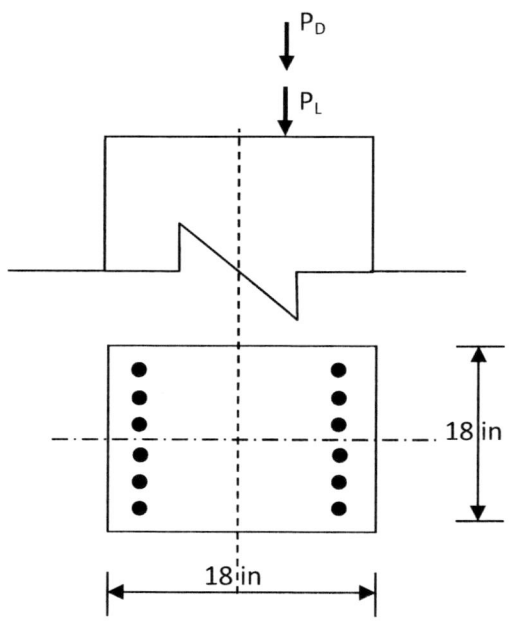

Problem 20

Interior concrete beams for an enclosed frame structure have the rectangular 12 inch x 24 inch section as shown in the figure. Use $f_c' = 5$ ksi and $f_y = 60$ ksi. What is the **nominal** moment capacity of the section?

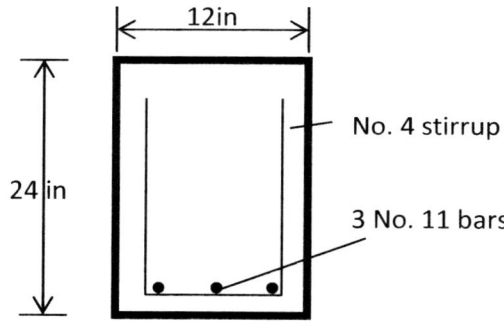

A. 380 kip-ft
B. 400 kip-ft
C. 417 kip-ft
D. 435 kip-ft

Problem 21

What is the required spacing of no. 4 stirrups in the high shear regions of the beam section shown? The design shear is V_u = 80 kips. Assume clear cover = 1.5 inch. Use f_c' = 4500 psi and f_y = 60000 psi

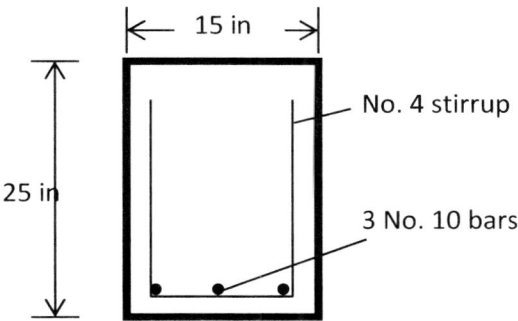

A. 9.0 inches
B. 4.5 inches
C. 4.25 inches
D. 8.5 inches

Problem 22

The load acting on a rectangular reinforced concrete column has an eccentricity e = 4 inches. Use f_c' = 4000 psi and f_y = 60000 psi. The column has dimensions 20 inch x 14 inch and is reinforced with 8 no.10 bars as main reinforcement, as shown. What is the maximum factored load P_u that the column can carry?

A. 650 kips
B. 790 kips
C. 985 kips
D. 2115 kips

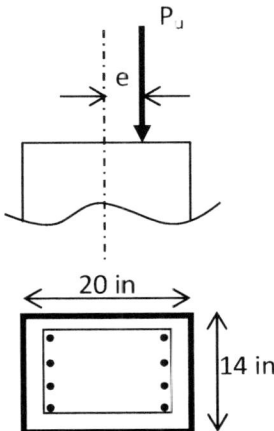

Structural Design Topics on FE Civil Examination

Problem 23
A rectangular reinforced concrete beam has a simple span L = 18 ft and a uniformly distributed (factored) load w_u = 5 k/ft. The beam section is rectangular with width = 12 inches and depth = 20 inches). Use f_c' = 5,000 psi and f_y = 60,000 psi. What is the required flexural reinforcement?
A. 2.5 in^2
B. 3.0 in^2
C. 3.5 in^2
D. 4.0 in^2

Problem 24
What is the largest factored moment that can be ignored in the design of a square reinforced concrete column that carries a factored compression load P_u = 600 kips? The column has a 15 inch x 15 inch cross section. Use f_c' = 4000 psi and f_y = 60,000 psi
A. 45 kip-ft
B. 60 kip-ft
C. 75 kip-ft
D. 90 kip-ft

Problem 25
What is the required reinforcement for an 18 inch x 18 inch reinforced concrete column (f_c' = 4000 psi, f_y = 60,000 psi) subjected to the following loads:

P_{DL} = 200 kips, P_{LL} = 300 kips. Assume the eccentricity of the load is 4 inches
A. 16.5 in^2
B. 14.5 in^2
C. 12.5 in^2
D. 10.5 in^2

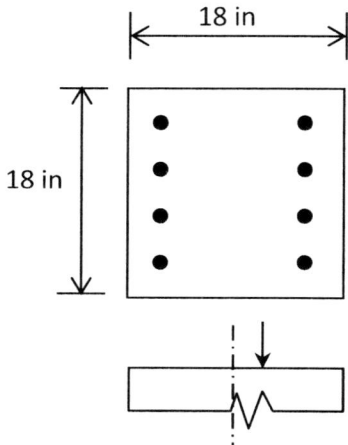

Structural Design Topics on FE Civil Examination

Problem 26

A 20 inch x 20 inch reinforced concrete column (f_c' = 4000 psi, f_y = 60,000 psi) is subjected to an eccentric load. The eccentricity of the load is 6 inches. The column is reinforced with 12 No. 11 bars distributed equally on two opposing faces. What is the maximum factored load that the column can carry?

    A. 650 kips
    B. 790 kips
    C. 890 kips
    D. 1005 kips

Problem 27

A square reinforced concrete column carries a factored compression load P_u = 600 kips. The column has a 15 inch x 15 inch cross section. The longitudinal reinforcement consists of 12 no. 10 bars. Use f_c' = 4000 psi and f_y = 60,000 psi. The maximum permitted longitudinal spacing of no. 3 ties is most nearly:

    A. 24 in
    B. 20 in
    C. 15 in
    D. 12 in

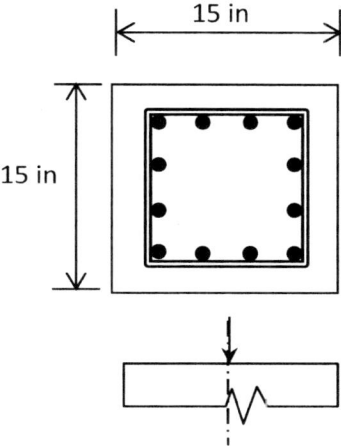

Problem 28

Find the governing net area for the tension member (7/8 inch thick steel plate) shown below.

    A. 6.21 in^2
    B. 6.74 in^2
    C. 6.85 in^2
    D. 7.04 in^2

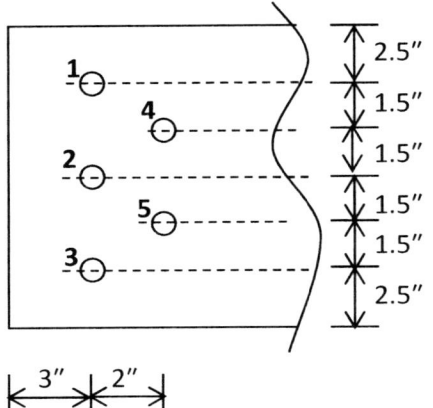

Plate thickness 7/8 inch
Bolt diameter 1 inch

Problem 29

A simply supported reinforced concrete beam spans L = 26 ft. The factored load on the beam is w_u = 7.2 kip/ft. The cross section of the beam if rectangular (width = 14 in., depth = 25 in.) Use f_c' = 4500 psi and f_y = 60000 psi. What is the total length of the zone where no shear reinforcement is required?

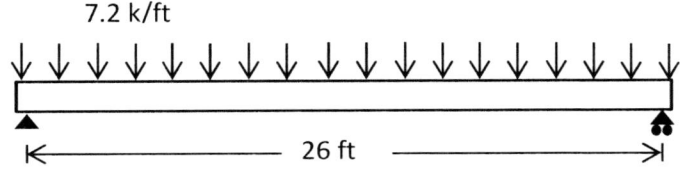

A. 40 in
B. 50 in
C. 60 in
D. 70 in

Structural Design Solutions

Structural Design Topics on FE Civil Examination

Solution 1

Total area = 12x1 + 18x¾ + 10x2 = 45.5 in²

The PNA is located such that it divides the area into equal halves. Half area = 22.75 in²
Since both flange areas are less than half the area, the PNA lies in the web.

If PNA is a distance y above the bottom edge, 20 + 0.75(y-2) = 22.75 → y = 5.667 inch

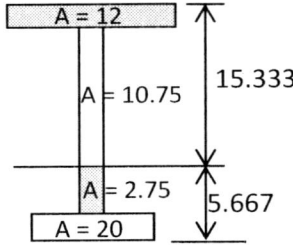

This line divides the section into the four sub-areas (rectangles) shown above.

Plastic section modulus is calculated as the sum of the first moments of these areas about the PNA:

Z = ΣA$_i$y$_i$ = 12x14.833 + 10.75x7.167 + 2.75x1.833 + 20x4.667 = 353.4 in³

Plastic moment capacity: $M_P = Z_x F_y = 353.4 \times 36 = 12723.2 \; kip - in = 1060.3 \; kip - ft$

Answer is B

Solution 2
Under these loads, A$_x$ = -240 k; A$_y$ = 175 kips, E$_y$ =265 kips
Using method of sections, F$_{BC}$ = 546.7 kips

Yield criterion: $0.9F_y A_g \geq 546.7 \Rightarrow A_g \geq \frac{546.7}{0.9 \times 36} = 16.9 \; in^2$

Fracture criterion: $0.75F_u A_e = 0.75F_u 0.75A_g \geq 546.7 \Rightarrow A_g \geq \frac{546.7}{0.75^2 \times 58} = 16.8 \; in^2$

Answer is C

Solution 3
For a C10x30, A$_g$ = 8.81 in²; t$_w$ = 0.673 in
Hole diameter = bolt diameter + ⅛ inch = ⅞ inch

Design strength (based on yield capacity): $\phi_t P_n = 0.9 F_y A_g = 0.9 \times 36 \times 8.81 = 285.4\ kips$

Net area no. 1: $A_{net,1} = 8.81 - 2 \times \frac{7}{8} \times 0.673 = 7.63\ in^2$

Net area no. 2: $A_{net,2} = 8.81 - 3 \times \frac{7}{8} \times 0.673 + 2 \times \frac{2^2}{4 \times 3} \times 0.673 = 7.49\ in^2$

Shear lag factor: $U = 1 - \frac{0.649}{4} = 0.84$

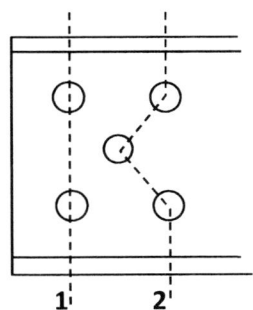

Design strength (fracture through effective net area): $\phi_t P_n = 0.75 F_u A_e = 0.75 \times 58 \times 0.84 \times 7.49 = 273.7\ kips$. This governs.

Answer is B

Solution 4
Since the beam is braced at midspan, L$_{unbraced}$ = 30/2 = 15 ft

From the Z$_x$ table extract in the handbook (page 156), we get the following parameters for a W16x67

$\phi_b M_p$ = 488 k-ft; L$_p$ = 8.69 ft; L$_r$ = 26.1 ft; ϕ_bBF = 10.4 kips

Since the unbraced length (L$_b$ = 15 ft) is between L$_p$ and L$_r$, the moment capacity $\phi_b M_p$ is given by:
$$\phi_b M_n = 488 - 10.4 \times (15 - 8.69) = 422.4\ k - ft$$

Max. Factored Moment Capacity = 422.4 kip-ft (approx.)

For a simple span, maximum moment for uniformly distributed load: $M_u = \frac{1}{8} w L^2$

$$\frac{1}{8} w L^2 = 422.4 \Rightarrow w = \frac{422.4 \times 8}{30^2} = 3.75\ kip/ft$$

Answer is B

Structural Design Topics on FE Civil Examination

Solution 5
P_u = 1.2(DL) +1.6(LL) = 1.2(200) + 1.6(215) = 584 kips

Required design strength = $\phi_c P_n$ = 584 kips

From page 155, for a W12x72 section, r_y = 3.04 in; A_g = 21.1 in^2
Slenderness ratio KL/r = 20x12/3.04 = 78.95
From page 159, $\phi_c F_{cr}$ = 28.5 ksi. Therefore $\phi_c P_n = \phi_c F_{cr} A_g$ = 28.5x21.1 = 610.8 k

Since this is a little over the target capacity (584 k), try the next lower size:

From page 155, for a W12x65 section, r_y = 3.02 in; A_g = 19.1 in^2
Slenderness ratio KL/r = 20x12/3.02 = 79.5
From page 159, $\phi_c F_{cr}$ = 28.35 ksi. Therefore $\phi_c P_n = \phi_c F_{cr} A_g$ = 28.35x19.1 = 541.5 k (NO GOOD)

Use W12x72 (capacity = 610 kips)

Answer is C

Solution 6
From page 155 of the FE reference handbook, gross area of a W18x71 is A_g = 20.8 in^2

The axial design capacity based on yield of the gross area is given by

$$P_u = 0.9 F_y A_g = 0.9 \times 42 \times 20.8 = 786.2 \; kips$$

The axial design capacity based on fracture of the net area is given by

$$P_u = 0.75 F_u A_e = 0.75 F_u (0.75 A_g) = 0.75 \times 60 \times 0.75 \times 20.8 = 702.0 \; kips. \text{ This governs.}$$

Normally, the gross area of the section is first reduced to the governing (minimum) net area and then the net area is reduced to the effective net area by taking into account the shear lag factor U. The first step requires knowledge of the number, size and arrangement of bolt holes and the second step requires knowledge of the connectivity of various parts of the section. Since these specifics are not given the question instructs to lump these two reductions into one (A_e = 0.75A_g). This assumption is consistent with the tables in the AISC manual.

Answer is A

Solution 7
Under the given symmetric load, the end reactions are 240 kips. The shear and bending moment diagrams are as shown below:

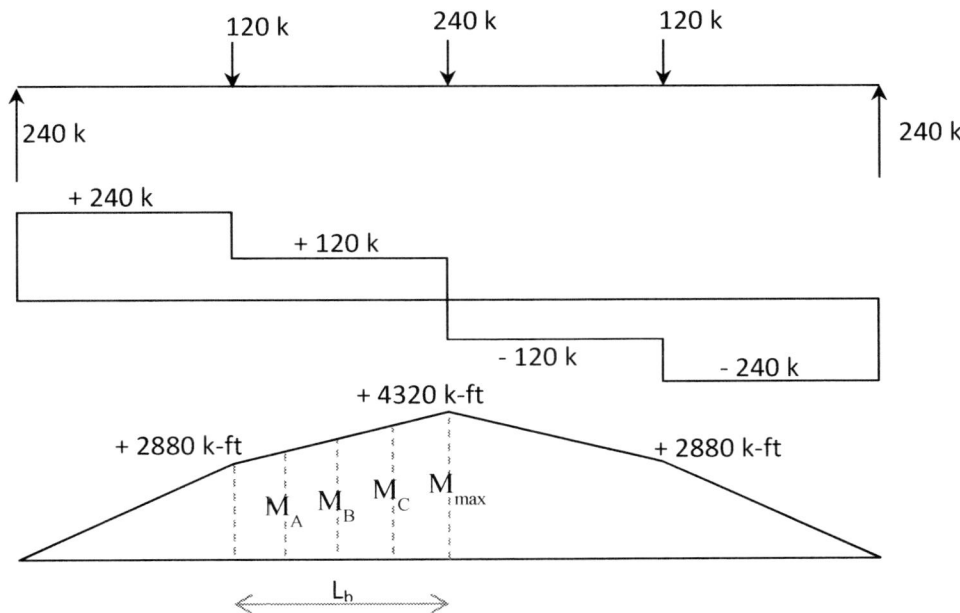

The cross beams serve to brace the compression flange against lateral buckling. The unbraced length is from L/4 to L/2 or from L/2 to 3L/4. The bending coefficient is given by:

$$C_b = \frac{12.5 M_{max}}{2.5 M_{max} + 3M_A + 4M_B + 3M_C} = \frac{12.5 \times 4320}{2.5 \times 4320 + 3 \times 3240 + 4 \times 3600 + 3 \times 3960} = 1.154$$

Answer is B

Solution 8

W12x50 section has cross sectional area A_g = 14.7 in²

$$4.71\sqrt{\frac{E}{F_y}} = 4.71\sqrt{\frac{29000}{38}} = 130.1$$

Euler buckling stress:

$$F_e = \frac{\pi^2 E}{(KL/r)^2} = \frac{\pi^2 \times 29000}{90^2} = 35.34 \; ksi$$

Since KL/r < 130.1, critical buckling stress:

$$F_{cr} = \left(0.658^{F_y/F_e}\right)F_y = \left(0.658^{38/35.34}\right)38 = 24.23 \; ksi$$

Nominal load capacity (compression): $P_n = F_{cr}A_g$ = 24.23 x 14.7 = 356 kips

Answer is A

Structural Design Topics on FE Civil Examination

Solution 9

$P_u = 1.4D = 140$ k
$P_u = 1.2D + 1.6L = 520$ k
$P_u = 1.2D + 1.6W + 1.0L = 658$ k

Answer is D

Note: When the FE Reference Handbook updates to the new load combinations from ASCE 7, the load factor for the wind load will change from 1.6 to 1.0

Solution 10
The maximum moment for a simple span carrying a uniformly distributed load is given by:
$$M_u = \frac{w_u L^2}{8} = \frac{4.8 \times 24^2}{8} = 345.6 \; kip-ft = 4147.2 \; kip-in$$
Since the compression flange has continuous lateral support: nominal moment capacity is:
$$\phi_b M_n = \phi_b M_p = 0.9 F_y Z_x$$
Thus,
$$0.9 F_y Z_x \geq 4147.2 \Rightarrow Z_x \geq \frac{4147.2}{0.9 \times 40} = 115.2 \; in^3$$

Using the Z_x table extract (page 156 in the FE Handbook), the lightest section is a W21x55

Answer is C

Solution 11
With compression flange braced at midspan, $L_b = 15$ ft
From the AISC design charts extract (page 157 of the FE handbook), for $M_u = 400$ kip-ft and $L_b = 15$ ft, the lightest section is W21x62 (first solid line vertically above this point)

Answer is D

Solution 12
$G_{top} = (100+120)/(350+380) = 0.3$
$G_{bottom} = (120+170)/(350+370) = 0.4$

Figure C-A7.2 (p. 158 of the FE Reference Handbook), K = 1.11

Answer is B

Structural Design Topics on FE Civil Examination

Solution 13

One of the options (for fracture to occur through the section) is on the normal section through TWO bolt holes. Once this is considered, there is no need to consider the other two hole options, which have one staggered segment and are therefore stronger.

$$A_{net,1} = 8 \times 0.75 - 2 \times \frac{7}{8} \times \frac{3}{4} = 4.69$$

The other option is to consider the three-hole section, with TWO staggered segments.

$$A_{net,2} = 8 \times 0.75 - 3 \times \frac{7}{8} \times \frac{3}{4} + \left(\frac{2^2}{4 \times 3} + \frac{2^2}{4 \times 1}\right) \times \frac{3}{4} = 5.03$$

Answer is C

Solution 14

For the W10x39, from page 155 of the FE handbook, r_x = 4.27 in and r_y = 1.98 in

From Table C-A-7.1 on page 158 of the FE handbook, the recommended effective length factor for pinned-fixed end conditions (case b) is K = 0.8 and for fixed-fixed end conditions (case a) is K = 0.65

For strong-axis buckling, effective length = 0.65x22 = 14.3 ft
Slenderness ratio KL/r_x = 14.3x12/4.27 = 40.2

For weak-axis buckling, effective length = 0.8x12 = 9.6 ft
Slenderness ratio KL/r_x = 9.6x12/1.98 = 58.2. This governs.

Answer is B

Solution 15

With only dead and live loads present, the governing load combination will be 1.2D + 1.6L. This factored loading is shown.

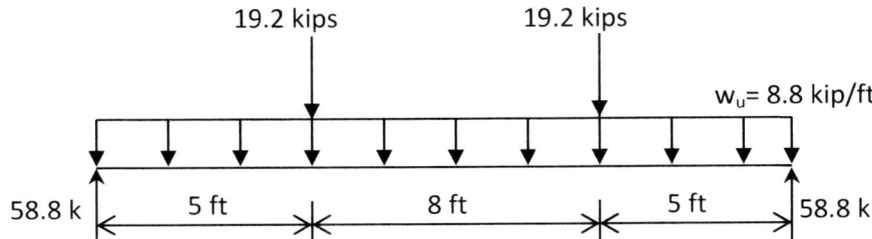

The loading is symmetric. Therefore, each support reaction is half the load. The maximum bending moment (at midspan) is the sum of two cases (both of which produce maximum moment at midspan).

Structural Design Topics on FE Civil Examination

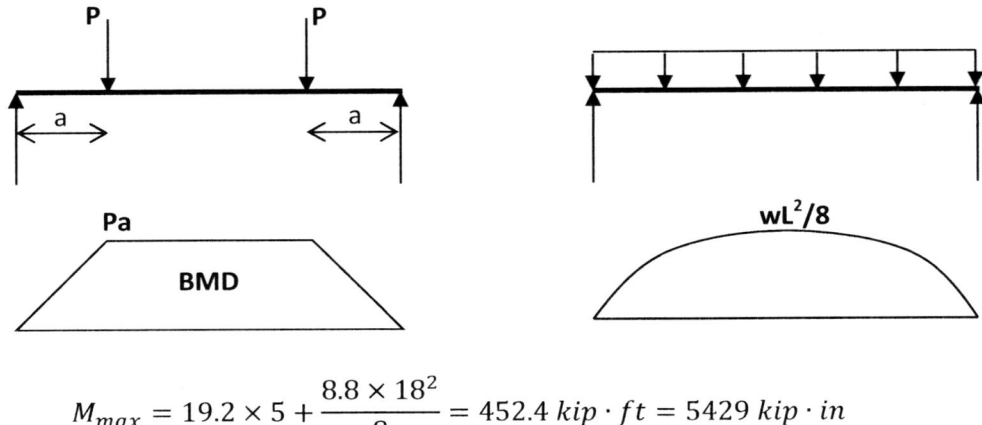

$$M_{max} = 19.2 \times 5 + \frac{8.8 \times 18^2}{8} = 452.4 \; kip \cdot ft = 5429 \; kip \cdot in$$

With continuous lateral support:

$$\phi_b M_n = \phi_b M_p = 0.9 F_y Z_x \geq 5429 \Rightarrow Z_x \geq 120.6 \; in^3$$

The lightest section is W21x55

Answer is A

Solution 16

Factored axial load: $P_u = 1.2 P_D + 1.6 P_L = 1.2 \times 300 + 1.6 \times 180 = 648 \; kips$

Factored moment: $M_u = 1.2 P_D e_D + 1.6 P_L e_L = 1.2 \times 300 \times 0 + 1.6 \times 180 \times 4 = 1152 \; kip \cdot in$

The dimensionless parameters to be used in the interaction diagram are:

$$K_n = \frac{P_u}{\phi f_c' A_g} = \frac{648}{0.65 \times 4 \times 320} = 0.78$$

$$R_n = \frac{M_u}{\phi f_c' A_g h} = \frac{1152}{0.65 \times 4 \times 320 \times 20} = 0.07$$

Assuming effective cover of about 2.5 inches, γh = 20 – 2x2.5 = 15 inches → γ = 0.75

For the above data, the column interaction diagram yields ρ_g < 1%. However, minimum of 1% steel must be used.

Therefore, A_s = 0.01x16x20 = 3.2 in²

Answer is A

Solution 17
Maximum reinforcement = 8%

P_u = 1.2 x 300 + 1.6 x 350 = 920 kips

$$\phi P_n = \phi \beta A_g [0.85 f'_c (1 - \rho_g) + f_y \rho_g]$$
$$= 0.75 \times 0.85 \times A_g [0.85 \times 4 \times (1 - 0.08) + 60 \times 0.08] = 5.054 A_g$$

A_g > 182 in²

Answer is C

Solution 18
If no. 4 stirrups are used and No. 10 bars as longitudinal reinforcement and clear cover is 1.5 inches, then effective depth d = 24 - 1.5 - 0.5 - 1.27/2 = 21.365 inches

Depth of neutral axis is calculated as: $c = \dfrac{A_s f_y}{0.85 \beta_1 f'_c b} = \dfrac{4 \times 1.27 \times 60}{0.85 \times 0.85 \times 4 \times 15} = 7.03\ in$

Tensile strain is calculated as: $\varepsilon_t = \dfrac{0.003(d-c)}{c} = \dfrac{0.003(21.365-7.03)}{7.03} = 0.0061$

Answer is B

Solution 19
The factored load is P_u = 1.2x220 + 1.6x400 = 904 kips

Assuming approximately 2 inches of effective cover, the center to center distance between parallel lines of reinforcement = 18 – 2x2 = 14 inches

Parameter γ = 14/18 = 0.78. Let us use the diagram for f_c' = 4 ksi, f_y = 60 ksi, γ = 0.80 (actually, this is the only column interaction diagram we have)

Area of steel A_s = 12x1.27 = 15.24 in², and gross area A_g = 18x18 = 324 in²

Reinforcement ratio ρ_g = 15.24/324 = 0.047

The parameter $K_n = \dfrac{P_u}{\phi f'_c A_g} = \dfrac{900}{0.65 \times 4 \times 324} = 1.07$

Using K_n = 1.07 and ρ_g ≈ 0.047 (visual interpolation between 0.04 and 0.05), we get e/h ≈ 0.17.

Therefore, the tolerable eccentricity e = 0.17 h = 3.1 inches

Answer is C

Solution 20

According to ACI 318, clear cover should be 1.5 inch.

Effective depth d = 24 − 1.5 − 0.5 − 1.41/2 = 21.3 inches

$\beta_1 = 0.8$; $A_s = 4.68 \text{ in}^2$

Depth of equivalent compression block: $a = \dfrac{A_s f_y}{0.85 f'_c b} = \dfrac{4.68 \times 60}{0.85 \times 5 \times 12} = 5.5 \text{ in}$

Nominal moment capacity: $M_n = A_s f_y \left(d - \dfrac{a}{2}\right) = 4.68 \times 60 \times \left(21.3 - \dfrac{5.5}{2}\right) = 5209 \text{ kip} \cdot \text{in} = 434 \text{ kip} \cdot \text{ft}$

Answer is D

Solution 21

Effective depth: $d = 25 - 1.5 - 0.5 - \dfrac{1.27}{2} = 22.37 \text{ in}$

Shear capacity of concrete section: $V_c = 2\sqrt{f'_c} bd = 2\sqrt{4500} \times 15 \times 22.37 = 45{,}019 \text{ lb} = 45.02 \text{ k}$

Required capacity of shear reinforcement: $V_s = \dfrac{V_u}{\phi} - V_c = \dfrac{80}{0.75} - 45 = 61.67 \text{ k}$

Required (maximum) spacing of no. 4 stirrups (A_v=0.4 in²):
$$s = \dfrac{A_v f_y d}{V_s} = \dfrac{0.4 \times 60 \times 22.37}{61.67} = 8.7 \text{ in}$$

Since $V_s < 4\sqrt{f'_c} bd = 90 \text{ k}$, spacing is not to exceed d/2 (11.2 in) nor 24 in.

Therefore, spacing in the maximum shear zone is not to exceed 8.7 in

Answer is D

Solution 22

For a tied column, e/h < 0.1 would allow us to use the small eccentricity equation.
Since e/h = 4/20 = 0.2, the eccentricity cannot be ignored.

Reinforcement ratio: $\rho_g = \dfrac{8 \times 1.27}{14 \times 20} = 0.036$

$\gamma h = 20 - 2 \times (1.5 + 0.5 + 0.635) = 14.73 \Rightarrow \gamma = \dfrac{14.73}{20} = 0.74; \text{ Use } \gamma = 0.8$

From the column interaction diagram on page 152 of the handbook, $K_n = 0.9$

$$K_n = \frac{P_u}{\phi_c f_c' A_g} \Rightarrow P_u = K_n \phi_c f_c' A_g = 0.9 \times 0.65 \times 4 \times 280 = 655.2\ kips$$

Answer is A

Solution 23

Assuming effective depth d ≈ h − 2.5 = 17.5 inches

Design moment: $M_u = \frac{w_u L^2}{8} = \frac{5 \times 18^2}{8} = 202.5\ kip \cdot ft$

This is a type of problem that is best done using design aids, which are not in the handbook. Thus, the quickest way would be try out answer choices.

Try $A_s = 4\ in^2$

Depth of compression block: $a = \frac{A_s f_y}{0.85 f_c' b} = \frac{4 \times 60}{0.85 \times 5 \times 12} = 4.7\ in$

Nominal moment capacity: $M_n = A_s f_y \left(d - \frac{a}{2}\right) = 4 \times 60 \times \left(17.5 - \frac{4.7}{2}\right) = 3635\ kip \cdot in = 303\ kip \cdot ft$

Design moment capacity: $\phi_b M_n = 0.9 \times 303 = 272.6\ kip \cdot ft$

This is significantly over target.

Try $A_s = 3\ in^2$

Depth of compression block: $a = \frac{A_s f_y}{0.85 f_c' b} = \frac{3 \times 60}{0.85 \times 5 \times 12} = 3.53\ in$

Nominal moment capacity: $M_n = A_s f_y \left(d - \frac{a}{2}\right) = 3 \times 60 \times \left(17.5 - \frac{3.53}{2}\right) = 2832\ kip \cdot in = 236\ kip \cdot ft$

Design moment capacity: $\phi_b M_n = 0.9 \times 236 = 212\ kip \cdot ft$

This is just about right.

Answer is B

Solution 24

A rectangular column will necessarily have lateral confinement in the form of ties. Therefore, according to the ACI, the maximum eccentricity that can be ignored is equal to 0.1h = 0.1 x 15 inches = 1.5 inches.

Therefore, the maximum factored moment that can be ignored is

$$M_u = P_u e = 600 \times 1.5 = 900\ kip \cdot in = 75 kip \cdot ft$$

Answer is C

Structural Design Topics on FE Civil Examination

Solution 25

$P_u = 1.2 \times 200 + 1.6 \times 300 = 720$ kips

Eccentricity is greater than 0.1h (4 inches > 0.1 x 18 inches). Therefore, the column must be designed for a combination of P_u and M_u (e/h = 4/18 = 0.22)

$$K_n = \frac{P_u}{\phi_c f'_c A_g} = \frac{720}{0.65 \times 4 \times 324} = 0.85$$

From the column interaction diagram, using K_n = 0.85 and e/h = 0.22, ρ_g = 5%

$A_s = 0.05 \times 324 = 16.2$ in^2

Answer is A

Solution 26

Eccentricity is greater than 0.1h (6 inches > 0.1 x 20 inches). Therefore, the column must be designed for a combination of P_u and M_u (e/h = 6/20 = 0.30)

Area of steel $A_s = 12 \times 1.56 = 18.72$ in^2, and gross area $A_g = 20 \times 20 = 400$ in^2

Reinforcement ratio ρ_g = 18.72/400 = 0.047

Assuming approximately 2 inches of effective cover, the center to center distance between parallel lines of reinforcement = 20 – 2x2 = 16 inches

Parameter γ = 16/20 = 0.80. Let us use the diagram for f_c' = 4 ksi, f_y = 60 ksi, γ = 0.80

From the column interaction diagram, for e/h = 0.30 and ρ_g = 4.7%, K_n = 0.76

$$\phi_c P_n = K_n \phi_c f'_c A_g = 0.76 \times 0.65 \times 4 \times 400 = 790 \; kips$$

Answer is B

Solution 27

Longitudinal spacing of ties is given as the minimum of:
1. Least column dimension = 15 inches
2. 16 times the diameter of longitudinal bars = 16 x 1.27 = 20.3 inches
3. 48 times the diameter of ties = 48 x 0.375 = 18 inches

Therefore, maximum ties spacing = 15 inches

Answer is C

Solution 28

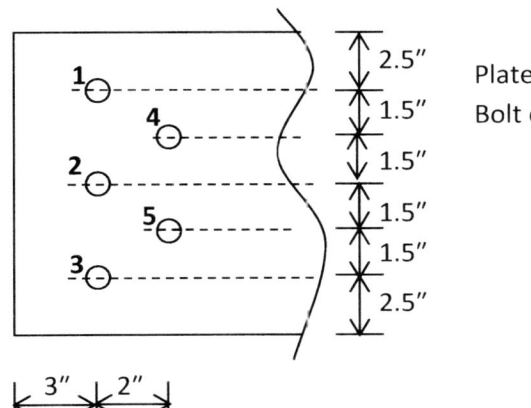

Plate thickness 7/8 inch
Bolt diameter 1 inch

Line 1-4-5: $A_{net,3} = 11 \times 0.875 - 3 \times 7/8 \times 9/8 + 1 \times 0.875 \times (2^2/4 \times 1.5) = 7.255$

Line 1-4-2-5: $A_{net,4} = 11 \times 0.875 - 4 \times 7/8 \times 9/8 + 2 \times 0.875 \times (2^2/4 \times 1.5) = 6.854$

Line 1-4-2-5-3: $A_{net,5} = 11 \times 0.875 - 5 \times 7/8 \times 9/8 + 4 \times 0.875 \times (2^2/4 \times 1.5) = 7.036$

Governing net area, $A_{net} = 6.85$ in^2

Answer is C

Solution 29

The effective depth, d ≈ 25 − 2.5 = 22.5 in

Shear capacity of concrete section, $V_u = 2\sqrt{f'_c}bd = 2 \times \sqrt{4500} \times 14 \times 22.5 = 42261.7\ lb$

$$\frac{1}{2}\phi V_c = 0.5 \times 0.75 \times 42.26 = 15.85\ kips$$

The distance on either side of the midspan, where this shear occurs = 15.85/7.2 = 2.2 ft

The total distance over which no shear reinforcement is required = 4.4 ft = 52.8 inches

Answer is B

Geotechnical Engineering

Geotechnical Topics on FE Civil Examination   **9-14 problems**
Approximately 9% of Exam

A. Geology
B. Index properties and soil classifications
C. Phase relations (air-water-solid)
D. Laboratory and field tests
E. Effective stress (buoyancy)
F. Stability of retaining walls (e.g., active pressure/passive pressure)
G. Shear strength
H. Bearing capacity (cohesive and noncohesive)
I. Foundation types (e.g., spread footings, deep foundations, wall footings, mats)
J. Consolidation and differential settlement
K. Seepage/flow nets
L. Slope stability (e.g., fills, embankments, cuts, dams)
M. Soil stabilization (e.g., chemical additives, geosynthetics)
N. Drainage systems
O. Erosion control

Problem 1

The sieve analysis result for a soil sample is shown in the table below. Atterberg tests resulted in: LL = 54, PL = 23. What is the USCS classification for the soil?

    A. GW-GC
    B. GW-GM
    C. GP-GM
    D. GP-GC

Sieve size	% passing
2 inch	95
1 inch	85
½ inch	60
No. 4	41
No. 10	31
No. 40	22
No. 200	10

Problem 2

The sieve analysis result for a soil sample is shown in the table below. Atterberg tests resulted in: LL = 54, PL = 23. What is the AASHTO classification for the soil?

    A. A-7-5
    B. A-2-7
    C. A-2-5
    D. A-7-6

Sieve size	% passing
2 inch	95
1 inch	85
½ inch	60
No. 4	41
No. 10	31
No. 40	22
No. 200	10

Problem 3

A cantilever retaining wall is shown. What is most nearly the active resultant per unit length of the wall?

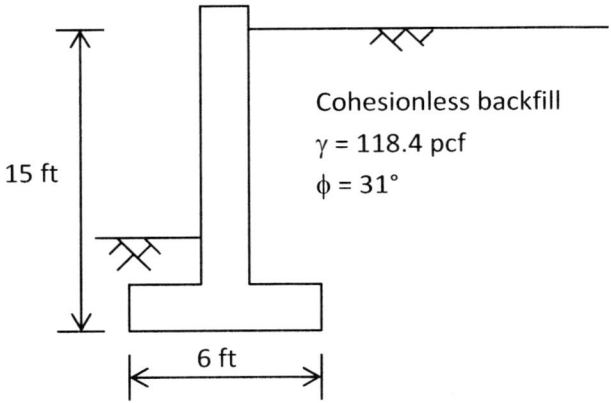

A. 280 lb/ft
B. 1900 lb/ft
C. 4260 lb/ft
D. 8530 lb/ft

Problem 4

Six soil samples are prepared from a borrow pit. Different amounts of water are added to the samples to vary (and measure) the water content. Specific gravity of soil solids = 2.66. The samples are prepared using Standard Proctor apparatus. The volume of the Proctor mold is 1/30 ft^3. Moist net soil weight and corresponding values of water content for the six samples are summarized in the table below.

Weight of soil (lb)	Water content (%)
3.20	12.8
3.78	13.9
4.40	15.0
4.10	15.7
3.70	16.6
3.30	18.1

The maximum dry unit weight is most nearly
A) 85 lb/ft^3
B) 90 lb/ft^3
C) 100 lb/ft^3
D) 115 lb/ft^3

Problem 5

A mass concrete gravity retaining wall (concrete unit weight = 140 pcf) is shown. Ignoring the contribution of the passive soil, the factor of safety for overturning is most nearly:

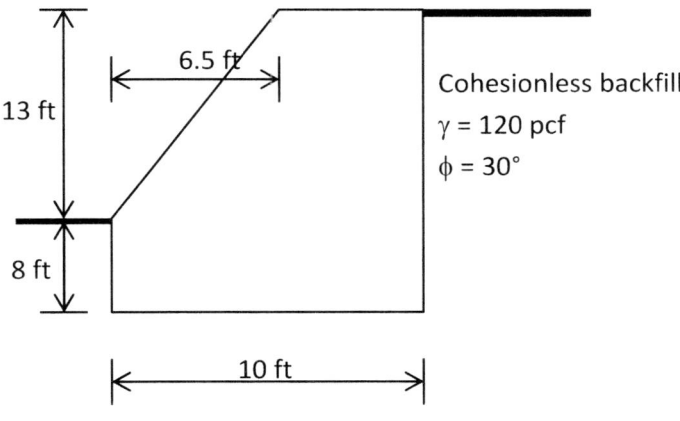

A) 1.6
B) 2.2
C) 2.8
D) 3.2

Problem 6

Sieve analysis and plasticity test results for a soil sample are shown below:

Sieve analysis	
Sieve size	% passing
No. 10	84
No. 40	51
No. 200	21

Atterberg limits	
Liquid limit (%)	Plastic limit (%)
19	15

According to the AASHTO soil classification system, the classification of this soil is:

A) A-2-4
B) A-7-5
C) A-1-b
D) A-3

Geotechnical Topics on FE Civil Examination

Problem 7

Given the phase diagram shown below, what is most nearly the porosity?
- A) 0.4%
- B) 3.3%
- C) 9.1%
- D) 30%

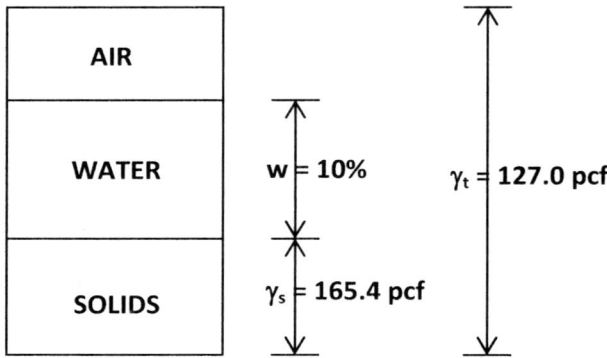

Problem 8

Laboratory tests on a soil sample generated the following results:

Sieve #	% Passing
#4	100
#10	95
# 20	92
#40	70
#100	40
#200	15
Liquid Limit	20
Plastic Limit	18

According to the Unified Soil Classification System, the classification of this soil sample is most nearly:
- A) SP
- B) CL
- C) SM
- D) SC

Problem 9

A clayey sand (SC) was compacted into a 1/30th cubic foot cylindrical Proctor steel mold with the following results:
  Weight of wet soil: 4.18 pounds
  Weight of dry soil: 3.67 pounds

If specific gravity of solids = 2.73, the percent saturation of this compacted sample is most nearly:
  A) 70%
  B) 50%
  C) 15%
  D) 85%

Problem 10

The concrete cantilever retaining wall pictured below has been backfilled with clean granular soil, is free to rotate and has good drainage so that hydrostatic pressure will not build up behind the wall. The backfill, foundation and concrete have the following properties:
  Concrete: γ_c = 150 pcf
  Granular backfill γ = 118 pcf
  K_A = 0.3
  K_P = 3.3
  μ (base of wall) = 0.5

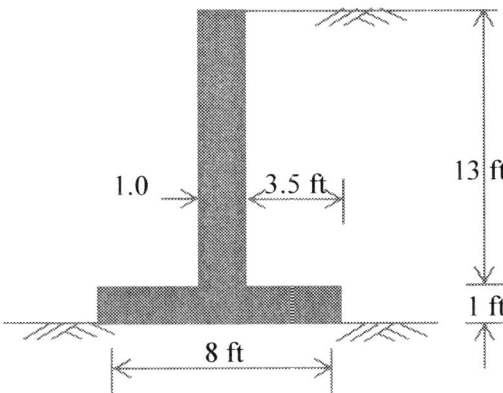

Assuming negligible friction between the wall and the backfill, the factor of safety against sliding is most nearly:
  A) 2.5
  B) 4.25
  C) 0.25
  D) 1.25

Geotechnical Topics on FE Civil Examination

Problem 11

Results from a standard Proctor compaction test from 6 soil samples from an excavation are tabulated below. The natural moisture content of the excavated material is 11%. The fill location requires 1.5 million cubic yards of soil compacted to a minimum 90% of the maximum Proctor dry density.

Sample	Net weight of soil	Moisture content (%)
1	3 lb 8 oz	13
2	3 lb 14.4 oz	14
3	4 lb 2.9 oz	15
4	4 lb 3.2 oz	16
5	3 lb 14.4 oz	18
6	3 lb 6.4 oz	20

The volume of water needed to increase the water content to the optimum value, is most nearly:

- A) 12 million gallons
- B) 16 million gallons
- C) 19 million gallons
- D) 24 million gallons

Problem 12

The following results are listed for a soil:

Percent passing No. 4 sieve (4.75 mm)	80
Percent passing No. 10 sieve (2.00 mm)	60
Percent passing No. 40 sieve (0.425 mm)	30
Percent passing No. 200 sieve (0.075 mm)	10

Liquid Limit   31
Plastic Limit 25

What is the classification of the soil according to the Unified Soil Classification System (USCS)?

- A) SM
- B) SP
- C) SW-SC
- D) SW-SM

Problem 13

Results from a sand cone test are listed below:

Weight of soil obtained from the test hole:	3.65 lb
Moisture content of soil from test hole:	17.3%
Maximum dry density (Standard Proctor):	122.3 lb/ft³
Unit weight of dry test sand:	84.7 lb/ft³
Initial weight of sand cone apparatus filled with test sand:	13.36 lb
Final weight of sand cone apparatus after sand fills test hole:	11.13 lb

The in-place percent compaction is most nearly
  A) 97
  B) 104
  C) 114
  D) 133

Problem 14

A dam of length 120 ft is constructed of an impermeable soil. The dam overlays a sand bed of thickness 6.5 ft as shown. The permeability of the sand bed is 9.5 ft/day.

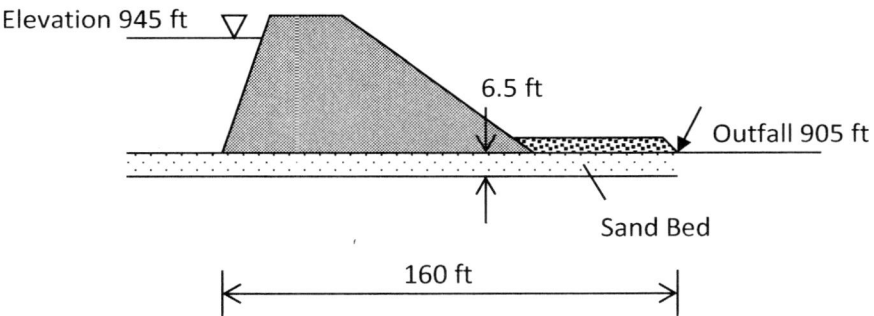

The discharge due to seepage is most nearly:
  A) 7.5 gallons per minute
  B) 9.6 gallons per minute
  C) 10.5 gallons per minute
  D) 11.0 gallons per minute

Problem 15

A soil sample has the following parameters:

Weight	66.8 lb
Volume	0.55 ft^3
Moisture content	19%
Specific gravity of solids	2.72

The degree of saturation (percent) is most nearly:
- A) 56
- B) 63
- C) 71
- D) 77

Problem 16

A concrete footing is subject to the following column loads:

Concentric load, P	80 kips
Moment due to wind, M	35 kip-ft

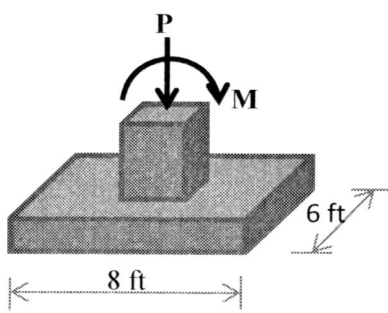

What is the maximum soil pressure under the footing?
- A) 1734 psf
- B) 2215 psf
- C) 2564 psf
- D) 2914 psf

Problem 17

The diagram below shows a soil profile which consists of a sandy fill layer (8 feet thick) overlying a layer of normally consolidated clay (thickness 12 ft). The ground water elevation is 6 ft below the ground surface. The unit weight of the sand above the GWT is 114 lb/ft³ and the saturated sand below the GWT has unit weight 120 lb/ft³.

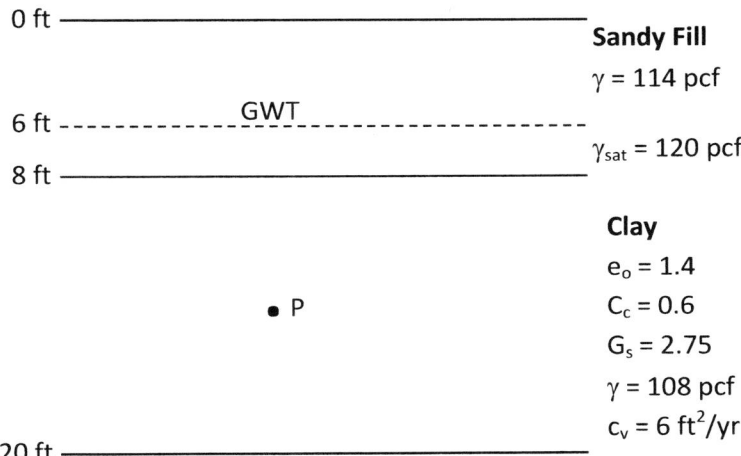

If a building applies a stress change of 670 psf at point P located at the center of the clay layer, the settlement caused by the consolidation of the clay layer (inches) is most nearly

A) 7.5
B) 6.0
C) 4.5
D) 9.0

Problem 18

A direct shear test is performed on a silty sand sample. Sample A tested at a vertical stress equal to 1,000 psf failed at a shear stress of 675 psf while sample B tested at a vertical stress of 3,000 psf failed at a shear stress of 2,025 psf. Based upon the results of this direct shear test the shear strength parameters for this silty sand are most nearly:

A. $c = 0$ psf and $\phi = 34°$
B. $c = 200$ psf and $\phi = 34°$
C. $c = 0$ psf and $\phi = 42.5°$
D. $c = 200$ psf and $\phi = 42.5°$

Problem 19

A 10 feet square footing embedded 3 feet into a sand profile has a total density, $\gamma_t = 115$ pcf and bearing capacity factors: $N_c = 0$, $N_q = 29.5$ and $N_\gamma = 27.4$. Neglecting shape factors, if the depth to the water table is 20 feet below the ground surface and the proposed column load equals 750 kips, the FS against bearing capacity failure is most nearly:

  A. 3.6
  B. 3.3
  C. 2.9
  D. 2.6

Problem 20

Water seeps through a sandy soil layer (20 inch thick, 30 inch diameter) and overflows through an outlet maintaining the outfall elevation of 50 inches, as shown below. As the water seeps out, the level of water drops in the fine bore tube from an elevation of 85 inch to 75 inch over a 35 minute interval. The hydraulic conductivity of the soil is most nearly

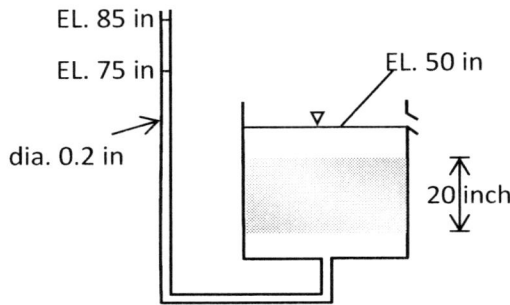

  A. 1.5×10^{-5} ft/hr
  B. 5.2×10^{-4} ft/hr
  C. 4.3×10^{-5} ft/hr
  D. 2.5×10^{-4} ft/hr

Problem 21

A soil sample has a water content of 20%, a degree of saturation of 60%, and a specific gravity of 2.68. The dry unit weight is most nearly:

  A. 82 lb/ft^3
  B. 85 lb/ft^3
  C. 88 lb/ft^3
  D. 91 lb/ft^3

Problem 22

A moist soil sample in a tare can is put on a balance and the mass of the soil plus can is found to be 48.30 g. After oven drying, the mass of the soil plus can is found to be 41.22 g. The mass of the empty tare can is 7.41 grams. The water content of the soil is most nearly:

A. 21%
B. 18%
C. 15%
D. 12%

Problem 23

A sample of dry sand has an in place dry unit weight = 121 lb/ft^3. When this sample is excavated and loosely placed in a laboratory apparatus, the unit weight is measured as 105 lb/ft^3. When the sample is then placed in a vibrating mold and packed into a dense state, the unit weight is observed to be 125 lb/ft^3. What is the relative density of the sand *in situ*?

A. 80.0%
B. 82.5%
C. 85.0%
D. 87.5%

Problem 24

Five pounds of moist soil has a water content of 20%. How many pounds of water must be added to increase the water content to 30%?

A. 0.34 lb
B. 0.42 lb
C. 0.73 lb
D. 0.87 lb

Problem 25

A fine-grained, inorganic soil sample has liquid limit of 45 and a plastic limit of 30. Classify the soil according to the Unified Soil Classification System.

A. CL
B. CH
C. ML
D. MH

Problem 26

The groundwater elevation at a site coincides with the top of a normally consolidated clay layer, as shown. During construction, the groundwater elevation remains constant. A preloading fill of 10 ft height is exerted over a 50 ft x 50 ft area as shown. The settlement due to the consolidation (inches) of the lean clay layer is most nearly:

A. 2.8 in
B. 3.9 in
C. 4.9 in
D. 6.1 in

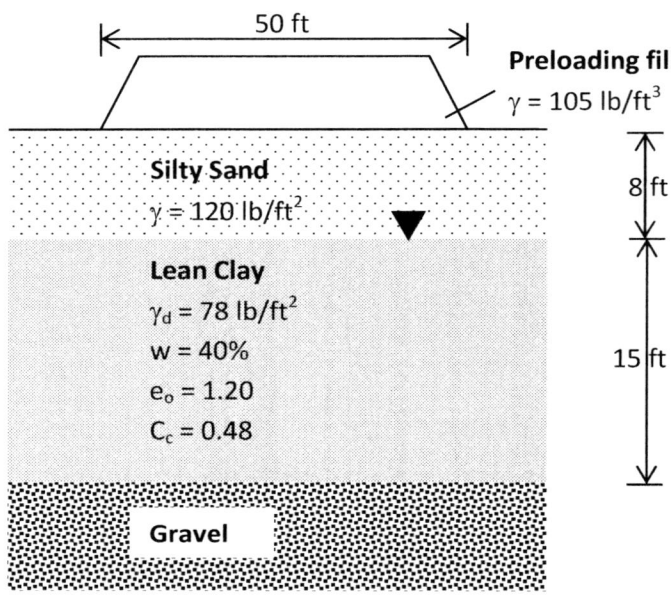

Problem 27

The retaining wall shown has a cohesionless backfill as shown. After a few years, the drainage behind the wall becomes clogged, resulting in the groundwater to rise to within 6 feet of the top of the backfill (as shown) during a flooding event. Under the flooded condition, the total lateral (horizontal) force acting on the wall is most nearly:

A. 2530 lb/ft
B. 3234 lb/ft
C. 5746 lb/ft
D. 6324 lb/ft

Geotechnical Topics on FE Civil Examination

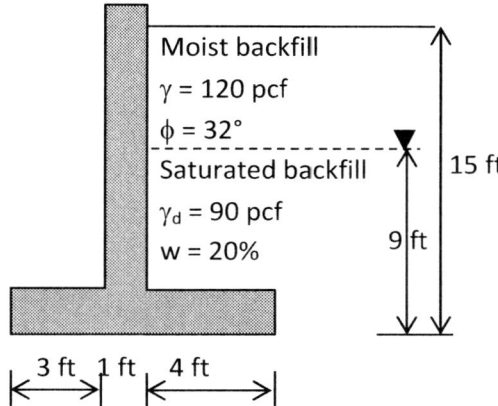

Problem 28

The soil profile shown below consists of a silty sand layer overlying a 12 ft thick layer of medium sand. A standard penetration test is conducted with a split spoon sampler, which is driven through an 18 inch penetration from depth of 10 ft to 11 ft 6 inches. The number of blows to drive the sampler through 6 inch penetration intervals are 12, 17 and 22 respectively.

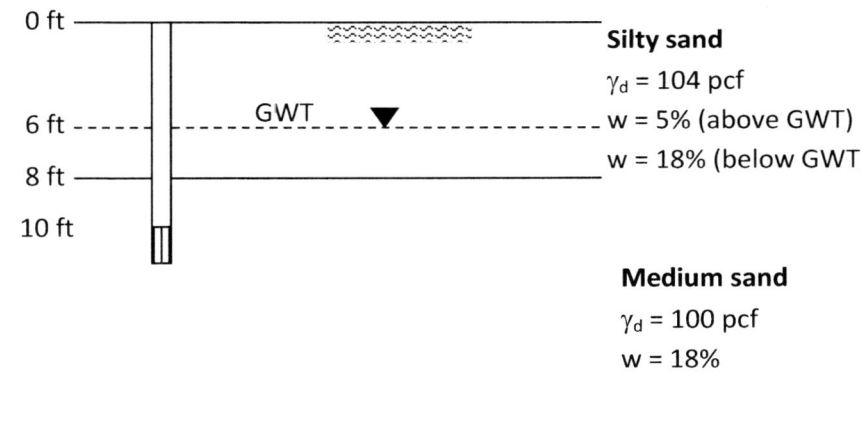

The field standard penetration resistance (N-value) is most nearly:
- A) 31
- B) 39
- C) 49
- D) 62

Geotechnical Topics on FE Civil Examination

Problem 29
Two samples of a particular soil are tested as follows:

Sample 1
Original volume = 0.5 ft³.
Net weight of soil = 62.3 lb.

Sample 2
Original volume = 0.3 ft³.
Net weight of dry soil (after oven drying) = 32.3 lb.

Specific gravity of solids = 2.65

How much water (lb) can be added to sample 1 before it bleeds or swells?
- A. 1.28 lb
- B. 2.45 lb
- C. 3.12 lb
- D. 3.89 lb

Problem 30

A cylindrical sample of clayey sand is tested in a triaxial apparatus. The following data are given for the undrained test.
- Sample diameter = 2 inches
- Sample length = 4 inches
- Confining pressure = 50 psi
- Axial load at failure = 240 lb
- Pore water pressure at failure = 16 psi.

The angle of internal friction of the sand is most nearly:
- A. 30°
- B. 32°
- C. 34°
- D. 36°

Problem 31

A retaining wall has a cohesionless backfill as shown. What is the active resultant on the wall?

A. 6500 lb/ft
B. 7250 lb/ft
C. 8125 lb/ft
D. 9050 lb/ft

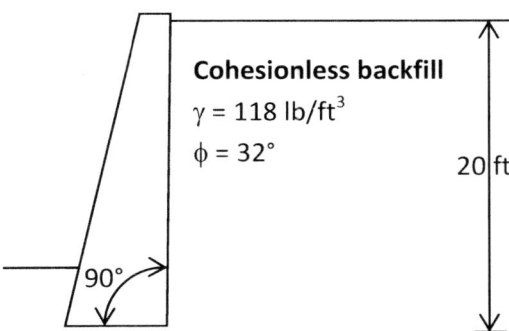

Problem 32

Grain size distribution for a soil sample is shown in the curve below. What is the USCS classification?

A. SW
B. GW
C. SP
D. SM

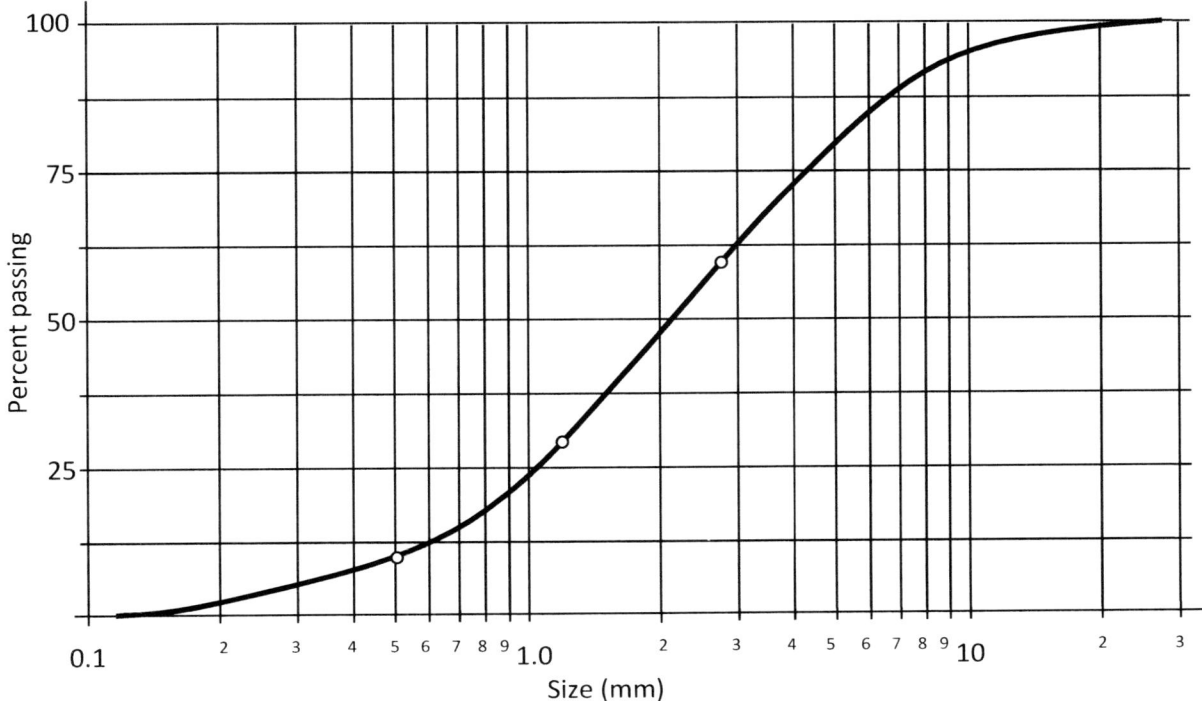

Geotechnical Topics on FE Civil Examination

Problem 33

A sample of wet soil weighs 37.6 grams. The sample is coated with wax (specific gravity = 0.9) and then weighed to be 40.9 g. The wax-coated sample is then completely immersed in water and found to weigh 16.5 g. Water content of the soil sample is 17.4% and specific gravity of solids is 2.70. What are (a) dry density (g/cm^3), (b) wet density (g/cm^3), (c) porosity and (d) percent saturation?

Problem 34

The flow net shown below describes the seepage into a long 20 feet deep and 40 feet wide excavation made in a 40 foot thick bed of silty sand having a coefficient of permeability K = 1x10^{-5} ft/sec. The sand bed is underlain by impermeable soil.

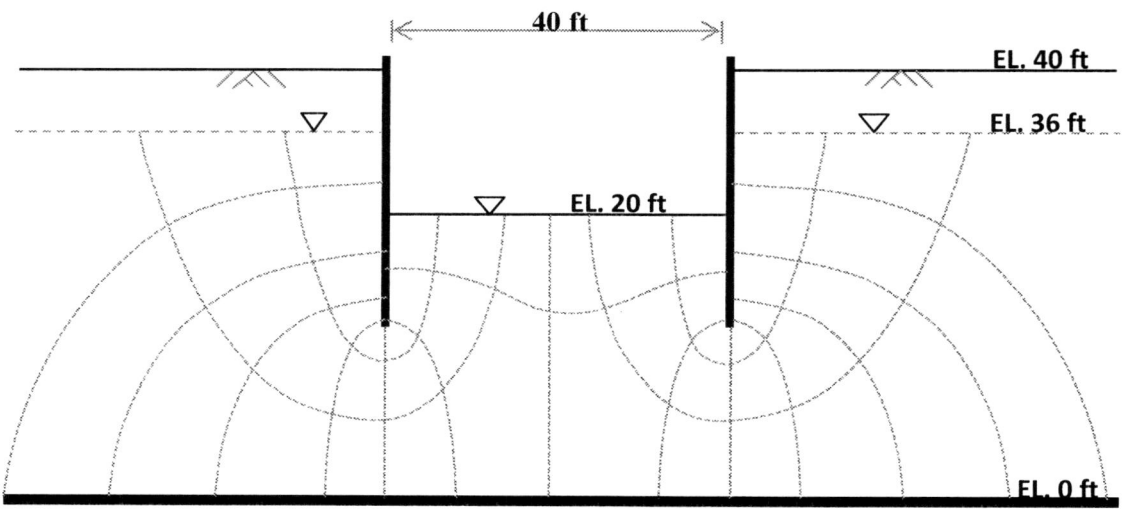

IMPERMEABLE LAYER

To maintain the water level at the base of the excavation, the quantity of water the contractor has to pump is most nearly:

A. 3.6 x 10^{-3} ft^3/min/ft
B. 7.2 x 10^{-3} ft^3/min/ft
C. 15.0 x 10^{-3} ft^3/min/ft
D. 30.0 x 10^{-3} ft^3/min/ft

Geotechnical Topics on FE Civil Examination

Problem 35
Seepage occurs through a saturated soil with unit weight = 124 lb/ft³. If the pressure difference creating the seepage forces is 20 lb/in² and the length of the seepage path is 320 ft, what is the factor of safety against seepage liquefaction?
- A. 2.3
- B. 5.1
- C. 6.9
- D. 8.2

Problem 36
What are expected values of compression and recompression index for clay with LL = 45% and PL = 15%?
- A. $C_C = 0.32$; $C_R = 0.05$
- B. $C_C = 0.32$; $C_R = 0.10$
- C. $C_C = 0.42$; $C_R = 0.08$
- D. $C_C = 0.42$; $C_R = 0.10$

Problem 37
A soil has the following properties:
    cohesion = 2,100 lb/ft²
    angle of internal friction = 20°
What is the shear strength of the soil when the effective normal stress in the soil is 2000 psf?
- A. 2,830 psf
- B. 2,785 psf
- C. 2,670 psf
- D. 2,510 psf

Problem 38
A concrete pile (diameter D = 18 inches, length = 40 ft) is embedded in a deep clay (cohesion = 2,300 lb/ft²) deposit. The bearing capacity factors are: $N_c = 9$, $N_q = 1$, $N_\gamma = 0$. The unit friction along the sides of the pile is 1400 lb/ft². What is the ultimate bearing capacity of the pile?
- A. 36,600 lb
- B. 160,000 lb
- C. 264,000 lb
- D. 300,000 lb

Geotechnical Engineering Solutions

Geotechnical Topics on FE Civil Examination

Solution 1

F_{200} = 10. This is less than 50, so it is predominantly a coarse grained soil (first letter G or S).
Coarse fraction = 90%
R_4 = 100 – 41 = 59. This is more than half of the coarse fraction. Therefore first letter is G.
D_{10} = No. 200 size = 0.075 mm
D_{30} = No. 10 size = 2.0 mm (slightly less)
D_{60} = 0.5 inch = 12.7 mm

$$C_u = \frac{D_{60}}{D_{10}} = \frac{12.5}{0.075} = 166.7$$

$$C_c = \frac{D_{30}^2}{D_{10}D_{60}} = \frac{2.0^2}{0.075 \times 12.5} = 4.3$$

Since F_{200} is between 5% and 12%, the soil has a dual classification. The first part of the classification is based on gradation. Since BOTH criteria ($C_u > 4$ and $1 < C_c < 3$) for GW are not met, the soil must be classified GP.

Plasticity Index: PI = 54 – 23 = 31
PI on the A-Line: PI = 0.73(LL – 20) = 24.8

GP-GM if PI < 0.73(LL–20) OR PI < 4
GP-GC if PI > 0.73(LL–20) AND PI > 7

Thus, the soil meets BOTH criteria for GP-GC

Answer is D

Solution 2

Since F_{200} < 35, the groups A-4, A-5, A-6 and A-7 are eliminated.

Also, the soil has significant plasticity (PI = 31), so A-1 and A-3 are eliminated. These designations are essentially for soils with no to low plasticity.

Soil meets criteria for A-2-7 (F_{200} < 35, LL > 40, PI > 10)

Answer is B

Geotechnical Topics on FE Civil Examination

Solution 3

Ignoring friction between backfill and the wall (Rankine): $K_a = \tan^2(45 - \varphi/2) = \tan^2(45 - 31/2) = 0.32$ Active earth pressure resultant: $R_a = \frac{1}{2}K_a \gamma H^2 = 0.5 \times 0.32 \times 118.4 \times 15^2 = 4262.4 \; lb/ft$

Answer is C

Solution 4

The calculations for unit weight and dry unit weight are shown for sample # 1

Weight of soil (lb)	Water content (%)	Unit weight (pcf)	Dry Unit weight (pcf)
3.20	12.8	3.2÷(1/30) = 96.0	96÷(1+0.128) = 85.1
3.78	13.9	113.4	99.6
4.40	15.0	132.0	114.8
4.10	15.7	123.0	106.3
3.70	16.6	111.0	95.2
3.30	18.1	99.0	83.9

The maximum dry unit weight = 114.8 pcf

Answer is D

Solution 5

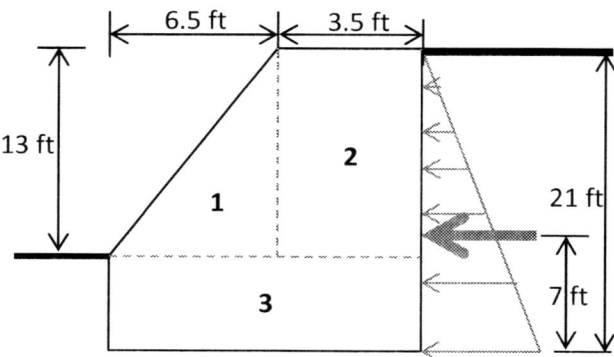

Weights of segments 1, 2 and 3 of the wall are: $140 \times \left(\frac{1}{2} \times 6.5 \times 13\right) = 5915 \; lb/ft$, $140 \times (3.5 \times 13) = 6370 \; lb/ft$ and $140 \times (8 \times 10) = 11200 \; lb/ft$ respectively

The stabilizing moment about the toe (tipping point) is given by:
$$5915 \times \frac{2}{3} \times 6.5 + 6370 \times 8.25 + 11200 \times 5 = 134184 \; lb \cdot ft/ft$$

For φ = 30°, K_a = 0.333

$$R_a = \frac{1}{2}K_a \gamma H^2 = 0.5 \times 0.333 \times 120 \times 21^2 = 8820 \; lb/ft$$

Overturning moment = 8820 x 7 = 61740 lb-ft/ft

FS = 134184/61740 = 2.17

Answer is B

Solution 6
Since F_{200} < 35, the groups A-4, A-5, A-6 and A-7 are eliminated.

Gradation requirements of groups A-1 and A-3 are not met.

LL = 19 and PI = 4 meets requirements for AASHTO Group A-2-4

Answer is A

Solution 7
Total unit weight = 127 lb/ft^3
Assume total volume V = 1 ft^3
Then, total weight W = 127 b.
Distribute this weight in 100:10 proportions (solid:water)
Weight of solids = 100/110 x 127 = 115.5 lb
Weight of water = 11.5 lb.
Volume of solids = 115.5/165.4 = 0.698 ft^3
Volume of voids = 0.302

Porosity = V_{voids}/V_{total} = 30%

Answer is D

Solution 8
F_{200} = 15. This is less than 50. Therefore it is predominantly a coarse grained soil (first letter G or S). However, since F_{200} > 12, the seond letter of the classification will depend on plasticity characteristics (LL and PI)

R_4 = 0. This means that the gravel fraction is negligible. Therefore first letter is S.

LL = 20, PI = 2, which is less than 4. This plots in the "ML" region of the Casgrande chart. Soil is classified as SM.

Answer is C

Solution 9
Weight of soil solids 3.67 lb
Since sp. gravity of soil solids = 2.73, volume of soil solids = 3.67÷(2.73x62.4) = 0.02154 ft³
Weight of water = 4.18 – 3.67 = 0.51 lb
Volume of water = 0.51÷62.4 = 0.00817 ft³
Total volume = 1/30 = 0.03333 ft³
Therefore, volume of air = 0.03333 – (0.02154 + 0.00817) = 0.00362 ft³

Degree of saturation: $S = \dfrac{V_{water}}{V_{voids}} = \dfrac{0.00817}{0.00817+0.00362} = 0.693$

Answer is A

Solution 10
Weight of wall = (13x1+8x1)x150 = 3150 lb/ft
Weight of soil = 13x3.5x118 = 5369 lb/ft
Total weight = 8519 lb/ft
Friction force = 0.5x8519 = 4260 lb/ft
K_A = 0.3
Active earth pressure resultant $R_a = ½ K_a \gamma H^2$ = 3469 lb/ft
FS = 4260÷3469 = 1.23

Answer is D

Solution 11

Sample	Net weight of soil	Moisture content (%)	Unit weight (pcf)	Dry Unit weight (pcf)
1	3 lb 8 oz = 3.50 lb	13	3.5 ÷ (1/30) = 105	105 ÷ 1.13 = 92.9
2	3 lb 14.4 oz= 3.90 lb	14	117	102.6
3	4 lb 2.9 oz= 4.18 lb	15	125.4	109.0
4	4 lb 3.2 oz= 4.20 lb	16	126	108.6
5	3 lb 14.4 oz= 3.90 lb	18	117	99.2
6	3 lb 6.4 oz= 3.40 lb	20	102	85.0

Maximum Proctor dry density = 109 pcf. Target dry density = 0.9x109 = 98 pcf
Target water content = 15%. Current water content (11%) needs to be increased by 4%
Total weight of solids in fill = $1.5 \times 10^6 \times 27 \times 98 = 3.97 \times 10^9$ lb
Water weight needed = $0.04 \times 3.97 \times 10^9$ lb = 1.588×10^8 lb
Volume of water needed = 19 million gallons

Answer is C

Solution 12

F_{200} = 10. Coarse fraction = 90. This is more than 50, therefore it is predominantly a coarse grained soil (first letter G or S).
R_4 = 20, which is less than half of the coarse fraction. Therefore first letter is S.
LL = 31, PI = 6

D_{10} = 0.075 mm; D_{30} = 0.425 mm; D_{60} = 2.00 mm
$C_u = D_{60}/D_{10}$ = 26.7; $C_c = D^2_{30}/(D_{10}D_{60})$ = 1.2

5 < F_{200} < 12: Soil has dual classification. Meets both criteria for SW (C_u > 6 and 1 < C_c < 3) and plots below the A-Line (0.73(LL-20) = 8; PI is less than 8

Soil is classified as SW-SM

Answer is D

Solution 13
Weight of test sand in test hole = 13.36 − 11.13 = 2.23 lb
Volume of test sand in test hole = 2.23÷84.7 = 0.02633 ft^3
Weight of soil obtained from the test hole = 3.65 lb
Unit weight of soil obtained from the test hole = 3.65÷0.02633 = 138.6 pcf
Dry unit weight of soil = 138.6÷1.173 = 118.2 pcf
Percent compaction = 118.2÷122.3 = 97%

Answer is A

Solution 14
Head difference = 945 − 905 = 40 ft
Length of seepage path = 160 ft
Hydraulic gradient = 40/160 = 0.25
Area of flow = 120 x 6.5 = 780 sq. ft
Permeability k = 9.5 ft/day = 0.0066 ft/min
Discharge Q = KIA = 0.0066 x 0.25 x 780 = 1.286 ft^3/min = 9.62 gal/min

Answer is B

Solution 15
Since the moisture content is 19%, the total weight of the soil can be divided into the solids fraction (100/119) and the water fraction (19/119).
Weight of soil solids = 100/119x66.8 = 56.1 lb
Since specific gravity of soil solids = 2.72, solids volume = 56.1/(2.72x62.4) = 0.33 ft^3
Volume of voids = 0.55 − 0.33 = 0.22 ft^3

Geotechnical Topics on FE Civil Examination

Weight of water = 66.8 − 56.1 = 10.7 lb
Volume of water = 10.7/62.4 = 0.17 ft³

Therefore, degree of saturation S = V_water/V_voids = 0.17/0.22 = 0.77

Answer is D

Solution 16
Concentric load = 80 k. Moment = 35 kip-ft. As a result, eccentricity e = M/P = 0.44 ft. This is less than B/6, so the entire footing is effective in compression.

Maximum soil pressure: $\sigma = \frac{P}{A} + \frac{Mc}{I} = \frac{80}{6\times 8} + \frac{35\times 4}{\frac{1}{12}\times 6\times 8^3} = 2.214 \; kip/ft^2$

Answer is B

Solution 17
Initial effective vertical stress at P = 6 x 114 + 2 x (120-62.4) + 6 x (108-62.4) = 1072.8 psf
After building load, effective vertical stress at point P = 1072.8 + 670 = 1742.8 psf

Settlement: $s = \frac{H\Delta e}{1+e_o} = \frac{HC_c}{1+e_o} \log_{10} \frac{P'_2}{P'_1} = \frac{144\times 0.6}{1+1.4} \log_{10} \frac{1742.8}{1072.8} = 7.6 \; in$

Answer is A

Solution 18
σ_1 = 1000
τ_1 = 675
σ_2 = 3000
τ_2 = 2025

Friction angle: $\tan \phi = \frac{\tau_2 - \tau_1}{\sigma_2 - \sigma_1} = \frac{2025 - 675}{3000 - 1000} = 0.675 \Rightarrow \phi = 34°$

Using coordinates of point 1: Cohesion: $c = 675 - 1000 \times \tan \phi = 0$

Answer is A

Solution 19
Depth of water table below footing = 20 − 3 = 17 ft, which is more than the footing width (10 ft). Therefore, the groundwater has no effect on the bearing capacity. Ignoring any cohesion, ultimate bearing capacity is given by:

Geotechnical Topics on FE Civil Examination

$$q_{ult} = cN_c + \gamma DN_q + \frac{1}{2}\gamma BN_\gamma = 0 + 115 \times 3 \times 29.5 + 0.5 \times 115 \times 10 \times 27.4$$
$$= 25{,}932.5 \: psf$$

Soil pressure due to column load + soil overburden = 750,000/100 + 115x3 = 7845 psf

FS = 25932/7845 = 3.3

Answer is B

Solution 20

The governing theory is for the falling head test. The area of the tube in which the liquid column is falling (a) is given by:

$$a = \frac{\pi \times 0.2^2}{4} = 0.0314 \: in^2$$

Cross-sectional area of the soil column:

$$A = \frac{\pi \times 30^2}{4} = 706.9 \: in^2$$

h_1 and h_2 must be measured from the outfall elevation (50 in). h_1 = 85 – 50 = 35. H_2 = 75 – 50 = 25. Elapsed time = 35 minutes = 0.583 hr

$$K = 2.303 \frac{aL}{A(t_2 - t_1)} \log_{10}(h_1/h_2) = \frac{2.303 \times 0.0314 \times 20 \times \log_{10}(35/25)}{706.9 \times 0.583}$$
$$= 0.000513 \frac{in}{hr} = 4.3 \times 10^{-5} ft/hr$$

Answer is C

Solution 21

Assume weight of solids = 100 lb
Weight of water = 20 lb (since water content = 20%)
Volume of soil solids = 100 ÷ (62.4 x 2.68) = 0.6 ft^3
Volume of water = 20 ÷ 62.4 = 0.321 ft^3
Since degree of saturation = 0.6, volume of voids = 0.321 ÷ 0.6 = 0.535 ft^3
Total volume = 0.6 + 0.535 = 1.135 ft^3
Dry unit weight = 100 lb ÷ 1.135 ft^3 = 88 pcf

Answer is C

Solution 22

Weight of can = 7.41 lb
Moist soil + can = 48.30 lb
Therefore, weight of moist soil = 48.30 – 7.41 = 40.89 lb
Dry soil + can = 41.22 lb
Therefore, weight of dry soil = 41.22 – 7.41 = 33.81 lb

Weight of water = 40.89 − 33.81 = 7.08 (same as 48.30 − 41.22)
Water content = 7.08 ÷ 33.81 = 0.21

Answer is A

Solution 23

The formula for relative density is:

$$D_r = \left(\frac{\gamma_{D,field}-\gamma_{D,min}}{\gamma_{D,max}-\gamma_{D,min}}\right)\left(\frac{\gamma_{D,max}}{\gamma_{D,field}}\right) = \left(\frac{121-105}{125-105}\right)\left(\frac{125}{121}\right) = 82.6\%$$

Answer is B

Solution 24

Moist weight of soil = 5 lb (proportioned as 100:20 – solids:water)
Weight of soil solids = 100/120x5 = 4.17 lb
To achieve 10% increase of water content, we must add 10% of weight of solids = 0.417 lb

Answer is B

Solution 25

Fine grained soil – use Casagrande Plasticity Chart.

LL = 45, PI = 45 − 30 = 15. This plots below the A-line. Soil classification is ML

Answer is C

Solution 26

The wet unit weight of the lean clay: $\gamma = \gamma_d(1+w) = 109.2\ pcf$

At the center of lean clay layer, the initial effective vertical stress:

$$\sigma_1' = 120 \times 8 + (109.2 - 62.4) \times 7.5 = 1311\ psf$$

The surface load due to the preloading fill is dissipated with depth as follows:

$$\sigma_v' = \frac{105 \times 10 \times 50^2}{(50+15.5)^2} = 612\ psf$$

At center of lean clay layer, the effective stress after preloading:

$$\sigma_2' = 1311 + 612 = 1923\ psf$$

Settlement due to consolidation: $s = \frac{0.48 \times 15 \times 12}{1+1.2} \times \log_{10}\left(\frac{1923}{1311}\right) = 6.13\ inches$

Answer is D

Solution 27

For vertical stem, horizontal backfill and no friction behind wall, the active earth pressure coefficient is:

$$K_a = \tan^2(45 - \varphi/2) = \tan^2(45 - 32/2) = 0.307$$

For soil layer 2, total unit weight = 90x1.2 = 108 pcf and submerged unit weight = 45.6 pcf

According to standard case shown in the FE Handbook, the lateral force components are:

$$P_W = \frac{1}{2}\gamma_w H_2^2 = \frac{1}{2} \times 62.4 \times 9^2 = 2527.2 \; lb/ft$$

$$P_{A1} = \frac{1}{2}\sigma_1' K_A H_1 = \frac{1}{2} \times 120 \times 6 \times 0.307 \times 6 = 663.1 \; lb/ft$$

$$P_{A2} = \frac{1}{2}(\sigma_1' + \sigma_2') K_A H_2 = \frac{1}{2} \times (720 + 1130.4) \times 0.307 \times 9 = 2556.3 \; lb/ft$$

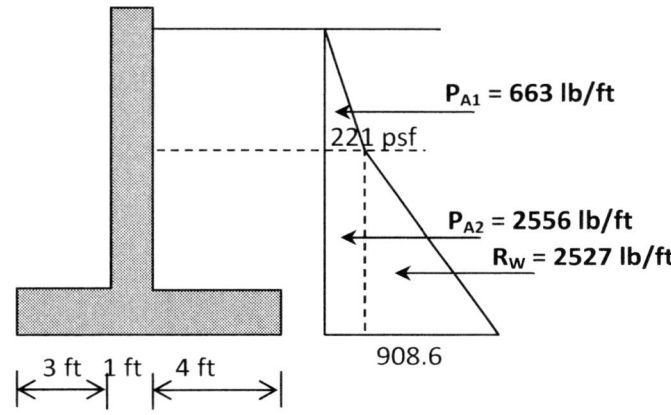

The total horizontal earth pressure force = 5746 lb/ft

Answer is C

Solution 28

The depth associated with this SPT result is at the center of the 2nd and 3rd penetration intervals, i.e. exactly 1 foot below the start depth for the test.

Field SPT N-value = 39

Answer is B

Solution 29

From sample 1, total unit weight = 62.3 ÷ 0.5 = 124.6 lb/ft^3

From sample 2, dry unit weight = 32.3 ÷ 0.3 = 107.7 lb/ft^3

Geotechnical Topics on FE Civil Examination

Water content: $w = \frac{\gamma}{\gamma_d} - 1 = \frac{125.6}{107.7} - 1 = 0.157$

Sample 1:
Weight of solids: $W_s = \frac{W_{total}}{1+w} = \frac{62.3}{1.157} = 53.85 \; lb$

Volume of solids: $V_s = \frac{53.85}{2.65 \times 62.4} = 0.326 \; ft^3$

Weight of water: $W_w = 62.3 - 53.85 = 8.45 \; lb$

Volume of water: $V_w = \frac{8.45}{62.4} = 0.135 \; ft^3$

Therefore, volume of air: $V_a = 0.5 - 0.326 - 0.135 = 0.039 \; ft^3$

This volume can be replaced by water, taking the soil to the saturated condition, beyond which the soil will bleed.

Weight of water that can be added = 0.039 x 62.4 = 2.45 lb

Answer is B

Solution 30

Cross sectional area: $A = \frac{\pi D^2}{4} = \frac{\pi \times 2^2}{4} = 3.14 \; in^2$

The 240 lb load represents an added axial load AFTER the confining pressure is exerted hydrostatically on the sample.

Axial stress at failure: $\sigma_1 = \frac{240}{3.14} + 50 = 126.4 \; psi$

Confining stress: $\sigma_3 = 50 \; psi$

Effective stresses: $\sigma_1' = 126.4 - 16 = 110.6 \; psi$; $\sigma_3' = 50 - 16 = 34 \; psi$

The distance from the origin to the center if the Mohr's circle is ½(σ_1' + σ_3') and radius of the Mohr's circle is ½(σ_1' - σ_3').

Therefore, angle of internal friction: $\sin \phi = \frac{\sigma_1' - \sigma_3'}{\sigma_1' + \sigma_3'} \Rightarrow \phi = \sin^{-1}\left(\frac{110.6-34}{110.6+34}\right) = 32°$

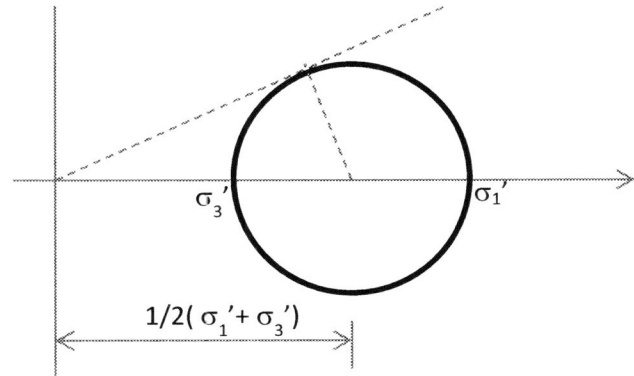

Answer is B

Solution 31

$$K_a = \tan^2(45 - \phi/2) = \tan^2(29) = 0.307$$

Active earth pressure resultant: $R_A = \frac{1}{2}K_a\gamma H^2 = \frac{1}{2} \times 0.307 \times 118 \times 20^2 = 7245\ lb/ft$

Answer is B

Solution 32

D_{10} = 0.5 mm
D_{30} = 1.2 mm
D_{60} = 2.9 mm

Uniformity coefficient: $C_u = \frac{D_{60}}{D_{10}} = \frac{2.9}{0.5} = 5.8$

Curvature coefficient: $C_z = \frac{D_{30}^2}{D_{10}D_{60}} = \frac{1.2^2}{0.5 \times 2.9} = 1.0$

F_{200} = 0 (smallest size is approx. 0.1 mm > 0.075 mm)

Coarse fraction = 100%. No. 4 sieve size = 4.75 mm. % passing no. 4 sieve ≈ 80%
R_4 = 100 – 80 = 20%. Therefore, the first letter is S (gravel frction 20%, sand fraction 80%)

Does not meet ALL criteria for SW soil (F_{200} < 5; C_u ≥6 AND 1<C_z<3)

Soil is classified SP.

Answer is C

Solution 33

Weight of wet soil = 37.6

Geotechnical Topics on FE Civil Examination

Since the water content = 17.4%, this can be split into dry soil (100/117.4x37.6 = 32.03 g) and water (5.57 g). Since the SG of soil solids is known (2.70), we also have volume of soil solids = 32.03÷2.7= 11.86 cc and volume of water = 5.57 cc.

Also, the buoyancy (apparent loss of weight on immersion) of the wax-coated sample = 40.9 – 16.5 = 24.4 g. Therefore, the volume of displaced water = volume of wax-coated sample = 24.4 cc

The weight of the wax = 40.9 – 37.6 = 3.3 g. This has a volume = 3.3÷0.9 = 3.67 cc

Therefore, the volume of the (uncoated) soil sample = 24.4 – 3.67 = 20.73 cc

Therefore volume of air = 20.73 – (11.86+5.57) = 3.30 cc

Based on these parameters: dry density ρ_d = 32.03÷20.73 = 1.545 g/cc
wet density ρ = 37.6÷20.73 = 1.814 g/cc
porosity n = V_{voids}/V_{total} = 8.87÷20.73 = 0.428
degree of saturation S = V_{water}/V_{voids} = 5.57÷8.87 = 0.628

Solution 34

K = 1 x 10^{-5} ft/sec

For each side, N_f = 3, N_e = 8, H = 16 ft

Flow rate (per unit length) q = 1 x 10^{-5} x 3/8 x 16 = 6 x10^{-5} ft^3/s/ft = 3.6 x10^{-3} ft^3/min/ft

Therefore, total seepage into the trench = 2 x 3.6 x10^{-3} ft^3/min/ft = 7.2 x10^{-3} ft^3/min/ft

Answer is B

Solution 35

The pressure difference can be converted to an equivalent head difference as: $H = \frac{\Delta p}{\gamma} = \frac{20 \times 144}{62.4} = 46.2\ ft$

The hydraulic gradient is calculated as: $i = \frac{H}{L} = \frac{46.2}{320} = 0.144\ ft/ft$

The critical hydraulic gradient is: $i_c = \frac{\gamma_{sat} - \gamma_w}{\gamma_w} = \frac{124 - 62.4}{62.4} = 0.987\ ft/ft$

Factor of safety against seepage liquefaction: $FS = \frac{i_c}{i_e} = \frac{0.987}{0.144} = 6.86$

Answer is C

Solution 36

According to the correlation between liquid limit and the compression index,
$$C_C = 0.009(LL - 10) = 0.009 \times (45 - 10) = 0.315$$
According to the correlation between compression index and the recompression index,
$$C_R = C_C/6 = 0.053$$

Answer is A

Solution 37

The shear strength of a c-f soil is calculated as: $\tau_F = c + \sigma_N \tan \phi = 2100 + 2000 \times \tan 20 = 2,828 \; psf$

Answer is A

Solution 38

The ultimate bearing capacity is composed of two components – side friction over the embedded surface area A_s, and point bearing on the tip area A_p

$$A_s = 2\pi RH = 2 \times \pi \times \frac{9}{12} \times 40 = 188.5 \; ft^2$$

$$A_p = \pi R^2 = \pi \times \left(\frac{9}{12}\right)^2 = 1.77 \; ft^2$$

Ultimate point bearing capacity: $Q_p = cN_c A_p = 2300 \times 9 \times 1.77 = 36,639 \; lb$

Ultimate side friction capacity: $Q_s = f_s A_s = 1400 \times 188.5 = 263,900 \; lb$

Total ultimate bearing capacity = 300,539 lb

Answer is D

Transportation Topics on FE Civil Examination

Transportation

Transportation Topics on FE Civil Examination   **8-12 problems**
Approximately 8% of Exam

A. Geometric design of streets and highways
B. Geometric design of intersections
C. Pavement system design (e.g., thickness, subgrade, drainage, rehabilitation)
D. Traffic safety
E. Traffic capacity
F. Traffic flow theory
G. Traffic control devices
H. Transportation planning (e.g., travel forecast modeling)

Problem 1
A horizontal circular curve is to connect a back-tangent bearing S42°30'W to a forward tangent bearing N70°W. If the degree of curve is 3°45' and the tangents intersect at station 50+22.30, what is the location of the PC?
- A. 35+87.30
- B. 40+01.40
- C. 41+67.80
- D. 43+47.90

Problem 2
A parabolic vertical curve is to connect a tangent of +5% to a gradient of –4%. If the PVI is a station 123+32.50 and the tangent offset at the PVT is 17.65 ft, the station of the PVC is most nearly:
- A. 120+32.98
- B. 120+81.32
- C. 121+07.74
- D. 121+36.39

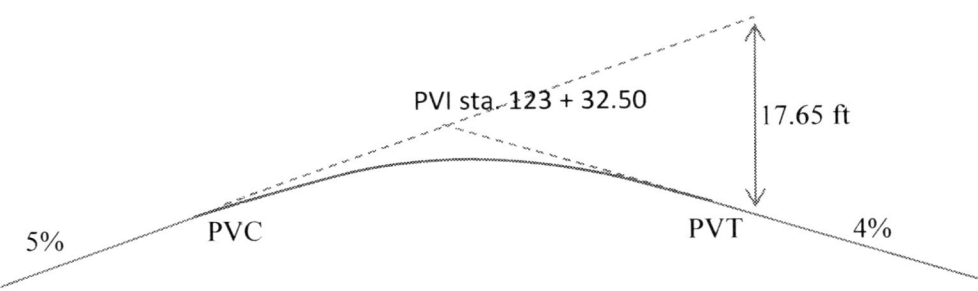

Problem 3
A parabolic vertical curve joins a grade of –5% to a grade of +3%. The PVC is at station 53+12.50 and the PVI is at station 60+09.00. Elevation of the PVI is 365.57 ft. The curve passes under a bridge structure at station 55+05.20. The bottom elevation of the bridge is 405.20 ft. The vertical clearance under the bridge (feet) is most nearly:
- A. 13.11
- B. 13.37
- C. 13.56
- D. 13.91

Problem 4
A parabolic vertical curve joins a grade of +6% to a grade of −4%. The length of the curve is 800 ft. What is the minimum stopping sight distance required on this curve?
- A. 380 ft
- B. 415 ft
- C. 450 ft
- D. 488 ft

Problem 5
A two-lane highway has a circular horizontal alignment with centerline radius = 750 ft. Lanes are 12 ft wide. An obstructing structure exists 10 ft from the inside edge of the roadway as shown. The available stopping sight distance for a driver in the inside lane (assume path of driver is along the centerline of the inside lane) is most nearly:
- A. 275 ft
- B. 305 ft
- C. 325 ft
- D. 356 ft

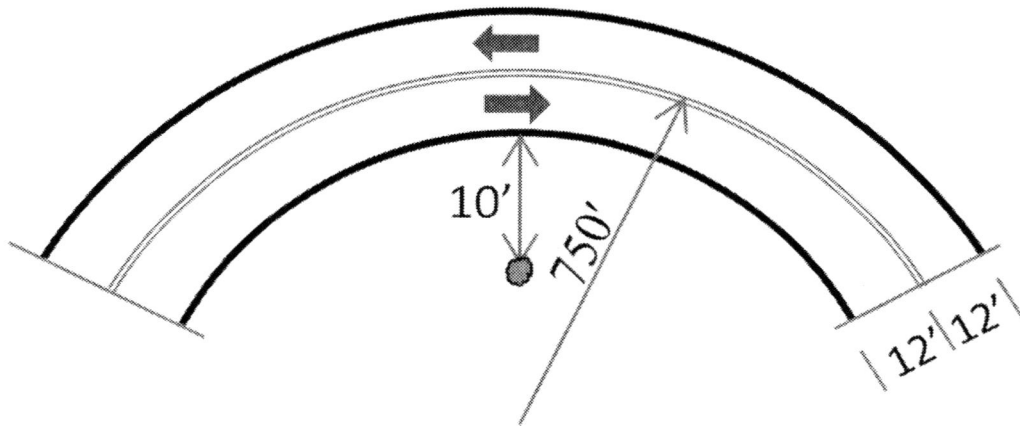

Problem 6
The findings of a speed survey are summarized below.

Speed Interval (mph)	Frequency
20 – 25	2
25 – 30	9
30 – 35	16
35 – 40	28
40 – 45	19
45 – 50	11
50 – 55	3

Transportation Topics on FE Civil Examination

The 85th percentile speed, in miles per hour is most nearly
- A) 43.2 mph
- B) 44.7 mph
- C) 46.1 mph
- D) 45.5 mph

Problem 7
Assuming driver perception-reaction time of 2.5 seconds and deceleration rate = 11.2 ft/s^2, the braking distance (feet) for a car on a 2 percent upgrade traveling at 40 mph is most nearly
- A) 145
- B) 167
- C) 177
- D) 307

Problem 8
A car accelerates uniformly from rest to its peak speed of 70 mph. The acceleration rate is 8 mph/sec. After traveling a certain distance at peak speed, the vehicle brakes to rest, decelerating uniformly at 10 mph/sec. If the total distance traveled is 0.5 miles, the average running speed (mph) is most nearly:
- A) 48.7 mph
- B) 51.2 mph
- C) 53.6 mph
- D) 57.4 mph

Problem 9
A horizontal curve is to be designed for a roadway where the design speed is 65 mph, the side friction factor is in the range 0.10 to 0.15, superelevation rate is in the range 0.08 to 0.10. For a safe design, the maximum degree of curvature (degrees) is most nearly:
- A) 3.6
- B) 4.1
- C) 4.7
- D) 5.1

Problem 10

A horizontal curve for a section of a highway has a design speed of 60 mph. The terrain restricts the radius of the curve to 1200 ft. If the side friction factor is 0.12, what is the required superelevation of the highway (percent)?

- A) 4
- B) 6
- C) 8
- D) 10

Problem 11

A parabolic crest curve is followed by a sag curve. The two curves are connected by a tangent section as shown. A bridge structure is located at station 40 + 55.00. The elevation of the low point on the bridge is 410.54 ft. The vertical clearance at station 40 + 55.00 is most nearly:

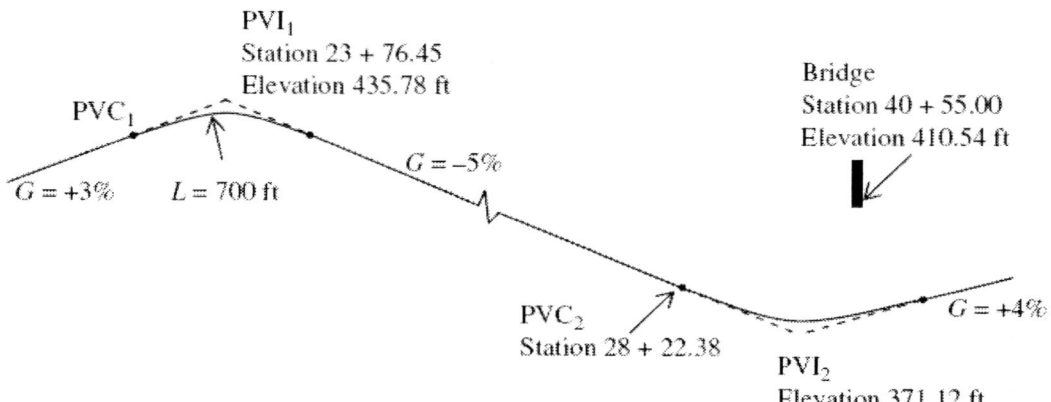

(A) 17 ft 9 in
(B) 18 ft 4 in
(C) 13 ft 6 in
(D) 14 ft 9 in

Problem 12

A horizontal (circular) curve has a radius of 1150 ft as shown below. The intersection angle at the center is 36°. The point P on the major chord is located such that AP = 215 ft. What is the length of the arc AQ?

Transportation Topics on FE Civil Examination

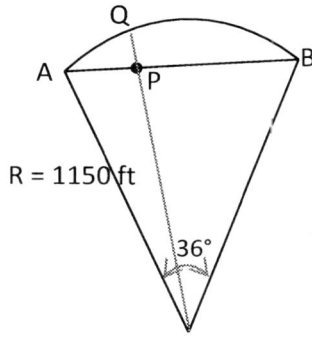

A) 213.45 ft
B) 214.76 ft
C) 214.92 ft
D) 215.34 ft

Problem 13

A horizontal curve is going to be constructed for a paved county road in northern Michigan. The recommended superelevation is 8%. The pavement is 20 ft wide with 4 ft shoulders. The legs of the proposed curve are perpendicular. A design speed of 60 mph is desired. What is most nearly the minimum radius needed to provide a design where there is no reliance on a lateral friction force?

    A. 1890 ft
    B. 2340 ft
    C. 2680 ft
    D. 3000 ft

Problem 14

A horizontal curve is to be constructed for a paved county road in northern Michigan. The recommended superelevation is 8%. The pavement is 20 ft wide with 4 ft shoulders. The legs of the proposed curve are perpendicular. The side friction factor for the design speed of 60 mph is 0.12. What is most nearly the minimum length of the curve?

    A. 1885 ft
    B. 2025 ft
    C. 2145 ft
    D. 2320 ft

Problem 15

A ramp is to tie into an existing road at elevation 1207.44 ft, sta 16 + 00 on a 3% downgrade. The vertical curve must clear an underground sewer by 4.5 ft. The sewer is 125

Transportation Topics on FE Civil Examination

ft back from the PVT, and the top of the sewer is at elevation 1204.69 ft. The grade leading into the vertical curve is + 6%. What is the required length of the vertical curve?

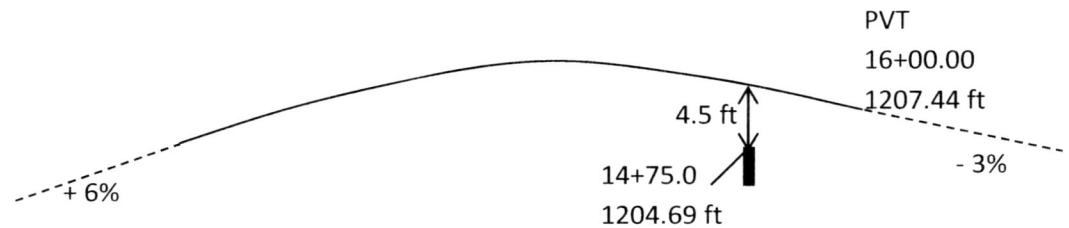

Problem 16

A stadium hosts an event with an audience of 40,000. Approximately 30% of the audience members are expected to use an adjacent light rail station following the event. It is anticipated that about 90% of the stadium empties in the first hour after the conclusion of the event. A dedicated pedestrian walkway connects the stadium to the light rail station. The effective width of the walkway is 32 ft. Assume the PHF (based on peak 15 minute flow) for the walkway is 0.88. The peak flow rate (ped/min/ft) on the walkway during the first hour is most nearly:
  A) 4.8
  B) 5.6
  C) 6.4
  D) 7.2

Problem 17
A weigh station records the following truck axle data:

Single Axles	
Axle load (kips)	Number
10	34
15	56
24	17
32	9

Double Axles	
Axle load (kips)	Number
15	11
24	35
32	22
40	5

What is the equivalent number of 18 kip axles?
  A. 100
  B. 150
  C. 200
  D. 250

Problem 18

The intersection shown below has the accident data tabulated in the table. What is the total rate of accidents at this intersection over the period 2009-2011?

A. 4.7 accidents per million entering vehicles
B. 5.2 accidents per million entering vehicles
C. 7.1 accidents per million entering vehicles
D. 8.9 accidents per million entering vehicles

Year	Number of accidents		
	Fatal	Injury	PDO
2009	3	13	28
2010	5	14	23
2011	2	21	31

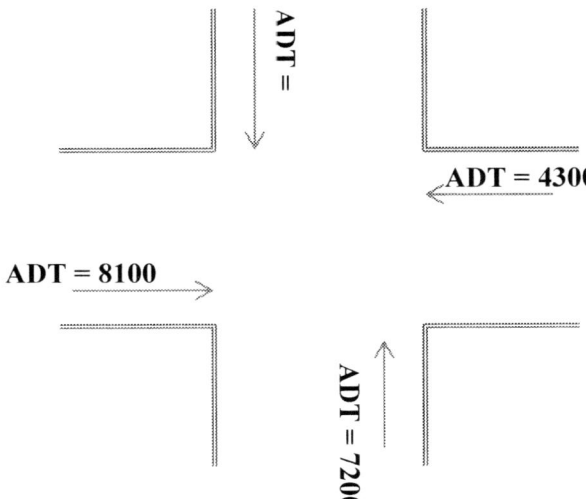

ADT values from 2009. Traffic expected to grow by 4% each year

Problem 19

A highway alignment consists of a circular horizontal curve with radius R = 850 ft. The length of the curve is 625 ft. If the design speed is 55 mph and the coefficient of side friction = 0.12, what is the required superelevation?

A. 6%
B. 8%
C. 10%
D. 12%

Transportation Topics on FE Civil Examination

Problem 20

The intersection shown below is signalized with a two phase signal cycle. The green phase in each direction is to be followed by a yellow clearance interval. The design speed for both approaches is 45 mph. Main Street is on level grade, while 3rd Avenue has a longitudinal grade of 5%. If the design vehicle length is 48 ft, reaction time = 1 second and deceleration rate = 10 ft/s^2, what is the length of the yellow interval required following the north-south green phase?

    A. 4 seconds
    B. 5 seconds
    C. 6 seconds
    D. 7 seconds

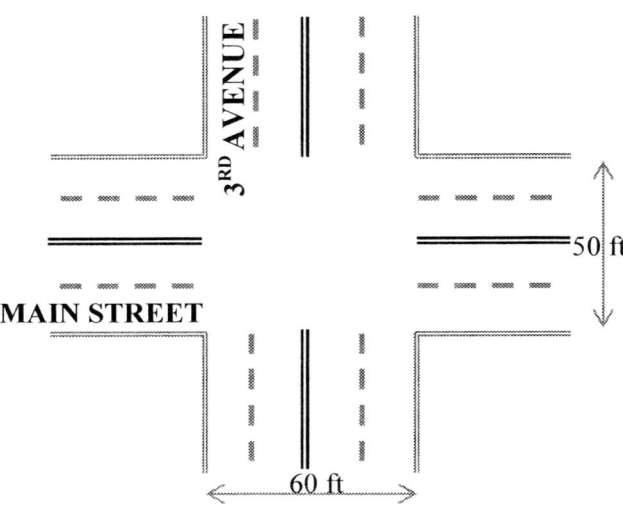

Problem 21

Earthwork estimates for a highway project are summarized in the following table of end areas at stations 100 ft apart. The total earthwork volume (yd^3) between stations 20 + 0.00 and 24 + 0.00 is most nearly:

    A) 6500
    B) 7000
    C) 7500
    D) 8000

Station	Area (ft^2)
20 + 00	405
21 + 00	576
22 + 00	432

23 + 00	378
24 + 00	630

Problem 22

A parabolic vertical curve joins a grade of –5% to a grade of +6%. The PVC is at station 53+12.50 and the PVI is at station 60+09.00. Based on rider comfort, what is the maximum recommended speed on the roadway?

    A. 65 mph
    B. 70 mph
    C. 75 mph
    D. 80 mph

Problem 23

A highway has a design speed of 60 mph. One portion of the alignment consists of a horizontal circular curve with radius 1200 ft. In order to provide a smoother transition into the curve at this design speed, the designers are proposing a spiral as a transition curve from the tangent to the circular curve. If the rate of increase of lateral acceleration = 2 ft/s^3, what should be the length of the spiral?

    A. 175 ft
    B. 285 ft
    C. 315 ft
    D. 375 ft

Problem 24

A new housing development will likely produce 800 trips during the a.m. peak hour. Most of the people who will live in the development will likely work in five zones scattered across the city. The sizes of the employment zones and the distances from the zones to the housing development are provided below.

Employment Zone	No. of employees	Distance (km)
1	2,000	2
2	4,000	5
3	12,000	6
4	50,000	10
5	8,000	15

Transportation Topics on FE Civil Examination

It may be assumed that the number of trips attracted to each zone is proportional to the total number of employees in that zone. The number of trips attracted to zone 3 from the housing development during the a.m. peak hour is most nearly:

A. 170
B. 160
C. 150
D. 140

Problem 25
A flexible pavement has two layers – a 4 inch thick asphalt surface course (layer coefficient = 0.40) and a 10-inch thick base course (layer coefficient = 0.20). What is the structural number of the pavement?

A. 3.0
B. 3.3
C. 3.6
D. 4.0

Problem 26
A highway has a peak flow rate of 1560 pcphpl (passenger cars per hour per lane). If the average speed is 45 mph, what is the headway (time gap) between successive vehicles?

A. 120 ft
B. 135 ft
C. 150 ft
D. 165 ft

Problem 27
A horizontal curve connects two tangents with a deflection angle of 56°. The degree of curve is 7°30'. If the PI is located at sta. 12 + 30.45, what is the location of the PT?

A. 14 + 60.21
B. 15 + 70.93
C. 14 + 52.84
D. 15 + 20.23

Problem 28

What are the latitude and departure of the line CA for the traverse shown below?

A. Latitude = − 532.13 ft; Departure = + 447.48 ft
B. Latitude = + 447.48 ft; Departure = − 532.13 ft
C. Latitude = + 447.48 ft; Departure = + 532.13 ft
D. Latitude = + 532.13 ft; Departure = − 447.48 ft

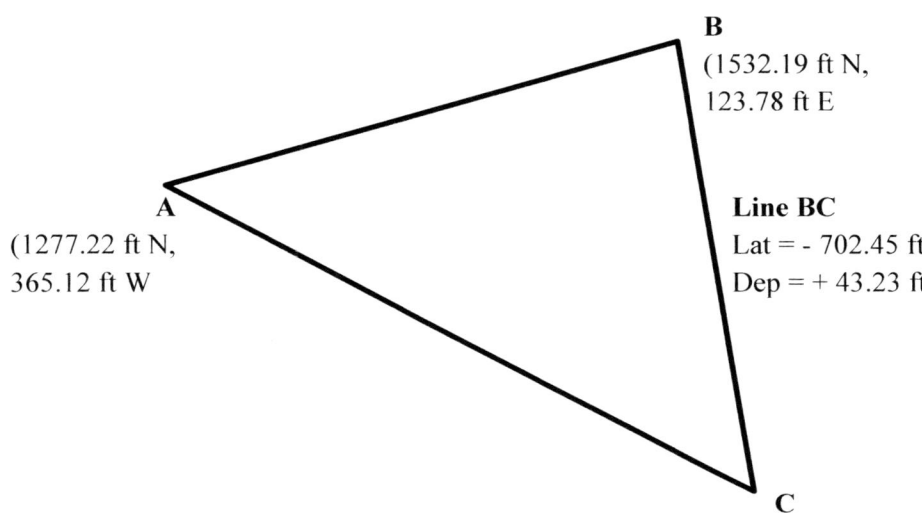

Problem 29

What is the appropriate performance grading for an asphalt binder which is subjected to:

　　　　　Average 7-day maximum pavement temperature　　55°C
　　　　　Mimimum pavement temperature　　　　　　　　- 20°C

A. PG 52 – 10
B. PG 55 – 20
C. PG 58 – 20
D. PG 58 – 22

Problem 30

A circular horizontal curve of radius 1025 ft has a back tangent with a bearing S 76°45′ W. The curve deflects left by a deflection angle of 56°. What is the chord distance from the PC to the PT?

A. 962 ft
B. 876 ft
C. 823 ft
D. 798 ft

Problem 31

An urban intersection had 23 crashes during the planning year 2001-2002. The ADT (all entering vehicles) for this year was 6400. Two specific countermeasures were implemented. They are described below:

Countermeasure 1
Widening of lanes
Expected reduction of crashes = 12%

Countermeasure 2
Eliminating curbside parking
Expected reduction of crashes = 32%

If the ADT is expected to increase by 3% every year, what is the number of crashes expected during the year 2011-2012?

A. 12
B. 19
C. 26
D. 31

Problem 32

What is the recommended gyratory compaction effort for an asphalt mix for the following conditions?

Average design high air temperature = 40°C
$W_{18} = 30 \times 10^6$

A. 106
B. 121
C. 139
D. 166

Problem 33

A parabolic curve has an approach grade of -4% and an exit grade of +6% as shown. A bridge overpass exists at station 32 + 23.78 as shown. The vertical clearance under the bridge is 14 ft 6 inch. The design speed for the highway is 70 mph. Assume that height of a truck driver's eye is 8.0 ft and the height of the obstruction to be sighted is 2.0 ft. What is the minimum length of curve required for adequate stopping sight distance under the obstruction?

A. 500 ft
B. 600 ft
C. 700 ft
D. 800 ft

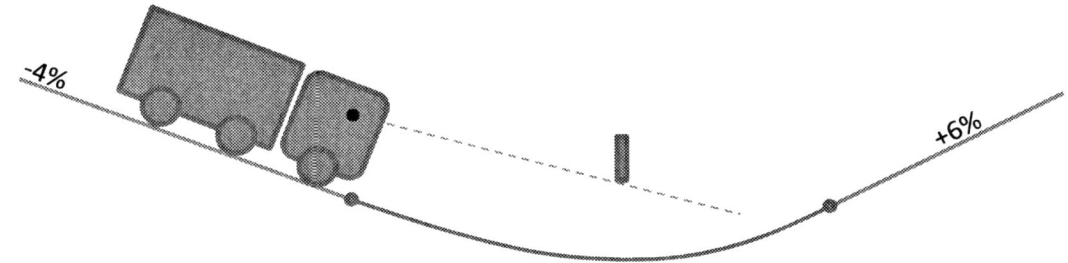

Problem 34
A 3 lane freeway has free flow speed = 70 mph and jam density = 130 veh/mi/lane. Assuming a linear relationship between speed and density, what is the maximum flow rate this freeway can carry?
- A. 2300
- B. 5600
- C. 6800
- D. 7200

Problem 35
Citizens of a small community have three choices for commuting to the employment zone defined as 'downtown', which is a distance of 17 miles away. The choices are (1) driving, (2) commuter rail and (3) a suburban bus line. The utility values for the three modes, based on a factored sum of attributes such as time, cost, etc. are -1.23 for driving, -2.11 for commuter rail and -1.89 for the bus line. If the total number of commuters originating from the community is 560, how many are expected to take the bus?
- A. 150
- B. 170
- C. 190
- D. 210

Problem 36
The following results are given from conducting tests on an asphalt binder as part of the Superpave protocol.

Dynamic Shear Rheometer

Test temperature °C	Dynamic Shear $G^*/\sin \delta$ kPa
58	1.92
64	1.08
70	0.81

Rolling Thin Film Oven Residue

Test temperature °C	Dynamic Shear $G^*/\sin \delta$ kPa
58	4.04
64	2.41
70	1.75

Pressure Aging Vessel

Test temperature °C	Creep Stiffness S MPa
-6	272
-12	304
-18	421

Based on these results, the recommended range of pavement temperatures where this asphalt can be used is:

 A. 55°C to -18°C
 B. 50°C to -24°C
 C. 65°C to -20°C
 D. 60°C to -26°C

Transportation Solutions

Solution 1

Azimuth of back tangent = 180° + 42°30′ = 222°30′

Azimuth of forward tangent = 360° − 70° = 290°00′

Deflection angle between tangents, I = 290°00′ − 222°30′ = 67°30′

Radius: $R = \dfrac{5729.578}{D} = \dfrac{5729.578}{3.75} = 1527.9\ ft$

Tangent length: $T = R \tan \dfrac{I}{2} = 1527.9 \times \tan \dfrac{67.5}{2} = 1020.9\ ft$

PC station = PI station − T = (50+22.30) − (10+20.90) = 40+01.40

Answer is B

Solution 2

The tangent offset at any location on a vertical curve = ½ Rx²

At the end of the curve (i.e. at the PVT) x = L, therefore tangent offset = $\dfrac{1}{2} \dfrac{G_2 - G_1}{L} L^2 = \dfrac{(G_2 - G_1)L}{2}$

For a crest curve, the vertical offset is negative, therefore: $\dfrac{(-4-5)L}{2} = -17.65 \Rightarrow L = 3.9222\ sta.$

Therefore, since the PVC is half the curve length upstream of the PVI:

Sta. PVC = sta. PVI − 1.9611 = 123.325 − 1.9611 = 121.3639   **(121 + 36.39)**

Answer is D

Solution 3

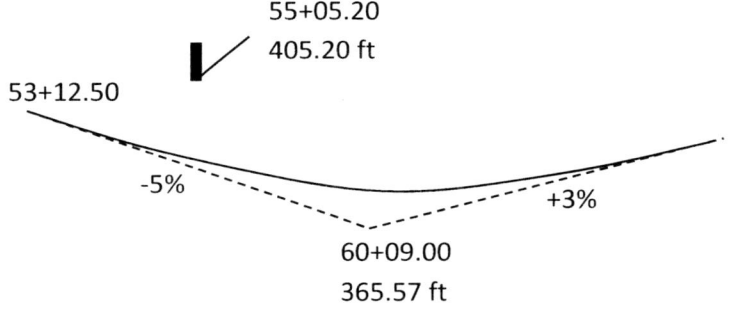

Distance from PVC to PVI = 6009.0 − 5312.50 = 696.50 ft

Length of curve = 2 × 696.50 = 1393 ft

Rate of grade change: $R = \dfrac{G_2 - G_1}{L} = \dfrac{3 - (-5)}{13.93} = 0.5743\ \%/sta$

Elevation of PVC: $y_{PVC} = y_{PVI} - G_1 \dfrac{L}{2} = 365.57 - (-5) \times 6.965 = 400.40$

Curve elevation at location of bridge (1.927 sta. ahead of PVC): $y = y_{PVC} + G_1 x + \dfrac{1}{2} R x^2 = 400.40 + (-5) \times 1.927 + \dfrac{1}{2} \times 0.5743 \times 1.927^2 = 391.83$

Vertical clearance = 405.20 − 391.83 = 13.37 ft

Answer is B

Solution 4

According to AASHTO Green Book criteria, stopping sight distance on crest vertical curves is:

$$L = \frac{AS^2}{2158} \quad for \quad S \leq L$$
$$L = 2S - \frac{2158}{A} \quad for \quad S > L$$

Try the first: $S = \sqrt{\frac{2158L}{A}} = \sqrt{\frac{2158 \times 800}{10}} = 415.5 \, ft$

This satisfies the corresponding criterion (S ≤ L)

Answer is B

Solution 5

Radius of roadway centerline = 750 ft
Radius of inside lane centerline = 750 – 6 = 744 ft
Middle ordinate distance (obstruction edge to centerline of inside lane) = 10 + 6 = 16 ft

$$S = \frac{R}{28.65} \cos^{-1}\left(1 - \frac{M}{R}\right) = \frac{744}{28.65} \cos^{-1}\left(1 - \frac{16}{744}\right) = 309.13 \, ft$$

Since 309 ft is the *available* stopping sight distance, we cannot choose 325 ft, but need to go *lower* to 305 ft

Answer is B

Solution 6

Total number of observations = 88
85% of observations = 74.8
Speed of 45 mph has an associated cumulative frequency = 74, and
speed of 50 mph has an associated cumulative frequency = 85

Interpolating, we have 85th percentile speed (corresponding to 74.8 observations) = 45.4 mph

Answer is D

Solution 7

Transportation Topics on FE Civil Examination

Question asks ONLY for Braking distance, given by: $\dfrac{V^2}{30\left(\frac{a}{32.2}\pm G\right)} = \dfrac{40^2}{30\left(\frac{11.2}{32.2}+0.02\right)} = 145\ ft$

Solution 8

For acceleration phase, time = 70÷8 = 8.75 sec
Acceleration rate = 8 mph/sec = 11.76 ft/s²
Distance = ½ at² = 0.5x11.76x8.75² = 450.2 ft
For deceleration phase, time = 70÷10 = 7.0 sec
Deceleration rate = 10 mph/sec = 14.7 ft/s²
Distance = ½ at² = 0.5x14.7x7² = 360.2 ft

Since total distance traveled = 0.5 mile = 2640 ft, this leaves distance for constant velocity phase = 2640 – 450.2 – 360.2 = 1829.6 ft

Time for constant velocity phase = 1829.6÷(1.47x70) = 17.8 sec

Total travel time = 8.75 + 17.8 + 7.0 = 33.53 sec

Average running speed = 2640÷33.53 = 78.73 fps = 53.6 mph

Answer is C

Solution 9

For a speed of 65 mph, the mimimum available value of (e + f) is 0.08 + 0.10 = 0.18

$$\dfrac{V^2}{15R} = 0.01e + f = 0.25 \Rightarrow R \geq \dfrac{65^2}{15 \times 0.18} = 1564.8\ ft$$

Degree of curve: $D = \dfrac{5729.58}{R} = \dfrac{5729.58}{1564.8} = 3.66°$ (not to be exceeded)

Answer is A

Solution 10

The required (minimum) superelevation is calculated as:

$$e \geq \dfrac{V^2_{mph}}{15R_{ft}} - f = \dfrac{60^2}{15 \times 1200} - 0.12 = 0.08$$

Answer is C

Solution 11

Distance to bridge structure from PVC_2 = 40.55 − 28.2238 = 12.3262 sta
Change in elevation between PVI_1 and PVI_2 = 435.78 − 371.12 = 64.66 ft
Distance between PVI_1 and PVI_2 = 64.66 ft ÷5% = 12.932 sta
Location of PVI_2 = 23.7645 + 12.932 = 36.6965 sta.
Distance from PVC_2 to PVI_2 = 36.6965 − 28.2238 = 8.4727 sta (which is L/2)
Therefore, length of curve 2 = 16.9454 sta
Rate of gradient change for curve 2 = 9/16.9454 = 0.53112 %/sta
Elevation of PVC_1 = 371.12 + 5 x 8.4727 = 413.48 ft
Elevation at sta 40.55 is
y = 413.48 + (−5)x12.3262 + 0.5 x 0.53112 x 12.3262^2 = 392.20 ft
Vertical clearance = 410.54 − 392.20 = 18.34 ft

Answer is B

Solution 12

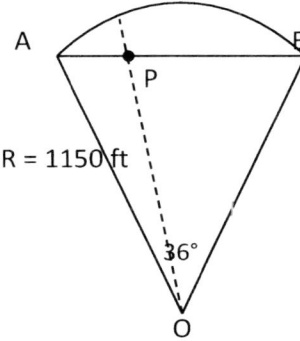

From triangle OAB, the angle OAB (which is the same as ange OAP) = 72°
From triangle OAP, using the law of cosines:
$$OP = \sqrt{1150^2 + 215^2 - 2 \times 1150 \times 215 \times \cos 72} = 1102.69 \, ft$$
Using law of sines:
$\frac{AP}{\sin \alpha} = \frac{OP}{\sin 72} \Rightarrow \alpha = 10.7° = 0.18675 \, rad$

The arc length = 1150 x 0.18675 = 214.76 ft

Answer is B

Solution 13

For a county road in northern Michigan (ice and snow prevalent) e = 8%

If there is no reliance of lateral friction, then the superelevation must be adequate for the centrifugal factor:

Transportation Topics on FE Civil Examination

$$e = \frac{V^2}{gR} = \frac{V_{mph}^2}{15R_{ft}} = 0.08 \Rightarrow R = \frac{60^2}{15 \times 0.08} = 3000 \, ft$$

Answer is D

Solution 14

Superelevation = 0.08

At V = 60 mph, the recommended side friction factor f = 0.12

Therefore, e + f = 0.20

$$\frac{V_{mph}^2}{15R_{ft}} \leq e + f = 0.20 \Rightarrow R \geq \frac{60^2}{15 \times 0.2} = 1200 \, ft$$

When the intersecting roads are perpendicular, I = 90°, length of curve: $L = \frac{RI}{57.29578} = \frac{1200 \times 90}{57.29578} = 1885 \, ft$

Answer is A

Solution 15

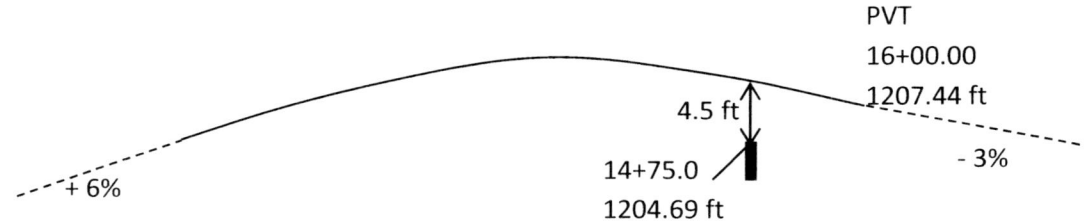

At the PVT, distance from PVC = L, elevation = 1207.44

$$1207.44 = y_{PVC} + 6 \times L + \frac{1}{2} \times \frac{G_2 - G_1}{L} \times L^2 = y_{PVC} + 6L - 4.5L = y_{PVC} + 1.5L$$

At point (on curve) above the top of the sewer, distance from PVC = L − 1.25, elevation = 1204.69 + 4.50 = 1209.19

$$1209.19 = y_{PVC} + 6 \times (L - 1.25) + \frac{1}{2} \times \frac{-9}{L} \times (L - 1.25)^2$$

$$= 1207.44 - 1.5L + 6L - 7.5 - \frac{4.5}{L} \times (L - 1.25)^2$$

Solving this equation, we get:

L = 3.516 sta = 351.6 ft

Transportation Topics on FE Civil Examination

Solution 16

Pedestrians using the walkway in the first hour = 0.9x0.3x40,000 = 10,800 ped/hr (hourly average)

Peak flow during the first hour = 10,800÷0.88 = 12,273 ped/hr = 204.5 ped/min

Peak flow rate = 204.5÷32 = 6.4 ped/min/ft

Solution 17

Single Axles				Double Axles			
Axle load (kips)	Number	LEF	N x LEF	Axle load (kips)	Number	LEF	N x LEF
10	34	0.0877	2.98	15	11	0.036	0.40
15	56	0.478	26.77	24	35	0.260	9.10
24	17	3.03	51.51	32	22	0.857	18.85
32	9	8.88	79.92	40	5	2.08	10.40
			161.18				38.75

The total ESAL (equivalent single axle loads) = 161.18 + 38.75 = 199.93

Answer is C

Solution 18

In year 2009, ADT = 26,300. This is equivalent to 9,599,500 veh per year

If the ADT grows by 4% ever year, total vehicles over 3 year (2009-2011) period can be calculated as the sum of a geometric series.

$$V = 9599500 \times \frac{1.04^3 - 1}{1.04 - 1} = 29.966 \; million$$

Total number of accidents = 44 + 42 + 54 = 140

Rate of accidents = 140/29.966 = 4.67 accidents per million entering vehicles

Answer is A

Solution 19

The superelevation requirement is governed by: $0.01e + f \geq \frac{V^2}{15R} = \frac{55^2}{15 \times 850} = 0.2373$

Therefore, 0.01e = 0.2373 − 0.12 = 0.1173

e = 11.73% (Use 12%)

Answer is D

Transportation Topics on FE Civil Examination

Solution 20

Design speed = 45 mph = 66 fps

The longer (and therefore, critical) value of the clearance interval will occur using the negative grade (G = - 5%)

The length of the yellow interval is given as: $y = t_R + \frac{v}{2a \pm 64.4G} = 1 + \frac{66}{2 \times 10 - 64.4 \times 0.05} = 4.93\ sec$

Yellow time of 5 seconds should be used.

Answer is B

Solution 21

Using the average end area method (trapezoidal rule), earthwork volume is calculated as:

$$V = \frac{1}{2} \times 100 \times [405 + 630 + 2 \times (576 + 432 + 378)] = 190{,}350\ ft^3 = 7{,}050\ yd^3$$

Answer is B

Solution 22

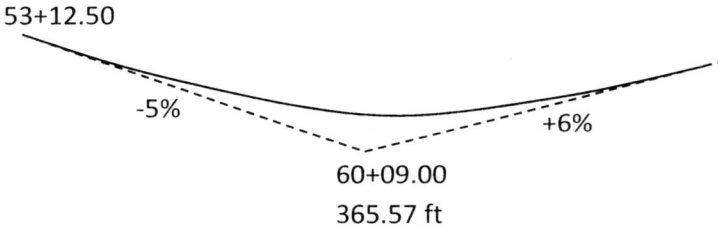

Distance from PVC to PVI = 6009.0 – 5312.50 = 696.50 ft
Length of curve = 2 x 696.50 = 1393 ft

Algebraic difference in grades: A = 6 + 5 = 11%

Minimum length of curve (based on rider comfort): $L_{min} = \frac{AV^2}{46.5}$

Therefore, max speed: $V = \sqrt{\frac{46.5L}{A}} = \sqrt{\frac{46.5 \times 1393}{11}} = 76.7\ mph$

Answer is C

Solution 23

Using C (rate of increase of lateral acceleration) = 2 ft/s³, the length of the spiral should be:

Transportation Topics on FE Civil Examination

$$L = \frac{3.15V^3}{RC} = \frac{3.15 \times 60^3}{1200 \times 2} = 283 \, ft$$

Answer is B

Solution 24

The 800 trips will be distributed according to weight factors that are proportional to employee population and inversely proportional to distance. These weight factors are presented in the table

Employment Zone (j)	Number of Employees (A_j)	Distance to Development $d_{ij} = 1/F_{ij}$	Factor $A_jF_{ij} = A_j/d_{ij}$
1	2,000	2	1000
2	4,000	5	800
3	12,000	6	2000
4	50,000	10	5000
5	8,000	15	533.33
			9333.33

Number of trips attracted to zone 3 = 2000/9333.33×800 = 171

Answer is A

Solution 25

The Structural number (SN) is calculated as: $SN = a_1D_1 + a_2D_2 + \cdots = 0.4 \times 4 + 0.2 \times 10 = 3.6$

Answer is C

Solution 26

Flow rate, q = 1560 pcphpl
Speed, S = 45 mph

Density, D = q/S = 1560/45 = 34.7 pc/mile/ln
Spacing between vehicles = 5280 ft/mile ÷ 34.7 pc/mile = 152 ft/pc

Answer is C

Solution 27

Degree of curve = 7.5°
Radius, $R = \frac{5729.58}{D} = 763.94 \, ft$

Transportation Topics on FE Civil Examination

Tangent length, $T = R \tan\left(\frac{I}{2}\right) = 763.94 \times \tan 28 = 406.19\ ft$

The PC is located this distance (T) behind the PI. Therefore, PC is located at (12 + 30.45) − (4 + 06.19) = 8 + 24.26

Length of curve: $L = \frac{100I}{D} = \frac{100 \times 56}{7.5} = 746.67\ ft$

The PT is located this distance (L) ahead of the PC. Therefore, PT is located at (8 + 24.26) + (7 + 46.67) = 15 + 70.93

Answer is B

Solution 28
Using the latitude and departure of line BC, coordinates of C are 1532.19 − 702.45 = 829.74 N and 123.78 + 43.23 = 167.01 ft E
Therefore, latitude and departure of line CA = coordinates of A − coordinates of C

Latitude = dfference in northings = 1277.22 − 829.74 = + 447.48 ft

Departure = difference in eastings = − 365.12 − 167.01 = − 532.13 ft

Answer is B

Solution 29
PG 58 is appropriate if 52°C ≤ T_{max} < 58°C
PG 58 − 22 is appropriate if minimum pavement temperature > -22°C

Answer is D

Solution 30
The length of the long chord is given by: $LC = 2R \sin\frac{I}{2} = 2 \times 1025 \times \sin\frac{56}{2} = 962.42\ ft$

Answer is A

Note: Even though bearing of back tangent and whether the curve deflects left or right are important details for the curve, they are not necessary to answer the question asked.

Solution 31
Growing at the rate of 3% every year, ADT after interval of 10 years = 6400×1.03^{10} = 8601
Crash reduction factor for countermeasure 1: CR_1 = 0.88
Crash reduction factor for countermeasure 2: CR_2 = 0.68

Overall crash reduction factor: $CR = CR_1 + (1 - CR_1)CR_2 = 0.12 + 0.88 \times 0.32 = 0.4016$

Therefore, number of crashes prevented in 2011-12: $N \times CR \times \frac{ADT_2}{ADT_1} = 23 \times 0.4016 \times \frac{8601}{6400} = 12.4$

It may be assumed that without the countermeasures, the number of crashes would increase in proportion to the ADT. This would mean 23x8601/6400 = 30.9

With the countermeasures, expected number of crashes = 30.9 – 12.4 = 18.5

Answer is B

Solution 32
For ESAL = 30 million and high air temp = 40°C, design N = 121

Answer is B

Solution 33
For a design speed S = 70 mph, stopping sight distance (on level grade, assuming reaction time = 2.5 seconds and deceleration rate a = 11.2 ft/s²) is:

$$SSD = 1.47 \times 2.5 \times 70 + \frac{70^2}{30\left(\frac{11.2}{32.2} + 0\right)} = 726.8 \; ft$$

According to the formula in the FE handbook,

$$L = \frac{AS^2}{800\left(C - \frac{h_1 + h_2}{2}\right)} = \frac{10 \times 726.8^2}{800 \times \left(14.5 - \frac{8+2}{2}\right)} = 695 \; ft$$

However, this solution is valid for the condition S < L (which is not satisfied here)

The other formula gives:

$$L = 2S - \frac{800}{A}\left(C - \frac{h_1 + h_2}{2}\right) = 2 \times 726.8 - \frac{800}{10} \times \left(14.5 - \frac{8+2}{2}\right) = 693.6 \; ft$$

Therefore, required curve length L = 694 ft

Answer is C

Solution 34
At optimum density, D_o = ½ D_j = 65 veh/mi/ln
Optimum speed S_o = ½ S_f = 35 mi/hr
Maximum flow rate = $S_o D_o$ = 35x65 = 2275 veh/hr/ln
For the entire 3-lane group, maximum flow rate = 6825 veh/hr

Answer is C

Transportation Topics on FE Civil Examination

Solution 35

The probability of selecting mode C (bus line) can be written:

$$P(C) = \frac{e^{U_C}}{e^{U_A} + e^{U_B} + e^{U_C}} = \frac{e^{-1.89}}{e^{-1.23} + e^{-2.11} + e^{-1.89}} = \frac{0.151}{0.292 + 0.121 + 0.151} = 0.268$$

Number of commuters expected to use the bus line = 0.268x560 = 149.9

Answer is A

Solution 36

From the dynamic shear rheometer, the minimum value of G*/sin δ should be 1.0 kPa. By interpolation, this is achieved at a temperature of 65.78°C

From the RTFO residue, the minimum value of G*/sin δ should be 2.2 kPa. By interpolation, this is achieved at a temperature of 65.91°C

Therefore, the maximum temperature is 65.78°C. These are specified in increments of 6°C (52°C, 58°C, 64°C, ...). Therefore, the maximum (7-day average) pavement temperature is 64°C

For the low temperature, one looks at the results of the pressure aging vessel (PAV). The maximum value of the creep stiffness S should be 300 MPa. By interpolation, this is achieved at a temperature of -11.25°C

The low temperature is set 10°C lower than this value. Therefore the lowest paement temperature is -21.25°C

Choices (A) and (C) are within these limits. However, (C) is the wider limit.

Answer is C

Note: Since the performance grading limits are discrete, this would actually be specified as PG64 –16

Environmental Topics on FE Civil Examination

Environmental Engineering

Environmental Topics on FE Civil Examination 6-9 problems
Approximately 6% of Exam

A. Water quality (ground and surface)
B. Basic tests (e.g., water, wastewater, air)
C. Environmental regulations
D. Water supply and treatment
E. Wastewater collection and treatment

Environmental Topics on FE Civil Examination

Problem 1
A stream has the following characteristics:
  Flow rate = 18 cfs
  Temperature = 12°C
  BOD_5 = 2.0 mg/L
  Deoxygenation rate constant (log 10 at 20°C) = 0.20 day^{-1}
  D.O. = 5.1 mg/L
A factory discharges a wastewater stream into the river at point A. The wastewater has the following characteristics:
  Flow rate = 750 gal/min
  Temperature = 37°C
  BOD_5 = 105 mg/L
  D.O. = 1.7 mg/L
  Kinetic temperature correction factor = 1.056
What is the ultimate BOD of the river-wastewater mix immediately downstream of point A?
  A. 10.7 mg/L
  B. 13.3 mg/L
  C. 14.8 mg/L
  D. 16.2 mg/L

Problem 2
A factory discharges a wastewater stream into the river at point A. The river-wastewater mix has the following characteristics:
  Flow rate = 20 ft^3/sec
  Average velocity = 4 ft/sec
  Temperature = 15°C
  D.O. = 4.8 mg/L
  Ultimate BOD = 15 mg/L
  At temperature of 15°C, saturation D.O. = 10.1 mg/L
  Deoxygenation rate constant (log 10 at 15°C) = 0.20 day^{-1}
  Reoxygenation rate constant (log 10 at 15°C) = 0.30 day^{-1}

What is the dissolved oxygen in the stream at a distance 5 miles downstream from point of mixing?
  A. 5.0 mg/L
  B. 4.7 mg/L
  C. 4.3 mg/L
  D. 2.0 mg/L

Problem 3

A wastewater treatment plant treats 3 MGD of wastewater using an array of primary clarifiers in parallel configuration. At any time, the plant manual requires one unit to be taken offline for maintenance. The wastewater has TSS = 180 mg/L. The maximum solids load on each clarifier is 800 lb-TSS/day. The number of clarifier units required is most nearly:

A. 5
B. 6
C. 7
D. 8

Problem 4

The schematic of an activated sludge process is shown below. The influent flow rate is 4 MGD. The primary clarifier removes 65% of the total suspended solids and 20% of the BOD_5. The primary sludge contains 6% solids. The quantity of primary sludge is most nearly:

A. 6,245 gallons per day
B. 8,125 gallons per day
C. 10,850 gallons per day
D. 12,920 gallons per day

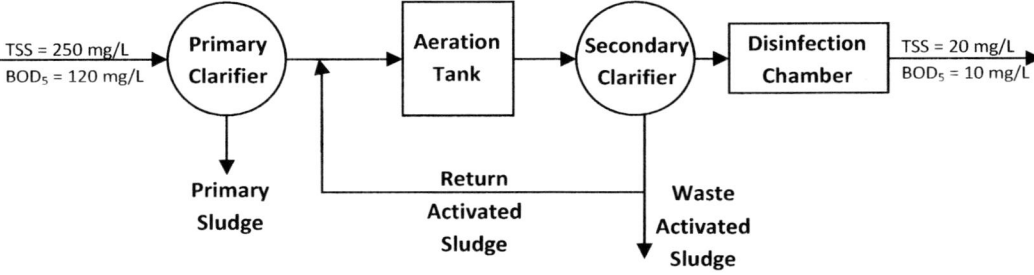

Problem 5

The schematic of an activated sludge process is shown below. The influent flow rate is 4 MGD. The primary clarifier removes 65% of the total suspended solids and 20% of the BOD_5. The primary sludge contains 6% solids. The concentration of biosolids in the activated sludge is 8000 mg/L. The quantity of waste sludge is most nearly:
   A. 26,400 gallons per day
   B. 33,800 gallons per day
   C. 38,300 gallons per day
   D. 42,900 gallons per day

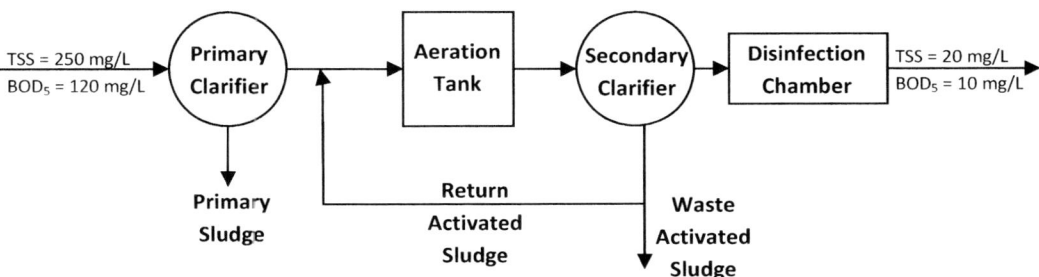

Problem 6

A secondary treated effluent from a 4.0 MGD wastewater treatment plant is discharged into a receiving stream. The wastewater has a BOD_5 of 20 mg/L. The receiving stream upstream from the point of wastewater discharge has a flow rate of 18 cfs and a BOD_5 of 4.0 mg/L. The BOD reaction rate (base-e at 20°C) is 0.23 day^{-1}. Reaeration and deoxygenation are the only major factors affecting the dissolved oxygen concentration in the stream after mixing with the wastewater effluent.

The ultimate BOD just downstream of the effluent discharge into the receiving stream is most nearly
   A) 4 mg/L
   B) 8 mg/L
   C) 12 mg/L
   D) 16 mg/L

Environmental Topics on FE Civil Examination

Problem 7
A trickling filter plant processes 2 MGD of domestic wastewater with 200 mg/L suspended solids and 150 mg/L BOD. The primary settling tank removes 50% of the suspended solids and BOD. If the mass of solids removed from the trickling filter is one-quarter of those removed from the primary settling tank, what is the total mass of solids removed each day?
  A. 2086 lbm/day
  B. 1669 lbm/day
  C. 250 lbm/day
  D. 3650 lbm/day

Problem 8
A water sample yields the following results:

Ca^{++}	60.0 mg/L
Mg^{++}	21.2 mg/L
Fe^{++}	2.2 mg/L
HCO_3^-	221.3 mg/L
Cl^-	33.5 mg/L

The hardness of the water sample, expressed in terms of mg/L of calcium carbonate, is most nearly
  A. 240.8 mg/L as $CaCO_3$
  B. 242.8 mg/L as $CaCO_3$
  C. 510.1 mg/L as $CaCO_3$
  D. 228.7 mg/L as $CaCO_3$

Problem 9
A water sample is tested with the following results:

Sample volume filtered = 200 mL
Mass of crucible and filter paper = 25.439 g
Mass of dry crucible, filter paper and solids = 25.645 g
Mass of crucible, filter paper and ignited solids = 25.501 g

Sample volume evaporated = 100 mL
Mass of dry evaporation dish = 275.41 g
Mass of dry evaporation dish + solids = 276.201 g
Mass of evaporation dish + ignited solids = 275.645 g

Environmental Topics on FE Civil Examination

The volatile dissolved solids concentration of the water sample is most nearly:
- A. 720 mg/L
- B. 1440 mg/L
- C. 4840 mg/L
- D. 5560 mg/L

Problem 10

A wastewater sample was incubated at 27°C for 7 days and the BOD was measured as 100 mg/L. The deoxygenation rate constant (base-10, 20°C) is 0.23 day^{-1}. Kinetic temperature correction factor = 1.047

The BOD for this sample, if incubated for 5 days at a temperature of 20°C, would be most nearly:
- A. 125 mg/L
- B. 95 mg/L
- C. 35 mg/L
- D. 20 mg/L

Problem 11

The flow rate treated at a wastewater treatment plant is 2 MGD. The concentration of total suspended solids (TSS) in the influent is 800 mg/L. The flow passes through a bank of filters, arranged in parallel. The maximum solids load on each filter is 10 lb. TSS/ft^2-day. If filter size is limited to 200 ft^2 and plant operation guidelines require at least two filters to be shut down at any time for backwashing, the number of filters needed is most nearly:
- A. 6
- B. 7
- C. 8
- D. 9

Problem 12

An industrial plant produces wastewater with the following characteristics:
Flow rate = 5000 gpm
Temperature = 37°C
Ultimate BOD = 80 mg/L
Lead concentration = 0.5 mg/L

Environmental Topics on FE Civil Examination

The stream into which the plant plans to discharge its wastewater has the following data:
    Flow rate = 60 ft³/sec
    Temperature = 14°C
    Ultimate BOD = 10 mg/L
    Lead concentration = 4 μg/L

If the EPA limit for lead in surface waters is 15 μg/L, the level of pretreatment (%) necessary at the plant (before discharging into the stream) is most nearly:
    A. 75%
    B. 80%
    C. 85%
    D. 0%

Problem 13

Results for a settling column analysis are summarized in the form of percent removal curves as shown below. The cumulative removal rate at a depth of 2 ft at t = 60 minutes is most nearly:

    A. 42%
    B. 53%
    C. 71%
    D. 77%

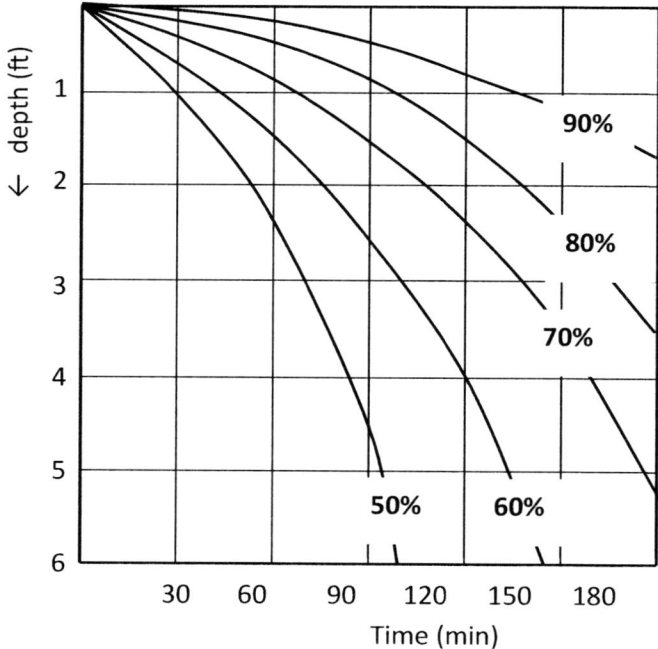

Environmental Topics on FE Civil Examination

Problem 14

Assuming an average wastewater flow rate of 100 gpcd, what is the peak wastewater flow rate generated by a community with a population of 20,000?

A. 2.0 MGD
B. 3.2 MGD
C. 4.2 MGD
D. 5.6 MGD

Problem 15

A standard BOD test conducted on a wastewater sample has the following data:
  Sample volume = 15 mL
  Volume of dilution water added = 285 mL
  Initial (at t = 0) dissolved oxygen concentration = 6.3 mg/L
  Final (at t = 5 days dissolved oxygen concentration = 2.5 mg/L
  Incubation temperature = 25°C
  Deoxygenation rate constant (base 10, 25°C) = 0.10

What is the ultimate BOD (mg/L)?

A. 75 mg/L
B. 90 mg/L
C. 110 mg/L
D. 135 mg/L

Problem 16

The percent removal of 30 μm particles in a cyclone precipitator is 50%. What is the percent removal of 20 μm particles?

A. 23%
B. 31%
C. 57%
D. 71%

Environmental Topics on FE Civil Examination

Problem 17

An incinerator receives air containing hexachlorobenzene (C_6Cl_6) at a concentration of 120 µg/m³. Assume air temperature = 20°C and pressure = 1 atm. If the concentration in the effluent is 1 ppb, what is the destruction and removal efficiency?

A. 75%
B. 80%
C. 85%
D. 90%

Problem 18

A community produces solid waste at the rate of 4 lb/capita/day. The table below shows the approximate composition of the waste collected from the community (population 20,000) as well as data about the energy recovery from each waste category.

Category	Fraction of total waste stream (%)	Moisture content (%)	Energy Recovery Btu/lb	Recycle rate (%)
Food waste	30	70	2,000	10
Paper	40	10	7,000	80
Metal	10	3	500	75
Plastics	20	2	12,000	80

What is the annual energy recovered through the recycling program?

A. 101 billion Btu
B. 111 billion Btu
C. 125 billion Btu
D. 146 billion Btu

Problem 19

A cyclone is used to remove suspended particles from an air stream. The cone has the following geometric properties:
 Body diameter = 1.2 m
 Body length = 1.9 m
 Cone length = 2.5 m
 Height of inlet = 0.55 m
 Width of inlet = 0.30 m
 Dust outlet diameter = 0.5 m

Environmental Topics on FE Civil Examination

What is the effective number of turns the gas makes in the cyclone?
- A. 4
- B. 6
- C. 8
- D. 10

Problem 20

Clay with hydraulic conductivity K = 1×10^{-9} m/s is used as liner material for a landfill cell. The void ratio of the clay is 0.25. If the hydraulic head is 2.7 m, how long does it take for leachate to penetrate the liner, which is 30 cm thick?
- A. 30 days
- B. 50 days
- C. 70 days
- D. 90 days

Problem 21

A chemical formed as a byproduct of wastewater treatment is to be removed by granulated activated carbon (GAC) adsorption. The Freundlich isotherm coefficients are:

K_f = 3.6 and 1/n = 0.70

If the original concentration of the chemical is 0.1 mg/L and the concentration in the effluent is to be 0.03 mg/L, how much GAC (lb/day) is required to treat 2.6 MGD of wastewater?
- A. 3 lb/day
- B. 5 lb/day
- C. 7 lb/day
- D. 9 lb/day

Problem 22

Assuming laminar settling of particles, how long will it take for a 0.1 mm diameter soil particle to fall 1.2 m vertically through water at 20°C (density of water = 998 kg/m³; viscosity = 0.001 Pa-s). Assume soil particles are spherical with specific gravity = 2.6
- A. 94 seconds
- B. 115 seconds
- C. 138 seconds
- D. 173 seconds

Problem 23

A specific form of activated carbon is being used for adsorbing a specific liquid contaminant. The following experimental data shown below was obtained for two different amounts of the activated carbon that were placed in 1 liter of solution initially containing 50 mg of the contaminant. What are the constants of the isotherm equation?

$$\frac{x}{m} = KC^{1/n}$$

x = amount of contaminant adsorbed (mg)
m = mass of activated carbon in solution (mg)
C = equilibrium concentration of contaminant in solution after adsorption (mg/L)
K, n = empirical constants

Amount of carbon (g)	Initial amount of contaminant (mg)	Amount of contaminant adsorbed (mg)
0.5	50	25
1.0	50	35

A. n = 3.21; k = 0.015
B. n = 1.43; k = 0.005
C. n = 1.22; k = 0.004
D. n = 0.70; k = 0.002

Problem 24

The schematic of an activated sludge process is shown below. The influent flow rate is 4 MGD. The quantity of sludge rejected from the primary clarifier and the secondary clarifier are 23,000 gpd and 87,000 gpd respectively. The volume of the aeration tank is 300,000 ft³. The concentration of biosolids in the aeration tank is 2500 mg/L and of the activated sludge is 8000 mg/L. The solids residence time (days) is most nearly:

A. 1.3 days
B. 3.3 days
C. 5.3 days
D. 7.3 days

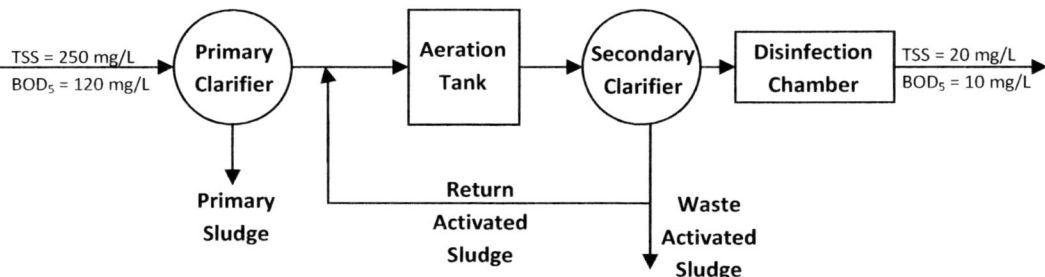

Environmental Topics on FE Civil Examination

Problem 25

An electrostatic precipitator has the following characteristics:

    Effective area of collection plates = 100,000 ft^2
    Flow rate of flue gas = 750,000 ft^3/min
    Drift velocity = 0.5 ft/sec

What is the collection efficiency?

    A. 93.4%
    B. 95.3%
    C. 98.2%
    D. 99.2%

Problem 26

A plug of a disninfectant is injected into a water disinfecting chamber. The concentration of the disinfectant at the inlet is 5 mg/L. The incident flow rate is 2 ft^3/sec and the volume of the chamber is 50,000 gallons. If the decay reaction is first order with a rate constant k = 0.35 day^{-1}, what is the concentration of the disinfectant at the outlet?

    A. 4.86 mg/L
    B. 4.90 mg/L
    C. 4.93 mg/L
    D. 4.96 mg/L

Problem 27

A rectangular sedimentation tank is 3 m wide x 12 m long. The depth of the tank is 4 m. It is estimated that the smallest particle of interest that must be settled out completely has a settling velocity of 0.1 mm/sec. What should be the peak flow rate that is incident to the tank?

    A. 0.016 m^3/sec
    B. 0.021 m^3/sec
    C. 0.027 m^3/sec
    D. 0.036 m^3/sec

Environmental Topics on FE Civil Examination

Problem 28

A water supply flow rate Q = 2 MGD contains CO_2 at a concentration of 2.7 mg/L. What is the dosage of lime $Ca(OH)_2$ required to reduce the CO_2 concentration to 1.6 mg/L?

- A. 14 kg/day
- B. 21 kg/day
- C. 28 kg/day
- D. 35 kg/day

Problem 29

Wastewater at a flow rate Q = 2 MGD is disinfected in a chlorination chamber. The concentration of free chlorine in the chamber is 2.0 mg/L. The wastewater has temperature = 15°C and pH = 6.5. What is the required volume of the chlorination chamber to achieve 3-log inactivation of Giardia Lamblia?

- A. 6400 ft³
- B. 5600 ft³
- C. 4800 ft³
- D. 4000 ft³

Problem 30

A water supply is to be disinfected immediately following a slow sand filtration process. What is the log inactivation requirement for viruses?

- A. 1.0
- B. 2.0
- C. 3.0
- D. 4.0

Environmental Engineering Solutions

Environmental Topics on FE Civil Examination

Solution 1
Wastewater flow rate = 750 gpm = 1.67 cfs

Immediately downstream of mixing location: $\overline{BOD_5} = \frac{18 \times 2 + 1.67 \times 105}{18 + 1.67} = 10.74 \frac{mg}{L}$

$$\overline{T} = \frac{18 \times 12 + 1.67 \times 37}{18 + 1.67} = 14°C$$

BOD rate constant: $k_{14} = k_{20} \times 1.056^{14-20} = 0.20 \times 1.056^{-6} = 0.144$

Ultimate BOD: $BOD_{ult} = \frac{10.74}{1 - 10^{-0.144 \times 5}} = 13.26 \frac{mg}{L}$

Answer is B

Solution 2

Initial oxygen deficit = 10.1 – 4.8 = 5.3 mg/L

Time for stream to travel 5 miles (26400 ft) at 4 ft/sec = 6600 sec (0.0764 day)

$$D_t = \frac{k_d L_o}{k_r - k_d}\left(e^{-k_d t} - e^{-k_r t}\right) + D_o e^{-k_r t}$$

$$= \frac{0.2 \times 15}{0.3 - 0.2}\left(e^{-0.2 \times 0.0764} - e^{-0.3 \times 0.0764}\right) + 5.3 \times e^{-0.3 \times 0.0764} = 5.40 \frac{mg}{L}$$

Therefore, 5 miles downstream, the oxygen deficit = 5.4 and D.O. = 10.1 – 5.4 = 4.7 mg/L

Answer is B

Solution 3
The total solids load (page 180 in handbook) in the influent: $X = 3 \times 180 \times 8.34 = 4503.6 \; lb/day$

Number of units needed (if all are operational): n = 4503.6÷800 = 5.6 (6 filters)

With the requirement of one offline printer at a time, we need 7 filters.

Answer is C

Solution 4
Assuming that the primary sludge, which contains 6% solids, essentially has the same specific gravity as water, we can convert the 6% solids to a concentration:

$$6\% = \frac{60 \; g}{1000 \; g} = \frac{60{,}000 \; mg}{L}$$

Environmental Topics on FE Civil Examination

> Note: If specific gravity of sludge is assumed to be nearly 1.0 (water), then this always works - multiply percent solids by 10,000 to get solids concentration in mg/L

Primary effluent (after 65% removal of TSS) contains TSS = 0.35x250 = 87.5 mg/L

Performing a summation of mass flow rates at the node representing the primary clarifier, we get

$$4 \times 250 = (4 - Q_{ps}) \times 87.5 + Q_{ps} \times 60,000 \Rightarrow Q_{ps} = 0.01085 \; MGD = 10,850 \; gpd$$

Answer is C

Solution 5
Note which branches of the flow diagram have known data. These are highlighted below.

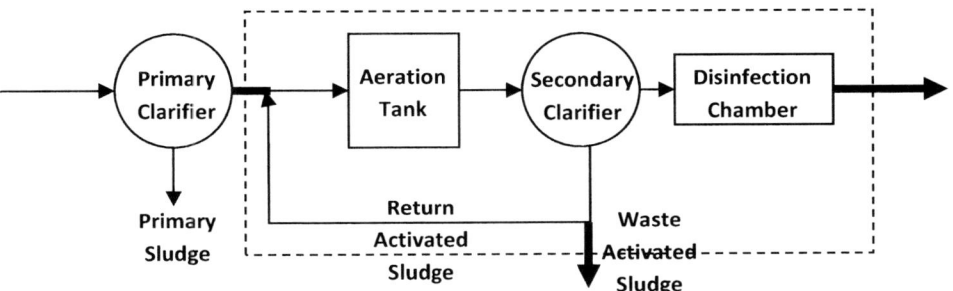

We further assume that the primary sludge quantity is negligible compared to the influent. This will allow us to assume that the flow rate out of the primary clarifier is essentially 4 MGD. Thus, if the quantity of the waste activated sludge is Q_w, then the quantity of the effluent is $4 - Q_w$.

Primary effluent contains TSS = 0.35x250 = 87.5 mg/L

Performing a summation of mass flow rates into and out of the control volume (dashed box above), we get

$$4 \times 87.5 = (4 - Q_w) \times 20 + Q_w \times 8,000 \Rightarrow Q_w = 0.0338 \; MGD = 33,800 \; gpd$$

Answer is B

Solution 6
4 MGD = 4x1.5472 = 6.19 ft³/s

Immediately downstream of mixing point, the BOD$_5$ is given as the weighted average

Environmental Topics on FE Civil Examination

$$\overline{BOD_5} = \frac{20 \times 6.19 + 4 \times 18}{6.19 + 18} = 8.09 \frac{mg}{L}$$

The ultimate BOD (mg/L): $BOD_{ult} = \frac{8.09}{1 - 10^{-0.23 \times 5}} = 11.84 \frac{mg}{L}$

Answer is C

Solution 7

50% of TSS influent = 0.5X200 = 100 mg/L

Mass of solids removed in primary settling tank = 2 x 100 x 8.34 = 1668 lb/day

Mass of solids removed in trickling filter = ¼ x 1668 = 417 lb/day

Total solids removed = 2085 lb/day

Answer is A

Solution 8

Using information in the Periodic Table (page 101) and page 191 of the Handbook, the equivalent weights of the relevant species are:
Ca^{++} 40.078/2 = 20.04 mg/L
Mg^{++} 24.305/2 = 12.15 mg/L
Fe^{++} 55.847/2 = 27.92 mg/L

Using the equivalent weight of $CaCO_3$ (50 mg/L), the give concentrations are converted to:

Ca^{++} 60.0x50/20.04 = 149.7 mg/L as $CaCO_3$
Mg^{++} 21.2x50/12.15 = 87.2 mg/L as $CaCO_3$
Fe^{++} 2.2x50/27.92 = 3.9 mg/L as $CaCO_3$

Hardness = 240.8 mg/L as $CaCO_3$

Answer is A

Solution 9

The suspended solids are in the fraction that is retained on the filter paper. The dissolved solids are in the fraction that passes through the filter paper.

The total volatile solids concentration (mg/L) of the water sample is calculated as the difference between

Mass of dry evaporation dish + solids = 276.201 g
Mass of ignited evaporation dish + solids = 275.645 g
Thus, in a 100 mL sample, the total volatile solids = 0.556 g = 556 mg

Environmental Topics on FE Civil Examination

VS concentration = 0.556g/100mL = 5560 mg/L
The volatile suspended solids concentration (mg/L) of the water sample is calculated as the difference between

Mass of dry crucible, filter paper and solids = 25.645 g
Mass of crucible, filter paper and ignited solids = 25.501 g
Thus, in a 200 mL sample, the suspended volatile solids = 0.144 g = 144 mg
VSS concentration = 0.144g/200mL = 720 mg/L

Therefore, volatile dissolved solids = 5560 – 720 = 4840 mg/L

Answer is C

Solution 10

k (base-10, 20°C) = 0.23 day^{-1}
k (base-10, 27°C) = 0.23×1.047$^{27-20}$ = 0.32

$$BOD_{ult} = \frac{BOD_7}{1 - 10^{-0.32 \times 7}} = 100.6 \ \frac{mg}{L}$$

$$BOD_5 = BOD_{ult}(1 - 10^{-0.23 \times 5}) = 93.5 \ \frac{mg}{L}$$

Answer is B

Solution 11

Q = 2 MGD
TSS = 800 mg/L
Suspended solids load = 2 x 800 x 8.34 = 13334 lb-TSS/day
Maximum solids load on each filter = 10 lb-TSS/ft^2-day
Total filter area required = 1333 ft^2 = 6.7 filters. Therefore 7 filters needed
Number of filters provided = 9
Answer is D

Solution 12

Q_{ww} = 5000 gpm
Lead concentration in untreated effluent = 0.5 mg/L = 500 µg/L
Lead concentration in treated effluent C_{ww} = ?

Q_r = 60 ft^3/sec = 26880 gpm

Environmental Topics on FE Civil Examination

Lead concentration = 4 μg/L
EPA limiting concentration = 15 μg/L

$$\frac{5000 C_{ww} + 26880 \times 4}{5000 + 26880} \leq 15 \Rightarrow C_{ww} \leq 74$$

The discharged C_{ww} = 500 must be reduced to 74. This implies 85% removal
Answer is C

Solution 13

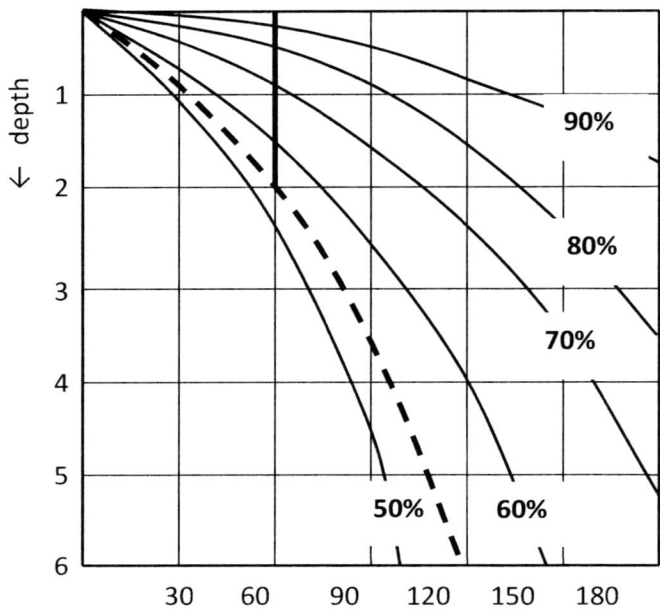

It seems that the iso-concentration line passing through the point of interest (2 ft, 60 min) corresponds to approximately 53% removal. This is shown by a dashed curve. The heavy vertical line extending to the top edge of the curve can be used to conduct the following weighted average.

$$\%R = \left(\frac{53 + 60}{2}\right) \times \frac{0.5}{2.0} + \left(\frac{60 + 70}{2}\right) \times \frac{0.6}{2.0} + \left(\frac{70 + 80}{2}\right) \times \frac{0.4}{2.0} + \left(\frac{80 + 90}{2}\right) \times \frac{0.3}{2.0}$$
$$+ \left(\frac{90 + 100}{2}\right) \times \frac{0.2}{2.0} = 70.9$$

Cumulative removal at depth of 2 ft at 60 min = 71%

Answer is C

Solution 14

According to either curve B or G on page 162, the peak factor is approximately 2.8

Therefore, peak flow rate = 2.8x100 = 280 gpcd

For a population of 20,000, the peak flow rate = 5.6 million gallons per day

Answer is D

Solution 15

The 5-day BOD is calculated as: $BOD_5 = \dfrac{DO_i - DO_f}{\dfrac{V_{sample}}{V_{total}}} = \dfrac{6.2 - 2.5}{15/300} = 76\ mg/L$

Ultimate BOD is calculated as: $BOD_{ult} = \dfrac{BOD_5}{1 - 10^{-kt}} = \dfrac{76}{1 - 10^{-0.1 \times 5}} = 111.1\ mg/L$

Answer is C

Solution 16

Efficiency: $\eta = \dfrac{1}{1 + (d_{pc}/d_p)^2} = \dfrac{1}{1 + (30/20)^2} = 0.31$

Answer is B

Solution 17

Molecular weight of C_6Cl_6 = 6x12+6x35.46 = 284.8 g/mol

Converting the influent concentration to ppb: $ppb = \dfrac{(\mu g/m^3) RT}{P \times MW} = \dfrac{120 \times 0.0821 \times 293.15}{1 \times 284.8} = 10.14$

Influent concentration = 10.14 ppb

Effluent concentration = 1 ppb

DRE = 9.14/10.14 = 90.1%

Answer is D

Solution 18

On a daily basis, total mass of solid waste produced by the community = 80,000 lb

In a year, total mass of solid waste produced by the community = 29.2 million lb

For food waste, annual mass = 29.2 million x 0.3 = 8.76 million lb

Amount recycled = 10% = 0.876 million lb

Energy recovery = 0.876x10^{6}x2000 = 1.75x10^9 Btu

Similarly, the other 3 categories contribute:

Paper: 29.2x10^6 x 0.4 x 0.8 x 7000 = 65.4x10^9 Btu

Metal: 29.2x10^6 x 0.1 x 0.75 x 500 = 1.1x10^9 Btu

Environmental Topics on FE Civil Examination

Plastics: $29.2 \times 10^6 \times 0.2 \times 0.8 \times 12000 = 56.1 \times 10^9$ Btu

Total annual energy yield = 124.4×10^9 Btu

Answer is C

Solution 19

The effective number of turns is calculated as: $N_e = \frac{1}{H}\left(L_b + \frac{L_c}{2}\right) = \frac{1}{0.55}\left(1.9 + \frac{2.5}{2}\right) = 5.73$

Answer is B

Solution 20

Porosity is given by: $\eta = \frac{e}{1+e} = \frac{0.25}{1+0.25} = 0.2$

The break-through time is given by:

$$t = \frac{d^2 \eta}{K(d+h)} = \frac{0.3^2 \times 0.2}{1 \times 10^{-9} \times (0.3+2.7)} = 6 \times 10^6 \; seconds = 69.4 \; days$$

Answer is C

Solution 21

Influent concentration C_o = 0.1 mg/L
Effluent concentration C_e = 0.03 mg/L

On a daily basis, the amount of solute adsorbed (based on the reduction in concentration from 0.1 mg/L to 0.03 mg/L) is:
$$(0.10 - 0.03) \times 2.6 \times 8.34 = 1.518 \; lb/day$$

According to the Freundlich isotherm:
$$X = \frac{x}{m} = K_f C_e^{1/n} = 3.6 \times 0.03^{0.7} = 0.309$$

But X = mass of adsorbed solute per mass of adsorbent.
Therefore, mass of adsorbent (GAC) required = 1.518/0.309 = 4.91 lb/day

Answer is B

Solution 22

Assuming laminar settling means Stokes law applies. Settling velocity is

$$v_t = \frac{g\rho(SG-1)d^2}{18\mu} = \frac{9.81 \times 998 \times (2.6-1) \times 0.0001^2}{18 \times 0.001} = 0.0087 \; m/s$$

Time to settle 1.2 m = 137.9 seconds

Answer is C

Solution 23

For sample 1, equilibrium concentration of adsorbate in the effluent C_e = 50 – 25 = 25 mg/L
and for sample 2, concentration C_e = 50 – 35 = 15 mg/L

Taking logarithms of the isotherm equation:
$$\log \frac{x}{m} = \log K + \frac{1}{n} \log C_e \quad \text{which can be written as } Y = b + mX$$

For sample 1
Amount of carbon, m = 500 mg
Amount of adsorbed contaminant, x = 25 mg

Y_1 = log(x/m) = log(25/500) = -1.30
X_1 = log C_e = log 25 = 1.398

For sample 2
Amount of carbon, m = 1000 mg
Amount of adsorbed contaminant, x = 35 mg

Y_2 = log(x/m) = log(35/1000) = -1.456
X_2 = log C_e = log 15 = 1.176

Slope (1/n) is calculated as: $\frac{1}{n} = \frac{Y_2 - Y_1}{X_2 - X_1} = \frac{-1.456 + 1.30}{1.176 - 1.398} = 0.70 \Rightarrow n = 1.42$

Y intercept (log K) is calculated as: $\log K = Y_1 - mX_1 = -1.3 - 0.7 \times 1.398 = -2.28 \Rightarrow K = 0.0053$

Answer is B

Solution 24

The effluent flow rate: $Q_e = Q_o - Q_{ps} - Q_{ss} = 4 - 0.023 - 0.087 = 3.89 \, MGD$

Concentration of biosolids in effluent: X_e = 20 mg/L

Volume of aeraton tank, V = 300,000 ft³ = 2.244 million gallons

Solids retention time: $\theta_c = \frac{VX}{Q_w X_w + Q_e X_e} = \frac{2.244 \times 10^6 \times 2500}{87000 \times 8000 + 3.89 \times 10^6 \times 20} = 7.25 \, days$

Environmental Topics on FE Civil Examination

Answer is D

Solution 25

Drift Velocity = 0.5 ft/s = 30 ft/min

Fractional collection efficiency: $\eta = 1 - e^{-WA/Q} = 1 - e^{-30 \times 100,000/750,000} = 0.982$

Answer is C

Solution 26

Volume of tank, V = 50,000 gallons = 6684.5 ft³

Retention time, t = V/Q = 6684.5/2 = 3342 seconds = 0.0387 day

For first order reaction, $C_t = C_o e^{-kt} = 5 \times e^{-0.35 \times 0.0387} = 4.93 \; mg/L$

Answer is C

Solution 27

Equating the hydraulic loading rate to the critical settling velocity:

$$\frac{Q}{A_{surface}} = v_o \Rightarrow Q = A_{surface} v_o = 3 \times 12 \times 0.1 \times 10^{-3} = 0.036 \; m^3/s$$

Answer is D

Solution 28

CO₂ removal = 2.7 − 1.6 = 1.1 mg/L

The reaction for CO₂ removal with lime is:

$$CO_2 + Ca(OH)_2 \rightarrow CaCO_3 + H_2O$$

Stoichiometrically, to react with 44 g of CO_2, we need 74 g of $Ca(OH)_2$. Thus, to react with a concentration of 1.1 mg/L of CO_2, we need 1.85 mg/L of $Ca(OH)_2$.

With a flow rate Q = 2 MGD = 2x10⁶ gallons/day = 7.57x10⁶ L/day

Lime dosage = 1.85x10⁻⁶ kg/L x 7.57x10⁶ L/day = 14 kg/day

Answer is A

Solution 29

At T = 15°C and pH = 6.5, to achieve 3-log inactivation of Giardia, using a free chlorine concentration of 2.0 mg/L, the required CT value = 69 min-mg/L

Environmental Topics on FE Civil Examination

Since C = 2.0 mg/L, required detention time, T = 69/2 = 34.5 min = 0.024 day

Detention time: $t = \frac{V}{Q} \Rightarrow V = Qt = 2 \times 0.024 = 0.048\ MG = 48{,}000\ gal = 6406\ ft^3$

Answer is A

Solution 30

For disinfection from viruses, the normal requirement is 4-log inactivation. However, for slow sand filtration, a log-inactivation credit of 2.0 ca be applied. Therefore, the resulting disinfection log inactivation requirement is 4.0 − 2.0 = 2.0

Answer is B

Construction

Construction Topics on FE Civil Examination **4-6 problems**
Approximately 4% of Exam

A. Construction documents
B. Procurement methods (e.g., competitive bid, qualifications-based)
C. Project delivery methods (e.g., design-bid-build, design build, construction mgmt, multiple prime)
D. Construction operations and methods (e.g., lifting, rigging, dewatering and pumping, equipment production, productivity analysis and improvement, temporary erosion control)
E. Project scheduling (e.g., CPM, allocation of resources)
F. Project management (e.g., owner/contractor/client relations)
G. Construction safety
H. Construction estimating

Construction Topics on FE Civil Examination

Problem 1
An excavator has a capacity of 3 yd^3. A single cycle of operation consists of excavation, travel (two-way) and transfer of excavated material. Cycle time for the excavator is 8 minutes. Efficiency factors are:

    Site   0.90
    Equipment & Operator 0.72

The daily production rate (yd^3/day) assuming an 8-hour workday is most nearly:
- A. 58
- B. 78
- C. 117
- D. 132

Problem 2
A room is 35 ft x 25 ft in plan. Ceiling height is 14 ft. Openings for doors and windows total 85 ft^2. The following data is given for plastering and painting operations.

    Plaster and paint crew:
        1 supervisor $30/hr
        1 laborer $12/hr
        2 painters $18/hr
        Plastering productivity 50ft^2/L.H.
        Painting productivity 150ft^2/L.H.

The labor cost for plastering and painting the room (walls and ceiling) is most nearly:
- A. $1125
- B. $1285
- C. $1385
- D. $1715

Problem 3

An activity on arrow network for a project is shown below. Numbers adjacent to arrows are activity durations (weeks). The minimum time to complete the project (weeks) is most nearly:

A. 12
B. 13
C. 14
D. 15

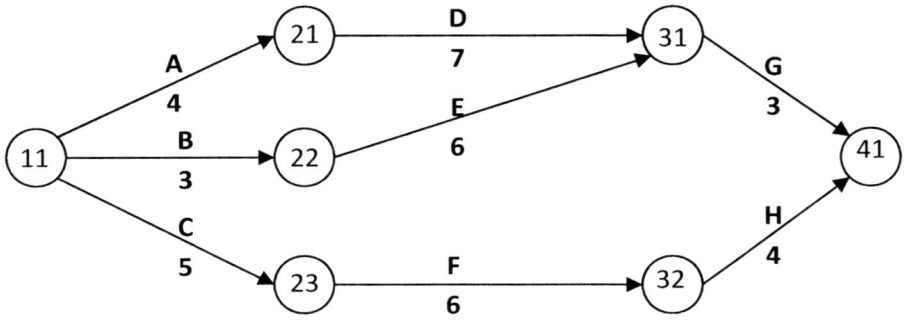

Problem 4

An activity on arrow network for a project is shown below. Numbers adjacent to arrows are activity durations (weeks). The early start date (week) for activity G is:

A. 11
B. 12
C. 13
D. 14

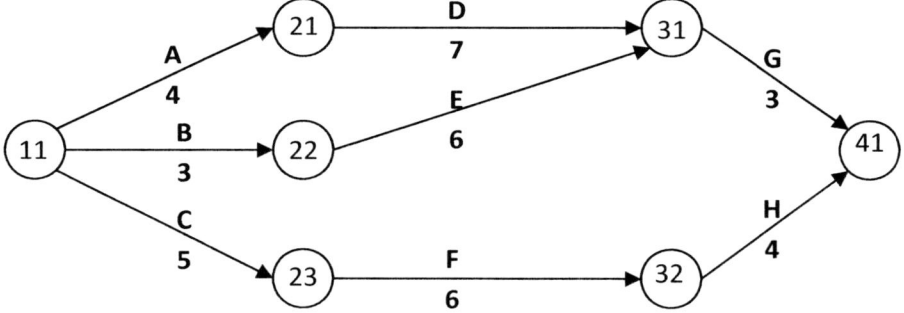

Problem 5

An activity on arrow network for a project is shown below. Numbers adjacent to arrows are activity durations (weeks). The total float (weeks) for activity G is:

A. 0
B. 1
C. 2
D. 3

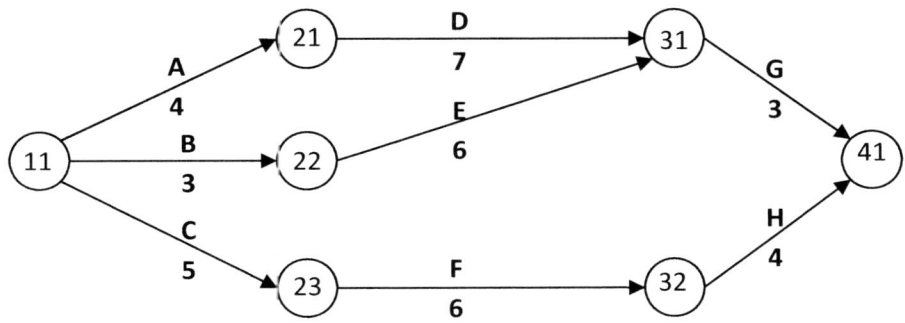

Problem 6

A contractor has the following options for a project lasting 18 months:

Option A: Monthly rental of excavation equipment at $15,000 per month + operating costs $2,000/month

Option B: Purchase equipment for $200,000

Maintenance costs $8,000/month

Resale value of equipment after 18 months = $120,000

Annual interest rate = 10%

The benefit:cost ratio of option B (purchasing) is most nearly:

A. 1.23
B. 1.32
C. 1.55
D. 1.67

Problem 7

The tasks within a project and their durations are shown below:

A	Preliminary design	5 months
B	Market analysis	1 month
C	Assembly line	2 months
D	CAD modeling	3 months
E	Marketing	2 months
F	Cost analysis	3 months
G	Prototype	4 months
H	Personnel training	2 months
I	Final price structure	1 month
J	Final Analysis & report	1 month

The activity on arrow representation of the project is also shown below.

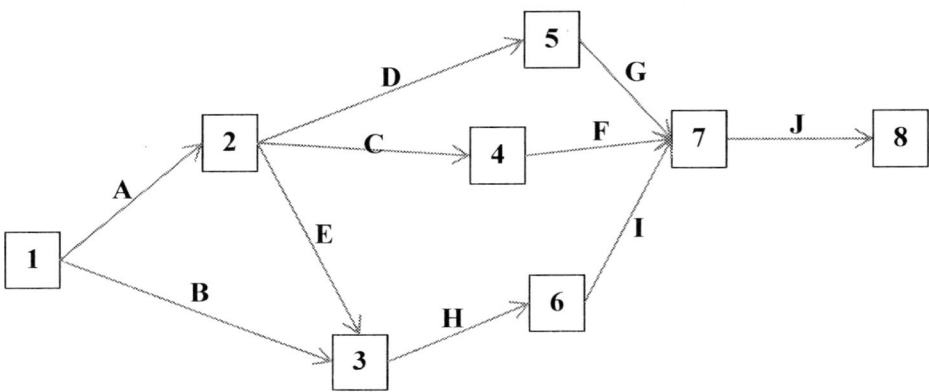

The critical path for the project is

A. ACFJ
B. ADGJ
C. BHIJ
D. AEHIJ

Problem 8

A contractor needs to bring in 4,200 yd^3 of select soil to replace unsuitable subgrade material for a new highway. The borrow site is located 2.6 miles away with an average round trip travel/loading/dumping time of 30 minutes. The soil has a unit weight of 125 lb/ft^3 and the dump truck drivers are on 10-hr workdays. The minimum number of 10-ton capacity trucks needed to complete the job within 8 working days is:

A. 4 trucks
B. 5 trucks
C. 6 trucks
D. 7 trucks

Problem 9

An excavator has a bucket capacity of 2.8 yd³. Its operation cycle consists of the following phases – (a) excavation time = 45 seconds, (b) travel time (two-way) = 4 minutes and (c) dumping/transfer time = 30 seconds. Assume an overall efficiency factor for the excavator = 85%.

The quantity of excavated material = 50,000 ft³ (bank measure). The material has the following properties:
Swell = 20%
Unit weight = 120 lb/ft³
Water content = 30%

The number of days required to complete the job, assuming 8-hour workdays, is most nearly:

    A. 9
    B. 10
    C. 11
    D. 13

Problem 10

A grade beam 3 ft wide by 2 ft deep must be poured around the perimeter of a building whose plan is shown below. The trench excavated for the grade beam has to have 1V:1H side slopes. Excavation is accomplished by a ¾ cu. yd. capacity trackhoe, having productivity of 9 yd³/hr. Assume a 8-hr workday, the number of days to complete the excavation activity is most nearly:

    A) 5
    B) 7
    C) 9
    D) 11

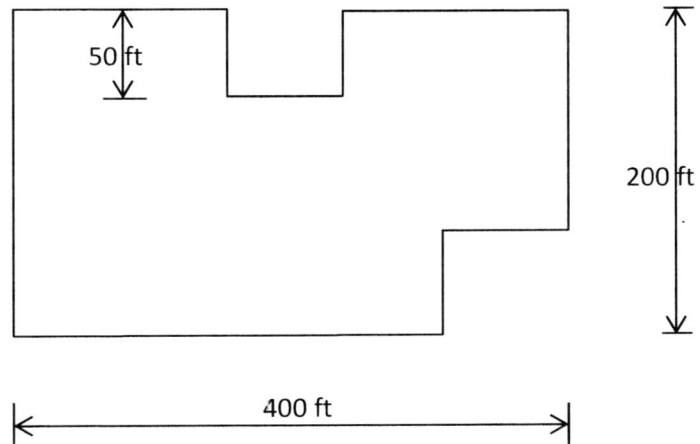

Construction Topics on FE Civil Examination

Problem 11

A contract has 90 days remaining until completion. Advance completion will be paid $10,000 bonus per day. The most critical activity duration can be shortened by employing more crews. There is a reduction in efficiency as the number of crews increase; that is, the number of schedule days saved is not directly proportional to the number of crews added. For each crew added, the cost is $2800 per day for labor and equipment. If crews must be added as a complete unit, how many crews should be added to maximize the profit?

    A. 0
    B. 1
    C. 2
    D. 3

Crew added	Added crew cost per day	Schedule days reduced
1	$2,800	20
2	$5,600	26
3	$8,400	30

Problem 12

A compacted fill is to be constructed with a total volume of 15,000 yd^3. The fill is to be compacted to a dry unit weight of at least 127 lb/ft^3 and a minimum water content of 10%. Soil in the borrow area has a dry density of 120 lb/ft^3 and an average water content of 8%. The amount of borrowed material that must be removed is most nearly:

    A. 15,250 yd^3
    B. 15,565 yd^3
    C. 15,875 yd^3
    D. 16,125 yd^3

Problem 13

An asphalt paving surfacing alternative is being evaluated using the present worth for future expenditures over an expected 40 yr life. The initial cost of the asphalt surface is $700,000. It will require overlays at several intervals during the expected life. The cost of the future overlays will be $252,000 at 10 years from construction, $332,000 at 17 years, $420,000 at 23 years, $530,000 at 30 years, and $671,000 at 40 years. The inflation rate is set at 4% annually for the analysis. What is the present worth of the asphalt alternative?

    A. $1,481,903
    B. $1,514,235
    C. $1,546,764
    D. $1,591,766

Construction Topics on FE Civil Examination

Problem 14
A new earth haul project requires moving of 323,000 ft³ (bank measure) of excavated material to a location 12 miles away. A bidding contractor had completed a similar project (size and scope) 2 ½ years ago. The proposed price for the job on record was $525.00 per dump truck load. Annual construction inflation factor is 3.2%. The contractor uses a fleet of dump trucks with 26 yd³ capacity (heaped). The excavated material has a swell factor of 25%. The contractor's bid ($) and the amount of earth moved (yd³) are most nearly:
   A. $261,280
   B. $301,875
   C. $314,400
   D. $326,600

Problem 15
An existing landfill is rectangular at the base plan dimensions 4000 ft x 2500 ft. The sides slope 3H: 1V. The height of the landfill is 12 ft. The landfill must be covered with cover soil to a depth of 18 inches. The amount of borrow soil (yd³) required to cover the top surface is most nearly:
   A) 220,000
   B) 325,000
   C) 525,000
   D) 650,000

Problem 16
The total duration of a project was estimated as follows:
552 working days at 6 days per week and 10 hours a day or work plus 30 days (10 hours per day) for bad weather, which would be worked on weekends and holidays.

The labor agreement defines the regular work day as 8 hour long. Labor cost for premium time is 75% for hours during the week and 100% for weekend work. What is most nearly the labor premium rate for the project?
   A. 1.21
   B. 1.33
   C. 1.45
   D. 1.63

Construction Topics on FE Civil Examination

Problem 17

A test strip shows that a steel-wheeler roller, operating at 3 mph, can compact a 0.5 ft. layer of material to a proper density in four passes. The width of the drum is 8.0 ft. The roller operates 50 min per hour. The number of rollers required to keep up with a material delivery rate of 540 bank cubic yards/hr is most nearly: (1 bank cubic yard = 0.83 compacted cy):

    A. 1
    B. 2
    C. 3
    D. 4

Problem 18

A construction project has the following information in the Plan of Work:

    Total duration = 113 days
    Total number of tasks = 23
    Number of critical tasks = 8
    Total budgeted cost (labor and materials) = $1.75 million

At the end of 100 days, the following cost parameters are calculated:

    Tasks completed = 15
    Budgeted cost of completed tasks = $1.37 million
    Actual cost of completed tasks = $1.35 million
    Critical tasks completed = 5

What is the estimated actual cost to complete the project?

    A. $1.698 million
    B. $1.712 million
    C. $1.725 million
    D. $1.756 million

Construction Solutions

Construction Topics on FE Civil Examination

Solution 1
The daily production rate (yd³), assuming a 8-hr workday, is most nearly:
In 8-hr workday, number of cycles = 480/8 = 60
Ideal production = 3 x 60 = 180 yd³
Actual production = 0.90x0.72x180 = 116.64 yd³

Answer is C

Solution 2
Crew labor rate:
$$\frac{1 \times 30 + 2 \times 18 + 1 \times 12}{4} = \$19.5 \ /L.H.$$
Area: $A = 2 \times (35 + 25) \times 14 + 35 \times 25 - 85 = 2{,}470 \ ft^2$

Labor cost:
$$2470 \ ft^2 \div \frac{150 \ ft^2}{LH} \times \frac{\$19.50}{LH} + 2470 \ ft^2 \div \frac{50 \ ft^2}{LH} \times \frac{\$19.50}{LH} = \$ \ 1{,}284.40$$

Answer is B

Solution 3
The paths through the project network are (a) A-D-G (b) B-E-G and (c) C-F-H. Of these, maximum duration = largest of 14 weeks, 12 weeks and 15 weeks.

Project duration = 15 weeks.

Answer is D

Solution 4
A has ES (early start) = 0, EF (early finish) = 4
D has ES = 4, EF = 11

B has ES = 0, EF = 3
E has ES = 3, EF = 9

G has ES = larger of EF = 11 (for D) and EF = 9 (for E). Therefore, ES date for G = 11 weeks.

Answer is A

Solution 5
A has ES = 0, EF = 4
D has ES = 4, EF = 11

Construction Topics on FE Civil Examination

B has ES = 0, EF = 3
E has ES = 3, EF = 9

G has ES = larger of EF = 11 (for D) and EF = 9 (for E). Therefore, ES date for G = 11 weeks.
G has EF = 14

C has ES = 0, EF = 5
F has ES = 5, EF = 11
H has ES = 11, EF = 15

Therefore all terminal tasks have LF = project duration = 15
Therefore, total float for G = LF – EF = 15 – 14 = 1 week

Answer is B

Solution 6

Pursuing option B has: Initial cost = $200,000
Monthly savings = $17,000 – 8,000 = $9,000
Resale value (after 18 months) = $120,000

Monthly interest rate (nominal) = 10/12 = 0.833%

$$\left(\frac{A}{F}, i, n\right) = \frac{i}{(1+i)^n - 1}$$

(A/F, 0.833%, 18 periods) = 0.051724

$$\left(\frac{A}{P}, i, n\right) = \frac{i(1+i)^n}{(1+i)^n - 1}$$

(A/P, 0.833%, 18 periods) = 0.060057

Converting everything to annuities (monthly):   Initial cost = 200,000×0.060057 = $12,011
Monthly benefit = 9,000
Cost offset (resale) = 120,000×0.051724 = $6,207

Benefit cost ratio: B/C = 9000/(12,011 – 6,207) = 1.55

Answer is C

Construction Topics on FE Civil Examination

Solution 7
ACFJ: length of path = 5+2+3+1 = 11 months
ADGJ: length of path = 5+3+4+1 = 13 months
BHIJ: length of path = 1+2+1+1 = 5 months
AEHIJ: length of path = 5+2+2+1+1 = 11 months

The critical path for the project is ADGJ (13 months)

Answer is B

Solution 8
10 tons = 20,000 lb = 20,000 ÷ 125 = 160 ft^3 = 5.93 yd^3

Thus, truck moves 5.93 yd^3 every 30 minutes. Thus, in a 10-hour workday, a single truck makes 600/30 = 20 trips, moving 20x5.93 = 118.52 yd^3. In 8 days, a single truck moves 948 yd^3. Total number of trucks needed = 4200/948 = 4.43. Use 5 trucks.

Answer is B

Solution 9
Cycle time = 5 min 15 sec = 5.25 min
Ideal volume turnover = 2.8 yd^3/5.25 min = 32 yd^3/hr
Actual volume turnover = 0.85x32 = 27.2 yd^3/hr = 216 yd^3/day
Excavated material = 50,000 ft^3 = 1.2x50,000 ft^3= 60,000 ft^3 (loose) = 2222 yd^3
The number of days required to complete the job = 2222÷216 = 10.3 days

Answer is C

Solution 10
Excavation for grade beam has a bottom width = 3 ft, 1:1 side slopes, which creates a top width = 3 + 2x2 = 7 ft. Cross section of trench = ½ (3+7) x 2 = 10 ft^2
Perimeter = 200x2 + 400x2 + 50x2 = 1300 ft
Volume of excavation = 10x1300 = 13000 ft^3 = 481.5 yd^3
Daily productivity = 9 yd^3/hr x 8hr/day = 72 yd^3
Number of days = 481.5÷72 = 6.7 days

Answer is B

Solution 11
By employing 1 extra crew unit, work will be completed in 90 – 20 = 70 days
Extra cost = 2800 x 1 x 70 = 196,000
Bonus = 10000 x 20 = 200,000

Net = 4,000 (Acceptable)

By employing 2 extra crew units, work will be completed in 90 − 26 = 64 days
Extra cost = 5600 x 1 x 64 = 358,400
Bonus = 10000 x 26 = 260,000
Net = − 98,400 (Unacceptable)

By employing 3 extra crew units, work will be completed in 90 − 30 = 60 days
Extra cost = 8400 x 1 x 60 = 504,000
Bonus = 10000 x 30 = 300,000
Net = − 204,000 (Unacceptable)

Answer is B

Solution 12
Fill: Dry unit weight = 127 lb/ft^3
Fill volume = 15,000 yd^3 = 405,000 ft^3
Weight of solids = 405,000 x 127 = 51,435,000 lb
Borrow soil: Dry unit weight = 120 lb/ft^3
Assuming no loss of soil solids, the volume of borrow soil needed = 51435000 lb ÷120 lb/ft^3
= 428,625 ft^3 = 15,875 yd^3

Answer is C

Solution 13
The present worth (thousands) is given by:

$$PW = 700 + 252 \times \left(\frac{P}{F}, 10\ yrs, 4\%\right) + 332 \times \left(\frac{P}{F}, 17\ yrs, 4\%\right) + 420 \times \left(\frac{P}{F}, 23\ yrs, 4\%\right)$$
$$+ 530 \times \left(\frac{P}{F}, 30\ yrs, 4\%\right) + 671 \times \left(\frac{P}{F}, 40\ yrs, 4\%\right)$$

$$PW = 700 + 252 \times 0.6756 + 332 \times 0.5134 + 420 \times 0.4057 + 530 \times 0.3083 + 671 \times 0.2083 = 1514.26$$

Therefore, present worth of all expenses = $1,514,260

Answer is B

Solution 14
Current bid price can be calculated by applying inflation (3.2%) factor to price on file (2½ yrs ago):

Construction Topics on FE Civil Examination

$$525 \times (1 + 0.032)^{2.5} = \$568$$

Excavated material 323,000 ft³ will swell to 323,000x1.25 = 403,750 ft³ = 14,954 yd³

This will occupy 14,954÷26 = 575 truckloads

Bid price should be 575 x 568 = $326,600 for the 14,954 yd³ of earth moved

Answer is D

Solution 15
The dimensions at the top of the landfill (depth = 12 ft) are 4000 – 2x3x12 = 3928 ft by 2500 – 2x3x12 = 2428 ft. Plan area at the top = 3928x2428 = 9,537,184 ft²
The volume of cover soil required = 9.5372x10⁶ x 1.5 = 1.431x10⁷ ft³ = 530,000 yd³

Answer is C

Solution 16
552 working days at 6 days per week = 92 weeks
Number of weekdays = 5x92 = 460

Number of regular weekday hours = 460x8 = 3680	Premium factor = 1.0
Number of extra weekdays hours = 460x2 = 920	Premium factor = 1.75
Number of weekend hours = 92x10 +30x10 = 1220	Premium factor = 2.0

Weighted average of premium: $\frac{3680 \times 1.0 + 920 \times 1.75 + 1220 \times 2.0}{3680 + 920 + 1220} = 1.328$

Labor premium = 33%

Answer is B

Solution 17
Material delivery = 540 yd³/hr (loose soil), which is equivalent to 540x0.83 = 448.2 yd³/hr compacted
Roller covers ground at 3 mph x 8 ft = 126720 ft²/hr. 0.5 ft thick layer gets compacted in 4 passes. Therefore each pass compact the equivalent of 0.125 ft, which means it compacts 15,840 ft³ (587 yd³) of soil per pass. This is ideal capacity. Working 50 minutes per hour, roller compacts 50/60x587 = 489 yd³/hr

Therefore, only 1 roller is needed to handle the delivery of the material.

Answer is A

Solution 18

Actual cost of work performed, ACWP = $1.35 million

Budgeted cost of work performed, BCWP = $1.37 million

Cost performance index, CPI = 1.37/1.35 = 1.0148

BAC = original project estimate = $1.75 million

Estimate to complete (millions of dollars), ACP = ACWP + (BAC − BCWP)/CPI = $1.35 + (1.75 − 1.37)/1.0148 = 1.724

Answer is C

Surveying Topics on FE Civil Examination

Surveying

Surveying Topics on FE Civil Examination **4–6 problems**
Approximately 4% of Exam

A. Angles, distances, and trigonometry
B. Area computations
C. Earthwork and volume computations
D. Closure
E. Coordinate systems (e.g., state plane, latitude/longitude)
F. Leveling (e.g., differential, elevations, percent grades)

Surveying Topics on FE Civil Examination

Problem 1

The table below shows differential leveling data using a transit level. The starting station (A) is of known elevation. Find the elevation of station D.

Station	B.S (m)	F.S. (m)	Elevation (m)	Notes
A	3.95	-	500.00	Benchmark
B	2.47	6.34		
C	3.81	5.51		
D	-	6.78		

    A. 508.40 m.
    B. 489.77 m.
    C. 510.23 m.
    D. 491.60 m.

Problem 2

The back-tangent to a horizontal circular curve has a bearing of N 34° 44′ 35″W. The deflection angle between tangents is 67° to the right. If the PC is located at coordinates 4453.51^m N, 643.29^m W, and the tangent length is 850.32^m, what are the coordinates of the PT?

    A. 5657.19 N, 888.18 W
    B. 5850.95 N, 643.29 W
    C. 5871.32 N, 674.06 W
    D. 4184.70 N, 147.33 E

Problem 3

EDM (electronic distance measurement) instrument is used to sight a prism located at station B. The distance is measured as 234.78 m and the zenith angle is 73° 32′ 30″. If the height of instrument (H.I.) is 565.23 m above sea level, what is the elevation of the prism at B? (Neglect curvature and refraction effects)

    A. 776.85 m above sea level
    B. 790.39 m above sea level
    C. 394.92 m above sea level
    D. 631.75 m above sea level

Surveying Topics on FE Civil Examination

Problem 4

A closed traverse ABCD is shown below. Which of the following statements is incorrect?
- A. The bearing of line AD is S 23° E
- B. The azimuth of line BC is 73°
- C. The latitude of line AD is negative
- D. The sum of the latitudes (for all 4 lines) is equal to the sum of the departures.

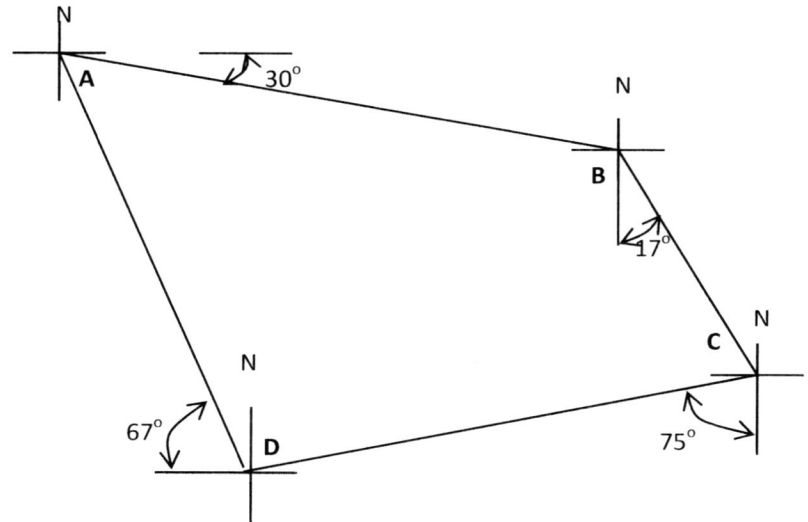

Problem 5

A triangular site ABC is surveyed. The table below shows latitudes and departures recorded in the field.

Segment	Latitude (ft)	Departure (ft)
AB	+ 250	+ 400
BC	− 520	+ 350
CA	+ 272	− 755

The Transit Rule for traverse closure says that corrections to latitudes and departures for each segment are to be done according to:

Latitude adjustment = $\frac{|LAT_i|}{\Sigma|LAT_i|} \times \Delta_y$

Departure adjustment = $\frac{|DEP_i|}{\Sigma|DEP_i|} \times \Delta_x$

What are the corrected latitudes and departures of segment BC?
- A. − 521.00, + 349.84
- B. − 519.00, + 351.16
- C. − 521.00, + 351.16
- D. − 519.00, + 349.84

Problem 6

A closed traverse ABCD is described below in terms of coordinates (northings and eastings of stations A, B, C and D). What is the area of the polygon ABCD?

A. 39.8 acres
B. 14.5 acres
C. 29.0 acres
D. 79.6 acres

	Northing (ft)	Easting (ft)
A	+520	− 350
B	+850	+350
C	− 450	+950
D	− 700	− 1150

Problem 7

The table below describes a traverse ABCDE. Determine the interior angle at C.

Line	Azimuth Angle	Bearing	Length (m)	Deflection
AB	132°23'45"	-	271.12	-
BC	-	-	289.18	52°34' left
CD	137°46'32"	-	362.15	-
DE	-	-	213.32	96°56'22" left

A. 130°11'08"
B. 122°03'13"
C. 121°45'17"
D. 120°39'23"

Problem 8

The table below shows data for a closed traverse ABCD. All necessary closure corrections have been applied. What is the bearing of line AD?

Segment	Length (ft)	Bearing
AB	561.87	S 30°11'08" W
BC	1023.65	N 28°41'38" W
CD	653.67	N 73°16'22" E
DA		

Surveying Topics on FE Civil Examination

A. N 76°09'16" W
B. N 13°50'44" W
C. S 13°50'44" E
D. S 76°09'16" E

Problem 9

An excavation plan is outlined in the figure below. Each grid square is 50 ft x 50 ft. The numbers are depth of cut (ft) at indicated locations. The total volume of cut (yd³) is most nearly:

A. 1250
B. 2500
C. 3400
D. 4600

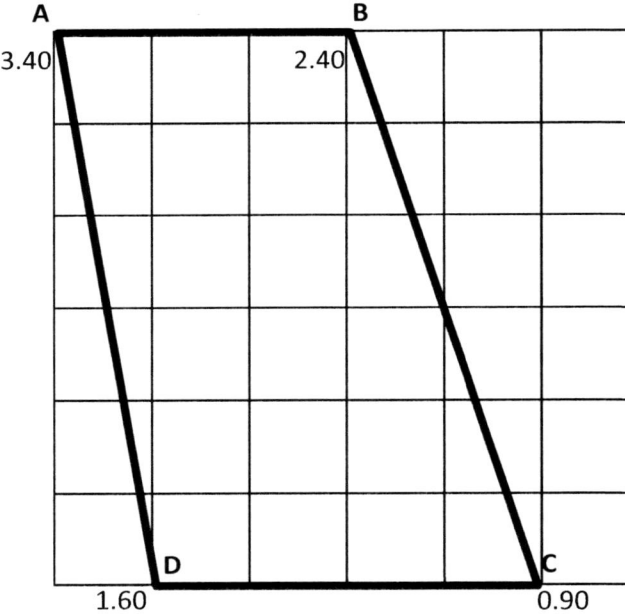

Problem 10

Earthwork estimates for a highway project are summarized in the following table of end areas at stations 100 ft apart. The total earthwork volume (yd³) between stations 20 + 0.00 and 24 + 0.00 is most nearly:

A. 6500
B. 7000
C. 7500
D. 8000

Station	Area (ft²)
20 + 00	405
21 + 00	576
22 + 00	432
23 + 00	378
24 + 00	630

Problem 11

For a particular site, the existing and the proposed ground profiles have been drawn to establish the following cross sectional areas at stations spaced at 25 ft intervals. What is the volume of earthwork between stations 204 + 0.00 and 205 + 50.00 using Simpson's Rule?

    A. 2662
    B. 2460
    C. 1662
    D. 1775

Station	End Area (ft²)
204 + 00.00	214.56
204 + 25.00	345.54
204 + 50.00	412.45
204 + 75.00	334.78
205 + 00.00	325.45
205 + 25.00	276.45
205 + 50.00	233.23

Problem 12

A distance is measured as 65.123 m using steel tape on a day when the ambient temperature is 28°C. The tape is held 'taut' by using a tension of 250 N. Use the following data:

    Standardization temperature = 20 °C
    Thermal expansion coefficient, $\alpha = 11.6 \times 10^{-6}$ /°C
    Modulus of elasticity of steel = 205 GPa
    Tape cross-sectional area = 3 mm x 0.5 mm
    The tape length is standardized while supported on the ground with tension = 30 N

What is the distance, corrected for temperature and axial tension?

    A. 65.132 m
    B. 65.129 m
    C. 65.117 m
    D. 65.114 m

Surveying Topics on FE Civil Examination

Problem 13

Cut and fill areas are shown at three stations 50 ft apart. What is the total earthwork volume between station 12 + 0.00 and 13 + 0.00?
  A. Cut 320 yd^3
  B. Fill 320 yd^3
  C. Cut 480 yd^3
  D. Fill 480 yd^3

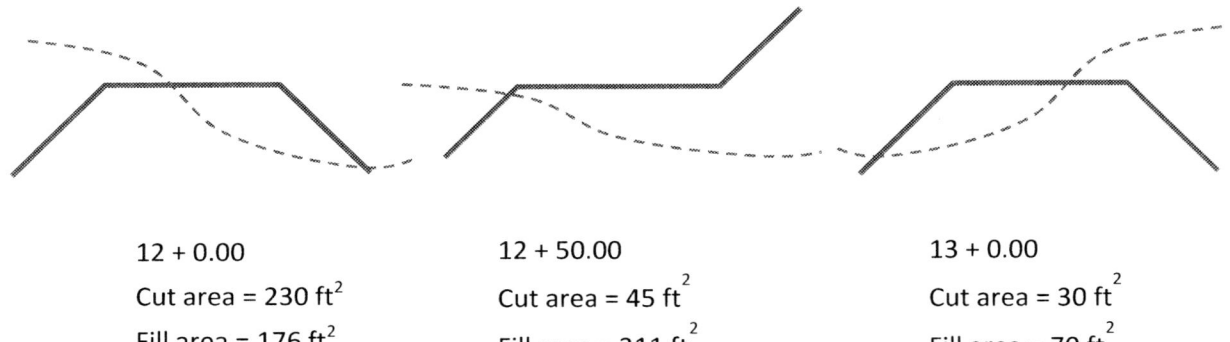

12 + 0.00	12 + 50.00	13 + 0.00
Cut area = 230 ft^2	Cut area = 45 ft^2	Cut area = 30 ft^2
Fill area = 176 ft^2	Fill area = 311 ft^2	Fill area = 70 ft^2

Problem 14

A surveyor is using an instrument that can only measure angles (no distance measurement). She is using this instrument to sight the top of a building, as shown below. From position A, she measures the zenith angle to be 77°45′ She then moves the instrument to position B, which is 100 ft closer to the building and measures the zenith angle as 73°30′. What is the height of the building?
  A. 61 ft
  B. 67 ft
  C. 81 ft
  D. 86 ft

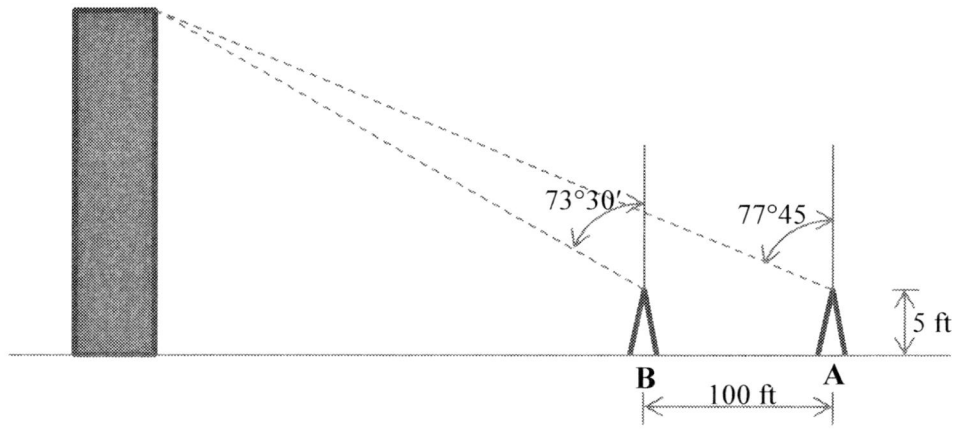

Problem 15

Points A, B and C are keypoints on a traverse. The distance from A to B is 387.65 ft and the bearing of line AB is S 75°45' E. The distance from B to C is 712.12 ft and the bearing of line BC is N 25°30' E. What is the length of line AC?

A. 723.5 ft
B. 784.6 ft
C. 843.4 ft
D. 911.3 ft

Problem 16

A 36 inch diameter concrete pipe (I.D. 36 in, O.D. 44 in) slopes at a longitudinal slope 0.5% as shown. The elevation of the pipe invert at A (sta. 34 + 45.30) is 238.15 ft above sea level. What is the soil cover over the pipe at location B (sta. 47 + 12.80) where the surface elevation is 239.23 ft?

A. 3.7 ft
B. 4.1 ft
C. 4.4 ft
D. 4.7 ft

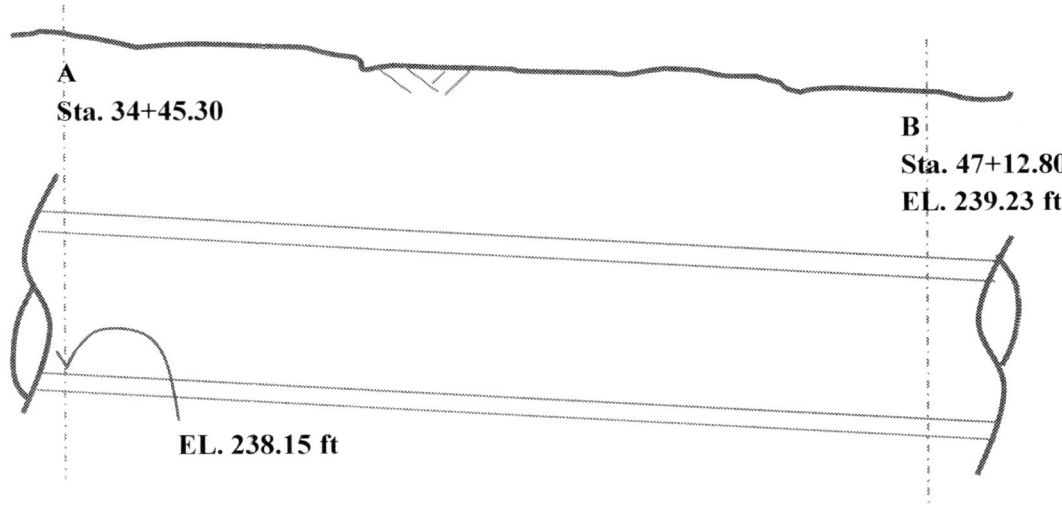

Problem 17

A benchmark station (A) is located at coordinates 135,765.23 ft N and 349,231.67 ft W within the state coordinate system. The elevation at the top of a peg at this station is 453.94 ft above sea level. Station B is sighted from instrument located at station A. Height of instrument is 4.76 ft. The elevation of the top of a building located at coordinates 136,052.44 ft N and 348,535.29 ft W is 595.21 ft. above sea level. What is the zenith angle of the line of sight from the instrument to the top of the building?

- A. 89°21'01"
- B. 86°37'23"
- C. 82°34'52"
- D. 79°43'42"

Problem 18

A closed traverse ABCD has the recorded latudues and departures as summarized in the table below.

Segment	Latitude (ft)	Departure (ft)
AB	+ 328.45	+ 702.29
BC	− 1301.48	+ 589.38
CD	− 238.93	− 2076.91
DA	+ 1210.89	+ 786.23

What is the closure correction?

- A. $\Delta X = + 0.99; \Delta Y = + 1.07$
- B. $\Delta X = + 1.07; \Delta Y = + 0.99$
- C. $\Delta X = − 0.99; \Delta Y = + 1.07$
- D. $\Delta X = − 1.07; \Delta Y = − 0.99$

Surveying Solutions

Surveying Topics on FE Civil Examination

Solution 1

Sum of all backsight values = 10.23

Sum of all foresight values = 18.63

Elevation of D = Elevation of A + Sum of backsight − Sum of foresight = 491.60 m

Answer is D

Solution 2

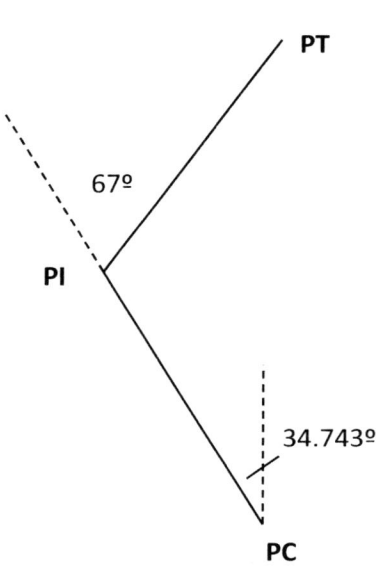

Bearing angle for forward tangent = 67º − 34º44′35″ = N32º15′25″E (32.257 deg)

Coordinates of PI:
Northing = 4453.51 + (850.32)cos(34.743º) = + 5152.23
Easting = − 643.29 − (850.32)sin(34.743º) = − 1127.88
Coordinates of PI: 5152.23 N, 1127.88 W

Coordinates of PT:
Northing = 5152.23 + (850.32)cos(32.357º) = + 5871.32
Easting = − 1127.88 + (850.32)sin(32.357º) = − 674.06
Coordinates of PT: 5871.032 N, 674.06 W

Answer is C

Solution 3

Zenith angle = 73º 32′30″ (73.542 deg)

Elevation Difference between sighting instrument and prism = (234.78)cos(73.542º) = + 66.52 m

Elevation of prism = Elevation of sighting instrument + 66.52 = 565.23 + 66.52 = 631.75 m

Answer is D

Surveying Topics on FE Civil Examination

Solution 4

Since the traverse is a closed one, sum of latitudes = 0 AND sum of departures = 0.
Therefore D is correct.
Line AD (from A to D) heads south. Therefore the latitude (which is considered positive with a northward heading) is negative. Therefore, C is correct.
Line AD is 23 degrees east of the south meridian. A is correct.
The azimuth of a line is measure clockwise from the north meridian. For line BC, azimuth = 180 – 17 = 163°
B is incorrect.

Answer is B

Solution 5

As may be seen, the closure errors are e_{LAT} = + 2.0 and e_{DEP} = – 5.0
Therefore, the corrections must be negative (for latitude) and positive (for departure)

Absolute values of latitudes and departures are shown in the table

Segment	|LAT|	|DEP|
AB	250	400
BC	520	350
CA	272	755
Sum	1042	1505

Therefore, for segment, BC, the corrections are:
Latitude adjustment = $\frac{520}{1042} \times -2.0 = -0.998 \, ft$
Departure adjustment = $\frac{350}{1505} \times +5.0 = +1.163 \, ft$
Therefore, the corrected values (for BC) are: latitude = 519.002; departure = 351.163

Answer is B

Solution 6

The area of a closed polygon is given by:

$$A = \frac{1}{2} |\Sigma y_i (x_{i-1} - x_{i+1})|$$

These are calculated in the table below:

Surveying Topics on FE Civil Examination

	Northing (ft)	Easting (ft)	$X_{i-1} - X_{i+1}$	$Y_i (X_{i-1} - X_{i+1})$
A	+520	−350	−1150 − 350	−780,000
B	+850	+350	−350 − 950	−1,105,000
C	−450	+950	+350 − (−1150)	−675,000
D	−700	−1150	+950 − (−350)	−910,000
				−3,470,000

Therefore the area of the polygon = 0.5×3,470,000 = 1,735,000 ft² = 39.83 acres

Answer is A

The calculation above can be quickly written by writing out all the coordinates (gray shaded cells in table below), repeating the first set of coordinates (+520, −350) at the end. The diagonal products are then grouped. One group yields the sum + 1,752,000 and the other group yields the sum − 1,718,000.

	+520	−350	
−297,500	+850	+350	182,000
−157,500	−450	+950	807,500
−665,000	−700	−1150	517,500
−598,000	+520	−350	245,000
−1,718,000			1,752,000

Area is given by: $A = \frac{1}{2}[1,752,000 - (-1,718,000)] = 1,735,000\ ft^2$

Solution 7

The azimuthal angles for all lines may be calculated starting with AB

Az(AB) = 132°23'45" (given)

Az(BC) = 132°23'45" − 52°34'00" = 79°49'45" (deflection angle is subtracted because line deflects left)

Az(CD) = 137°46'32" (given)

Interior angle at C = Azimuth(BC)−Azimuth(CD) +180° = 79°49'45" − 137°46'32" + 180º = 122°03'13"

Answer is B

Surveying Topics on FE Civil Examination

Solution 8

In the table below, the NS and EW projections of each line segment are calculated and listed (easting and northing positive)

Segment	Length (ft)	Bearing	Northing	Easting
AB	561.87	S 30°11'08" W	-485.68	-282.51
BC	1023.65	N 28°41'38" W	897.94	-491.49
CD	653.67	N 73°16'22" E	188.14	626.01

In order for the traverse to close perfectly, line DA must have northing = -600.40 and easting = +147.98

Therefore, line AD has northing = +600.40 and -147.98

$$\tan\theta = \frac{147.98}{600.40} \Rightarrow \theta = 13.85°$$

Bearing of line AD = N 13.85 W = N 13°50'44" W

Answer is B

Solution 9

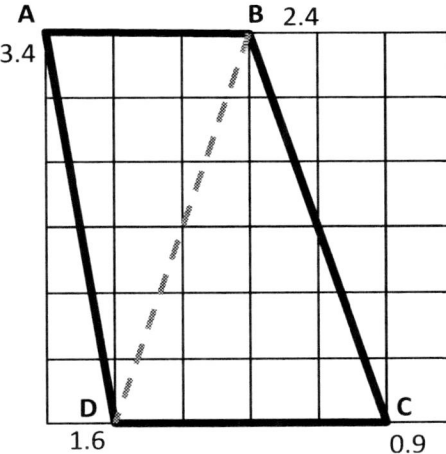

Drawing the diagonal BD allows us to calculate the areas ABD and BCD as 9 squares and 12 squares respectively (1/2 base times height).

A_{ABD} = ½bh = 0.5x150x300 = 22,500 ft² d_{ave} = ⅓(3.4+2.4+1.6) = 2.43 ft   V = 22,500x2.43 = 54,750 ft³

Surveying Topics on FE Civil Examination

A_{BCD} = ½bh = 0.5x200x300 = 30,000 ft² d_{ave} = ⅓(2.4+0.9+1.6) = 1.63 ft   V = 30,000x1.63 = 49,000 ft³

Total volume = 103,750 ft³ = 3842.6 yd³

Solution 10

Using the average end area method (trapezoidal rule), earthwork volume is calculated as:

$$V = \frac{1}{2} \times 100 \times [405 + 630 + 2 \times (576 + 432 + 378)] = 190.350 \, ft^3 = 7,050 \, yd^3$$

Answer is B

Solution 11

Using Simpson's rule, earthwork volume is calculated as:

$$V = \frac{1}{3} \times 25 \times [214.56 + 233.23 + 4 \times (345.54 + 334.78 + 276.45) + 2 \times (412.45 + 325.45)] = 47,922.25 \, ft^3 = 1,774.9 \, yd^3$$

Answer is D

Solution 12

Temperature correction: $\alpha L \Delta(T - T_o) = 11.6 \times 10^{-6} \times 65.123 \times (28 - 20) = +0.00604 \, m$

Tension correction: $\frac{(P-P_o)L}{AE} = \frac{(250-30) \times 65.123}{(0.003 \times 0.0005) \times 205 \times 10^9} = +0.00283 \, m$

Corrected length = 65.123 + 0.00604 + 0.00283 = 65.132 m

Answer is A

Solution 13

Cut volume (positive earthwork): $V = \frac{50}{2} \times (230 + 30 + 2 \times 45) = +8,750 \, ft^3$

Fill volume (negative earthwork): $V = \frac{50}{2} \times (176 + 70 + 2 \times 311) = -21,700 \, ft^3$

Net earthwork volume (FILL) = 21,700 - 8750 = 12, 950 ft³ = 479.6 yd³

Answer is D

Solution 14

Assuming the distance from B to the front of the building to be 'X', we have the following relations:

Surveying Topics on FE Civil Examination

$$\tan 16.5 = \frac{Y}{X} \Rightarrow Y = X \tan 16.5 = 0.2962X$$

$$\tan 12.25 = \frac{Y}{X + 100} \Rightarrow Y = X \tan 12.25 + 21.71 = 0.2171X + 21.71$$

Equating the two expressions for Y, we have: $0.2171X + 21.71 = 0.2962X \Rightarrow 0.0791X = 21.71 \Rightarrow X = 274.5 \, ft$

Therefore, Y = 0.2962X = 81.3 ft

Height of building = 86.3 ft

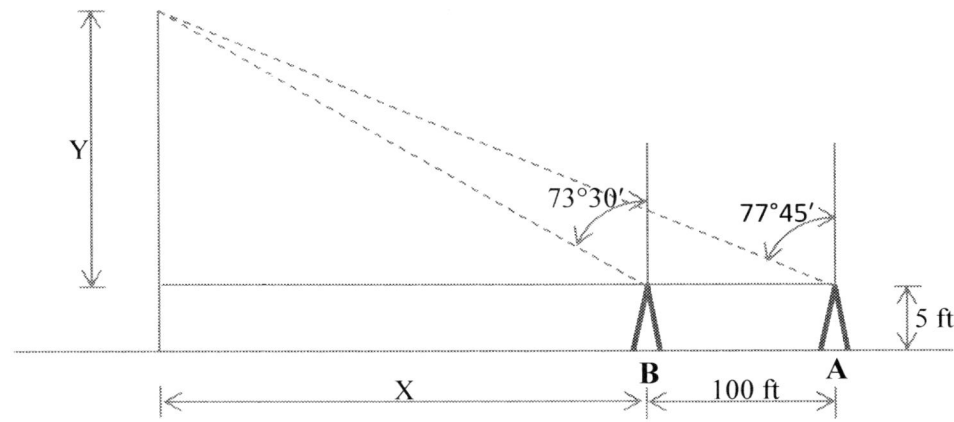

Answer is D

Solution 15

Since B is the vertex point (common to both rays), we can say that line BA (opposite to AB) has bearing N 75°45' W (azimuth 284.25) and line BC has azimuth 25.5.

Thus the included angle at B is 360 + 25.5 – 284.25 = 101.25

Length AC (by the cosine rule) is:
$$L_{AC} = \sqrt{387.65^2 + 712.12^2 - 2 \times 387.65 \times 712.12 \times \cos 101.25} = 843.35 \, ft$$

Answer is C

Solution 16

Distance from A to B = 4712.80 – 3445.30 = 1267.5 ft
Change in elevation = 0.005 x 1267.5 = 6.34 ft

Invert elevation at B = 238.15 − 6.34 = 231.81 ft
Pipe thickness = (44 − 36)/2 = 4 inches. Therefore, top of pipe is 40 inches above invert.
Therefore, elevation of top of pipe at B = 231.81 + 40/12 = 235.14 ft

Therefore, cover at location B = 239.23 − 235.14 = 4.09 ft

Answer is C

Solution 17

Elevation of instrument = 453.94 + 4.76 = 458.70 ft
Using north as 'Y', east as 'X' and elevation as 'Z' coordinate:
Coordinates of the instrument at A are: (−349,231.67, + 135,765.23, +458.70)

Coordinates of the top of building at B are: (−348,535.29, + 136,052.44, +595.21)

Elevation difference: Y = 595.21 − 458.70 = 136.51 ft
Horizontal distance: $X = \sqrt{(349231.67 - 348535.29)^2 + (135765.23 - 136052.44)^2} = 753.28\ ft$

Vertical angle: $\alpha = \tan^{-1}\left(\frac{Y}{X}\right) = \tan^{-1}\left(\frac{136.51}{753.28}\right) = 10.272$
Azimuth angle = 90 − 10.272 = 79°43'42"

Answer is D

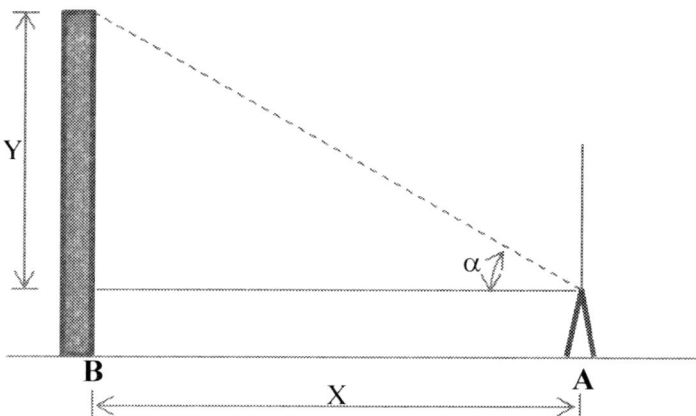

Solution 18

As may be seen, the closure errors are e_{LAT} = − 1.07 and e_{DEP} = + 0.99
Therefore, the corrections must be positive (for latitude, Y) and negative (for departure, X).

Answer is C